## EKNATH EASWARAN

Born into an ancient matrilineal Hindu family in Kerala state, South India, Eknath Easwaran regards his mother's mother as his spiritual teacher. She taught him by her selfless example how to find complete fulfillment in the family context.

Easwaran was chairman of the English department of a well-known Indian university when he came to the U.S. on the Fulbright exchange program. Here, as in India, his humor and humanness soon made him a teacher of enormous appeal. In 1961 he established the Blue Mountain Center of Meditation in Berkeley, California – "to move," as he puts it, "from education for degrees to education for living." As the Center's director Easwaran has taught meditation in the greater San Francisco Bay Area to those who want to lead active, spiritually fulfilling lives in the midst of family, friends, and society.

Easwaran brings to this volume a rare combination of literary skill, scholarship, and spiritual wisdom. His Sanskrit comes from one of the purest traditions in India, and for almost twenty years he followed a successful career as a writer, lecturer, and teacher of English literature. But it is essentially the stamp of personal experience that makes Easwaran's presentation of the spiritual life so effective. In this book, without philosophy or metaphysics, he illustrates the practicality of the Bhagavad Gita with familiar anecdotes from daily living.

Besides *The Bhagavad Gita for Daily Living,* Easwaran has written *Meditation, The Mantram Handbook, Gandhi the Man,* and over twenty other titles on living the spiritual life in the home and the community.

राग‌द्वेषवियुक्तैस्तु विषयानिन्द्रियैश्चरन् । आत्मवश्यैर्विधेयात्मा प्रसादमधिगच्छति ॥६४॥
प्रसादे सर्वदुःखानां हानिरस्योपजायते । प्रसन्नचेतसो ह्याशु बुद्धिः पर्यवतिष्ठते ॥६५॥

*But when you move amidst the world free from attachment and aversion alike, there comes the peace in which all sorrows end; and you live in the wisdom of the Self.*

*—BHAGAVAD GITA 2:64–65*

THE BHAGAVAD GITA
FOR DAILY LIVING, VOLUME 1

# The End of Sorrow

BY EKNATH EASWARAN

NILGIRI PRESS

©1975 by the Blue Mountain Center of Meditation
First paperback edition 1979
Fifteenth printing March 2008
All rights reserved. Printed in the United States of America
ISBN-13 : 978-0-915132-17-1
ISBN-10 : 0-915132-17-6

The Blue Mountain Center of Meditation, founded
in Berkeley, California, in 1961 by Eknath Easwaran,
publishes books on how to lead the spiritual life in the
home and the community. For information please write
to Nilgiri Press, Box 256, Tomales, California 94971.
On the Web at www.nilgiripress.org

This volume originally appeared in a hardcover edition
which is available under the title *The Bhagavad Gita
for Daily Living, Chapters 1 through 6,* published by
the Blue Mountain Center of Meditation.

Library of Congress Cataloging in Publication Data
will be found on the last page of this book.

# Table of Contents

*To my Teacher*
EKNATH CHIPPU KUNCHI AMMAL
*my Grandmother & my Playmate*

# A Living Tree

This practical commentary on the Bhagavad Gita, one of the greatest scriptures of the world, has grown out of the weekly talks given by Sri Eknath Easwaran[1] to a group of his devoted students and friends in Berkeley. The talks, beginning in May 1968, have been carefully recorded and transcribed weekly with the help of many members of Easwaran's āshram, or spiritual family. The transcribed lectures were then compiled and edited under Easwaran's close supervision.

The Gita class, like all of Easwaran's classes, is primarily a preparation and inspiration for the practice of meditation as well as a commentary on a particular scripture. Group meditation follows the hour-long talk, in which Easwaran usually covers one or two verses from the Gita. In these impromptu talks, he may apply the verse to the biggest challenges facing the world today or direct his comments to solving the personal problem of a friend in the audience. But whether talking about local incidents in Berkeley or international issues, his unchanging purpose is to inspire his listeners to practice the Gita in their daily life and to make the Gita a driving force in their consciousness. The purpose of this book is to enable Easwaran's readers, also, to translate the timeless values of the Gita into their daily living through the practice of meditation.

Easwaran began studying Sanskrit, the language of the ancient Hindu scriptures, at the age of ten in his village school in Kerala

---

1. *Easwaran* is the given name by which he is known among his friends; *Eknath* is the name of his ancestral family. *Sri* is used in India as a respectful form of address.

state, India. He also studied Sanskrit at his ancestral Shiva temple
under a priest from a community which is well known in India for
its pure Sanskrit tradition. Thoroughly familiar with the Gita in the
original Sanskrit, Easwaran is also perfectly at home in English,
though Malayalam is his mother tongue. In interpreting the scriptures, however, he relies on neither his Sanskrit nor his English
scholarship, but on his experience in meditation and his personal
practice of the spiritual life. He grew up in a large joint family in
the matrilineal tradition of Kerala, and he considers his mother's
mother, the flower of the Eknath family, his spiritual teacher.

It is said that every spiritual teacher has a particular context in
which he or she flourishes best. Easwaran is an educator. Formerly, he would say, it was education for scholarship, education for
degrees; now it is education for living. Before he came to the United
States he was chairman of the Department of English at the University of Nagpur and was devoted to his students and the literature he
taught them. After coming to this country on the Fulbright exchange program in 1959, Easwaran began giving talks on meditation and the spiritual life, and the response was so great that in 1960
he established the Blue Mountain Center of Meditation in Berkeley
to carry on his work of teaching meditation. Since that time, except
for one return to India, he has been giving ongoing classes each
week on the practice of meditation and commenting on the writings
of the great mystics of all religions, including the *Yogasūtras* of
Patanjali, the *Little Flowers* of St. Francis, the writings of Meister
Eckhart, the Upanishads, the *Bhaktisūtras* of Nārada, the Dhammapada of the Buddha, the Sermon on the Mount, Thomas a Kem-
pis's *Of the Imitation of Christ,* and the Bhagavad Gita. He also
teaches courses on meditation and on Mahatma Gandhi for the
University of California Extension, Berkeley. In Nagpur, he likes
to tell us laughingly, he had a reputation for always dragging Sri
Ramakrishna into his lectures on Shakespeare and Shaw. Now, in
these talks on the Gita, it is Shakespeare who illustrates the teachings of Sri Ramakrishna and St. Francis. The content has changed,
but the context in which Easwaran flourishes cannot be very different: a small but extremely devoted group, perhaps eighty to a hun-

dred, mostly young people of the sort who gravitate to a university town, gathered around in a semicircle to drink in the words of a man who is talking not about something he has read or something he has thought out, but about something he has experienced in his own life.

So this is a very special kind of book. Easwaran likes to say that it has grown like a tree because it issues directly from his life, which is so completely rooted in the Gita that every day he gains a deeper understanding of its teachings during even the most commonplace experiences: sharing ice cream with the āshram children in Santa Rosa, walking with friends down Telegraph Avenue in Berkeley, watching a mime with his wife in San Francisco's Union Square. Every Tuesday night in class this tree would flower, and we would hear these incidents retold as precise, profound illustrations of the Gita's applicability to our modern world. You can follow these incidents in this book, week by week, and at the same time you can trace the growth of the Blue Mountain Center of Meditation itself: the long months of looking for an āshram site, the building and remodeling when Ramagiri Ashram was acquired, the arrival of Easwaran's mother and nieces from India. The result is a living document which, as Easwaran says, is still growing even now, and which will continue to grow as it is read and absorbed by others into their own lives.

Easwaran has chosen to comment on the eighteen chapters of the Gita in three volumes, each volume covering six chapters. It is said that these three parts of the Gita illustrate the profound truth of the Upanishads, *Tat tvam asi:* "That thou art." The first six chapters are an exposition of *tvam,* 'thou,' the Ātman, and reveal the nature of our real, eternal Self. The second six chapters concern *Tat,* 'That': Brahman, the supreme Reality underlying all creation. The last six chapters explain *asi,* 'is,' the relationship between *tvam* and *Tat:* the identity of the Self within and the supreme Reality, which unites all existence into one whole. The Gita develops this truth, "That thou art," in practical terms: by discovering our real Self, we realize the indivisible unity of life and become united with the Divine Ground of existence.

Easwaran would like to convey his appreciation to everyone who has helped with this book, including those who have attended the Gita talks with sustained enthusiasm over the years. He wishes to express his deep love to all the members of his spiritual family who have assisted in translating, recording, transcribing, editing, and printing this commentary on the Gita.

In turn we, the editors, speaking for everyone who has helped, feel that working on this book has been a great privilege. Nachiketa, the student in the Katha Upanishad, tells Yama, "A teacher of this, another like you, is not to be found. No other boon is equal to this at all." The combination of enlightenment and practical, effective teaching in these pages is rare indeed, difficult to find in the modern world.

THE EDITORS

# The Bhagavad Gita
# for Daily Living

There is no significant problem in life which cannot be referred to the Bhagavad Gita for a perfect solution. The Gita is one of the most powerful of the Sanskrit scriptures of ancient India, but in my eyes it is neither philosophy nor theology, metaphysics nor poetry. It is a practical manual for daily living in any age, in any religious tradition, and my commentary is an attempt to apply its teachings specifically to the problems facing us in modern life.

Today there is an urgent need for such a manual. We see this reflected in our newspapers, magazines, books, movies, and television programs, but most of all in our daily living. Life has never seemed more futile. In spite of all our technological advances and material prosperity, we have no peace of mind and live in fear and anger in the midst of increasing violence. We are caught in the lurid dream that the pursuit of pleasure will lead us to joy, the pursuit of profit will lead us to security, and most of us have no other purpose in life than this driving urge to bring about our own private fulfillment even if it is at the expense of other persons, races, or countries.

The Bhagavad Gita shows us how we can awaken from this dream. In Sanskrit, the language of the Gita, the underlying Reality of life is called by a simple but very powerful name: *advaita,* 'not two.' In the words of a lovable mystic of modern India, Meher Baba, "You and I are not 'we'; you and I are One." There is no division, no fragmentation in life at all; no matter how much we may appear to differ on the surface, the welfare of each one of us is inseparable from the welfare of all others. Even on the level of the body, we know that in cancer the whole organism is eventually destroyed when even a single cell begins to pursue its own course independently of the rest. Similarly, the Bhagavad Gita tells us, you and I cannot fulfill ourselves by going our own way. We can find lasting fulfillment only by contributing to the joy and fulfillment of others, in which our own joy and fulfillment are included. This is not a philosophical platitude, but a practical principle which we must learn to live by if our civilization is to survive.

Every mystic will interpret the scriptures in accordance with the urgent needs of the times. Though the Bhagavad Gita is timeless, it too must be interpreted in accordance with the needs of the times—the *yugadharma* in Sanskrit, the 'special law of the age.' In commenting on the Gita, I always stress the indivisible unity of life because this is the need of our time. I do not stop with the family of man, but extend this unity to all life and to the environment as well. It is the urgent need of our time to recognize the unity of all forms of life, and the intimate relationship between water, earth, air, plants, and all creatures. I am a vegetarian not only because my ancestors were, but also because I perceive this unity. Ecologists have begun to tell us that there is an interpenetrating relationship among all things which we can violate only at our peril. Jacques Cousteau, who has devoted his life to studying the oceans of the earth, tells us: "We forget that all life-cycles are one. Environment is one too. There is no such thing as an environment of a single species, of man for example." Spiritual living and sound ecological practice go together. A vegetarian diet respects this partnership among all forms of life and meets man's nutritional needs with a minimum demand on the earth's resources.

Salvation, Self-realization, *nirvāna, moksha*—these are just different words for the same discovery of the unity of all life. This is what we have come into life to accomplish, and until we have accomplished this, we have not attained fulfillment. Even one person attaining this goal elevates the entire consciousness of mankind. As Philo of Alexandria said: "Households, cities, countries, and nations have enjoyed great happiness when a single individual has taken heed of the Good and Beautiful. Such men not only liberate themselves; they fill those they meet with a free mind." In the Hindu spiritual tradition there is an unbroken continuity of illumined men and women who have verified the supreme goal in their lives. There is always someone with us in India to embody the ideals of spiritual living, and through their personal life such people are able to inspire those around them to follow the supreme goal. When they write a commentary on the scriptures, it is in the light of their own experience and enables us to practice their teachings in our daily life.

My own approach to the spiritual life appeals to many men and women today, partly because I have not retired from the world—I live very much as a family man, a good husband, son, and friend—but also because I have tried to combine the best of West and East. I live together with forty friends at our āshram, or spiritual community, and though I have heavy responsibilities in guiding our work, I take time for recreation. I go with friends to the theater; I am fond of Western and Indian classical music; I like to take the children to the ice cream parlor and the dogs to the beach for a run. But perhaps what appeals most deeply is that I understand the difficulties of living in the modern world. Before taking to meditation, in my ignorance of the unity of life, I too committed most of the mistakes that even sensitive people commit today. As a result, I understand how easy it is to make those mistakes, and I know how to guide and support those who are trying to learn a wiser way of living.

I am a believer in the little man and do not look to governments and corporations to set the world right. In India, the tropical sun dries up almost all vegetation during the hot season, and a shade tree is a precious shelter from the deadening heat. The leaves of the tamarind tree are very small, but they are packed so closely together that they give better shade than the large leaves of the banana tree. My Grandmother, my spiritual teacher, used to point to the tamarind tree and remind me that a large number of little people, working together closely, can accomplish much more than a few big people. The Lord within, whether we call him Krishna, Christ, the Buddha, or Allah, is the source of all power, and when we live for others in accordance with the unity of all life this power flows into our hands, enabling us to take on the biggest problems facing the modern world. In Hindu mythology, Ganesha, the elephant god, is the symbol of the Lord's power. The elephant is a huge, strong creature, but very gentle. Often he does not know his own strength. His eyes are so small that in India we say he thinks he is only a small creature, not capable of much. He never knows his own size. My Gita commentary is aimed at ordinary men and women who think they are small, who do not realize their real stature.

Even if it takes us a whole lifetime to learn to practice the teachings of the Gita, we shall have made a valuable contribution in life. You and I can make a contribution to the spiritual evolution of humanity by learning to resolve the terrible civil war described vividly in the Gita. This war is continually raging within every one of us, and the two armies in conflict are all that is selfish in us pitted against all that is selfless in us. It is a lifelong struggle between the demonic and the divine.

The Bhagavad Gita, which is found in the Hindu epic the *Mahābhārata,* is the most influential scripture to come down the ages in India. It is the quintessence of the Upanishads, giving us their perennial wisdom in a manner that can be systematically practiced. The Upanishads, which come at the end of the Vedas and are among the oldest, most revered Hindu scriptures, contain flashing insights into the nature of life and death. The Gita gives order to the insights of the Upanishads and tells us how to undertake spiritual disciplines to become aware of the supreme Reality always.

My surmise is that the Gita was originally an Upanishad which has been inserted into the *Mahābhārata,* its first chapter serving as a bridge between the epic story and the upanishadic teaching in chapters two through eighteen. Perhaps this interpretation cannot be substantiated by scholarship, but in the traditional invocation to the Gita we find this verse:

> *Sarvo 'panishado gāvo*
> *dogdhā gopālanandanah*
> *Pārtho vatsah sudhīr bhoktā*
> *dugdham gītāmritam mahat*

> All the Upanishads are cows
> milked by Krishna, the cowherd boy,
> and Arjuna is the calf.
> Those who are wise and pure drink the milk,
> the supreme, immortal nectar of the Gita.

The Gita also uses the dialogue form of the Upanishads and is especially similar to the Katha Upanishad, where Yama, the King of Death, teaches the teenager Nachiketa how to attain immortality through Self-realization. In the Gita, the dialogue is between Sri Krishna (a full incarnation of Vishnu, the Preserver in the Hindu Trinity) and Arjuna, a young prince who represents you and me. Arjuna is a man of action, living in the midst of society and confronting essentially the same problems that challenge us today. His friend and spiritual teacher, Sri Krishna, is the Lord of Love who dwells in the depths of our consciousness. He is the Ātman, our real Self.

To practice the teachings of the Bhagavad Gita no amount of intellectual study can be of much help, because intellectual knowledge, by its very nature, has little power to transform character, conduct, and consciousness. Meditation is the mighty instrument which enables us to bring the timeless teachings of the Gita into our life, day by day, step by step.

In the Hindu scriptures meditation is called *Brahmavidyā*, the supreme science, in which all human desires are completely fulfilled. If we practice meditation sincerely, systematically, and with sustained enthusiasm, our physical and emotional problems find their solution, all of our artistic and creative capacities come to full maturity, and we are able to contribute to the welfare of our family and community. We live in the world as integral members of our society, and by transforming ourselves, we transform those with whom we live. This is joyful living; it is not running away from problems but facing problems with a quiet confidence and unfailing insight that come to us day by day in the practice of meditation.

In order to bring the teachings of the Gita into our daily lives and to practice meditation, we must observe the simple rules of right living. On the strength of my own small spiritual experience, let me indicate here the eight-point program which I have found extremely useful in my own life. This body of disciplines, which can enable us to fulfill the supreme goal of life, Self-realization, can be followed by every person capable of some resolution, some endurance, and some sense of dedication.

## THE EIGHTFOLD PATH

*1. Meditation.* First comes the practice of meditation. You begin by devoting half an hour every morning as early as convenient to the practice of meditation. Do not increase this half-hour period, but if you want to meditate more, have half an hour in the evening also.

Have a room in your home for meditation, or a special corner, and keep it as austere as possible. A quiet, cool, well-ventilated room is best. Have pictures of the great spiritual teachers if this appeals to you.

If you want to sit in a straight-back chair, one with arms is best; or sit cross-legged on the carpet. Sit with spinal column erect, and eyes gently closed. As concentration deepens you may begin to relax and fall asleep; if so, draw yourself up and move away from your back support so that you can keep the spine, neck, and head in a straight line.

Have an inspirational passage memorized, such as the Prayer of St. Francis of Assisi, the second or twelfth chapter of the Bhagavad Gita, the Twenty-third Psalm, the first chapter of the Dhammapada of the Buddha, the Beatitudes of the Sermon on the Mount, or a selection from the Upanishads. Go through the words of the passage in your mind as slowly as you can, letting each word drop singly into your consciousness. Do not follow any association of ideas, but keep to the words of the inspirational passage. When distractions come, do not resist them, but try to give more and more attention to the words of the prayer. If you find that your mind has wandered away completely, go back to the first word of the prayer and begin again. Keep adding to your repertoire of inspirational passages from the scriptures of all religions to prevent dryness in meditation.

The secret of meditation is that you become what you meditate on. When you use the second chapter of the Gita in meditation, you are driving the words deeper and deeper into your consciousness, so that one day, perhaps after many years, they will become an integral part of your consciousness.

2. *Japam.* Japam is the silent repetition of the mantram, or Holy Name, in the mind. The popular etymology of the Sanskrit word *mantram* is from *manas,* 'mind,' and *tri,* 'to cross over': "that which enables us to cross the tempestuous sea of the mind." Every religion has its mantram. The very name of Jesus is a mantram; so is *Hail Mary,* which calls on the Divine Mother whose children we all are. *Om mani padme hum* is a great Buddhist mantram; *mani* means 'jewel'—the Self—and *padme,* 'the lotus of the heart.' Jews may use the Shema or *Barukh attah Adonai,* 'Blessed art thou, O Lord'; Muslims repeat the name of Allah or *Bismillah ir-Rahman ir-Rahim,* 'In the name of God, the Merciful, the Compassionate.' And one of the oldest, simplest mantrams in India is *Rāma,* from the root *ram,* 'to rejoice,' signifying the source of all joy.

When you are angry, afraid, or anxious, repeat the mantram to still the agitation rising in your mind. Anger and fear are power rising within us, and by the repetition of the Holy Name we can put anger and fear to work, harnessing them for the benefit of ourselves and others rather than allowing them to use us destructively.

At bedtime, repeat the mantram in your mind until you fall asleep. In the morning you will feel refreshed in body and mind.

Whenever you get a moment, while waiting for a bus or while walking, use this time to repeat the mantram. Boredom is a great source of problems to people who do not know what to do with their time. We may smoke, for example, just because we do not know what to do with the odds and ends of time in our day.

The mind is very much like the restless trunk of an elephant. In India elephants often walk in religious processions which wind through the streets of the town on their way to the temple. The trunk of the elephant is a restless thing, always moving, and as the temple elephant is taken through the narrow streets of the bazaar, it is usually tempted by the coconuts, bananas, and other produce displayed in the stalls on either side. As it walks, if the shopkeeper doesn't watch, it picks up a coconut and puts it in its mouth. There is a loud crack, and that is the last of the coconut. Then from the next stall it takes a whole bunch of bananas. It doesn't peel them, but just puts the whole bunch inside, and it's gone. But the wise mahout, the man in charge of the elephants, knows their habits, so as the procession begins he gives the elephant a short bamboo stick to hold in its trunk. The elephant holds the bamboo firmly and walks through the streets without confiscating anyone's property.

This is what we do when we repeat the mantram: we slowly give a mantram-stick to the mind, and instead of wanting to smoke or overeat, it has something to hold on to. Gradually, this makes the mind firm, secure, steadfast, and proof against tension.

*3. Slowing down.* Millions in our modern world suffer because they are constantly pushed and hurried. Hurry makes us tense and causes us to make mistakes and do a poor job. The remedy for hurrying is to get up earlier, so that we can begin the day without tension and set a slow, leisurely pace for the day. When we are concentrated and slow we do not make mistakes; we do a much better job, which in the long run is much more economical than hurrying and making mistakes. In order to slow down we may need to eliminate some unnecessary activities from our day.

*4. Ekāgratā, 'one-pointedness.'* The practice of meditation is a systematic exercise in concentration, which will finally become a permanent, spontaneous state. It is a great aid to meditation if you practice being one-pointed during your day. Give your complete attention to whatever you are doing; particularly in conversation, give your complete attention to the person with whom you are talking. After much practice, you should be able to make your mind one-pointed, concentrating on whatever task is at hand.

Almost all of us suffer from a mind which is many-pointed, and we are usually not able to bring all our concentration to bear on a given problem or task. For example, background music while eating, while studying, while working, prevents us from being fully aware of what we are eating, studying, or working at. Smoking while watching a movie curtails our capacity to appreciate the movie, because our mind is two-pointed. When we do only one thing at a time, we are healing the divisions in our consciousness, and when we can give our complete attention to another person, he cannot help but respond by giving his complete attention to us.

5. *Sense restraint.* This does not mean sense-negation or sense-denial but training the senses to be obedient servants. We begin to train the senses by exercising discriminating restraint in our choice of movies, television programs, books, and magazines, and by eating nourishing food in temperate quantities rather than things that appeal to our taste but have no nutritional value. It is good to have a light meal in the evening and our heaviest meal at breakfast and to eat plenty of fresh vegetables and fruits. Avoid overcooked, deep-fried, strongly flavored, and heavily spiced foods.

The training of the senses takes a long time, but finally it will enable us to have mastery over our deepest drives, our strongest powers. When the senses are trained, the body becomes healthy, strong, and beautiful.

6. *Putting others first.* When we go after our own pleasure and profit, dwelling on ourselves and ignoring the needs of those around us, we are constricting our consciousness and stunting our growth. People who are driven by anger, for example, are usually those who are full of self-will, who cannot put the other person first. Seldom do they have lasting relationships; seldom are they able to live at peace with themselves and with those around them. But the person who has little or no self-will is secure and by his calmness and steadfastness is able to help those who are agitated to become calm. In the home it is particularly the privilege of the woman by her personal example to help the members of her family to be patient, enduring, and forgiving. I place so much emphasis on the family context because it gives us countless opportunities every day for expanding our consciousness by reducing our self-will or separate-

ness. This need not mean following the wishes of the other person always, but when it seems necessary to differ, this must be done tenderly and without the slightest trace of resentment or retaliation.

*7. Reading the scriptures.* My suggestion here is to read the scriptures and great mystics of all religions. If you want to know about the mystical tradition, go direct to the great mystics, rather than relying on books about mysticism. This devotional reading can be an inspiration and encouragement on the spiritual path, but even here it is better to read a few books slowly and well than many books quickly. All knowledge is within, and the practice of meditation enables us to draw upon this knowledge. Through carefully selected spiritual reading we can be inspired by the spiritual awareness of the mystics of all religions and ages.

*8. Satsang,* or association with spiritually oriented people. It is of great importance for all of us to draw inspiration from someone who is able to interpret the sacred scriptures and the great mystics in the light of his own personal experience. It is a difficult task to practice meditation for many years, day in and day out, and we all need the support and companionship of people meditating together. This is the great advantage of a spiritual community, or āshram, where those dedicated to the practice of meditation live together with a spiritual teacher. In your own home, it is very good if members of the family can meditate together.

If we want to make the discovery that will fulfill all our desires and establish us in abiding joy, bringing to our life limitless love, wisdom, and beauty, then the mystics have described the path for us to follow. By following these simple rules of right living and practicing meditation regularly, we can learn to fulfill the supreme goal of life, which is to discover experientially that all life is one.

The Bhagavad Gita for Daily Living

# CHAPTER ONE

# The War Within

धृतराष्ट्र उवाच
धर्मक्षेत्रे कुरुक्षेत्रे समवेता युयुत्सवः ।
मामकाः पाण्डवाश्चैव किमकुर्वत संजय ॥१॥

DHRITARASHTRA:[1]
*1. O Sanjaya, tell me what happened at Kurukshetra,
on the field of dharma, where my family and the
Pāndavas gathered to fight.*

"The Gita," says Mahatma Gandhi, "is not a historical discourse. A physical illustration is often needed to drive home a spiritual truth. It is the description not of war between cousins, but between two natures in us—the Good and the Evil." Volumes have been written about the battle which is said to have taken place on the field of Kurukshetra, located north of Delhi, but for the spiritual aspirant, the battle described in the Bhagavad Gita is not limited to a particular historical setting. Sri Krishna's message is as valid today as it was centuries ago, and it will continue to be so tomorrow, for it describes the eternal truth of life that the fiercest battle we must wage is against all that is selfish, self-willed, and separate in us. Today when the world is being torn asunder by war, when violence stalks our streets and invades our homes, when anger disrupts our relationships and separateness pervades our consciousness, Sri Krishna's immortal words, given to us in the Gita, are of urgent practical value. The violence we see about us is a reflection of the anger and

1. Dhritarāshtra, a blind king, is the father of the forces of darkness. His name means "he who has usurped the kingdom."

self-will burning deep within us. Most of us carry a conflagration around with us in the depths of our consciousness, and many of us are skilled tacticians in guerilla warfare right in our own homes. The war the mystics of all the world's great religions talk about is not the one erupting in the Middle East or in Southeast Asia that makes newspaper headlines; it is the one erupting from the fierce self-will afflicting all of us, estranging individuals, families, communities, races, and nations.

Once I was on a train going from Delhi to Simla, high on the Himālayas, and on the way we passed through Kurukshetra, the historical battlefield of the Bhagavad Gita. My fellow passengers were talking about the tremendous battle which took place there, and when we arrived at the scene, they eagerly climbed out to have a look. To me there was no need to disembark, because I already had an inkling that the real battlefield in the Gita was right inside each passenger on the train. The language of battle is often found in the scriptures, for it conveys the strenuous, long, drawn-out campaign we must wage to free ourselves from the tyranny of the ego, the cause of all our suffering and sorrow. By setting before us the inspiring ideal of the victorious man or woman as one who has conquered himself or herself, the mystics urge us on to fight this battle and eradicate all that is selfish in us.

How can we ordinary men and women, living in the midst of our family and society, achieve such a victory? In the Gita Sri Krishna gives us the precious jewel of spiritual wisdom, of immediate practical value to everyone's life. He tells us how we can learn to fight the battle against self-will and separateness through the practice of meditation and its allied disciplines, and he shows us how in our own daily lives we can gain the will and the wisdom to transform anger into compassion, fear into courage, and greed into tireless striving for the welfare of others.

संजय उवाच

दृष्ट्वा तु पाण्डवानीकं व्यूढं दुर्योधनस्तदा ।
आचार्यमुपसंगम्य राजा वचनमब्रवीत् ॥२॥

पश्यैतां पाण्डुपुत्राणामाचार्य महतीं चमूम् ।
व्यूढां द्रुपदपुत्रेण तव शिष्येण धीमता ॥३॥

अत्र शूरा महेष्वासा भीमार्जुनसमा युधि ।
युयुधानो विराटश्च द्रुपदश्च महारथः ॥४॥

धृष्टकेतुश्चेकितानः काशिराजश्च वीर्यवान् ।
पुरुजित्कुन्तिभोजश्च शैब्यश्च नरपुङ्गवः ॥५॥

युधामन्युश्च विक्रान्त उत्तमौजाश्च वीर्यवान् ।
सौभद्रो द्रौपदेयाश्च सर्व एव महारथाः ॥६॥

अस्माकं तु विशिष्टा ये तान्निबोध द्विजोत्तम ।
नायका मम सैन्यस्य संज्ञार्थं तान्ब्रवीमि ते ॥७॥

भवान्भीष्मश्च कर्णश्च कृपश्च समितिंजयः ।
अश्वत्थामा विकर्णश्च सौमदत्तिस्तथैव च ॥८॥

अन्ये च बहवः शूरा मदर्थे त्यक्तजीविताः ।
नानाशस्त्रप्रहरणाः सर्वे युद्धविशारदाः ॥९॥

अपर्याप्तं तदस्माकं बलं भीष्माभिरक्षितम् ।
पर्याप्तं त्विदमेतेषां बलं भीमाभिरक्षितम् ॥१०॥

अयनेषु च सर्वेषु यथाभागमवस्थिताः ।
भीष्ममेवाभिरक्षन्तु भवन्तः सर्व एव हि ॥११॥

SANJAYA:[2]

*2. Having surveyed the forces of the Pāndavas arrayed for battle, Duryodhana,[3] the prince, approached his teacher and spoke.*

2. The entire dialogue of the Bhagavad Gita is reported to us by Sanjaya, who sees what is taking place on the battlefield within through his power of divine vision.

3. Duryodhana, eldest son of Dhritarāshtra, is the leader of the forces of darkness.

*3. "O my teacher, look at this mighty army of the
Pāndavas; it has been assembled by your gifted disciple, the son of Drupada.*

*4–6. "There are heroic warriors and great archers
who are the equals of Bhīma and Arjuna: Yuyudhāna,
the mighty Virāta, Drupada, Dhrishtaketu, Cekitāna,
the valiant king of Kāshī, Purujit, Kuntibhoja, the
great leader Shaibya, the powerful Yudhāmanyu, the
valiant Uttamaujas, the son of Subhadrā, and the
sons of Draupadī; all these command mighty chariots.*

*7–8. "You who are the best of the brahmins, listen
to the names of those who are distinguished among us:
Bhīshma, Karna, and the victorious Kripa; Ashvat-
thāma, Vikarna, and the son of Somadatta.*

*9. "There are many others, too, heroes giving up their
lives for my sake. They are all proficient in war and
armed with a variety of weapons.*

*10. "Our army is unlimited and commanded by
Bhīshma; theirs is small and commanded by Bhīma.*

*11. "Let everyone take his proper place and stand
firm supporting Bhīshma."*

Religion is realization of the unity of life; this is the supreme purpose for which we have come into the human context. Our intellectual orientation, useful though it is in helping us solve some of our
problems, tends to make us forget that the scriptures of the great religions are meant to be personally experienced in daily life. I appreciate the scholarly editions of the Gita, the Bible, or the Dhammapada that abound in footnotes and appendices, but I always ask myself: will this approach show me how to translate the teachings of
Sri Krishna, Jesus the Christ, or the Compassionate Buddha into
my own life? Will it prepare me to undertake the long, exhausting
war I have come into this world to win?

Sri Krishna insists we do the actual fighting in this battle ourselves, but with his infinite mercy, he outlines the battle plan and
gives us the maps, weapons, and strategies necessary to win. The

first tip the Gita gives us is on the nature of the contesting armies, the Kauravas and the Pāndavas. The Kauravas are usually identified with the forces of darkness that bring about death and despair, and the Pāndavas with the forces of light which bring abiding joy and unshakable security. The ancient Sanskrit scriptures throw a flood of light on this dichotomy by describing it as a choice between *preya* and *shreya*. *Preya*, the passing pleasure that seems pleasing to the senses but soon fades into its opposite, is what we choose when we indulge in injurious physical habits or retaliate against others. *Shreya*, the good that leads to lasting welfare for the whole, is what we choose by cultivating healthy habits, by bringing conflicting parties together, and by putting the happiness of those around us first. These two conflicting forces are very much in evidence in the world today: on the one hand we have made great strides towards eliminating poverty and disease, but on the other hand, we have stockpiled sufficient arms to kill every man, woman, and child on the face of the earth several times over. We seek peace and freedom for all, but we are letting the selfish pursuit of personal profit and pleasure destroy our families, our communities, and even our society. As Sri Ramakrishna, the great saint who lived in India in the last century, was fond of saying, "If you want to go east, don't walk towards the west." Such is the confusion of our lives that we have forgotten there is this choice to be made at all, and in fact we no longer know whether we are running east or west.

Another set of beautiful Sanskrit terms for describing the perennial opposition between the forces that elevate us and those that bring about our downfall is *nitya* and *anitya*. *Nitya* refers to that which is eternal and unchanging, and this is what we seek by forgiving those who harm us and supporting those who differ from us. *Anitya* is that which fades away and brings suffering in its wake, and this is what we seek when we give in to an angry impulse or do what leads to self-aggrandizement at the expense of our family, community, and society. When we fight others, whether physically or in the mind, we harm them and ourselves, but when we fight all that is base and self-willed in us, we bring lasting joy to everyone. This is a central theme in all the great scriptures. We can all learn

to conquer hatred through love by drawing on the power released
through the practice of meditation to throw all our weight, all our
energy, and all our will on the side of what is patient, forgiving, and
selfless in ourselves and others.

तस्य संजनयन्हर्षं कुरुवृद्ध: पितामह: ।
सिंहनादं विनद्योच्चै: शङ्खं दध्मौ प्रतापवान् ॥१२॥
तत: शङ्खाश्च भेर्यश्च पणवानकगोमुखा:।
सहसैवाभ्यहन्यन्त स शब्दस्तुमुलोऽभवत् ॥१३॥
तत: श्वेतैर्हयैर्युक्ते महति स्यन्दने स्थितौ ।
माधव: पाण्डवश्चैव दिव्यौ शङ्खौ प्रदध्मतु: ॥१४॥

*12. Then the powerful Bhīshma, the grandsire,
oldest of all the Kurus, in order to cheer Duryodhana,
roared like a lion and blew his conch horn.
13. And after Bhīshma there was a tremendous
noise of conchs and cowhorns and pounding on
drums.
14. Then Sri Krishna and Arjuna, who were standing
in a mighty chariot yoked with white horses, blew
their divine conchs.*

In this greatest of all battles between the forces of good and evil,
Arjuna represents you and me, and Sri Krishna, the Lord of Love
enshrined in the heart of every creature, is his best friend, his dearest companion, and above all, his beloved teacher and guide. Sri
Krishna is not someone outside us, swinging between Neptune and
Uranus; he is closer to us than our body, nearer to us, as the Sufi
mystics put it, than our jugular vein. The word *Krishna* comes from
the Sanskrit root *krish,* 'to draw'; Krishna is the one inside us who is
drawing us to himself all the time. The title *Sri* means 'Lord.' Sri
Krishna is eternal and omnipresent; he is our real Self. Whether
we call him the Christ, the Buddha, or Allah, he is the supreme Reality underlying consciousness and uniting all creation.

पाञ्चजन्यं हृषीकेशो देवदत्तं धनंजयः ।
पौण्ड्रं दध्मौ महाशङ्खं भीमकर्मा वृकोदरः ॥१५॥
अनन्तविजयं राजा कुन्तीपुत्रो युधिष्ठिरः ।
नकुलः सहदेवश्च सुघोषमणिपुष्पकौ ॥१६॥
काश्यश्च परमेष्वासः शिखण्डी च महारथः ।
धृष्टद्युम्नो विराटश्च सात्यकिश्चापराजितः ॥१७॥
द्रुपदो द्रौपदेयाश्च सर्वशः पृथिवीपते ।
सौभद्रश्च महाबाहुः शङ्खान्दध्मुः पृथक्पृथक् ॥१८॥
स घोषो धार्तराष्ट्राणां हृदयानि व्यदारयत् ।
नभश्च पृथिवीं चैव तुमुलो व्यनुनादयन् ॥१९॥

*15. Sri Krishna blew the conch named Pāncajanya, and Arjuna blew that called Devadatta. The mighty Bhīma blew the huge conch Paundra.*

*16. Yudhishthira, the king, the son of Kuntī, blew the conch Anantavijaya; Nakula and Sahadeva blew their conchs as well.[4]*

*17–18. The king of Kāshī, the leading bowman, the great warrior Shikhandī, Dhrishtadyumna, Virāta, the invincible Sātyaki, Drupada, all the sons of Draupadī, and the son of Subhadra with the mighty arms all blew their conchs.*

*19. And the noise tore through the heart of Duryodhana's army. Indeed, the sound was tumultuous, echoing throughout heaven and earth.*

The tumult and confusion of warfare are the same no matter what the times or circumstances, no matter who the contestants or what the issues involved. In ancient India it was the mighty bowman and the strong elephant, today it is the missile and the tank, but the dreadful disruption of life which results is the same in both cases. As the Compassionate Buddha said more than two thousand years

4. Yudhishthira, Bhīma, Nakula, and Sahadeva are Arjuna's brothers.

ago, "Hatred will never cease by hatred at any time. Hatred ceases only through love. This is an eternal law." We can never bring an end to violence by using violent means; far from resolving conflicts, hostility and retaliation drive people further apart and make havoc of life.

The tragedy of self-will is that it leads to increasing insecurity, ill health, loneliness, and despair. This cannot but be the discouraging prognosis for those who pursue personal profit, power, prestige, and pleasure at the expense of the welfare of their family and community. In the beautiful words of St. Francis of Assisi, "It is in giving that we receive; it is in pardoning that we are pardoned." Most of us suffer from the mistaken belief that it is in grabbing that we receive, it is in venting anger that we improve our relationships, and it is in having our own way that we find fulfillment. Unfortunately happiness escapes us the more we clutch at it by manipulating those around us and accumulating more material possessions. Security is not found in a stockpile of weapons but in mutual trust and respect among individuals, races, and nations; peace is not found in asserting our rights over others but in assuring the lasting welfare of our extended circle of family and friends. This is the great insight that comes in meditation: on the spiritual path there is no possibility of defeat, for the Lord—called Sri Krishna by some and the Christ by others—is in the depths of our consciousness to support us, guide us, and help us win the war against our self-will.

One of the glorious names for Sri Krishna, used here and elsewhere throughout the Gita to remind us of the complete, unending joy lying within us, is Hrishīkesha, 'he whose hair stands on end with joy.' The name used here for Arjuna should also inspire us: Dhananjaya, 'conqueror of wealth.' This is the perfect epithet for the person who meditates, for he discovers that real wealth comes from giving freely of himself to others. We do not learn to do this overnight; we do not go to sleep selfish one evening and wake up the next morning with every trace of self-will gone. The battle against the ego is a long, agonizing affair that may take our entire lifetime. When we accept this challenge, all the boredom goes out of life; every day brings new tests of our endurance, strength, and desire to win the battle. All our angry, aggressive instincts are harnessed to the effort; instead of anger using us, we control it and use it as a source of tremendous power. We can take heart from the great mystics who have successfully met this challenge. As the Buddha declared twenty-five hundred years ago: "One man may conquer in battle a thousand times a thousand men, but if another conquers himself, he is the greatest of conquerors." It is only a mystic who can understand what struggle is required to extinguish self-will, to gain the patience that will not be exhausted by any attack and the forgiveness that will bear even with those who slander him.

अथ व्यवस्थितान्दृष्ट्वा धार्तराष्ट्रान्कपिध्वजः ।
प्रवृत्ते शस्त्रसंपाते धनुरुद्यम्य पाण्डवः ॥२०॥
हृषीकेशं तदा वाक्यमिदमाह महीपते ।
अर्जुन उवाच
सेनयोरुभयोर्मध्ये रथं स्थापय मेऽच्युत ॥२१॥
यावदेतान्निरीक्षेऽहं योद्धुकामानवस्थितान् ।
कैर्मया सह योद्धव्यमस्मिन्रणसमुद्यमे ॥२२॥
योत्स्यमानानवेक्षेऽहं य एतेऽत्र समागताः ।
धार्तराष्ट्रस्य दुर्बुद्धेर्युद्धे प्रियचिकीर्षवः ॥२३॥
संजय उवाच
एवमुक्तो हृषीकेशो गुडाकेशेन भारत ।
सेनयोरुभयोर्मध्ये स्थापयित्वा रथोत्तमम् ॥२४॥
भीष्मद्रोणप्रमुखतः सर्वेषां च महीक्षिताम् ।
उवाच पार्थ पश्यैतान्समवेतान्कुरूनिति ॥२५॥
तत्रापश्यत्स्थितान्पार्थः पितॄनथ पितामहान् ।
आचार्यान्मातुलान्भ्रातॄन् पुत्रान्पौत्रान्सखींस्तथा ॥२६॥
श्वशुरान्सुहृदश्चैव सेनयोरुभयोरपि ।
तान्समीक्ष्य स कौन्तेयः सर्वान्बन्धूनवस्थितान् ॥२७॥
कृपया परयाविष्टो विषीदन्निदमब्रवीत् ।

अर्जुन उवाच
दृष्ट्वेमं स्वजनं कृष्ण युयुत्सुं समुपस्थितम् ॥२८॥
सीदन्ति मम गात्राणि मुखं च परिशुष्यति ।
वेपथुश्च शरीरे मे रोमहर्षश्च जायते ॥२९॥

*20–21. Then, O Dhritarāshtra, lord of the earth,
having seen your son's forces set in their places and
the fighting about to begin, Arjuna spoke these words
to Sri Krishna.*

ARJUNA:
*21–22. O Krishna, drive my chariot between the
two armies. I want to see those who desire to fight with
me. With whom will this battle be fought?
23. I wish to see those assembled to fight for
Duryodhana, those who desire to please the evil-
minded son of Dhritarāshtra by engaging in war.*

SANJAYA:
*24–25. Thus Arjuna spoke, and Sri Krishna,
driving his splendid chariot between the two armies,
facing Bhīshma and Drona and all the kings of the
earth, said: "Arjuna, behold all the Kurus gathered
together."
26–29. And Arjuna, as he stood between the two
armies, saw fathers and grandfathers, teachers, uncles,
and brothers, sons and grandsons, in-laws and
friends. Seeing his kinsmen established in opposition,
Arjuna fell into confusion and mournfully spoke
these words:*

ARJUNA:
*O Krishna, I see my own relations here with the desire
to fight, and my limbs are weak; my mouth is dry, my
body is shaking, and my hair is standing on end.*

One of the best definitions of confusion is doing what is unnecessary and failing to do what is necessary. This is our condition in life

when we clash with our family and friends and fail to fight our worst enemy, our own self-will and separateness. Arjuna is beginning to realize that the battle he must wage is against what he has always considered to be a part of himself. Faced with the task of ridding his consciousness of every trace of selfish desire, Arjuna, like you and me, moans and groans to Sri Krishna: "How can I possibly fight these people, my best pals, with whom I have painted Hastināpura red?"

We have been so conditioned to search for happiness in sense-pleasure that defying these urges appears to be a denial of life itself. Actually the opposite is true. As we progress on the spiritual path, our vision begins to clear and our passions begin to come under our control, and we discover that we have been pursuing agitation instead of joy and accumulation instead of security. The curious thing is that we are convinced we can isolate pleasure as our own private possession, although it has escaped our grasp time and again. We may have failed in the past, but the next time we think we will succeed for sure, and we go on trying. The other day, while going for a walk, we saw two Alsatians that reminded me of our flair for chasing pleasure and profit. These two dogs were trying to catch a rainbow over a water sprinkler so they could take it home to their doghouse. One after the other they would come, jump into the spray, and snap at the rainbow hovering there. As soon as one had finished his jump, the other one would follow right on his heels as if to say, "You don't know how to do it. Let me show you," over and over again. This is what you and I do when we try to catch the rainbow that is personal pleasure, power, profit, and prestige. Even though we go through the experience many times, we do not seem able to learn from it. The Gita very compassionately says that the sooner we learn this lesson in life, the better it will be.

It is not surprising that we follow passing pleasure instead of abiding joy when we consider the extensive influence of the mass media and the widespread use of advertising. From childhood onwards we are conditioned to believe that we are our body, senses, and mind, and that happiness lies in satisfying their whims and desires. We have become so accustomed to telling Mr. Ego "You say,

I do" that the very idea of questioning his authority by training the senses and changing our attitudes makes us tremble in anxiety. In meditation we begin to suspect that the ego is really a tyrant who has usurped the throne from our real Self, called the Ātman in Sanskrit, which is the source of all wisdom and beauty in life. Once this suspicion arises, the days of the ego's tyranny are numbered, and the cloud of confusion which has blinded us begins to be dispelled.

गाण्डीवं स्रंसते हस्तात्त्वक्चैव परिदह्यते ।
न च शक्नोम्यवस्थातुं भ्रमतीव च मे मनः ॥३०॥
निमित्तानि च पश्यामि विपरीतानि केशव ।
न च श्रेयोऽनुपश्यामि हत्वा स्वजनमाहवे ॥३१॥
न काङ्क्षे विजयं कृष्ण न च राज्यं सुखानि च ।
किं नो राज्येन गोविन्द किं भोगैर्जीवितेन वा ॥३२॥

*30. My skin is burning, and the bow Gāndīva has slipped from my hand. I am unable to stand, and my mind seems to be whirling.*
*31. The signs are evil for us. I do not see that any good can come from killing our relations in battle.*
*32. O Krishna, I do not desire victory, or a kingdom, or pleasures. Of what use is a kingdom, O Govinda,[5] or pleasure, or even life?*

Arjuna is suffering from a very contemporary malady, paralysis of the will. This is the crux of many of our problems. We say we want to put an end to war, yet we go on making missiles, guns, tanks, and bombs, and arming other countries in the name of peace. We are alarmed about violence, yet we let our children watch hour after hour of violent television programs. We are concerned about pollution, but we pour pollutants by the ton into our rivers and oceans;

5. *Govinda*, a popular name for Sri Krishna, means 'leader of the cowherds'. As a young man Sri Krishna lived in a village of cowherds called Vrindāvana, and many legends are told of his pranks and exploits there.

we make the air unfit to breathe and strip the earth of irreplaceable resources. Even when we can clearly see the urgency of stopping pollution and putting an end to violence, we lack the will and the wisdom to translate our desire into effective action.

Though Arjuna deplores this state of inertia and self-pity, he is unable to shake it off. This is often our problem too; we can diagnose our shortcomings and even give a brilliant synopsis of the world's woes, but as long as our knowledge is limited to intellectual analysis, we will not have the capacity to make the world more peaceful; we will not be able to prevent pollution or even bring together estranged families and friends. It is the deeper will and wisdom which come through meditation that enable us to tap the creative resources and untiring energy lying latent in our consciousness.

Looking at the opposing army, Arjuna is plunged into confusion. His special bow, Gāndīva, slips from his grasp, and his mind reels at the prospect of fighting. This confrontation comes to all of us who are in earnest about putting an end to the cause of our sorrow and suffering, our petty little personality driven by self-will. Success on the spiritual path requires the highest kind of courage we can muster, for every ounce of our strength and resolution will be tested. It was my spiritual teacher, my mother's mother, who showed me through the example of her own life that it is the nonviolent person who cannot be frightened; the violent person can always be threatened with greater violence. If you want to see real bravery, look at the person who is patient under attack, who will not retaliate, who will suffer rather than inflict suffering on others. This is the heroic ideal Jesus the Christ gives us to follow: "Love your enemies, bless them that curse you, do good to them that hate you, and pray for them which despitefully use you, and persecute you, that ye may be the children of your Father which is in heaven." Sri Krishna, in his infinite grace, helps Arjuna find this source of strength within himself, just as he enables us, when we turn to him, to become patient when attacked, forbearing when provoked, and loving when hated. This is the way we grow fearless and strong enough to grapple with the grave problems that threaten our world.

येषामर्थे काङ्क्षितं नो राज्यं भोगाः सुखानि च ।
त इमेऽवस्थिता युद्धे प्राणांस्त्यक्त्वा धनानि च ॥३३॥
आचार्याः पितरः पुत्रास्तथैव च पितामहाः ।
मातुलाः श्वशुराः पौत्राः श्यालाः सम्बन्धिनस्तथा ॥३४॥
एतान्न हन्तुमिच्छामि घ्नतोऽपि मधुसूदन ।
अपि त्रैलोक्यराज्यस्य हेतोः किं नु महीकृते ॥३५॥
निहत्य धार्तराष्ट्रान्नः का प्रीतिः स्याज्जनार्दन ।
पापमेवाश्रयेदस्मान् हत्वैतानाततायिनः ॥३६॥
तस्मान्नार्हा वयं हन्तुं धार्तराष्ट्रान्स्वबान्धवान् ।
स्वजनं हि कथं हत्वा सुखिनः स्याम माधव ॥३७॥
यद्यप्येते न पश्यन्ति लोभोपहतचेतसः ।
कुलक्षयकृतं दोषं मित्रद्रोहे च पातकम् ॥३८॥
कथं न ज्ञेयमस्माभिः पापादस्मान्निवर्तितुम् ।
कुलक्षयकृतं दोषं प्रपश्यद्भिर्जनार्दन ॥३९॥
कुलक्षये प्रणश्यन्ति कुलधर्माः सनातनाः ।
धर्मे नष्टे कुलं कृत्स्नमधर्मोऽभिभवत्युत ॥४०॥
अधर्माभिभवात्कृष्ण प्रदुष्यन्ति कुलस्त्रियः ।
स्त्रीषु दुष्टासु वार्ष्णेय जायते वर्णसंकरः ॥४१॥

*33–34. Those for whose sake we would desire a kingdom, or pleasures, or happiness—teachers, fathers, sons, even grandfathers, uncles, in-laws, grandsons, and others with family ties—they are engaging in this battle, renouncing their wealth and their lives.*
*35. Even if they were to kill me, O Krishna, I would not want to kill them, not even to become ruler of the three worlds. How much less for the earth alone?*
*36. O Krishna, what satisfaction could we find in killing Dhritarāshtra's sons? We would become sinners by slaying these men, even though evil.*

*37. The sons of Dhritarāshtra are related to us;*
*therefore, we should not kill them, O Mādhava. How*
*can we gain happiness by killing members of our*
*own family?*
*38–39. Though they are overpowered by greed and*
*do not see evil in the decay of the family or the sin in*
*injuring friends, we see the evil which comes from the*
*destruction of the family. Why shouldn't we turn*
*away from this sin?*
*40. When a family declines, ancient traditions are*
*destroyed. With them are lost the spiritual foundations*
*for life, and the entire family loses its sense of unity.*
*41. O Krishna, where there is no sense of unity the*
*women of the family become corrupt. With the cor-*
*ruption of the women, O Vārshneya, society is*
*plunged into chaos.*

To realize the unity underlying all life and live in harmony with this awareness, we do not have to quit our jobs, leave our family, drop out of school, or turn our back on society. Living in the midst of our extended circle of family and friends provides the perfect context for learning to see the Lord in everyone, everywhere, every minute, for in these deep personal relationships we can easily forget ourselves, our comforts, and our conveniences in ensuring the joy of others. This is a straightforward way of reducing our self-will, which is the only obstacle standing between the Lord and us.

In these verses Arjuna has addressed Sri Krishna very appropriately by using two of his family names: Mādhava, 'son of the Madhu clan'; and Vārshneya, 'he who belongs to the family of the Vrishnis.' The family has always been a symbol of unity and selfless love in spite of the serious problems that have afflicted it from time to time. Arjuna's confusion over his family responsibility is ours as well, for we have let competition and self-interest tear our families apart. Husband and wife compete against each other, parents and children compete, sister and brother compete; even the grandparents are trying to get into the act. This competitive tendency has spread from the home to the school and campus, to organizations, and of course to international relationships. It breeds distrust, suspicion, and jealousy wherever it goes. As our security increases through meditation, we find we do not need to compete, for the source of joy and wisdom is right within us. Competition has so distorted our vision that we are defensive towards even our dear ones, but as our meditation deepens, we see what lasting joy there is in trying to complete one another rather than compete against one another.

If just one person in a family takes to the spiritual life, he or she can slowly transform the home from a battleground into a citadel of strength for family and friends alike. This is particularly true when the woman takes to meditation, for she is in an advantageous position to support and inspire others with her selfless love, patience, and forbearance. Over a period of time, her quiet example will enable her partner, parents, children, and friends to grow strong and secure. My Grandmother used to tell the girls in my ancestral family that it was their privilege to light up the home with their generosity and forgiveness; she showed them in her own personal life how everyone cannot but respond to such a woman, and how family and friends eagerly return to such a home. We should bear in mind that this concept of family loyalty and unity is not limited just to parents and children; those who deeply care for each other's welfare are a family in the best sense of the word, and it is by extending our capacity to love and support to a widening circle of friends that we transform our life into a permanent force for good in the world. Anandamayi Ma, the great woman saint of modern India whom my wife, Christine, and I have had the blessing of meeting, expresses this awareness of unity when she says: "The different organs of the human body fulfill different functions; some more noble certainly than others, but for the good of the body they must all be cared for. In the same way, try to treat with equal love all the people with whom you have relations. Make a habit of this and soon you will perceive that all humankind is as your family. Thus the abyss between 'myself' and 'yourself' will be filled in, which is the goal of all religious worship."

संकरो नरकायैव कुलघ्नानां कुलस्य च ।
पतन्ति पितरो ह्येषां लुप्तपिण्डोदकक्रियाः ॥४२॥

*42. Social chaos is hell for the family, and for those
who have destroyed the family as well. It disrupts the
process of spiritual evolution begun by our ancestors.*

The perennial truth expressed in the scriptures, which we can realize in our own lives, is that all creation is evolving towards the unitive state. Any sensitive person can appreciate the grandeur of this
process; just observe a hive of bees at work, or walk through a forest, or live with a selfless person, and you cannot but be profoundly
moved by the way every aspect of creation can work with all the
rest as a unit in perfect harmony. This truth has far-reaching application in our daily life. On the one hand, every time we violate the
unity of life by venting our anger on those around us, or by harming
our fellow creatures, we work against this evolution; on the other
hand, every time we forgive others, do what benefits them, or alleviate the distress of any creature, we contribute towards this evolution. By striving to live in accord with this unity we bring about the
fulfillment of all creation, which of course includes our own, but by
going our separate ways, we obstruct the evolution of consciousness
towards the unitive state.

The unity underlying life is so complete and pervasive that when
we inflict suffering on the smallest creature, we injure the whole.
When we refrain from habits that harm others, when we take up
jobs that relieve suffering, when we work to put an end to anger and
separateness, we strengthen the whole. John Donne reminds us of
this when he says, "No man is an island entire of itself; every man is
a piece of the continent, a part of the main; if a clod be washed
away by the sea, Europe is the less, as well as if a promontory were,
as well as if a manor of thy friends or of thine own were; any man's
death diminishes me, because I am involved in mankind; and therefore never send to know for whom the bell tolls, it tolls for thee."

There is nothing more important in life than learning to express this unity in all our relationships: with our family and friends, with our colleagues and fellow workers, with other communities and countries, with other races and religious groups, and with other creatures. This is the way we come to see the presence of the Lord.

दोषैरेतैः कुलघ्नानां वर्णसंकरकारकैः ।
उत्साद्यन्ते जातिधर्माः कुलधर्माश्च शाश्वताः ॥४३॥
उत्सन्नकुलधर्माणां मनुष्याणां जनार्दन ।
नरकेऽनियतं वासो भवतीत्यनुशुश्रुम ॥४४॥

*43. The timeless spiritual foundations of the family
and society are destroyed by these terrible deeds
which violate the unity of life.
44. It is said that those who have lost sight of this
unity dwell in hell.*

Arjuna is beginning to see the terrible consequences of disunity. We have a tendency to think of heaven and hell as physical domains located on some celestial map, when really they describe our state of being right here on earth. This is the practical meaning of unity and separateness in our daily living; we have a taste of heaven every time we forget ourselves in ensuring the joy of others, and we have a bitter dose of the other place when we think or behave unkindly.

Violence, war, pollution, estrangement, and insensitivity to our fellow creatures are external manifestations of the disunity seething in our consciousness. Because we live on the surface level of life we are often unaware of the anger and fear burning deep within us. It is only after practicing meditation for some years that we learn to descend into the depths of our consciousness where we can observe these negative forces at work and put an end to their disruptive activity. Right from the first days of our sādhana, the spiritual disciplines we practice begin, however slowly, to transform our character, conduct, and consciousness. When the divisiveness which has been agitating us and making life difficult begins to mend, we get immediate evidence in our daily life: our health improves, long-

standing personal conflicts subside, our mind becomes clear and
our intellect lucid; an unshakable sense of security and well-being
follows us wherever we go, and whatever challenges loom before us,
we know we have the will and the wisdom to meet them effectively.

Unification of consciousness can turn the most ordinary of us
into a spiritual force; this is the power of the unitive state that we
enter in the climax of meditation, called *samādhi* in Sanskrit, when
our heart, mind, and spirit come to rest in the Lord. Swami Ramdas,
a delightful saint whom we met in his āshram in South India, summarizes this in simple, clear words: "All sādhanas are done with a
view to still the mind. The perfectly still mind is universal spirit."

अहो बत महत्पापं कर्तुं व्यवसिता वयम् ।
यद्राज्यसुखलोभेन हन्तुं खजनमुद्यताः ॥४५॥

*45. This is a great sin! We are prepared to kill
our own relations out of greed for the pleasures of
a kingdom.*

It is easy to see why Arjuna represents you and me so well, for with
a few well-chosen words he is able to point right to the cause of our
disrupted relationships and increasing insecurity. With dismay he
tells Sri Krishna how he fears the devastating consequences of not
keeping in mind the unity underlying all life. For personal pleasure
and profit we are willing to sacrifice the welfare of our family and
friends, our society and environment. In Arjuna's time, it was greed
for a kingdom; in ours it is greed for a higher salary, a prestigious
home, and a partner who will always agree with our opinions. As
long as we seek to be lord and master over our petty personal kingdom, we bar the door to the Lord of Love within us, and confusion
and chaos reign. This is the inevitable consequence of violating the
unity of life by attempting to go our own separate way.

The Bible tells us we cannot love both God and Mammon at the
same time, and in the spiritual tradition of India, great sages like Sri
Ramakrishna will remind us that for Rāma—the source of abiding
joy—to come into our lives, Kāma—the craving to satisfy our per-

sonal desires—must go. Our capacity for joy is so great that going after passing pleasure is like throwing a peanut in an elephant's mouth and expecting him to be full. We are so trapped in our self-willed existence that we do not realize how clouded our judgment is and how tragically we waste the gift of life trying to acquire another car, which will pollute our environment, or enjoy an extra gourmet meal, which will add to our weight and injure our health.

The English mystic William Law describes how most of us go through life under the illusion that satisfying selfish desires can bring happiness: "A life devoted to the interests and enjoyments of this world, spent and wasted in the slavery of earthly desires, may be truly called a dream, as having all the shortness, vanity, and delusion of a dream; only with this great difference, that when a dream is over nothing is lost but fictions and fancies; but when the dream of life is ended only by death, all that eternity is lost, for which we were brought into being." As long as we have not seen someone who has conquered all that is self-willed in himself, we will find it hard to believe that we can cast off this spell of separateness and awake to the unity of life. But in the world's great religions, we have mystic after mystic showing us that this is possible if we are willing to change the direction of our lives through the practice of meditation. In our own time we have the inspiring example of Mahatma Gandhi, who attained the unitive state and helped many others undertake the struggle against all that is selfish and separate. His real name was Mohandas K. Gandhi, but in India we prefer to call him by the title Mahātmā, 'the great soul,' because by reducing himself to zero he was able to identify himself with the four hundred million suffering people of India and bring about not only their political emancipation but a spiritual renewal as well. Sometimes he is known as Gandhiji, the *ji* being added to his name as a sign of affection and respect. Such was Gandhiji's spiritual stature that he could transform little people made of clay into heroes and heroines. During India's struggle for independence, we had a leader from the North-West Frontier Province whose people were very brave and enduring, but also rather violent. Gandhi had the daring to go into their midst and tell them that if they really were brave they would throw away their guns and learn to fight nonviolently. Their leader, Khan Abdul Ghaffar Khan, responded to Gandhi's challenge and transformed himself into such an invincible combination of courage and gentleness that he became known as the Frontier Gandhi.

Even one person standing against violence, whether it is in the home, in the community, or between nations, can become a source of inspiration for everyone who comes in contact with him. The words from the Sermon on the Mount are not just to be illuminated in manuscripts; the Dhammapada is not just to be inscribed on *stūpas;* the Bhagavad Gita is not just to be etched on palmyra strips and carried in our hip pocket as a talisman. The man or woman who practices the teachings of these great scriptures will become aware of the unity of life, and this awareness will give constant strength and inspiration to those who seek to turn anger into compassion, fear into courage, and selfishness into self-forgetfulness in the joy of the whole.

यदि मामप्रतीकारमशस्त्रं शस्त्रपाणयः ।
धार्तराष्ट्रा रणे हन्युस्तन्मे क्षेमतरं भवेत् ॥४६॥

*46. If the sons of Dhritarāshtra, weapons in hand,
attack me in battle, and if they kill me unarmed and
unresisting, that would be better for me.*

My spiritual teacher, my Grandmother, did not know how to read or write, but she knew Sri Krishna, and she gave me the message of the Gita in language that all of us can remember. All life is a battlefield, she used to tell me; whether we like it or not, we are born to fight. We have no choice in this, but we do have the choice of our opponent and our weapon. If we fight other people, often our dear ones, we cannot but lose, but if we choose to fight all that is selfish and violent in us, we cannot but win. There is no such thing as defeat on the spiritual path once we join Sri Krishna, but if we try to fight against him, we shall never know victory.

When we fight others, we are harming everyone; when we fight all that is base and self-willed in us, we are benefiting everyone. This is the constant theme of the great scriptures. We need not be impressed by anyone who recites the scriptures or observes all the outer rituals of religion, but we cannot help being impressed by someone who can forgive, who can forget harm done to him or turn his back on his own personal profit and prestige for the welfare of all. From the Old Testament we have these words: "He that is slow to anger is better than the mighty; and he that ruleth his spirit, than he that taketh a city." It is the same theme as in the Hindu and Buddhist scriptures. "He that is slow to anger is better than the mighty." Conversely, he that is quick to anger is the weakest, most pathetic, and most harmful of men.

Unfortunately, in our day anger is considered to be part of expressing oneself, a vital means of communication. We have anger groups, called by other names, and we have anger seminars, called by other names, in which people agitate one another and send each other out as harmful influences into their homes and society. We have anger books, anger plays, and even films glorifying the angry man. After attending a violent movie like this, someone may come to us with virulent words and fling these words at us like lances. But if we can sit secure and patient and, after he has exhausted himself, comfort him by our patience, win him over by our love, we are practicing the words of the Bible: "Blessed are the peacemakers, for they shall be called the children of God."

The capacity to be patient, to bear with others through thick and thin, is within the reach of anyone who will practice meditation and put the welfare of those around him before his own. We do not realize what tremendous energy for selfless living we have lying dormant within us. Because we see the world through eyes of separateness, we think of ourselves as frail, fragmented creatures, with hardly any strength to stand up in life and make our contribution. But when we take to the spiritual path and start putting into practice the wise, compassionate counsel Sri Krishna gives us in the Gita, we shall discover our real stature and be able to contribute in good measure to life.

संजय उवाच
एवमुक्त्वार्जुनः संख्ये रथोपस्थ उपाविशत् ।
विसृज्य सशरं चापं शोकसंविग्नमानसः ॥४७॥

SANJAYA.

*47. Overwhelmed by sorrow, Arjuna spoke these*
*words. And casting away his bow and his arrows, he*
*sat down in his chariot in the middle of the battlefield.*

Arjuna, like you and me, wants to contribute to his family's happiness and his country's welfare, but he falls despondent at Sri Krishna's feet because he does not know how to make this contribution. Sri Krishna has not yet opened his divine lips to reveal himself to Arjuna as the supreme Teacher, but he will soon do so in the second chapter, giving Arjuna the practical instruction and guidance he needs to shake off this depression and inertia.

My ancestral family used to render a community service by staging a performance of Kathakali, the traditional dance drama of Kerala, in the open courtyard of our home under the warm evening sky of spring. Everyone was welcome, and hundreds of people would come from the village and surrounding neighborhood to see these stories from India's spiritual tradition enacted, to refresh their memory of the scriptures and deepen their devotion to the Lord who is always present in our consciousness. During the opening scenes the children would fall asleep on their mothers' or grandmothers' laps, but as soon as Sri Krishna is about to come on stage the mothers awaken them and they sit up with eyes wide open. Everyone gets ready: people who were nodding become alert, and those who were talking become silent. We concentrate the moment we hear Sri Krishna is coming, because he is our real Self. So for me, the real Gita begins with the second chapter where the Lord begins to teach. When we see Sri Krishna, it is a reminder that beneath all our surface deficiencies and seeming drawbacks, there is always present in our hearts the source of all joy and security who is the Lord.

To discover the Lord within is the supreme purpose of life, worthy of all our time, energy, resources, and dedication. For most of us, pain and suffering are necessary to make us grow up. Like little children learning to walk without support, we have to learn to walk without clutching at pleasure or profit. Watch a child learning to walk; it can be a pathetic sight to watch the little one get up only to fall down again and again. It is tempting to say out of sympathy, "Alfred, don't bother to get up. Just lie there and we'll bring everything to you." But this would permanently stunt poor Alfred's capacity for living.

It is reassuring to remember that many before us have learned to stand up to life's challenges; the mystics of both East and West tell us in inspiring words how all boredom and drabness go out of life in this greatest of all adventures. We must learn to be vigilant constantly; we cannot lapse into lack of watchfulness for one minute. Swami Ramdas describes the joy of rising to this challenge: "There is no greater victory in the life of a human being than victory over the mind. He who has controlled the gusts of passion that arise within him and the violent actions that proceed therefrom is the real hero. All the disturbances in the physical plane are due to chaos and confusion existing in the mind. Therefore to conquer the mind through the awareness of the great Truth that pervades all existence is the key to real success and the consequent harmony and peace in the individual and in the world. . . . The true soldier is he who fights not the external but the internal foes."

All the capacity for fighting, all the aggressive capacity we waste in conflict with others, can be harnessed through the practice of meditation to fight against our own self-will and separateness. This is a twenty-four-hour fight, because even in our dreams we can learn to dispel fear and anger. But it will take many, many years of valiant and unceasing resistance to win the peace that passeth all understanding.

When we meditate every morning we are putting on armor for the day's battle against our own impatience, inadequacy, resentment, and hostility. Of course, it is going to be extremely painful and distressing when we have to put all around us first and ourselves

last, but at night when we go to bed there is such a fierce joy in the
knowledge that we have contributed in some measure to the joy and
growth of our family and community, even though we have suffered
deeply ourselves. Often, however, when we have to choose to suffer
ourselves rather than bring suffering to others, we do exactly what
Arjuna does at the end of this chapter: we moan that we will not,
cannot fight.

Without the grace and guidance of the Lord none of us can win
this battle. In inspiring words, Sri Krishna will rouse us to action by
reminding us that our real Self is pure, perfect, and untainted, no
matter what our past errors. It does not matter what mistakes we
may have committed or what trouble we may have brought on ourselves and others out of our ignorance; if we surrender ourselves
completely to the Lord of Love who is always present in the depths
of our consciousness, we will discover that these mistakes never
touched us. We can throw away the ugly ego mask at last if we will
turn our face to the Lord, take to meditation, and do everything
possible to bring peace and security to our world.

इति अर्जुनविषादयोगो नाम प्रथमोऽध्यायः ॥१॥

CHAPTER TWO

# The Illumined Man

संजय उवाच
तं तथा कृपयाविष्टमश्रुपूर्णाकुलेक्षणम् ।
विषीदन्तमिदं वाक्यमुवाच मधुसूदनः ॥१॥

SANJAYA:

*1. These are the words that Sri Krishna spoke to Arjuna, whose eyes were burning with tears of self-pity and confusion.*

Right from the beginning of the second chapter Sri Krishna reveals himself as the perfect spiritual teacher, striking a strong note intended to shock Arjuna out of his despondency. When Sri Krishna, silent until now, opens the dialogue, there are no soft words, no honeyed phrases. He pours withering contempt upon Arjuna, who has been weeping and protesting that he cannot fight against his senses, passions, and self-will. No spiritual teacher fails to resort to this method of shocking and strengthening us with strong words when occasion demands—and of course, when opportunity calls for it, supporting us with tender, compassionate, and loving words also.

Once I went to my spiritual teacher, my Grandmother, complained to her that I was in great sorrow, and asked her why people should cause me suffering. You should not picture my Granny as a sweet old lady seated in a rocking chair, knitting. There were times when she would take me to task and use language that would hurt and yet strengthen me. She could be very harsh, particularly to those who were close to her. This was the mark of her love. And on this occasion, she pricked my bubble with ease by pointing out that I was not suffering from sorrow, but from self-pity. When I grieve

for others, that is sorrow, which is ennobling and strengthening.
But when I grieve for myself, it is not really sorrow; it is the debilitating emotion called self-pity.

Immediately, like a true friend, Lord Krishna tells Arjuna to
stop behaving like a water buffalo, which if it sees a pool of mud
will go and roll in it over and over again until it is completely
covered with mud. In order to live like a human being, to lead the
spiritual life, Sri Krishna insists, Arjuna must stop wallowing in
self-pity. To apply this to ourselves, we have only to look into our
minds to see how much of our time we spend in dwelling upon what
our father did to us, what our mother did to us, or what our husband said five years ago on a certain rainy morning. This is what
goes on in the witches' caldron seething in our consciousness.

Arjuna has beautiful eyes, but he has been sulking like a little
child, and shedding so many tears of self-pity that he cannot see
anything clearly. Our eyes, when full of self-pity, see even those
who are dear to us as very cruel, as persecutors—not because they
are like that, but because the tears of self-pity have clouded our vision. As the Buddha puts it: "'He abused me, he beat me, he defeated me, he robbed me,' in those who harbor such thoughts hatred will not cease. 'He abused me, he beat me, he defeated me, he
robbed me,' in those who do not harbor such thoughts hatred will
cease." In the next verse Lord Krishna will tell Arjuna to silence
this "she did this to me, he did this to me" refrain in his consciousness so that he can hear the Lord. Sri Krishna has to shock. He has
to be severe to get Arjuna out of this morass. This is the way he
shows his love.

श्री भगवानुवाच
कुतस्त्वा कश्मलमिदं विषमे समुपस्थितम् ।
अनार्यजुष्टमस्वर्ग्यमकीर्तिकरमर्जुन ॥२॥

SRI KRISHNA:
*2. This despair and self-pity in a time of crisis is
mean and unworthy of you, Arjuna. How have you
fallen into a state so far from the path to liberation?*

Sri Krishna looks with severity at Arjuna, who is overwhelmed by the horror and agony of self-naughting, and says, "Where does this depression, despair, and self-pity come from, Arjuna? Get rid of these things. They have no place where I live in your heart of hearts."

The Lord uses the word *anārya,* which means 'unworthy,' to refer to Arjuna, whose conduct has not been fully worthy of himself as a human being. You and I, by coming into the human context, have evolved beyond the animal stage. What distinguishes us from the animal level is our capacity to forget our own petty, personal satisfactions in bringing about the happiness of all those around us.

On one occasion when I was in college, a group of college friends and I were discussing the usual topics that young men talk about when my spiritual teacher overheard a few key words, mostly about personal pleasure, profit, and prestige. She was just coming from the cow shed, which she cleaned with her own holy hands every morning. The cows provided us with milk, butter, and yogurt, and therefore she considered it a necessary part of hospitality to make the home of the cows clean, to give them proper food, and to guard them against sickness. So, just as she was coming out of the cattle shed, she heard us all talking in this vein. She never wasted time on many words. She caught hold of one of my cousins, who was the ringleader, and told him, "You get in the cow shed. That is where you belong. We will give you plenty of hay, cotton seeds, and rice water." Because of her great love for us, she could shock us with these strong words without hurting us at all.

It is not enough if we walk on two legs, part our hair, and go about in a new suit. That does not make us a human being. The capacity to forget our own personal pleasures, and to bless those who curse us—these are what mark a human being.

Arjuna cowers now because there is lightning darting out of the eyes of the Lord when he says *asvargya:* "You have locked the door of the kingdom of heaven within by refusing to eliminate your ego, by failing to turn your back upon self-will and separateness." The Lord shocks Arjuna out of his torpor by using these strong words, and when he has been pulled out of his despondency and despair, Sri Krishna continues in the third verse:

क्लैब्यं मा स्म गमः पार्थ नैतत्त्वय्युपपद्यते ।
क्षुद्रं हृदयदौर्बल्यं त्यक्त्वोत्तिष्ठ परंतप ॥३॥

*3. It does not become you to yield to this weakness.
Arise with a brave heart, and destroy the enemy.*

Sri Krishna asks Arjuna to come out of this whirlpool in which he has been caught, saying, "It is unworthy of you. You are a blessed human being now and you cannot say that these challenges are too great to face."

When the senses are driving us, we cannot make the excuse that we are unable to resist. We cannot say that just because there is food nearby we must eat. We cannot say that everybody smokes, therefore we must smoke; everybody drinks, therefore we must drink. However difficult circumstances may be, however formidable the challenges may be, we can be certain that because the Lord is within us we have the infinite resources of his love and wisdom to meet the challenge. When our dear ones are agitating us, we cannot complain that we cannot live with them, because the Lord will answer: "Why can't you? I am in you. Draw upon Me to return love for hatred, goodwill for ill will."

Having thus made short work of Arjuna's ego, Sri Krishna now tells him to get up, to rise to his full stature, to straighten his head until it reaches the stars with the whole sky as a crown. He says, "Arjuna, you have such valor in you because I live in you; all you need do is to draw upon Me and you can destroy the enemy completely." He ends the verse by addressing Arjuna as *parantapa*, 'destroyer of the foe,' which is the ego.

अर्जुन उवाच
कथं भीष्ममहं संख्ये द्रोणं च मधुसूदन ।
इषुभिः प्रति योत्स्यामि पूजार्हावरिसूदन ॥४॥
गुरूनहत्वा हि महानुभावान्
    श्रेयो भोक्तुं भैश्यमपीह लोके ।
हत्वार्थकामांस्तु गुरूनिहैव
    भुञ्जीय भोगान्रुधिरप्रदिग्धान् ॥५॥

ARJUNA:

*4. How can I ever bring myself to fight against
Bhīshma and Drona, who are worthy of reverence?
How can I, Krishna?*
*5. Certainly it would be better to spend my life
begging than to kill these great and worthy souls; if I
killed them, every pleasure I found would be tainted.*

Even though Sri Krishna has been taking Arjuna to task for be-
moaning his helplessness and his inability to conquer his own sense
cravings and selfish urges, Arjuna still feels that the senses are his
friends. He turns to Sri Krishna and says, "What kind of counsel are
you giving me? These senses are good, steady friends of mine. I
should receive them with hospitality and give them everything they
ask for. I am shocked that you should use such unspiritual language
and ask me to defy the clamor of my senses."

In our own daily life we can see how much conflict we have
where the senses are concerned. When the eyes want to see something agitating, we feel we must show them all kinds of violent
sights. When the ears want to hear raucous music that will agitate
the mind and damage our hearing, we tell the Lord, "You don't expect us to say no, do you?" Since we do not want to be cruel to our
ears, we take them to all kinds of parties where the din is so great it
lifts the roof. Then food—what the palate demands *must* be good for
the body. Highly spiced, deep-fried, overrefined—this is the stuff the
palate enjoys; so we conclude that it is very good for the body.

In the early part of our spiritual development this conflict is likely to come to all of us because we have given license to our senses most of the time. Similarly, we have never consciously tried to go against our self-will, and therefore even the discipline of putting our family and friends first is going to take a long time to master. We are likely to complain to the Lord that by asking us to put other people first all the time, he is making our path too difficult. "Why should I inflict violence on my self-will?" we moan. "This agitates my mind, making meditation difficult."

न चैतद्विद्म: कतरन्नो गरीयो
    यद्वा जयेम यदि वा नो जयेयु:।
यानेव हत्वा न जिजीविषाम-
    स्तेऽवस्थिता: प्रमुखे धार्तराष्ट्रा: ॥६॥

*6. I don't even know which would be better, for us to conquer them or for them to conquer us. The sons of Dhritarāshtra have confronted us; but why would we care to live if we kill them?*

Arjuna now raises a question which many of us may be tempted to ask when we are having difficulties on the spiritual path. He says, "After all, even if I conquer the senses, how do I know that I will be able to control my mind? And even if I control my mind, how do I know that I will be able to eliminate the ego? This is all speculation. I am not convinced that all this is so carefully connected. It appears too logical. What does it matter if I conquer my senses or my senses conquer me? What is the use of rising to the summit of human consciousness and conquering the world if I am not there to enjoy it—if my senses are detached, my mind cannot get excited, and there are no more likes and dislikes?"

It seems to Arjuna that he is being asked to throw himself into an even more painful, agitating state. He is completely bewildered, and now breaks down and asks for spiritual guidance from Sri Krishna, the Lord of Love, who has been listening quietly and compassionately all the while.

कार्पण्यदोषोपहतस्वभावः
पृच्छामि त्वां धर्मसंमूढचेताः ।
यच्छ्रेयः स्यान्निश्चितं ब्रूहि तन्मे
शिष्यस्तेऽहं शाधि मां त्वां प्रपन्नम् ॥७॥

*7. My will is paralyzed, and I am utterly confused.*
*Tell me which is the better path for me. Let me be your*
*disciple. I have fallen at your feet; give me instruction.*

Arjuna tells Sri Krishna, "I am your disciple. Now be my teacher and instruct me." In the orthodox Hindu tradition, until we ask the teacher to be our guru, showing our readiness to receive his guidance on the path of meditation, he does not offer to do this for us. It is a great moment in the Gita when for the first time Arjuna declares himself the devoted disciple of Sri Krishna and asks him to be his beloved teacher. The word *guru* means 'one who is heavy,' so heavy that he can never be shaken. A guru is a person who is so deeply established within himself that no force on earth can affect the complete love he feels for everyone. If you curse him, he will bless you; if you harm him, he will serve you; and if you exploit him, he will become your benefactor. It is good for us to remember that the guru, the spiritual teacher, is in every one of us. All that another person can do is to make us aware of the teacher within ourselves. The outer teacher makes us aware of the teacher within, and to the extent we can be loyal to the outer teacher, we are being loyal to ourselves, to our Ātman. We are told in the scriptures to select a teacher very carefully. We should not get carried away by personal appearance—because we like his hair style or his saffron robe. We have to listen carefully, judge carefully, and then make our own decision. Once we make a decision and select an outer teacher who is suited to our spiritual needs, we must be completely loyal to him.

If I may refer to my own small example, I have committed the innumerable mistakes that most of us commit in our modern civilization, but in giving all my love to my Grandmother, I was able to attain some spiritual awareness. When the disciples love the guru, it is this love that unifies their consciousness. At the time when we are ready for it, the spiritual teacher will step aside to show us that all the love we have been giving him has been directed to our own Ātman. The guru, who has become complete in himself, does not need anyone's love to make him secure; it is in order to unify the consciousness of the disciple that the relationship exists.

If you are prepared to undertake the long journey, the teacher will give you the map and all necessary instructions, but you have got to do the travelling yourself. That the teacher cannot provide. The purpose of visiting a spiritual teacher is to be reminded that there is a destination, there is a supreme goal in life, and we all have the innate capacity to undertake the journey. When people used to sit in the presence of Sri Ramana Maharshi and praise him, he would just smile as if to say, "There is no Sri Ramana Maharshi. I am just a little keyhole through which, when you fix your eye with complete concentration, you can see the beckoning, irresistible vision of the Lord."

The Lord is most eager to meet us. He is much more eager than we are. He has been waiting and waiting for millennia, and we are standing him up. Every minute he is looking to see whether there is anybody coming home at last, and finally, after millions of years of evolution, when all our toys are broken, we decide reluctantly to turn back. When we go back like this after millions of years of separation, the Lord tells us out of his infinite love, "What good boys and girls to have come on your own." In this verse Arjuna begins to turn to the Lord, by asking him to lead him forward on the path to Self-realization.

न हि प्रपश्यामि ममापनुद्याद्
यच्छोकमुच्छोषणमिन्द्रियाणाम् ।
अवाप्य भूमावसपत्तमृद्धं
राज्यं सुराणामपि चाधिपत्यम् ॥८॥
संजय उवाच
एवमुक्त्वा हृषीकेशं गुडाकेशः परंतपः ।
न योत्स्य इति गोविन्दमुक्त्वा तूष्णीं बभूव ह ॥९॥

*8. What can overcome a sorrow that saps all my*
*vitality? Even power over men and gods or the wealth*
*of an empire seems empty.*
SANJAYA:
*9. This is how Arjuna, the great warrior, spoke to*
*Sri Krishna. With the words, "O Govinda, I will not*
*fight," he became silent.*

Arjuna, taking his bow and arrows and putting them away, looks silently at the ground. His actions tell the Lord, "I am not going to fight because I do not have the strength, the will, or the wisdom to turn all my endeavor toward the conquest of myself." It is impossible for any of us to take on the ego, which is really a formidable foe, without undergoing tremendous spiritual disciplines. When, in the early stage of their meditation, people complain to me about difficulties in controlling the palate, or giving up smoking or drinking, the Job's consolation that I give them is that these are just preliminaries. The fight has not begun yet; you are just clearing the arena. The real fight begins only when the ego, huge and ferocious, comes onto the field.

Yesterday I was listening to a reading from the Bible about the combat between David and Goliath, which I took as a firsthand description of the spiritual life. Goliath comes and tells the armies of Israel to send their best man; if their man wins, then Goliath and his followers will serve the Israelites, but if Goliath wins, then the Israelites will become the servants of their enemy. The description of Goliath is impressive and terrifying. His armor is invulnerable. He stands on the field like a giant. When David comes up with his five little stones and his puny sling, Goliath gets furious and says, "What are you trying to do, catch a dog?" David takes a little pebble and hits Goliath with a fatal blow right on the center of his forehead. I interpret such stories spiritually. One of the Shiva mantrams is called *pancākshara*, the 'five-lettered' mantram, and for me the five pebbles that David was carrying were a five-lettered mantram with which he was able to defeat his own ego.

The ego's size can be gauged by our anger, and the further we get into the depths of our consciousness, the more we shall see what anger surges in us when our self-will is violated. To defeat this colossal ego will take a long, long period of struggle with many reverses. But finally, the Gita and the scriptures of all religions assure us, through the grace of the Lord we will be able to eliminate our ego and extinguish our self-will, which is the only barrier between us and the Lord.

तमुवाच हृषीकेशः प्रहसन्निव भारत ।
सेनयोरुभयोर्मध्ये विषीदन्तमिदं वचः ॥१०॥

*10. As they stood between the two armies*
*Sri Krishna spoke with a smile to Arjuna, who*
*had fallen into despair.*

The Lord, Sri Krishna, does not get angry or agitated while listening to Arjuna's many objections, but smiling with great affection for his disciple and friend, he now begins to teach.

श्री भगवानुवाच
अशोच्यानन्वशोचस्त्वं प्रज्ञावादांश्च भाषसे ।
गतासूनगतासूंश्च नानुशोचन्ति पण्डिताः ॥११॥

SRI KRISHNA:
*11. You speak sincerely, but your sorrow has no*
*cause; the wise grieve neither for the living nor for*
*the dead.*

It is a marvelous line where the Lord implies: "You speak very wise words, but your action is just the opposite of wise. You say you want joy, but the direction in which you are going is towards sorrow. You say you want fulfillment, but what you are going after every day is frustration." Sri Krishna is now implying all this to Arjuna by pointing out that the way he uses words is one thing, but the way he lives is another.

Do we want joy, security, and fulfillment? This is the question you and I have to ask ourselves first, and then we must move towards these goals. We all say we want peace. There is no individual that says he does not want peace, no nation that says it does not want peace. But if we want peace, we must do the things that make for peace. If we do the things that make for war, only war will come. Bismarck, the Iron Chancellor of Germany, used to say, "I do not want war; I only want victory." On the individual level, too, we are tempted to say, "I don't want to fight with my parents, but I want to have my way. I don't want to have any conflict with my partner, but I want to have my way." In answer to statements like these, Sri Ramakrishna would say, in a childlike outburst, "If you want to go east, you mustn't go west." It is not enough if we talk about peace; we must work for it. Even today, after more than two thousand years of recorded history scarred by frequent wars, all the countries on the face of the earth say they long for peace but keep producing armaments, keep suspecting other countries. The Lord of Love therefore asks you and me through Arjuna, "If you want peace, why don't you work for peace?"

In the second line the Lord, in strong words, gives us the secret of our nature. Arjuna has been talking about death, saying that he does not want to be killed, that he does not want to kill, but Sri Krishna reminds him that it is only the body which is born and which dies. You and I were never born, nor will we ever die, because our real Self is not limited by our physical body. We are spirit eternal, infinite, and immutable. This is the great discovery we make in the climax of meditation, that we are not the body, senses, mind, or intellect, but supreme spirit.

When Sri Ramana Maharshi's body was about to be resolved

back into the five elements at the time of his death in 1950, all India wept for him, saying, "You are leaving us, you are going away." His simple reply was, "Where can I go? I am everywhere. How can I leave you?" This is the supreme experience of unity that comes to us in samādhi. No adventure in the external world, however great, can ever be compared to the experience of Sri Ramana Maharshi seated on his little bamboo cot, going beyond time, place, and circumstance and seeing the cosmos as one, all creation as one in the Lord.

न त्वेवाहं जातु नासं न त्वं नेमे जनाधिपाः ।
न चैव न भविष्यामः सर्वे वयमतः परम् ॥१२॥

*12. There has never been a time when you and I and the kings gathered here have not existed, nor will there be a time when we will cease to exist.*

We are now getting into one of the central themes of the Gita. Looking at Arjuna compassionately, the Lord tells him, "You have always been; you will always be." This is the realization we have to make in life—that we are immortal, that we have everlasting life. Jesus in the Christian scriptures often says, "I have come to bring you everlasting life." It is into this experiential discovery that we shall move in the course of our meditation. As our meditation deepens, we shall find we are delivered from time into the Eternal Now.

One of the ways to test our progress on the spiritual path is to see how much we are able to free ourselves from the oppressive pressure of time. The clock is the most eloquent symbol of the tyranny of time. I sometimes speculate that before long we may be wearing watches with only one hand, showing a second divided into sixty subseconds. When we make an appointment we will say, "Come at two seconds and thirty-nine subseconds after two thirty." This is the direction in which we are moving as we become more and more conscious of time. I notice that if at a traffic signal the automobile in front delays ten seconds, immediately the other drivers begin using the horn. I always ask, "What is the harm if that person repeats the mantram for ten seconds and gives us all a chance to slow down?"

The constant craze for going faster, faster, faster throws us more and more into consciousness of time; and curiously enough, when we are oppressed by time, we make many mistakes. It is possible to do our work and attend to our duties without in any way being oppressed by time, and when we work free from the bondage of time we do not make mistakes, we do not get tense, and the quality of our living improves.

One of the easiest ways to free yourself from the tyranny of time is to get up early in the morning. When we used to go for our walks in Oakland in the morning, I would invariably see a few people— usually the same people—making a dash to catch the bus as if they were participating in the Olympics. Often they would be too late, and I always wanted to ask, "Why do you want to run to miss the bus? You might as well walk slowly and miss it." This is the irony. You run and you still miss the bus, and in addition, the expression you direct at the bus driver is far from loving. You think that he has been doing it on purpose—just waiting until he saw you coming, then stepping on the gas.

This simple step of starting the day early in the morning gives you an opportunity to get up leisurely, take a short walk, and then have your meditation. In meditation, also, do not be aware of time. The moment you become aware of time in meditation, there is an unfavorable factor introduced. When we were having our large class of four or five hundred people on campus, the first night in meditation a few people kept looking at their watches, which I did not object to. But I did begin to protest when they started listening to see if the watches were still ticking. Once you start meditating, forget about time. There is no need to check the clock; you can learn to time the length of the meditation fairly well by the length of the passage you are using.

In order to regain our birthright of eternal life we have to rise gradually above the physical level. Any habit that ties us to the body through a sensory bond eventually has to be thrown away.

Right at the outset of the spiritual life we must begin to rid ourselves of physical habits, such as smoking, drinking, and overeating,
which will impede our progress. This is not at all a moral or ethical
problem; it is a question of spiritual engineering. As long as we tie
ourselves to the body by stimulating the senses, and especially by
building relationships on the physical level, we cannot realize this
legacy of everlasting life.

देहिनोऽस्मिन्यथा देहे कौमारं यौवनं जरा ।
तथा देहान्तरप्राप्तिर्धीरस्तत्र न मुह्यति ॥१३॥

*13. As the same person inhabits the body through
childhood, youth, and old age, so too at the time of
death he attains another body. The man of wisdom
is not deluded by these changes.*

Just as the body, with which all of us identify ourselves, changes
from childhood to youth to old age, similarly, Sri Krishna says
against the background of reincarnation, we acquire a new body
when we pass from one life into another after the last great change
called death. There is no need to subscribe to the theory of reincarnation to lead the spiritual life, but it cannot be easily dismissed with
a shrug of the shoulders as a feverish product of the tropical imagination. There is a wealth of evidence based upon scientific research
available to those who want to understand this subject before pro-
nouncing a verdict on it. Somerset Maugham, who came to India in
the late thirties and had the glorious opportunity of meeting Sri
Ramana Maharshi, from whom he drew the saint in his novel *The
Razor's Edge,* says that even for a nonbeliever it is very difficult to
attack the philosophical structure on which reincarnation is based.

One of the common questions about the theory of reincarnation
that people ask is, "How is it we do not remember anything of our
previous lives?" Sri Krishna is now implying that just as it is very
difficult to remember even our childhood in this life, it is impossible
for most of us to remember our past lives. If the Lord were to ask us

what we were doing on our birthday when we were one year old, we would say that we do not remember. If he said, "Then you didn't exist," we would object to his teasing and say, "Of course we existed. We received presents and great love from our parents on that day."

Sri Krishna now hints to Arjuna, "Just take your thoughts back to your childhood and look at yourself as a child." If we go back as far as we can to our childhood and picture ourselves as we were then, what our needs, ambitions, hopes, and desires were, we just cannot believe that it is the same person. Today what makes us happy is money, and to a child money means nothing, gold means nothing. One of my cousins, when she was going to the elementary school in our village, had a beautiful gold necklace made by our village goldsmith. One day when she was about eight she came home at noon for lunch, and her mother was alarmed to see that the necklace was not around her neck. "Have you lost your gold necklace, our family treasure?" she asked. And the little girl smiled and said, "No, mommy, I haven't lost it. I traded it for a mango." Somebody had offered her a mango, which was much more important, much more enjoyable, and she had just given the necklace away.

In these verses we are being led gradually to the question of death. I think it is Dr. Carl Jung who tells us that in the deep consciousness of most people there is a great fear of death, even among those who say they want to die. One of the most beneficial effects of meditation is that as our meditation deepens, we gradually lose our fear of death. This is the proof that we are rising above physical consciousness. If we talk about death to a great mystic like Sri Ramana Maharshi, who attained illumination at age seventeen, he will just chuckle quietly and say, "I died when I was seventeen." When at the time of samādhi we lose our 'I,' our separate ego, that *is* death. This is the experience of St. Paul when he says, *Not I, not I, but Christ liveth in me.* Even intellectually we can ask ourselves the question: when our 'I' is wiped out, who is there to die? As we keep putting the happiness of others first all the time, our little 'I' is erased, and with the elimination of the little finite 'I,' the Immortal 'I,' which is the Lord of Love, is revealed in our consciousness.

मात्रास्पर्शास्तु कौन्तेय शीतोष्णसुखदुःखदाः ।
आगमापायिनोऽनित्यास्तांस्तितिक्षस्व भारत ॥१४॥

*14. When the senses contact sense objects,
Kaunteya,[1] we experience cold or heat, pleasure
or pain. These are fleeting, they come and go.
Bear them patiently, Arjuna.*

Sri Krishna is now telling Arjuna the nature of the stimulus and response relationship that our body, senses, and mind have with the
finite world. When the material object that is the body comes in
contact with other material objects, such as the dollar, then there
is some kind of relationship established with which we have nothing
to do at all. Sri Krishna, as I imagine him, now almost seems surprised and asks Arjuna, "Why should you get elated or depressed if
one material object has its physical reaction with another material
object?"

Depression has become one of the scourges of the modern world.
Here the Gita can give immediate advice: when you are getting excited, when good things are happening to you, when fortune is
smiling on you and you want to go on talking, telling everyone
about how happy you are, that is the time not to get elated. On such
occasions of elation—when your play is on Broadway, when your
novel is on the best-seller list, when people are wanting your autograph—I am usually a bit of a wet blanket and say, "Now is the time
not to jump up. Don't pick up the telephone. Don't call people. Just
keep repeating the mantram." When the mind is getting agitated,
when the waves of elation are starting to rise, do not give them a
chance.

Elation expresses itself in many ways in many people. We have
some friends for whom the danger signal is the tendency to talk
constantly; for others it is grandiose visions of the future. Apparently modest, apparently humble people can have such grand visions
of the future that it is difficult to remind them how ordinary most of

1. Here Sri Krishna addresses Arjuna by the familiar name *Kaunteya,* 'the
son of Kuntī.' Kuntī is Arjuna's mother.

us are in the present. People with a talent for writing, drama, music, or painting, however mediocre, may get caught on such occasions in the visualization of scenes of great grandeur. They see audiences looking adoringly at them, fighting for their autograph, and in their elation they actually believe that these things can come true. The Gita suggests that when we conjure up elated visions of grandeur, we should guard ourselves against this kind of excitement. If we keep our equilibrium when good things happen, then when fortune frowns, as she surely will because that is her nature, we can sit back with fortitude and forbearance and remain secure.

When you are in a depression, do not withdraw into yourself. There are people with the best intentions who say, "We don't want to come and force our depression on others." This is another trick of the mind, which tells you, "Since you're in a depression now, why not confine yourself to your little cell?" This is likely to make you more and more depressed. When despondency comes, I would suggest a smile. Even if it does not look quite like a real smile, it does such good for everyone, because even a smile comes from a deeper level of consciousness. If you can at least repeat the mantram and smile, the great process of relaxation begins.

Not allowing ourselves to get elated is neither callousness nor passivity; it leads us into a deeper level of awareness where we find we are completely secure and joyful. Anything that tends to make us elated is inevitably going to throw us into depression, and one of my grievances against psychedelic drugs is the very deceptive state of euphoria into which they lead us. In order to guard ourselves against elation and the following state of deprivation, we cannot allow our senses to be stimulated unduly.

In the language of the Gita, not only elation and depression, not only pleasure and pain, but everything in life is a duality; and in order to attain samādhi, one of the magnificent disciplines taught by Sri Krishna is evenness of mind. He will say, *Samatvam yoga ucyate:* "Yoga is evenness of mind."

यं हि न व्यथयन्त्येते पुरुषं पुरुषर्षभ ।
समदुःखसुखं धीरं सोऽमृतत्वाय कल्पते ॥१५॥

*15. The person who is unaffected by these, who is the same in pleasure and pain, is truly wise and fit for immortality. Assert your strength to realize this, Arjuna.*

The Lord of Love begins to tell us how we can prepare ourselves for reclaiming our birthright of everlasting life. In the scriptures of all religions this promise of eternal life is given, but people usually understand it only as a very inspiring metaphor, not to be taken with scientific gravity. The mystics say that it is time that is an illusion; eternity is the reality.

How is it that you and I see people, very often our own dear ones, dying around us, and yet never ask ourselves the question: "Is this one day going to happen to me, too? Is there no way by which I can transcend death?" In my beautiful village in Kerala state, whenever a death took place, which is not infrequent in a poor country like India, my Grandmother would always insist that I accompany her to the scene of sorrow, even when I was still an impressionable and sensitive child. As I sat by the side of dying people while my Grandmother held their hand, it used to torture me. Even in my dreams, I long remembered the sight of all this agony I witnessed during the days when I was growing up at my Granny's feet.

Later on, when through her blessing I began to turn inwards, I realized why she had taken me to those scenes of great bereavement. It was to make me ask if there were any way to transcend death. Her grace enabled me to know that in the midst of life I am in death, and it made me want above everything else to go beyond death, to attain immortality in this very life. As my meditation deepened, I was able to harness even the fear of death, turning it into power to help me to overcome death.

As I began to recall the words of my spiritual teacher, it began to dawn upon me for the first time that man is not mortal. When Einstein was asked how he discovered the law of relativity, he said that it was by questioning an axiom accepted by all the world, and the scriptures say the stage will come in your meditation when you will begin to question whether death is inevitable. This is not an intellectual question at all, but an experience in which some lurking suspicion comes into your consciousness and whispers that you are not mortal. Once you hear that, there is great hope, and a great desire to turn your back upon all lesser desires so that you can use all your capacity to make the supreme discovery that you are eternal.

In every religion, the great founders will promise us everlasting life. In the Bhagavad Gita it is enunciated in very clear terms. The Gita says that as long as we identify ourselves obsessively with our body, we will keep falling into the jaws of death. In meditation we can very skillfully minimize this obsessive identification with the body. On many levels, in many ways, we can practice the spiritual disciplines which will gradually lift us above physical consciousness, giving us a continuing sense of freedom and a continuing sense of progress on the spiritual path.

नासतो विद्यते भावो नाभावो विद्यते सतः।
उभयोरपि दृष्टोऽन्तस्त्वनयोस्तत्त्वदर्शिभिः ॥१६॥

*16. The impermanent has no reality; reality lies in the eternal. Those who have seen the boundary between these two have attained the end of all knowledge.*

The main difficulty with Arjuna, as with all of us, is that he looks upon himself as the body, as the biochemical mechanism with which all of us identify ourselves. Sri Krishna is trying to help Arjuna break through this wrong identification to remind him that he is not the perishable body, which is only the house in which he dwells. He is the imperishable Ātman.

In this verse Lord Krishna distinguishes between what is real and what is unreal. With the far-reaching spiritual penetration of the Sanskrit scriptures, the Gita says that whatever perishes is not real. Whatever exists in reality, exists always. That which comes into being today and passes away a hundred years from now cannot truly be said to exist. In this sense the body, which is conditioned by time, is unreal.

Mahatma Gandhi, who studied Sanskrit while in jail, pointed out that the Sanskrit word *sat* has two meanings: the first is 'truth,' and the second is 'that which is.' When asked for a definition of God, Gandhi said, "Truth is God. God alone is and nothing else exists." During the campaign to free India of British domination, he told the oppressed millions of India that evil has no existence in itself; we support evil, therefore it exists, but if we withdraw our support, it ceases to exist. In the example of his own life, Gandhi applied this truth on the practical level in his campaigns of nonviolent resistance against British exploitation.

Those who see the supreme Truth, the Lord, in their own consciousness, says Sri Krishna, know that that which is not real has no existence, and that which is real has no nonexistence. Arjuna just gets confused. He looks at his body, he looks at Sri Krishna's body, he looks at Sri Krishna's peacock feather, and he just cannot believe that all this is an optical illusion. This is why the Lord limits the vision of the unreality of the passing phenomenal world only to the great mystics, who have realized that beneath the apparent, impermanent world, the world of separate fragments, there lies the changeless Reality called God. But this vision does not apply to the vast majority of human beings. As long as we believe we are a separate fragment, as long as we identify ourselves with our body, we have to deal with the phenomenal world which is very real to us. I am real. Every one of us is real. Even after we realize the truth that all life is one, we can continue the activities of the workaday world, establishing personal relationships with loving artistry. We learn to show our love to each individual in the way that is most correct for that special relationship, though never forgetting the underlying unity of all.

अविनाशि तु तद्विद्धि येन सर्वमिदं ततम् ।
विनाशमव्ययस्यास्य न कश्चित्कर्तुमर्हति ॥१७॥

*17. Realize That which pervades the universe and is indestructible; no power can affect this unchanging, imperishable Reality.*

Sri Krishna is driving into Arjuna's consciousness the great truth that he is neither the perishable body, nor the changing senses, nor the unsteady mind, nor the wavering intellect, but the Ātman, as immutable and infinite as Brahman itself. The Lord of Love tells Arjuna the nature of that which pervades the cosmos. All that we see in life is pervaded by the immortal, immutable, infinite Reality we call God.

अन्तवन्त इमे देहा नित्यस्योक्ताः शरीरिणः ।
अनाशिनोऽप्रमेयस्य तस्माद्युध्यस्व भारत ॥१८॥

*18. The body is mortal, but he who dwells in the body is said to be immortal and immeasurable. Therefore, O Bhārata,[2] fight in this battle.*

This body of ours will come to an end, but we, the Ātman, are eternal. Here again there is the reminder that we have no end, and therefore never should confuse ourselves with the perishable body. The body is changing from moment to moment, and even in the few minutes you have been reading these words, the body has already moved closer to the great change called death. The mind is subject to even more rapid changes. We have only to look at our desires and moods to see how much the mind is subject to change. In Sanskrit the word for the phenomenal world is *samsāra,* 'that which is moving intensely'—being born, dying, being born again, dying again.

Whenever we cling to anything that is continually changing, we will become more and more insecure with the passage of time.

2. Bharata was the first universal emperor of ancient India. By addressing Arjuna as Bhārata, 'descendent of Bharata', Sri Krishna is reminding him of his nobility and his Indian citizenship.

When we identify ourselves obsessively with the body, every morning begins to pose a threat as we get older and move into the latter half of life. Every morning we look in the mirror to see if there are new wrinkles on the face, bags under the eyes, or grey showing in our hair. Even it, with the advance of modern surgery, these bags and wrinkles can be removed, after ten or twenty years the same fate will come to us. Such is the paradox of life: when we cling to the body, it loses its beauty, but when we do not cling to it, and use the body as an instrument given to us to serve others, even on the physical level it glows with health and beauty, as we can see from the lives of many great mystics. When Sri Ramakrishna walked along the streets of Calcutta, legends say people were dazzled by his beauty. His spiritual radiance was so great that it would shine through the body. Ramakrishna did not like drawing the attention of people, so with his childlike simplicity he got an old blanket and covered his body when going out. When our consciousness becomes pure, even the body begins to reflect its light.

The body is the temple of the Lord and must be looked after with care. Even at the age of seventy-seven, my Grandmother had a beautiful, healthy body because she was always aware that this temple had to be kept in good order, swept with the mantram broom, and purified through the daily practice of meditation and discriminating restraint of the senses. We show respect for the Lord within by keeping the body healthy, clean, and beautiful. Any attempt to misuse the body, or to indulge the senses at the expense of the body, is a violation of the divine presence. Where books, movies, television, and our eating habits are concerned, we must be vigilant to see we are not indulging the senses at the cost of the health of our body or mind. Even with those who are making progress on the spiritual path, the senses can play havoc if vigilance is relaxed. In order to transform our belief that we are the changing body to identification with the Ātman, we begin by governing the senses very carefully for many years. This is not done in an ascetic spirit, or for the purpose of mortification, but to see that every day we give the body what is needed to sustain it as a spiritual instrument.

Just as we purify the physical body, called *sthūlasharīra* in Sanskrit, with vigilant care of the senses, healthy physical exercise, and repetition of the mantram, we purify the subtle body, *sūkshma-sharīra,* by cultivating healthy thoughts. Thoughts are the food of the subtle body of samskāras, our mental and emotional conditioning.[3] We are eating this food all the time, and every time a thought rises in the mind we have added either to the nutrition of the subtle body or to its malnutrition. The unhealthy effect on the mind of anger, resentment, and hostility is so great that it can cause far-reaching damage even on the physical level. To keep the subtle body pure and healthy we must first and foremost cultivate the virtue of forgiveness.

य एनं वेत्ति हन्तारं यश्चैनं मन्यते हतम् ।
उभौ तौ न विजानीतो नायं हन्ति न हन्यते ॥१९॥
न जायते म्रियते वा कदाचि-
न्नायं भूत्वा भविता वा न भूयः ।
अजो नित्यः शाश्वतोऽयं पुराणो
न हन्यते हन्यमाने शरीरे ॥२०॥

*19. One person believes he is the slayer, another believes he is the slain. Both these are ignorant; there is neither slayer nor slain.*
*20. We were never born, we will never die; we have never undergone change, we can never undergo change. Unborn, eternal, immutable, immemorial, we do not die when the body dies.*

Sri Krishna continues to explain our real nature in this verse, which is a favorite of mystics in India. *Na jāyate,* we were never born; *na mriyate vā,* therefore we will never die; *nā 'yam bhūtvā bhavitā vā*

---

3. A samskāra is a latency or a tendency in our personality, conditioned by experiences in this and former lives. It is almost always a negative term, implying rigidity and lack of freedom. A very strong samskāra might be called an obsession. *Samskāra* comes from the root *kri,* 'to do' or 'make', plus the prefix *sam,* 'fully', 'completely'; therefore the word implies that something is fully formed, elaborated, or rigid.

*na bhūyah,* we have never undergone any change, and we will never undergo any change. *Aja,* never born; *nitya,* eternal; *shāshvata,* immutable. And finally, in a flash of subtle humor, the Lord adds *purāna,* 'the ancient one': compared to us the Himālayas are like a newborn baby. When the world was not, when the galaxies were not, we were already greybeards faltering with a staff.

The play of the Lord, in which he assumes a body and seems to pass through childhood, youth, and old age, is beautifully portrayed in Kerala in the Guruvayur Temple, dedicated to Lord Krishna. Sri Krishna is worshipped there in three different forms during the three periods of the day. In the morning if you go to the temple you will see a little baby Krishna in a cradle being fed, bathed, and sung to sleep. Most children like to go for the morning service. They see that the Lord is even younger than they, and they have such compassion for him, and feel so protective, that they do not want any harm to come to the little one. This protective feeling towards the Lord as a little boy is very good discipline for spiritual awareness. At noon Sri Krishna is a young man straight as a palm tree, outgoing and very vigorous. You see Lord Krishna as the embodiment of physical fitness at its best. You find the peacock feather, the garland of wildflowers, the yellow silk dhoti, and the bamboo flute. Young people like to visit the temple at noon, when it is easy for them to identify with the Lord. In the evening, when the sun is about to set and tropical India is at its artistic best, the old people like to go and see the Lord, who, hardly able to stand up with a staff, is ready to shed the body. The different images serve to remind you that these are all changes which affect only the body, and that you should learn to rise above the physical level so that you do not get caught in the cycle of change.

वेदाविनाशिनं नित्यं य एनमजमव्ययम् ।
कथं स पुरुषः पार्थ कं घातयति हन्ति कम् ॥२१॥
वासांसि जीर्णानि यथा विहाय
नवानि गृह्णाति नरोऽपराणि ।
तथा शरीराणि विहाय जीर्णा-
न्यन्यानि संयाति नवानि देही ॥२२॥

*21. Realizing That which is indestructible, eternal,
unborn, and unchanging, how can we slay or cause
another to slay?*
*22. As we abandon worn-out clothes and acquire
new ones, so when the body is worn out a new one
is acquired by the Self, who lives within.*

In this homely verse, Sri Krishna says that just as when our clothes
become old and tattered we throw them away to put on new ones,
similarly, when this body has become unfit for serving others,
it is time to throw it away. We should not cling to it. When Sri
Ramana Maharshi's body was about to fall away and thousands of
his disciples begged him to continue on, he said, "No, this body is
no longer able to serve you. As long as it can serve you, I will retain
it, but when the time comes when it can no longer serve you, I am
going to lay it aside."

One of the facts about my Granny's life that I do not usually refer to is her attitude towards death. For her, death was not a painful topic because she believed so firmly that our real Self cannot
die. In other words, even though we cannot but grieve when our
dear ones pass away, the mystics tell us that underneath this grief
we should always remember that death is only a change of rooms.
They are speaking mostly against the background of transmigra-
tion, or reincarnation. We should all be aware, though, that the
spiritual life does not depend on our acceptance of reincarnation,
nor does meditation require that we subscribe to the theory of trans-
migration of souls. Whether we believe in one life or in a million
lives, the supreme goal is valid; the basis of meditation remains

valid for all. I would strongly discourage trying to speculate about previous or future lives; this life is headache enough. Let us confine our attention to this life and try as far as our capacity goes to learn to love the Lord here and now.

नैनं छिन्दन्ति शस्त्राणि नैनं दहति पावक: ।
न चैनं क्लेदयन्त्यापो न शोषयति मारुत: ॥२३॥
अच्छेद्योऽयमदाह्योऽयमक्लेद्योऽशोष्य एव च ।
नित्य: सर्वगत: स्थाणुरचलोऽयं सनातन: ॥२४॥
अव्यक्तोऽयमचिन्त्योऽयमविकार्योऽयमुच्यते ।
तस्मादेवं विदित्वैनं नानुशोचितुमर्हसि ॥२५॥

*23. The Self cannot be pierced by weapons or burned by fire; water cannot wet it, nor can the wind dry it.*
*24. The Self cannot be pierced or burned, made wet or dry; it is everlasting and infinite, standing on the motionless foundations of eternity.*
*25. The Self is unmanifested, beyond all thought and beyond all change; knowing this, you should not grieve.*

Arjuna still does not grasp what Sri Krishna means by "our real Self, our Ātman." In this particular verse, the Lord is trying to awaken Arjuna, and all of us, to the truth of our existence. In referring to our real personality, which is divine, he uses three words beginning with *a,* which means 'not': *avyakto 'yam, acintyo 'yam, avikāryo 'yam. Avyakta* means 'that which is not expressed,' 'that which remains concealed.' Our real personality is not revealed at all; it is very cunningly concealed. It is *acintya,* or unthinkable, because it is beyond the dualities of conceptual thinking. It is *avikārya,* beyond all change. Our real personality never grows because it is ever perfect. It is never enriched because it is always full. If we try to understand the applicability of these three terms to our own personality, we may begin to suspect that it lies beyond the fleeting body, beyond the turbulent senses, beyond the restless mind, beyond the clouded intellect.

*Avyakta* comes from the word *vyakta,* which means 'completely expressed,' 'manifested.' We all look upon ourselves as only our apparent personality, the body-mind complex, never realizing our real personality, which is the infinite, immortal, immutable Ātman. If someone were to ask us what we consider our personality, we would be likely to say that our height is six foot three, our weight two hundred twenty pounds. To this a sage like Sri Ramana Maharshi would say, "I did not ask you the dimensions of your house; I want you to tell me what your real personality is." If we tell him that we have two million in the bank, the illumined man will say, "You haven't answered my question." If we add that we have won the Nobel prize, he would still say, "Don't beat about the bush."

Meister Eckhart summarizes the truth of the Ātman beautifully when he points out that the seed of God is latent in all of us. In Sanskrit it is called the Ātman; Meister Eckhart prefers to use the homely expression "the seed of God." He says that just as apple seeds grow into apple trees and pear seeds into pear trees, God seeds grow into God trees. The word *avyakta* implies that our only purpose in life is to reveal the divine personality that is concealed in all of us. The seed has to be helped to germinate, the weeds have to be removed regularly, and then the plant becomes a God tree.

The question then arises as to how we can reveal this hidden divinity in our everyday life. To see what noxious weeds keep the seed of our true divinity from growing, we have only to look at people who are insecure, who dwell upon themselves. Such people look at everything, everyone, through their own personal needs; these are the people who say they are very, very sensitive. In my early days in Berkeley, one of the expressions that I heard often when I visited Telegraph Avenue was "I'm so sensitive." According to this interpretation, "insensitive" refers to anybody who treads on my corns, although when I tread on another's corns, I don't even know it. In the language of the mystic, being sensitive means being sensitive to the needs of others. You will find that the more you attend to the needs of others, in your own family for example, the less you will get hurt, agitated, or hostile over seemingly trivial things.

In a movie my wife and I saw recently, one that had been highly praised by critics, the daughter could not sleep one night just because her mother had repeated one question twice: "Have you forgotten my candy?" The daughter thought that her insomnia that night was a result of utter sensitiveness. Now, my mother often repeats herself half a dozen times—repetition runs in our family. And I don't say she is casting aspersions on my integrity. I just say she knows I am an absentminded professor, and I am likely to forget things. As long as we are deeply convinced that our parents want only our happiness, that our partner or our children want only to add to our joy, things are not likely to upset us. My mother uses curt language at times, but under no circumstances would it occur to me to think that she is trying to vent some pent-up hostility or to take it out on me, say, because the milkman diluted the milk more than he is permitted to. Wherever there is not this deep faith in those around us, I think that no attempt at courtesy, no attempt to repeat the right words and phrases, will bring about clear communication. Whenever we get agitated or apprehensive in daily relationships, because of some remark, some act of omission or commission from those around us, the very best thing we can do is use the mantram.

All of us are trying to build our personality on the short span of time in which we thrash about in the sensory world. During the Anglo-Saxon period, a few Christian emissaries came to England to preach the gospel of Christ. One of the Anglo-Saxon kings, Edwin, took counsel with his advisors over the new faith. It must have been a bitter winter evening, with snow outside and torches lighting up the hall, for the answer Edwin received is as evocative as it is thoughtful. "My lord," one man replied, "it has often seemed to me that we live like a swallow that suddenly darts through this hall at dinnertime and passes out again through a far window. It comes from the darkness and returns to darkness; for only a short while is it warm and safe from the winter weather. That is how I regard our life. I don't know where I have come from; all I know is a little span of light, until I pass again into the darkness beyond. If this new faith can tell us truly what lies before and after, I think it most worthy of being followed."

The Gita says that outside of this life we come from infinity and go again into infinity. This short spell in between, called *vyakta,* the finite, the mortal, the physical spell, has hypnotized us so that we say, "My personality lives only for one hundred years, from the time my body was born until the time it will die." But in the first word of this verse, *avyakta,* we are reminded that our life is infinite. Jesus constantly reminds the people not only of ancient Judea but of the whole modern world that we can have everlasting life by rising above the physical level of consciousness. This is a great challenge that can set the imagination of man on fire if he can understand that it is possible to rise so high above physical consciousness and fragmentation that he can see not only what goes on in the lighted hall, but also what is outside in the infinite darkness beyond death.

The second word is *acintya.* Because our real Self, our divine personality, is beyond all the dualities of conceptual thinking, it can only be revealed when the turbulent factory of the mind has become completely still. For most of us, the mind factory keeps working twenty-four hours, day in and day out, without a holiday, and without any strikes either. There is only overtime. All of us must have experienced moments when we have begged, "If only I could stop thinking. If only I could close down, put up a little note, 'Don't enter here. It's a misdemeanor.'" If we could, we would find ourselves beginning to reveal our true identity. One of the unfortunate trends of our modern civilization is described by that learned phrase, *Cogito ergo sum:* "I think, therefore I am." The mystic says, "I have stopped thinking; therefore I am." You can see the diametrical contrast. We are all under the impression that if we go beyond thinking, we are nowhere. If the mind is closed down, we fear we will be out of a job: "What will I do? How will I spend my time? What will I dream about in my sleep?" The answer is: why do you want to dream? Why do you want to go after personal profit and personal pleasure? It is in forgetting yourself, and in serving others, that you really come to life.

One of the constant reproaches that used to be flung at me in my early days of meditation was, "You have such a fascinating personality. Why do you want to throw it away? Look at your intellect, razor sharp; why do you want to blunt it? Look at your mind, so active, so productive; why do you want to still it?" It is not even possible for most of us to suspect that at present we have no personality. Most of us cannot reveal even one ray of the magnificence within us. This is why Sri Ramana Maharshi and other mystics will not take us seriously when we say we live. The mystics tell us that if we can only succeed in throwing away this mask which has become part of our face, the physical-psychical mask that we now call our personality, then all our magnificent capacity for loving, acting, and serving will come into our lives.

अथ चैनं नित्यजातं नित्यं वा मन्यसे मृतम् ।
तथापि त्वं महाबाहो नैनं शोचितुमर्हसि ॥२६॥
जातस्य हि ध्रुवो मृत्युर्ध्रुवं जन्म मृतस्य च ।
तस्मादपरिहार्येऽर्थे न त्वं शोचितुमर्हसि ॥२७॥
अव्यक्तादीनि भूतानि व्यक्तमध्यानि भारत ।
अव्यक्तनिधनान्येव तत्र का परिदेवना ॥२८॥

*26. O mighty Arjuna, even if you believe the
Self to be subject to birth and death, you should
not grieve.*
*27. Death is inevitable for the living; birth is
inevitable for the dead. Since these are unavoidable,
you should not grieve.*
*28. Every creature is unmanifested at first, and then
attains a manifestation, O Bhārata. When its end has
come, it once again becomes unmanifested. What
is there to lament in this?*

In spite of all the Lord's assurances about the immortality of the Self, there still lurks in Arjuna's consciousness the thought: "I am the body; when the body dies, I die." This is one of the occasions in the Gita when Sri Krishna teases Arjuna, telling him that even if he believes he is the body, even then he should not be afraid of death, because death is the natural consummation of the body's span of life. The Lord is forcing Arjuna to break through his wrong identification with the body, which is only the house in which he dwells.

Through the practice of meditation, we will acquire the delightful incapacity to associate people very much with their physical appearance. If someone asks me, "How tall is Jeff?" I have to take time to try to picture him, then use a mental tape and try to remember his height. This is a healthy sign. Particularly when someone asks me how old a person is, it takes a certain amount of time for me to recall. When we do not associate people with their physical appearance, with their age, we are beginning to associate them with the Ātman. The more we dwell upon the physical appearance and age of others, the more we are conscious of our own appearance and age. The mystics tell us we should be concerned less about these details of packaging and concerned more with the contents. When I look at people, I like to look at their eyes. These are the windows into the contents, which is the Lord. Gradually, as we become more and more conscious of the Ātman, we will be looking straight at people through their eyes and deep into the Lord of Love who is within.

आश्चर्यवत्पश्यति कश्चिदेन-
माश्चर्यवद्वदति तथैव चान्यः।
आश्चर्यवच्चैनमन्यः श्रृणोति
श्रुत्वाप्येनं वेद न चैव कश्चित् ॥२९॥

*29. The glory of the Self is beheld by a few, and a few speak of its glory; a few hear about this glory, but there are many who listen without understanding.*

Sri Krishna passes on to a verse for which there is a close parallel in the parables of Jesus. Sri Krishna says that people in their response to the spiritual life seem to fall into various categories. Similarly,

Jesus tells this parable: *Hearken; Behold, there went out a sower to sow: And it came to pass, as he sowed, some fell by the wayside, and the fowls of the air came and devoured it up. And some fell on stony ground, where it had not much earth; and immediately it sprang up, because it had no depth of earth: But when the sun was up, it was scorched; and because it had no root, it withered away. And some fell among thorns, and the thorns grew up, and choked it, and it yielded no fruit. And other fell on good ground, and did yield fruit that sprang up and increased; and brought forth, some thirty, and some sixty, and some an hundred.* (Mark 4:3–8)

It is a beautiful presentation. *And it came to pass, as he sowed, some fell by the wayside, and the fowls of the air came and devoured it up.* Unless there is a window open in our consciousness, some entry into the deeper state of consciousness, we will be unmoved by even the most eloquent presentation of the spiritual life. Somewhere in our consciousness there must be the suspicion that the passing toys of the world can never satisfy us. Even intelligent, educated, successful people, after listening to a talk on the spiritual life and meditation, may turn to their friends and ask, "What is he talking about?" In such people there is no window open; they are skimming, however successfully, on the surface of life. Very often they may ask, "Why do we need meditation?" Or, after I have waxed eloquent on what meditation can do in transforming all that is ugly into all that is beautiful in our consciousness, some good people have come up and said, "We don't need meditation because we *are* beautiful. You folks need this transformation; evidently you have quite a lot to transform." Still others of this tribe will say, "We are always happy. We get up happy; we go to bed happy; even in our dreams we are happy." One of our friends on the Blue Mountain used to tell me to call such people "smiling cabbages." When Jesus talks about the seeds falling by the wayside and the fowls devouring them, he is talking mostly about people in whom the words go in one ear and out the other.

In order to grow, you need sorrow; in order to become loving, you very often need distress, and turmoil is often required to release your deeper resources. Unless you have suffered yourself, it is not easy for you to understand those who are suffering acutely. Unless you have gone through some of the distressing vicissitudes of life, you cannot easily sympathize with others. Many people, even when they have gone through a good deal, suffer from a convenient amnesia with the passage of time. The older person has a tendency to forget some of the things he did when he was young. That is why he condemns the failings of the younger generation too readily. His own past sufferings should enable him to understand, sympathize, and help.

*And some fell on stony ground, where it had not much earth; and immediately it sprang up, because it had no depth of earth.* This is the second category. In Sanskrit there is a word—*ārambhashūra,* 'those who are heroes at the beginning'—which applies to many of us. The first time we hear a good talk on meditation, we really catch fire. On one occasion a young fellow came up at the end of my talk and said, "This is what I've been looking for all my life." I am still looking for him. Others, on the way home, get a deerskin, a Patanjali pillow, Mysore incense, and Ravi Shankar records, all in preparation for meditation. But after this upsurge of enthusiasm has exhausted itself in shopping, meditation is forgotten. It is not enough if we content ourselves with the preliminaries; we have to see that it is not a temporary infatuation, which passes away within a few days. Jesus must have met quite a number of this type in ancient Jerusalem, because he goes into greater detail: *But when the sun was up, it was scorched; and because it had no root, it withered away.*

*And some fell among thorns, and the thorns grew up, and choked it, and it yielded no fruit.* This is the third type. When we were in Berkeley twelve years ago, we tried to have a vegetable garden at the back of our house. We had tomatoes, corn, and pumpkins. My agricultural advisor was a young British friend who knew even less about gardening than I did; his main advice to me was, "Give the weeds a chance." I listened to him carefully, and between us we got one ear of corn, a few tomatoes, and pumpkins which I was told would not be edible at all. The weeds had really prospered; they choked out the corn, the tomatoes, and the pumpkins. In meditation, even though we meditate regularly in the morning, if we do not take care to pull out the weeds that are rampant in the garden of the mind, spiritual seeds are not likely to thrive. On Lee Street, where we reside, we have one of the best lawns, thanks to our friend Sumner. The dandelions which used to form the majority on the lawn are now disappearing. The dandelions are rather attractive, and they also have a place in the scheme of existence, but on our street they are not looked upon with favor. In the early days, our neighbors must have found it a little disquieting when these dandelions came up so quickly. Sumner would come and pull up the weeds, and as soon as he walked away the dandelions would say, "Is Sumner gone? Let's come up." We didn't know about their habits, so we had just been pulling off the flowers and throwing them away. Later Sumner explained that their roots go deep, and unless something drastic is done at the root, it is not possible to prevent the dandelions from coming up.

*And other fell on good ground, and did yield fruit that sprang up and increased; and brought forth, some thirty, and some sixty, and some an hundred.* There is sometimes a suspicion that the spiritual life is rather selfish. In the early days, when we try to make meditation the basis of our life and retire from some of our former activities and former cronies, it is not unlikely that we will be branded as unsociable. On such occasions we can strengthen ourselves by remembering that the practice of meditation is not going to benefit us alone. We may not be able to reach thousands, as does a great mystic like Sri Ramakrishna; but each of us, as our spiritual awareness deepens, can help a few members of our family and a few friends to find their center of gravity within.

देही नित्यमवध्योऽयं देहे सर्वस्य भारत ।
तस्मात्सर्वाणि भूतानि न त्वं शोचितुमर्हसि ॥३०॥

*30. The Self of all beings, living within the body, is
eternal and cannot be harmed. Therefore, you should
not grieve.*

In my village, where death was not uncommon, most people on
their death bed would send for my Grandmother just to have her sit
by their side. They would hold her hand or look into her eyes, which
said, "There is no death." For her, the dissolution of the body was
not death at all. At the time of samādhi, this is the realization the
lover of God attains. When he becomes united with the Lord in his
heart, he goes beyond identification with the body. The physical
nexus is cut once and for all, and afterwards, though he looks after
the body very carefully, he knows that it is just an instrument to be
used to convey the truth of immortality to all those ready to receive
it.

The body is not me; it is only the jacket which I wear. When this
jacket is torn and tattered, the time has come for me to throw it
away and put on a new jacket. Sri Krishna asks, "What is there to
grieve about? What is so tragic about putting on a new jacket? Do
you want to keep an old jacket that lets in cold air, makes you uncomfortable, and can no longer be used to serve others?"

When you are able to go deep into meditation and rise above
physical consciousness, it will seem as though you can just take off
the body as you would take off a jacket and leave it on the hanger
until you finish meditating. If sometime in meditation you go very
deep into your consciousness, after going home you may even find
that you have left your jacket at the āshram. Mystics in India have
been victims of this divine phenomenon at the most inopportune
times. Once, while walking on the streets of Calcutta, Sri Ramakrishna heard a song about the Divine Mother, or saw someone
seated in meditation with eyes closed, and had such a sudden transformation of consciousness that he dropped his dhoti. The dhoti is
wrapped very gently around the hips. It is not meant for sudden at-

tacks of higher states of consciousness; it is meant for the secular way of life. I can imagine Ramakrishna's embarrassed disciples gathering around him and asking, "Blessed One, where is your dhoti?" and he, in sublime simplicity, answering, "You ask me where is my dhoti? I ask you where is my body!"

Body consciousness is the obstacle to divine awareness, and every day we must ask ourselves what is likely to decrease our identification with the body. Whatever increases physical consciousness cannot be an aid to the spiritual life. Overeating, for example, intensifies body consciousness. Every time we are tempted to eat something because of an advertisement or an old samskāra, we should ask ourselves if the body needs it or if it will merely stimulate the palate. Once we start retraining our sense of taste, which is in the mind, we can enjoy green salad and fruits as the greatest of delicacies. Skipping a meal, especially when we have eaten a little more than is necessary at the previous meal, is another way of lessening body consciousness. Other aids for lessening physical consciousness are giving up harmful habits such as smoking, drinking, the use of drugs, and overindulgence of any kind. The Gita does not ask you to do this for puritanical reasons; it says that if you want to rise above physical consciousness, these are the things you have to throw away. Once this obsessive physical identification has been broken through, you feel so good, so high, all the time that you cannot imagine using any artificial aid to be a few inches high when you are now almost the height of the cosmos.

स्वधर्ममपि चावेक्ष्य न विकम्पितुमर्हसि ।
धर्म्याद्धि युद्धाच्छ्रेयोऽन्यत्क्षत्रियस्य न विद्यते ॥३१॥
यदृच्छया चोपपन्नं स्वर्गद्वारमपावृतम् ।
सुखिनः क्षत्रियाः पार्थ लभन्ते युद्धमीदृशम् ॥३२॥
अथ चेत्त्वमिमं धर्म्यं संग्रामं न करिष्यसि ।
ततः स्वधर्मं कीर्तिं च हित्वा पापमवाप्स्यसि ॥३३॥
अकीर्तिं चापि भूतानि कथयिष्यन्ति तेऽव्ययाम् ।
संभावितस्य चाकीर्तिर्मरणादतिरिच्यते ॥३४॥

भयाद्रणादुपरतं मंस्यन्ते त्वां महारथाः ।
येषां च त्वं बहुमतो भूत्वा यास्यसि लाघवम् ॥३५॥
अवाच्यवादांश्च बहून्वदिष्यन्ति तवाहिताः ।
निन्दन्तस्तव सामर्थ्यं ततो दुःखतरं नु किम् ॥३६॥
हतो वा प्राप्स्यसि खर्गं जित्वा वा भोक्ष्यसे महीम् ।
तस्मादुत्तिष्ठ कौन्तेय युद्धाय कृतनिश्चयः ॥३७॥

*31. Considering your dharma, you should not
vacillate. For a warrior there is nothing higher than
a war against evil.*

*32. O Arjuna, the warrior who is confronted with
such a war should be pleased, for it has come of itself
as an open gate to heaven.*

*33. But if you do not participate in this battle
against evil, you will be violating your dharma and
your honor, and you will incur sin.*

*34. The story of your dishonor will be repeated by
people endlessly; and for a man of honor, dishonor is
worse than death.*

*35. These brave charioteers will think you have
withdrawn from battle out of fear; those who formerly
esteemed you will treat you with disrespect.*

*36. Your enemies will ridicule your strength and
say things that should not be said. What could be more
painful than this?*

*37. Death means the attainment of heaven;
conquest means the enjoyment of the earth. Therefore
rise up, Kaunteya, with the resolution to fight.*

Now Sri Krishna begins giving specific instruction to Arjuna, a very
practical man who is a little impatient with all the philosophical
touches the Lord has been adding. He looks ready for the supreme
teaching, and Lord Krishna, who knows when the time is right,
plunges into the great verse:

सुखदुःखे समे कृत्वा लाभालाभौ जयाजयौ ।
ततो युद्धाय युज्यस्व नैवं पापमवाप्स्यसि ॥ ३८ ॥

*38. Having made yourself alike in pain and pleasure, profit and loss, victory and defeat, engage in this great war and you will be freed from sin.*

*Tato yuddhāya yujyasva. Yuddhāya* means 'for battle,' for the great war. We are all born to fight the ego, to do battle against the three phalanxes of the ego's formidable army: fear, which is the infantry; anger, which is the cavalry; and lust, most powerful of all, which is the elephantry. The language of the Gita is really appropriate when it describes this as a long, drawn-out war. If we talk in terms of one life, then all our life this war will rage; if we talk in terms of a million lives, against the background of evolution, this war has been going on all the time. The war is between what is selfish in me and what is selfless in me: what is impure in me pitted against what is pure in me, and what is imperfect against what is perfect.

*Sukhaduhkhe same kritvā.* Here is the way to embark upon this war against all that is death in yourself so that you may have immortal life. *Sukha* is pleasure; *duhkha* is pain. Make yourself alike in pleasure and pain. Here is one of the central themes of the Bhagavad Gita. Even if you fight with all your might, the ego will always win, you will always die again, the cycle of birth and death will go on and on, unless you succeed in being alike in pain and pleasure. When I used to hear this from my Grandmother, I would always make the same practical objection: "I don't know how to do this. I like pleasure, and I don't like pain." In answer, her smile seemed to say, "How original of you!" This is everybody's problem; it is the human condition to be pleased by pleasure, and to be displeased by pain. This is why Sri Krishna says, *Sukhaduhkhe same kritvā:* transform your mental state into perfect equanimity if you do not want to die. When you get the firm resolve not to die, when there is no price you are not prepared to pay in order to transcend death, then you have the unfailing motivation for carrying out this great discipline of being alike in pleasure and pain.

When pleasant things happen to us, the mind immediately gets agitated, and we say, "I am pleased; I am happy." We wrongly identify ourselves with this passing wave of mental agitation called pleasure, and because we identify with the wave of pleasure, we cannot help identifying with the passing wave of pain also. When something is a little more pleasant, the mind gets a little more agitated and becomes excited. If we repeatedly get caught up in the same experiences of pleasure and excitement, they become samskāras; the mind becomes more turbulent, and we get caught more and more in the cycle of birth and death.

Suppose someone praises us, "Look at your hair: gleaming like molten gold. Look at your eyes: Mediterranean blue. Look at your lips: ruby from the mines of Golconda." When somebody praises our appearance, almost all of us respond in the same way; immediately our mind becomes agitated. The point Sri Krishna makes is not that we have to tell people, "Don't praise me; I am trying to make my mind calm." What Sri Krishna says is to be grateful if someone declares that you are irresistible, but do not depend for your security on that; do not allow your mind to be affected. The way to remain calm when good things are happening to you, when people are praising you, is to repeat the mantram. As soon as someone looks appreciatively at your appearance, start repeating *Rāma, Rāma, Rāma.* I know it is dampening, but as long as you are vulnerable to praise, you will be vulnerable to condemnation also.

Most of us do not realize how much we depend upon other people's approval for our security. The time may come on the spiritual path, as it came many times in the life of Gandhi, when people withdraw their appreciation and their support because we are not going the way they want us to go. When we are established within ourselves, criticism, even condemnation, will not shake our security, will not make us hostile. We can function beautifully alone, against the whole world if necessary. If criticism is destructive, we can ignore it; when it is constructive, we can benefit from it.

More than once the people of India refused to follow Gandhi, particularly in the early days. "You are an ascetic," they said. "You are a dreamer; you are impractical. We cannot follow you." Gandhi would always answer, in effect, "I am not asking you to follow me. If you want me, my terms are complete nonviolence. If you are not prepared for that, look for another leader." Many times he said this, and many times the people of India said, "All right, we are going to look for another leader." But after some days they would return to him. This is what faith in oneself means: if necessary, I will go alone. What do I want when I know the Lord is within me? Whose criticism am I afraid to face?

The Lord continues to emphasize the duality of life in the word *labhālabhau*, 'profit and loss.' Today you may get fifty percent on your investment; tomorrow you may lose fifty percent. Be alike in gain and loss, not only in terms of money, but in terms of time, energy, and effort. Personal profit agitates the mind and gets you selfishly involved. "How much is it going to bring me? If it brings me fifty percent it is a philanthropic enterprise. If it brings me loss it is not good business." Even though you may have a high code of personal conduct, the mental agitation continues when you are attached to profit. In whatever you are doing, says Sri Krishna, keep your equanimity. He uses one more word, *jayājayau*, 'victory and defeat.' Make your mind alike in victory and defeat, in gain and in loss, in pain and in pleasure; then you will go beyond death to the supreme state.

एषा तेऽभिहिता सांख्ये बुद्धियोंगे त्विमां शृणु ।
बुद्ध्या युक्तो यया पार्थ कर्मबन्धं प्रहास्यसि ॥३९॥

*39. You have heard the intellectual explanation*
*of sānkhya, O Pārtha.*[4] *Now listen to the principles*
*of yoga; by practicing these you can break*
*through the bonds of karma.*

Arjuna is an intelligent man who has been taught by the best teachers in ancient India, and Sri Krishna therefore tries to satisfy his intellectual needs to some extent. This kind of intellectual background to the spiritual life is called *sānkhya*, which literally means 'count-

4. Another matronymic for Arjuna, meaning 'son of Pritha.'

ing' or 'listing.' First the spiritual teacher lists carefully the benefits of meditation and spiritual disciplines; but listening to these theories is not enough. The disciple must begin their practice. The theory is called *sānkhya;* the actual practice is *yoga.* The word *yoga* often has been misunderstood, especially in the West, as the practice of certain physical exercises. These exercises are not yoga; they are *āsanas.* Neither is music or dancing yoga. There may be musicians in India who say their music is yoga, but it is not. There may be dancers who claim their dancing is yoga, but I am afraid it is not. Yoga is the practice of meditation and the allied spiritual disciplines. When the senses are stilled, when the mind is stilled, when the intellect is stilled, when the ego is stilled, then the state of perfect yoga is reached.

Arjuna, having accepted Sri Krishna as his teacher and listened carefully to his initial instruction, is now ready to hear in detail about the actual practice of spiritual disciplines.

In this verse the Lord promises Arjuna that if he practices these disciplines—bases his life on meditation, repeats the Holy Name, restrains his senses intelligently, and puts the welfare of all those around him first—then he shall go beyond the law of karma. The law of karma is not a concept limited to only the Hindu and Buddhist traditions; no one has stated this law in clearer terms than Jesus the Christ: *As ye sow, so shall ye reap.* If we contribute to the suffering of those around us, we cannot escape the law which will bring this suffering back to us. Similarly, if we begin to keep the welfare of others in view, and contribute to it every day, we are contributing to our own joy as well.

In the ultimate analysis, our resentments and hostilities are not against others. They are against our own alienation from our native state, which is cosmic consciousness, Krishna-consciousness, or Christ-consciousness. All the time we are being nudged by some latent force within us. Somebody is trying to remind us what our native state is, and all the time we are under this pressure from within. Our senses are turned outwards, and we are adepts at personal profit and pleasure, so we do not like to hear these little reminders; but the needling goes on. When we get tense, it is easiest to vent our frustration by making cracks at our children, our wife, or our husband—it is just a matter of geographic proximity. When we attack other people, when we become a source of trouble to others, it is not because we want to add to their trouble; we have just become an object of trouble to ourselves. Our nerves are tense; we cannot sleep properly; we cannot sit down and meditate. Our partner is close by, our parents are close by, our neighbor is next door, so why not go and get them agitated? We succeed in agitating seven people, and each of them is now prepared to agitate seven more. Agitation, particularly the form that follows the precept "Express your anger; explode your anger on society," is infectious, and this chain of retribution will eventually bring our agitation back to us. When we are agitated, when we are ready to burst our anger upon others, the immediate solution is to go for a long walk repeating the mantram.

नेहाभिक्रमनाशोऽस्ति प्रत्यवायो न विद्यते ।
स्वल्पमप्यस्य धर्मस्य त्रायते महतो भयात् ॥४०॥

*40. On this path effort never goes to waste, and there is no failure. Even a little effort toward spiritual awareness will yield protection from the greatest fear.*

For me this is one of the most memorable verses in the Gita, and it will take a lifetime on the spiritual path to appreciate its applicability to every aspect of human life. When we meditate on the Lord within for even a short time every day, this effort is not wasted. Even if we meditate only thirty minutes every morning, and try to practice the allied spiritual disciplines to a small extent during the day, this can go a long way in guarding us against many fears, known and unknown, which lurk in our consciousness. Most of us have fears of losing what we believe gives us security. Those who go after money are doing so under the impression that this is the way to become secure. They are the victim, the toy, of the stock exchange. There are others who are afraid of losing their youth. Beauty has nothing to do with age. We can be beautiful in childhood, in youth, and in old age to the extent we are unselfish. To be secure, we must find the source of security within ourselves. The advice given by Sri Krishna in the Gita is simple and profound: if times are bad today, try to contribute the best you can to the welfare of those around you. If times are good today, also try to contribute the best you can to the welfare of those around you. You can serve others no matter if times are good or bad. This is the choice we make in order to find security within ourselves.

व्यवसायात्मिका बुद्धिरेकेह कुरुनन्दन ।
बहुशाखा ह्यनन्ताश्च बुद्धयोऽव्यवसायिनाम् ॥ ४१॥

*41. Those who follow this path, Arjuna, who resolve deep within themselves to seek Me alone, attain singleness of purpose. For those who lack resolution, the decisions of life are many-branched and endless.*

Sri Krishna says to look at the life of the man of the world, whose mind is many-pointed, like a grasshopper jumping from one blade of grass to another. Every day he keeps making decisions, most of them wrong. This is the natural pattern of worldly life when we go after personal pleasure, profit, prestige, and power. In comparison, in the spiritual life only one major decision is necessary. If, after turning to meditation, we look back upon our past, upon the innumerable wrong decisions we have made in seeking fulfillment in the world without, going down one blind alley after another, and contrast this with our present development, where everything is being subordinated to reaching the supreme goal, we see that now our consciousness is slowly being unified.

We are all granted a reasonable margin in life to make our experimentation with personal pleasure, but one day we must begin to suspect that it is not going to fulfill our deepest need, which is for Self-realization. When we begin to have this suspicion, when it is already at work deep inside, we may still resist it for a while. We are all ego-centered, and it is only natural that when our old props are being taken away we fear that we are going to lose out. None of us need have any qualms if now and then a little voice whispers,

"See what you are missing." Even after taking to meditation we are likely to have a few reservations. We may have a secret hope that in one of the rooms in our consciousness some old cravings can find an occasional welcome—we can leave the key under a stone, and they can just slip in; we do not have to invite them, but if they come we need not be inhospitable. In other words, we are all human.

In order to find the freedom of being able to function everywhere, under both hostile and favorable circumstances, to be able to reach the goal of Self-realization, we have to make the decision to find the Lord, and to subordinate everything else to union with him. If we can make this decision to base our life on meditation, to repeat the mantram as often as we can, to restrain the senses vigilantly, and to put the welfare of those around us first, the Gita says we need have no doubts about the outcome. We need not be anxious about the results; this is the Lord's responsibility. Self-realization comes through the grace of the Lord, who is ever present within.

यामिमां पुष्पितां वाचं प्रवदन्त्यविपश्चितः ।
वेदवादरताः पार्थ नान्यदस्तीति वादिनः ॥४२॥
कामात्मानः स्वर्गपरा जन्मकर्मफलप्रदाम् ।
क्रियाविशेषबहुलां भोगैश्वर्यगतिं प्रति ॥४३॥
भोगैश्वर्यप्रसक्तानां तयापहृतचेतसाम् ।
व्यवसायात्मिका बुद्धिः समाधौ न विधीयते ॥४४॥

*42–43. There are ignorant people who speak flowery words and take delight in the letter of the law, saying that there is nothing else, O Pārtha: whose hearts are filled with selfish desires, whose idea of heaven is their own enjoyment, and who engage in myriad activities for the attainment of pleasure and power. The fruit of their actions is continual rebirth.*
*44. Those whose minds are swept away by the pursuit of pleasure and power are incapable of following the supreme goal and will not attain samādhi.*

One of the beauties of the Bhagavad Gita is that it does not say "You should do this" or "You should not do that." Sri Krishna simply says that if you want joy, security, wisdom, then this is the path. If you want sorrow, insecurity, and despair, then that is the path. He gives both the maps in graphic detail, and tells you that it is for you to decide where you want to go.

In these strong verses Sri Krishna describes those who will not see samādhi. Those who say there is nothing other than this world, who say there is no God, no other life than eating, drinking, making merry, and dying—such people will not attain samādhi. When people say they are atheists, I usually feel a little amused, because even to say that one is an atheist requires a definite experience. In order to say that there is no one in our deeper consciousness, we have to go there, knock on the door, and find that no one is at home. Of those who tell me they are atheists, I ask, "Don't you believe in yourself?" Their answer is, "Of course." "Then," I say, "you believe in God." When the Gita uses the terms "God" or "Lord," *Īshvara* or *Bhagavān,* it is not referring to someone "out there." It is referring to someone who is inside us all the time, who is nearer to us than our body, dearer to us than our life.

When our heart is full of selfish desires and sense cravings, we cannot see the underlying principle of existence which is divine. This is the significance of the word *kāmātmānah,* 'one whose soul is clouded over by selfish desires.' Ramakrishna was fond of saying that Rāma, the principle of abiding joy, and Kāma, selfish desire, cannot live together. This is difficult for most of us to understand because we usually feel that even if Rāma has to be brought in, Kāma can be given a little closet, or some little corner with a drapery so that he isn't visible. Every mystic worth the name says it must be Rāma *or* Kāma; we cannot have both together. Here, too, we have to be prepared for a long period of development before Kāma finally packs up his belongings and leaves without any forwarding address. Let us not get agitated if, after a long time on the spiritual path, we still feel some of our old cravings. As our spiritual awareness deepens, we will come not to identify ourselves with those desires. Then a big desire may come and crawl like a rat across the stage of our consciousness, but we will just calmly sit and watch. It is when we identify with the desire that there is trouble. For a long period, I would suggest that when old desires and urges come, when the old samskāras come into play, the very best way to deal with them is to go for a long, brisk walk repeating the mantram.

त्रैगुण्यविषया वेदा निस्त्रैगुण्यो भवार्जुन ।
निर्द्वन्द्वो निपयसरपस्यो नियोगक्षेम आत्मवान् ॥४५॥

*45. The scriptures describe the three gunas. But you should be free from the action of the gunas, established in eternal truth, self-controlled, without any sense of duality or the desire to acquire and keep.*

It is difficult to translate the word *guna;* the English word "quality" is only a rough equivalent. According to the cosmological theory presented in the Gita, everything in the universe is a combination of the three gunas—sattva, rajas, and tamas—in varying proportions. We human beings, also, are considered to be varying combinations of sattva, 'law'; rajas, 'energy'; and tamas, 'inertia.' Evolution is from tamas to rajas to sattva. This far-reaching concept not only accounts for the way in which human beings conduct themselves in daily life, but also gives guidelines as to how we can proceed on the path of evolution by transforming tamas into rajas and rajas into sattva.

Let us first take our good old companion tamas, inertia. Tamas shows itself in not wanting to move, not wanting to act—in other words, in wanting to be a stone just lying on the road. It is all right for a stone to be inert; that is its dharma. But it is not all right for you and me to be inert, to try to avoid problems, to say, "What does it matter?" When I hear the phrase "well adjusted," I do not always take it as a favorable comment. Mahatma Gandhi has said that to be well adjusted in a wrong situation is very bad; in a wrong situation we should keep on acting to set it right. When Gandhi, at the peak of his political activity, was asked in a British court what his profession was, he said, "Resister." If he was put in a wrong situation, he just could not keep quiet; he had to resist, nonviolently but very effectively, until the situation was set right.

In order to transform tamas into rajas there is a series of simple steps we can all take in our daily life. Postponement is one of the valuable allies of tamas. One of the ways to tackle inertia and expedite its transformation into rajas is never to delay anything. "Immediately" is one of the favorite words of the mystics, who live completely in the present. Jesus often used the word "forthwith."

Concentration is perhaps the most effective way of transforming tamas into rajas. Those who have a tangible element of tamas can work only for a little while. Even if they are enthusiastic, they will begin work with gusto, but at the end of thirty minutes their morale collapses. They often complain they are bored. The answer to boredom is to give a little more attention to what we are doing; any job, the moment we attend to it completely, becomes interesting. If a job bores us, we should not yield to tamas, but should give more attention to our work and try to increase our span of concentration. This not only helps us get over tamas, but helps our meditation as well.

The transformation of rajas into sattva is not extraordinary either, for all of us have an element of sattva in us. We all have this capacity for some degree of forgiveness and friendship in our relationships. It is already there; we just have to extend it slowly to include a wider and wider circle. There is no human being who does not have an element of tamas, and there is none who does not have an element of sattva. As tamas becomes transformed into rajas, particularly as our meditation deepens, there is more and more energy available to us; there is more capacity for productivity, for action, and for service. We must harness this newly released energy in order to transform it into sattva. One reason why I emphasize that we should have plenty of physical exercise, and should work at our job or studies with concentration, is that this enables us to harness all this energy. If we meditate regularly but do not take regular exercise, do not work at a suitable job, and do not give at least some of our time to selfless service without thought of return, there is a possibility that this energy may become too much for us.

Though there is a vital need for hard work, we should take care in our fast-paced modern world to see that we do not get caught in work. This is one of the real dangers against which we should be on guard. There are people who become victims of work, who carry their work from their office or campus into their living room, then into the dining room while they eat, and then into the bedroom to dream about in their sleep. We should do our work with concentration and yet be able to drop it with complete detachment at a minute's notice. This frees us from tension and enables us to give our very best.

The characteristics of the man established in sattva are calmness, compassion, and complete fearlessness. When the mind is agitated, judgment is likely to be clouded; therefore the Gita says we should never undertake any action when angry or afraid. Such action is not likely to be correct or effective. Any time our mind is agitated, the repetition of the mantram is a great help in calming our agitation, and when the mind is calm, judgment is clear.

Another characteristic of sattva is the capacity to forgive. Most of us perhaps are not even dimly aware of how, under the surface level of consciousness, old resentments keep burning, old hostilities keep flaming up. A sudden agitation, or a sudden depression, is often caused by old resentments which we still harbor in the depths of our consciousness. We cannot learn to forgive by reading books about forgiveness. I once saw a big book entitled *The Dynamics of Forgiveness,* and I could not help wondering what the author would have done to me if I had written a strong review against it. He probably would have come to the Center and given me a piece of his mind. Writing books about forgiveness, reading about forgiveness, and talking about forgiveness do not enable us to forgive. When we rely upon our own capacities, I do not think it is easy for us to forgive, but when we repeat the mantram, the Holy Name, we are calling upon the Lord to help us transform all our resentments into love.

Finally Sri Krishna concludes that it is not enough if we transform tamas into rajas and rajas into sattva; we must go beyond sattva also. Going beyond the three gunas means going beyond time, space, and causality—going beyond death into eternity, immortality, and infinity, here and now.

यावानर्थ उदपाने सर्वतः संप्लुतोदके ।
तावान्सर्वेषु वेदेषु ब्राह्मणस्य विजानतः ॥४६॥

*46. Just as a reservoir is of little use to people when the country is flooded all around, so the scriptures are of little use to the illumined man or woman, who sees the Lord everywhere.*

When the whole countryside is flooded, as it is during the monsoon in my native state of Kerala, where is the need for a little reservoir to get water from? In the villages of India, during the heavy monsoon period, all the tanks, pools, rivers, and wells are filled up with water. But as the summer sets in, wells begin to dry up; tanks and pools dry up, and people in the village have to walk long distances to the river to have their baths and fetch water. In the dry season not even a bucketful of water is wasted.

As long as the living waters of spiritual awareness are not flowing all the time within, you have to get little pots of water from outside. This evening you bring a little pot here to meditation class, and take it home full. By tomorrow the pot is empty, and you have to come again in the evening to see that it is filled up once more. Now all this is necessary, but when the living fountain from within bursts forth, when the love of the Lord who is ever present within wells up, why would you want pots? Why would a person want pools who is in the midst of the limitless sea of love? At that time, you do not need to meditate; you do not need the scriptures. You do not need to repeat the mantram, because it will go on in your consciousness ceaselessly. This is the great ideal to be attained; but for the present we must be regular about our meditation, repeat the mantram regularly, restrain our senses discriminatingly, and be careful to put the welfare of others first.

कर्मण्येवाधिकारस्ते मा फलेषु कदाचन ।
मा कर्मफलहेतुर्भूर्मा ते सङ्गोऽस्त्वकर्मणि ॥४७॥

*47. You have the right to work, but never to the*
*fruit of work. You should never engage in action for*
*the sake of rewards, nor should you long for inaction.*

"You have only the right to act; you have no right to the fruit thereof." This line is often quoted by people who do not want to act, who get overpowered by circumstances and say, "What is the use? Everything is going to the dogs." But Sri Krishna is really trying to tell us here, "If you throw yourself heart and soul into a selfless undertaking, using the right means, the purest means that are available to you, I'll be responsible for the outcome." We all have to use our judgment, weighing the pros and cons before we select a selfless goal, assessing our capacity thoughtfully, and then selecting the right means. According to the great mystics, wrong means can never bring about a right end and right means can never fail to bring about a right end. This is why Gandhi has said, "Full effort is full victory."

Gandhi followed the path of karma yoga or selfless service, which requires the capacity to be perfectly detached from results and undaunted by reverses. When he returned to India from South Africa in 1915, the country had been in political bondage for nearly two hundred years, and nobody believed him when he said that through the grace of the Lord he could lead us to freedom without firing a shot, without using any means of violence. Everywhere he went, he identified himself with the people. He woke them from their long stupor, and within a little more than three decades, a very short period for a nation, the country became politically independent because of the tremendous capacity of nonviolence to win respect and cooperation even in Britain.

Gandhi was subject to the severest criticism, not only in foreign countries but in India as well. Composite photographs and scandalous stories were published in the papers. It is a painful experience when those who have supported us turn against us. Very few can remain calm and considerate when the crowd is crying for their down-fall. This happened many times to Gandhi, and I do not remember even one occasion when he lost confidence in himself or in the final goal. At the same time he was very firm, saying, in effect, "If you are not prepared to be nonviolent, I do not want to have anything to do with you." He was prepared to wage the fight alone, because he knew that the Lord would use him as a humble instrument if he used right means for attaining a right goal.

The second line warns us not to interpret Sri Krishna's words as a counsel for inaction. There is sometimes a dangerous tendency in the contemplative life to withdraw, to retire into our ivory tower, to ignore the tremendous need for all of us to contribute selflessly to solve the problems of the world. Every one of us has a debt to pay in life, and anyone who drops out of society, who turns his back on the problems of the world, is incapable of leading the spiritual life. The Gita is a forceful call to action—but to action in which the right goal is pursued by the right means.

योगस्थः कुरु कर्माणि सङ्गं त्यक्त्वा धनंजय।
सिद्ध्यसिद्ध्योः समो भूत्वा समत्वं योग उच्यते ॥४८॥

*48. Perform work in this world, Arjuna, as a*
*man established within himself—without selfish*
*attachments, and alike in success and defeat. For*
*yoga is perfect evenness of mind.*

Here Sri Krishna defines yoga in a single word, *samatvam:* 'to be equal,' to be completely serene. This is yoga. The man established in yoga, the illumined man, is equally loving to those who support him and to those who attack him, equally concerned about the welfare of all around him, regardless of their attitude and actions. Besides my Granny, the one person I have seen in life who never allowed himself to be shaken by the attacks of unfavorable circumstances was Mahatma Gandhi, who is a source of inspiration as to how you and I can free ourselves from dependence upon public applause and appreciation. Following Gandhi's example we can develop such calmness and such confidence in the Ātman that during reversals of fortune, which will inevitably come to all of us, we can maintain our equanimity and tranquility. We do not need any external support because we are complete in ourselves. We need not be downcast when people withdraw their support, or even attack us, because we can draw upon the Lord within to face any challenge.

Sri Krishna tells Arjuna, *Yogasthah kuru karmani:* "First become established within yourself, be united with Me; then begin a career of selfless service." Do not be intimidated by heavy odds, by changing winds of fortune, or by the vacillations of people. *Sangam tyaktvā:* do not worry about the results, thinking, will this come about? How long will it take? Will the results be delayed? Do not be anxious about all this because you have nothing to do with results. This is the secret of Gandhi, who embodies the ideal of karma yoga for the twentieth century. From the Gita he learned to throw himself into an undertaking for a selfless goal, to use right means, and never to be anxious about the results.

Sri Krishna says *siddhyāsiddhyoh:* be alike in victory and defeat. What does it matter if you have won temporarily, or have been defeated temporarily? When victory comes, do not get elated; do not let the ego get inflated; do not go about saying, "I have won; I have defeated my opposition." Instead, remain calm, remain considerate, and remember that the Lord has given you victory. When defeat comes, do not moan, but grit your teeth and increase your effort, using right means to attain a selfless goal. This is yoga; this is the spiritual life: being alike in pain and pleasure, victory and defeat, praise and censure.

The Gita is a call for enthusiastic, selfless action. Sri Krishna impresses upon us that by practicing meditation daily, by repeating the mantram daily, we too can learn to establish ourselves within Him and then throw ourselves into tireless service for our family, community, country, and world.

दूरेण ह्यवरं कर्म बुद्धियोगाद्धनंजय ।
बुद्धौ शरणमन्विच्छ कृपणाः फलहेतवः ॥४९॥

*49. Seek refuge in the attitude of detachment and
you will amass the wealth of spiritual awareness. The
man who is motivated only by desire for the fruits of
his action, and anxious about the results, is miserable
indeed.*

"Miserable" is the word used here to describe people who are
caught in results. Such people do not have any peace of mind; they
are consumed with the anxiety, "Am I going to fail? Am I going to
succeed?" They begin to use unscrupulous means once they become
afraid of not achieving the results they desire. Sri Krishna tells us
through Arjuna: "Whatever you do, therefore, do not get caught
in the result. That is for Me to give; as long as you use right means
and strive for a selfless goal, you can be sure that I shall give you
the right results."

Even after we have selected a selfless goal and the right means,
and have thrown ourselves into the endeavor, we have to free ourselves from anxiety about the results, which is the most difficult part
of the discipline for all of us. If I may take an example from our own
work, when I started looking for an āshram over ten years ago, I
could not help being somewhat entangled in the results. Now,
through long, strenuous years of detaching myself, and through the
hard discipline of reminding myself that the results are not in my
hands, that the world does not belong to me, that not even a leaf of
the tree in the back yard belongs to me, I have been relieved of all
anxiety and agitation. Today I take a great deal of interest in finding
a suitable āshram—read the papers, underline the property that is
likely to be of interest to us, go to these places and ask, "What is the
temperature like? Do many motorcycles come this way?" I do everything possible to further our work, but I do not get at all apprehensive. I do not get at all anxious about the results because I know
these are in the hands of the Lord, and it is for him, who knows our
needs and our difficulties, to give us the right place at the right time.

This is detachment: throwing oneself completely into selfless work, and yet knowing the results are always in the hands of the Lord.

बुद्धियुक्तो जहातीह उभे सुकृतदुष्कृते ।
तस्माद्योगाय युज्यस्व योग: कर्मसु कौशलम् ॥५०॥

*50. When consciousness is unified, all vain anxiety is left behind. There is no cause for worry, whether actions proceed well or ill. Therefore, devote yourself to the disciplines of yoga, for yoga is skill in action.*

"Yoga is skill in action." When we become detached from results and work hard without thought of profit or prestige, deeper resources come to us. We see our way clearly; we do not waver when difficulties come. Selfish motives hide our goal, for when we are attached to results, when we are worried about the outcome, we do not see the goal; we see only the opposition and the obstacles before us. Most of the time we just do not know what to do when caught in a wrong situation in which we should not rest content. Feeling unequal to the difficult circumstances, we become resigned. But no matter how complicated and explosive the situation may be, there is always something we can do. Many small people working together can take on even the biggest problem of our age—violence. Sri Krishna repeats over and over again, "Do not get caught in the results. I am in you; therefore keep on striving, and at the right time I shall give you victory."

कर्मजं बुद्धियुक्ता हि फलं त्यक्त्वा मनीषिण: ।
जन्मबन्धविनिर्मुक्ता: पदं गच्छन्त्यनामयम् ॥५१॥

*51. The wise, who have unified their consciousness and abandoned the attachment to the fruits of action which binds a man to continual rebirth, attain a state beyond all evil.*

Sri Krishna continues to tell us the secrets of karma yoga, the path of selfless action. Whatever the situation, we can act if we do not get caught in results; karma yoga can be practiced against the heaviest odds if we do not allow the ego to get us caught in attachment to results. Prior to Gandhi, even people who had seen and grieved over the political bondage of India could not bring themselves to act because they thought the situation was impossible. They could not act because even before taking the first step they were already caught in results. We too, when faced with problems, have a tendency to think, "There is nothing we can do about it." The secret of karma yoga is never to accept a wrong situation, a situation in which you are exploited, discriminated against, or manipulated, because it is bad not only for you but for the exploiter as well. In the early days, before India's independence, I myself used to see how young British men coming to India, fair-minded and interested in doing a good job for the benefit of the people, would gradually lose their fairness and come to believe they were superior, sent to civilize the people of Asia. This is a deterioration in character that no exploiter can escape. We all know, even in our own personal life, that with a selfish person if we yield an inch, he will ask for a yard. With the selfish person, therefore, it is necessary quietly to say no. This is the great art of nonviolent resistance, where you love the person, you respect him, but you will not allow him to exploit you, because it is bad for him just as it is bad for you. Wherever we find a wrong situation—in our personal life, in our country's life, or in our world's conflicts—we all have a duty to work to correct it.

In karma yoga every reverse will send you deeper into your own resources. This is one of the marvelous changes in perspective that comes over you in deepening spiritual awareness. When an obstacle is coming you say, "Come on. Let it be a big reverse, because then it will drive me deeper." You lose your fear of defeat. You learn to use defeat and disappointment to deepen your resources. Lord Krishna says, therefore, "Do not be afraid if out of my love for you I send you a few defeats. On the surface level you have no weapons, but when I send you defeat after defeat, then you will be able to draw upon your deeper awareness where my resources will be open to you."

यदा ते मोहकलिलं बुद्धिर्व्यतितरिष्यति ।
तदा गन्तासि निर्वेदं श्रोतव्यस्य श्रुतस्य च ॥५२॥
श्रुतिविप्रतिपन्ना ते यदा स्थास्यति निश्चला ।
समाधावचला बुद्धिस्तदा योगमवाप्स्यसि ॥५३॥

*52. When your mind has overcome the confusion*
*of duality, you will attain the state of holy indifference*
*to things you hear and things you have heard.*
*53. When you are unmoved by the confusion of*
*ideas, and your mind is completely united in love*
*for the Lord of Love, you will attain the state of*
*perfect yoga.*

The Sanskrit word used here for "confusion" is *moha,* the duality
of the sensory experience, beyond which lies the unitive state of
samādhi. When we cease to pursue sensory pleasure in the hope of
finding lasting joy, which the senses will never be able to give,
we come to have what the Catholic mystics call "holy indifference." This is not a negative state, but a very positive one in which
we learn to make the mind undisturbed and equal under all circumstances. When the mind is calm it is ready for samādhi.

अर्जुन उवाच
स्थितप्रज्ञस्य का भाषा समाधिस्थस्य केशव ।
स्थितधीः किं प्रभाषेत किमासीत व्रजेत किम् ॥५४॥

ARJUNA:
*54. Tell me of those who live always in wisdom,*
*ever aware of the Self, O Krishna; how do they talk,*
*how sit, how move about?*

This question of Arjuna's introduces the glorious eighteen stanzas
which, as Gandhi points out, hold the key to the interpretation of
the entire Bhagavad Gita. Gandhi, a devoted student of the Gita,
was especially drawn to these last eighteen verses of the second
chapter. I have seen him meditating on them with such intense con-

centration that as I watched, I could see the great stanzas coming to life in a human being. When Gandhi said that the Gita describes the war going on within, scholars in many countries, including India, would not take him seriously. In reply, Gandhi only asked them to look at these verses and see what reference there is to the conquest of international enemies, the conquest of enemies outside. In every verse of this passage we have clear proof that the battle referred to is within, between the forces of selfishness and the forces of selflessness, between the ferocious pull of the senses and the serene tranquility of spiritual wisdom. I strongly recommend these verses to be memorized for use in meditation because they gradually can bring about the transformation of our consciousness. The secret of meditation is that we become what we meditate on, and when every day we use these verses with the utmost concentration we are capable of, gradually we will become what they describe as the God-conscious person. If I might refer to my own small spiritual endeavor, before taking to meditation I was subject, as most normal people are, to all kinds of cravings and foibles that naturally led me to make many mistakes. But due to the spiritual awareness emanating from these verses, I have been able to surmount these obstacles. It is because of this small personal experience that I recommend all of you use these verses in your meditation.

What Sri Krishna is really trying to do in the first part of the Gita is to rouse Arjuna's interest, to prepare him for receiving instruction, and to make him ask this practical question. Without this preparation it is difficult to communicate spiritual wisdom. When I give my introductory talk on meditation, sooner or later there will be someone in the audience to say, "How do you do it?" In the early days I had to restrain myself from saying "Hurray!" because this is what I had been waiting for. Arjuna now begins to ask the same kind of question, which Sri Krishna has been waiting impatiently to hear.

Here Arjuna calls the Lord by a very charming name: *Keshava,* 'he who has beautiful, infinite hair.' In the Upanishads there is a marvelous simile that describes the entire cosmos as hair growing out of the Lord's head. In order to understand the beauty of this

name *Keshava,* you really have to go to India, and to Kerala more
than any other state, where women have the longest, richest, black-
est hair. Early morning when they go to the temple pool to have
their bath, it is a gorgeous sight to see their hair cascading down
their backs, sometimes reaching even to the knees. Long black hair
has always been considered a great mark of beauty, and when Arjuna uses this loving term, Sri Krishna must be blushing under his
deep blue complexion.[5]

Arjuna asks, *Sthitaprajnasya:* "Tell me about the man who is
firmly established in himself." *Kā bhāshā:* "What kind of man is
he?" *Samādhisthasya:* "Tell me a few words about his samādhi;
how does he live in union with you?"

Sri Krishna wants Arjuna to be more explicit, and probably the
look in the Lord's eyes makes Arjuna feel he is expected to be more
precise. Arjuna gets the point and says, *Sthitadhīh kim prabhāsheta
kim āsīta vrajeta kim:* "How does he talk? How does he sit? How
does he walk, move about, and conduct himself in the everyday vicissitudes of life?" It is a marvelous question, in which Arjuna by
implication is telling the Lord not to recommend the study of the
scriptures, not to give him papers published on the subject, not to
impart some spiritual gossip, but to give clear signs as to how he
can recognize the illumined man who lives in complete union with
the Lord.

श्री भगवानुवाच
प्रजहाति यदा कामान्सर्वान्पार्थ मनोगतान् ।
आत्मन्येवात्मना तुष्टः स्थितप्रज्ञस्तदोच्यते ॥५५॥

SRI KRISHNA:
*55. They live in wisdom who see themselves in all
and all in them, whose love for the Lord of Love has
consumed every selfish desire and sense craving
tormenting the heart.[6]*

5. Sri Krishna is usually depicted as blue. The scriptures say he is *megha-
shyāma,* 'dark like a cloud'. His color may suggest the all-encompassing sky.
6. The last eighteen verses of Chapter 2 make an ideal passage for medita-

He is established within himself in whose heart every selfish desire
has been completely eliminated. The word the Lord uses here is
*kāma,* which I translate as 'selfish desire.' Though the dictionary
gives other meanings as well, the significance of the word is selfishness, especially as it expresses itself in cravings on the sensory level.
The Lord is very particular about his words in this verse: *kāmān
sarvān,* 'all selfish desires.' Not a trace of any selfish desire, which
agitates all human minds, may remain. Sri Krishna looks compassionately at Arjuna, whose eyes reveal his thought: "Does it mean
*all?*" This is why I say that Arjuna represents you and me perfectly;
we, too, feel that Sri Krishna must mean just the majority of desires,
that a few must be allowed.

There is no human being, unless he belongs to the category of
Jesus, the Buddha, Sri Ramakrishna, or Sri Ramana Maharshi, who
does not have some taint of selfishness in his consciousness. Sri
Ramana Maharshi will say that selfishness is I-ness. He also says
that the I-thought is the mind. When in the Christian tradition St.
Paul says, *Not I, not I, but Christ liveth in me,* he is also showing us
that if we could tirelessly endeavor to expunge the I-concept from
our consciousness, purification would be complete. In Sanskrit the
word used for separateness and selfishness is *ahamkāra: aham*
means 'I'; *kāra* means 'maker.' This 'I-maker' shows itself in many,
many ways in daily conduct and behavior, particularly in our intimate personal relationships.

Anything we can do to subordinate our profit, our pleasure, and
our prestige to the welfare of all those around us naturally results in
the reduction of I-consciousness. When we keep imposing our self-
will on, for example, our partner—very often unwittingly and under
the impression that we are defending our rights—to that extent we
actually are adding to our separateness, building up a higher wall
between our partner and ourself. In the early days of almost all married relationships there is this tendency to stand on our rights, and
to get so agitated when our rights are violated that we naturally

tion. This translation of verses 55–72 has been done especially for this purpose. It appears in its original verse form on pp. 393–4.

build a higher and higher wall under the impression that we are de-
molishing it. Right from the early days of marriage, or of any relationship, we must try to forget about rights and remember duties if
the relationship is to last.

One of my favorite poets when I was professor of English was
Milton, who has given the world a spiritual masterpiece in *Paradise
Lost*. There is a moving sonnet by Milton on his blindness which
concludes with the lines:

> God doth not need
> Either man's work or his own gifts. Who best
> Bear his mild yoke, they serve him best. His state
> Is kingly: thousands at his bidding speed,
> And post o'er land and ocean without rest;
> They also serve who only stand and wait.

I interpret this "standing and waiting" as inexhaustible patience, as
bearing with people, particularly in close personal relationships.
When everything around us is swirling, when we feel our feet are
slipping, we get terrified. We fear that we are going to be swept
away, and even with our very good intentions, we are not sure
whether unkind words may not come out of our mouth, whether unkind actions may not come from our body. It is when everything is
uncertain like this, when the whirlpool is going round and round,
that we must be able to draw upon enormous patience to stay firm
and steadfast. This is the significance of the word *sthitaprajna*, 'established in wisdom.' On every occasion where there is resentment,
resistance, and hostility around us, let us not use it as an opportunity
for making ourselves more uncertain, more unstable, and more insecure by taking it out on the other person and retaliating. Let us
instead forgive and help the other person to overcome his problems,
which means we will also be helping to eliminate our separateness.

The capacity to yield is not defeatism; it is not weakness. It is
immense strength whereby you are able to get over your demands,
your claims, the shrill voice of your ego, to contribute even to those
who oppose you, ridicule you, attack you. Without forgiveness, I do
not think anyone can enjoy life. In order to enjoy life completely, it

is not a bank balance or material possessions that is required, but an immense capacity to forgive those who injure you and are hostile to you. St. Francis of Assisi puts it perfectly when he says that he who has not learned to forgive has lost the greatest source of joy in life.

We can recognize the person who is united with the Lord of Love, ever present in us all, because he has been enabled by the grace of the Lord to come out of the forest of selfish desires in which most of us seem to be wandering, unable to find our way. Life on the egoistic level, on the physical level, is called *samsāra,* which is from the root *sri,* 'to move.' *Samsāra* is that which is moving all the time, the ceaseless flux of life in which we cannot stand anywhere. Everywhere is movement; everywhere is change and flux. This is the cycle of birth and death, whether we believe in reincarnation or only in evolution.

In one of the great scriptural stories of Hinduism, the ferocity of the senses is brought out with terrible humor. A man who is very body-conscious, as we all are, was being pursued by a tiger. The man, panic-stricken, ran as fast as he could until he reached the brink of a precipice. There, just when he thought the tiger was about to pounce upon him, he saw a mango tree below him and leaped down onto it, finding shelter on one of the middle branches. The tiger was standing on top of the precipice looking down with its tongue hanging out. The man breathed a sigh of great relief and started to climb down the trunk of the tree. He looked down and there was another tiger looking up at him. This is *samsāra.* In this most precarious position—death above, death below—the man sees a mango. "Ha!" he says. "Just what I've been looking for." At that moment tigers, life, death, *samsāra,* all disappear, just for the few moments' satisfaction of a sense craving. It is a terrible story because this is what sense craving can do to us. At the particular moment when there is a fierce sensory craving, even though we are being submerged under it, it is good to remember that the nature of the mind, the nature of desire, is to change. If we can hold out and resist the temptation, we are free.

दुःखेष्वनुद्विग्नमनाः सुखेषु विगतस्पृहः ।
वीतरागभयक्रोधः स्थितधीर्मुनिरुच्यते ॥५६॥

*56. Not agitated by grief or hankering after
pleasure, they live free from lust and fear and anger.*

This second verse in the inspiring picture Sri Krishna is painting
of the illumined man is of extreme importance in daily life, because
according to the Gita the very texture of this life is one of duality—
pain and pleasure, success and defeat, birth and death. Like most of
you, in my earlier days, I also held on to the hope that I would be
able to isolate pleasure, take it home, keep it on my table, and throw
out pain. This has been the hope of every ambitious person, but up
to this day no one has succeeded. Anyone who goes after pleasure,
honesty demands, cannot complain when he comes across pain. If
you do not want pain, do not go after pleasure either.

When we hear this from the Gita, we immediately get frustrated
because we believe, on the evidence of the intellect and senses,
that we have a choice of either pain or pleasure. There is no choice.
But when we do not go after pleasure, we do not have to be on intimate terms with pain; we go beyond the duality of pain and pleasure,
into a state of tranquility, serenity, security, and abiding joy. Beyond
pleasure and pain there is this realm of abiding joy that is called, to
use Gandhiji's phrase, *Rāmarājya,* the Kingdom of Rāma. We just
do not want to go there. We want to live in the border kingdom
where we are haunted by pain and pleasure.

Sri Krishna does not use mystical terms here; he does not go in for
exaggerated language. He asks, "Don't you want to be *sthitadhī?*"
This means: aren't you tired of being a plaything of the forces of
life, of being pushed by pleasure here and pulled around by pain
there? Aren't you tired of being dependent upon other people's
praise, afraid of other people's censure, trying to manipulate people
and to return unkindness for kindness?

We all need joy, and we can all receive joy in only one way, by
adding to the joy of others. This is the simple teaching of the Gita:

do not complain against the Lord, and do not complain against fate; if you are miserable, it is because you have added to the misery of others. If you are very happy, it is because you have added to the happiness of others. Sri Krishna says that no matter what may have taken place in your past, here is the choice you have today; why don't you make it? Often our way of translating this into action is to write in our diary, "Today I began a life of putting other people first," and to have a sticker on the back of our car saying "Put Others First" and a button saying "I Put Myself Last." This is all very easy, but it does not add to security; it does not add to anybody's joy except that of the manufacturer of the sticker and button.

We have been dwelling upon ourselves so long, caught for so long in our own needs, urges, impulses, and conditioning, that we should be patient with ourselves while undergoing the discipline of gradually subordinating our personal profit and pleasure to the needs of those around us. This is the first and last of the spiritual disciplines, and it is not a matter of high IQ. It is a matter of high WQ, Will Quotient.

In order to strengthen the will, start early morning when you want a third piece of toast. Just push it away, and you have increased your will. From breakfast onwards this goes on, and every time you can say no to the craving of the palate you have added to the will just a little. Now just imagine: breakfast, lunch, high tea, dinner, and midnight snack; five attempts at strengthening the will every day—in one month, one hundred fifty opportunities. When you do not yield to the craving of the palate, after a long period of discipline the great day will come when you will realize that these cravings were a thorn in your flesh.

An even more effective way of increasing your will is to put the comfort and convenience of other people first in situations where you are used to putting yourself first. In many little matters every day it is very painful to make these concessions. It is not too difficult to be a hero on a great stage, but to be a hero when nobody is looking except your cat is extremely difficult. When there is an immense upsurge of self-will saying, "This is how I want it to be. Not you, not you, but me!" that is the time to give, particularly to your par-

ents, to your husband or wife, to your children, and to your friends.
That is the time to yield, and yield, and yield. You will find, beautifully enough, that when you start practicing this others start doing
the same. This is the advantage of a spiritual family where every
body is putting the welfare of everybody else first—everybody is
first.

I do not indulge in too much sympathy when I see someone is
growing up, even though he or she groans a little. Whenever I see
somebody growing up and standing on his or her own feet, it is a day
of jubilation for me. Tears, sighs, and groans are a part of the process
of growth; so Sri Krishna says that when suffering comes, we should
remember that we can use it to increase our spiritual awareness. It
is said that pain is the only teacher you and I will accept, and without this stern teacher, none of us would grow up to our full stature.
When we are suffering, we may be tempted to say, "If the Lord
wants me to lead the spiritual life, I would expect him to be more
cordial and more hospitable, instead of hitting me and making me
cry. This is no way to treat a devotee." The Lord is extremely fond
of us, but he has no sense of false pity. He wants us to grow out of
our selfishness and separateness to be united with him, and he knows
suffering is often the only language you and I understand.

य: सर्वत्रानभिस्नेहस्तत्तत्प्राप्य शुभाशुभम् ।
नाभिनन्दति न द्वेष्टि तस्य प्रज्ञा प्रतिष्ठिता ॥५७॥

*57. Fettered no more by selfish attachments,*
*they are not elated by good fortune or depressed*
*by bad. Such are the seers.*

*Sarvatrā 'nabhisneha:* his wisdom is unshaken, he is deeply rooted
in himself, who has no trace of selfish attachment on any level. In
all the mystical teachings, we are told it is our identification with
the ego, our obsessive attachment to our self-will, which is responsible for the friction, frustration, and futility in our lives. The most
unfortunate part of this tragedy is that as long as we are caught in
the ego trap we will always maintain we are free. With a certain de-

gree of progress in meditation, we come to realize with great alarm how even in the most endearing of human relationships there is the tendency to impose our self-will unwittingly and unconsciously on those around us.

There is a Sanskrit saying that gives the key as to how we can remove the taint of egoism in our relations with our children. According to this Hindu saying, until the child is five we should treat the little one as a god or goddess. This does not mean that we give up our power of authority, but that we give the children all the attention and affection we can, hugging them, carrying them, and keeping them physically close to us. Such affection is essential for maintaining unity on the physical level, and children respond to it easily. These five years of intense physical intimacy and intense emotional love reassure them more than any other experience—more than any words can—and in later life they will be able to draw upon this security they received in early childhood.

Three or four days ago, while we were seated in a restaurant, we saw a couple come in with a little baby, probably a few months old. Both of them were expressing their love for the little one and smoking the whole time. It is not enough if we talk about loving our children; we have to show our love in our personal life in every way, and this can be very, very difficult. If we want to be a loving parent, we cannot afford to smoke, because it is a bad example we are setting before the child. If we want to be a loving parent, we cannot afford to drink; we cannot afford to be selfish. It is an extremely serious responsibility to be a good father or mother. Those parents who can put their children's welfare first all the time, and can teach by their personal example of vigilantly restraining the senses and adding to the welfare of others, may rest assured that their children will follow their example when they grow up.

It is good to remember the words of Jesus: *Unless you become like a little child again, you cannot enter the kingdom of heaven.* As Wordsworth puts it: "Heaven lies about us in our infancy"; and when we fail to set an example before our children, we are violating their divinity.

One day when Sri Krishna was a little boy, his mother was churning curds into butter in an earthen pot, using a wooden pestle which she moved round and round by means of a rope. Little Krishna was up to mischief as usual, and when his mother tried to get him to behave like an obedient child, he was defiant. She took the rope she was using and said, "If you don't stop your mischief, I'm going to tie your arms." Little Gopala opened his rosebud of a mouth and put out his arms. The mother came up and tried to tie his hands, but the rope would not reach. She got another rope, but it also was not long enough. Soon everybody on the street had become interested. They all brought ropes and tied them together until the rope was very, very long, yet it would not reach around the wrists of the boy because of the infinity of the Lord present in him. With his slender hands he held the whole cosmos. Consciousness of this divinity of children can enable all parents to lead lives of reasonable sense restraint and utter selflessness in order to inspire their little ones to realize the divinity ever present within them.

After five, until the age of sixteen, the Sanskrit injunction tells us to treat our child as a servant. It sounds harsh, but the more I see of life, the more I appreciate the utility of this training in obedience. In modern psychology, it is said that growing young people get puzzled when their parents cannot take a positive stand. Even though the teenager may slam the door in anger, I think he cannot help appreciating parents who can draw a line very intelligently and tenderly, showing him he must learn to discriminate in life. It is during the years five to sixteen that children are going to rebel, and it is during these years that they must learn to obey their parents so they can learn to obey the Ātman later on. In their daily life the parents have to approximate themselves to the image of the Ātman. This is why parenthood is an extremely valuable aid to meditation.

From sixteen on, the saying concludes, your children are your equal. Afterwards do not try to push them about; do not throw your weight about, but try to explain. Appeal to their sense of reason; try to make them understand your position, and make a great effort to understand theirs. It is because parents and growing young people find themselves unable to be detached from their opinions that there is conflict, and obsessive identification with opinions can be the worst kind of attachment. The parents are not their opinions, nor are the children theirs.

If we are prepared to listen with respect to opinions that are different from ours, it is not impossible that once in a way we will find the other party is right. If we can go to our parents with the attitude that we will not contradict them because they may be right, we will find our feeling of hesitation and apprehension is lost. They will appreciate this; our father may even say to our mother, "You know, the boy may be right." In most personal friction this simple discovery of "you may be right, I may be wrong" can go a long, long way to facilitate communication and bring about better understanding. One of the unmistakable signs of spiritual awareness is the cheerful capacity to say, "I was wrong"; and it will save us a lot of trouble in life if we can make that very daring statement, "I don't know."

यदा संहरते चायं कूर्मोऽङ्गानीव सर्वशः ।
इन्द्रियाणीन्द्रियार्थेभ्यस्तस्य प्रज्ञा प्रतिष्ठिता ॥ ५८॥

*58. Even as a tortoise draws in its limbs, the wise*
*can draw in their senses at will.*

Sri Krishna uses the simile of the humble tortoise. In Kerala, it is very common for children to get excited when they see a tortoise. They gather around it and playfully hit it with their bamboo sticks. So as soon as a tortoise sees children coming, he issues an order immediately to all his limbs, his head, and his tail, "Return. Get inside." When the children come, the tortoise just waits patiently inside his bamboo-proof shell until they are tired of playing. I was reminded of this simile years ago when we went to the zoo. The lions and tigers, the panthers and leopards were all in cages, but a huge tortoise was wandering around unattended. On his back was written, "Don't report me to the management—I am free." If you have developed the capacity to withdraw your senses immediately when there is danger, then you are completely free. You can go anywhere and live in the midst of any agitation. When the situation is serious you just say, "Withdraw," and the gates are closed. As Sri Krishna says in this verse, *Tasya prajnā pratishtitā:* "That man is unshaken and firmly established in Me, the Lord of Love, who can withdraw his senses at will from sensory objects."

Most of us are unaware of how mercilessly our senses are being exploited by today's mass media. It requires some progress in meditation to become aware of how much we have become tyrannized by the siren song of the mass media: "Stimulate your senses, and you will find joy." Aldous Huxley went to the extent of calling the anonymous advertisement copywriter the apostle of our modern civilization.

On the sexual level, for instance, we have been subjected to relentless conditioning. Somebody has only to bring a matchbox in his pocket and we are on fire. There is no point in saying that we are a wicked generation; this is how we are conditioned—by the movies we see, by the magazines we read, by the television we watch, by the conversation we indulge in. In advertisements, sex is the motif that is played over and over again. None of us need be guilt-laden, therefore, if we find that preoccupation with sex has become extreme. The Gita says that there is only one way to dehypnotize ourselves, and that is to get some measure of control over the senses. Until this has been accomplished, it is not advisable to attend sensate movies, where old memories, slowly fading, are refreshed. This does not mean we have to give up movies altogether. What I do, when I find one of these scenes coming on where people start taking off their clothes, is to close my eyes and have a little nap. There is no point in thinking of these movies as "wicked." "Silly" is a better word for the childish illusion that by taking off our clothes we can reveal our beauty, which is only revealed when we rise above physical consciousness.

It is necessary also to be very discriminating in the books and magazines we read. When I go to the store and look at magazine covers, I envy my Grandmother her illiteracy. Most of the magazines that people read by the million cause more agitation, insecurity, and despair than we can imagine. I would suggest that we choose only those books that add to our self-knowledge, our self-respect, and our sense control.

If we want to be able to withdraw our senses at will, we should train them in such a way that they listen immediately to the slightest command we give them. What often obstructs this is our diffidence and agitation. We should have confidence in our capacity to train the senses. In disciplining the senses, do not get angry with them, but be courteous and say "Please" and "I beg your pardon." This is the kind of artistry I always recommend on the spiritual path. Do not do things by force, but with patience.

In training the eyes, we can begin by not staring at things in which we are likely to be caught. For most of us, the shop window may exercise a certain pull, particularly for those who have been used to buying things in order to maintain their security. The spell of attraction is broken when we realize that by buying things and giving presents we are not likely to become secure, and relationships are not likely to be repaired. The ear, also, can be trained not to listen to what is harmful, especially to gossip. The time will come when we can actually close our ears and not hear what is going on. I suggest that when there is unkind talk, unsavory gossip, we can always get up and walk out, or, even better, we can say something in praise of the person who is being attacked.

In order to understand the full import of this verse, we have to see where attachment to sense objects has brought our civilization. I am an admirer of science, and I know that the modern world needs the wise help of technology to solve many of its material problems, but the misuse of science and technology has brought us to a very serious pass. Today's paper carried a brilliant article by one of the foremost authorities in the country on the pollution of the environment. The writer traces the environmental crisis directly to our excessive attachment to objects, showing that we have produced for the sake of production, multiplied things for the sake of multiplying things, without any reference to their wise use or their necessity in our daily life. This is a serious pronouncement, and all of us should pay it more than lip service.

We are all aware of the terrible impact of the automobile on our environment. There are a number of simple ways we can help relieve this problem. The first is by walking more. Some years ago, when

my wife and I were first walking around Lake Merritt, the only
company we had was the seagulls and a black dog. Now we just
keep bumping into people; old, middle-aged, and even little ones
have started walking. A second suggestion, which is also beginning
to be practiced, is to form car pools. There may be practical problems with this. We may have to wait three minutes for one person,
five for another, but we can look upon these little inconveniences as
part of our sādhana, as an opportunity for repeating the mantram
while we wait. Third, we can all avoid travel that is unnecessary. We
do not need to travel around the world when the source of all joy
and all beauty is right within us.

We can be discriminating, too, in the way we furnish our homes.
In Kerala, even in well-to-do homes, there is very little furniture,
just a few pieces of teak or ebony. Teak is not expensive there; it
grows in abundance, as does redwood here in California. The rooms
are beautiful, austere, with just a few touches here and there. Once
we begin to exercise our judgment in these matters, we shall see
many other avenues in which we can simplify our life yet maintain
all its comfort, joy, and beauty.

In a world where natural resources are limited, we should not
waste a single particle of anything. When we were on the Blue
Mountain, my wife and I met often with a British Quaker friend,
Mary Barr, who had been close to Gandhi. She had so deeply im-
bibed this lesson from Gandhi that if I left two or three grains of rice
on my plate, she would say, "Don't waste," and I would obediently
pick up every last grain and put it in my mouth. Similarly, with regard to clothing, it is possible to be very attractively dressed with a
select wardrobe, and it is possible to be very unattractively dressed
with a vast wardrobe. There are many people, I am told, who have
sentimental attachments to clothing with a story—this dress they
wore in Acapulco in 1959, or that jacket in which they hitchhiked
to New York. Give these to someone who needs clothing. Get rid of
these attachments. These are the ways in which we can help relieve
the state of emergency which overproduction and overconsumption
have brought us to. Ultimately, you and I are responsible. If we do
not buy, they cannot make; if we do not buy, they cannot sell.

By meditating and leading the spiritual life we are showing how we can make the ecological emergency disappear. Sri Krishna says: "I am the source of all the joy, all the love, all the wisdom, and all the beauty within you. You do not need these external attachments. Just have enough to keep your family in comfort, and whatever else you have, give to those who need."

विषया विनिवर्तन्ते निराहारस्य देहिनः ।
रसवर्जं रसोऽप्यस्य परं दृष्ट्वा निवर्तते ॥५९॥

*59. Though aspirants abstain from sense pleasures, they will still crave for them. These cravings all disappear when they see the Lord of Love.*

If we remember Patanjali's[7] definition of *dharana,* the first stage in meditation, it may give us some idea of the behavior of the senses in the early years of our sādhana. Patanjali with his unfailing spiritual accuracy says that dharana is the effort to confine the mind in a limited area. Imagine the mind to be a dog. If I take a dog to the store and chain him outside while I go in, telling him, "I'll be out in two minutes—just a few groceries and I am done," the dog will expect me to come back soon. When he does not see me coming out, he will start going round and round, howling and putting his paws on the glass, trying to see me. After a while, when I still have not come out, the dog will finally become tired of looking. After a lot of restlessness, after walking about and whining, he will turn around three times and then lie down. The mind is very much like that. It has got to run about and howl a little, then stand up and see who is inside and what is coming out. But after a while it will turn around three times and lie down.

The senses, too, are very restless. They are so turbulent, and have been indulged so long, that even when you are beginning to restrain them, by eating only when hungry and only what is nourishing,

7. A famous teacher of meditation in ancient India, around the second century B.C. He is the author of the *Yogasūtras,* aphorisms teaching the practice of meditation and allied disciplines.

they still may rebel. Though you may be having only a meager breakfast, a spare lunch, and a pauper's dinner, you are still thinking about what makes a sumptuous meal, and mentally you are eating a long list of items. In your external consumption of food there may be extreme restraint, but for a long, long time the old sense cravings and selfish desires are going to be there in the mind. Sri Krishna is very compassionate. When you are restraining the senses, he admires you for that, and he does not hold it against you if once in a while you are tempted to say, "If only I hadn't taken to meditation!"

What is required for a long time is our conscious effort, our sustained discipline, in restraining the senses. Gradually these noxious weeds of sense cravings will begin to wither away if we do not yield to them. Even though the desires may arise in the mind, if we subject the senses to an external discipline, the desires will gradually cease to agitate our minds through the practice of meditation.

Listening to people who are subject to compulsive habits of eating is sometimes a little like science fiction. They say they are just walking along, thinking about what passage to memorize for meditation, and all of a sudden an unseen hand pulls them inside. Before they know where they are, the door has closed on them and they are in the restaurant. For such compulsive cases, what I would say is even if you are being pulled in the doorway, try a judo twist. In this way you can actually manage to come out and start running. When you are nearing a bakery, if you are not quite sure whether you are bakery-proof, make a dash for it. It helps your physical system, you get vigorous exercise, and you conquer temptation, too. So in the case of bakeries, candy shops, and restaurants, for all those who do not mind a certain amount of curiosity on the part of passers-by— *run.*

In samādhi, when we see the Lord, the source of all joy, then we do not need any other source of pleasure. When we see the source of all beauty, then we do not need any other source of beauty. When we see the source of all love, we do not need any other source of love. In samādhi, Sri Krishna says, we become complete; all the vacancies are filled, and there is no more craving.

When we consistently practice this exhilarating discipline of discriminating sense restraint, the time will come when we shall see for ourselves that the connection between our senses and the sense objects is cut. It is a glorious day that we can mark on our calendar as Deliverance Day, and celebrate every year because it brings such relief. Then we can go everywhere in freedom; there is no compulsive liking or disliking. We are free to choose.

यततो ह्यपि कौन्तेय पुरुषस्य विपश्चितः ।
इन्द्रियाणि प्रमाथीनि हरन्ति प्रसभं मनः ॥ ६०॥

*60. For even of one who treads the path, the stormy senses can sweep off the mind.*

Even though we are trying our best to lead the spiritual life, the senses are so fiercely turbulent that if we yield to them for a little while, and a little while more, we will be swept away. *Vipashcitah indriyāni pramāthīni:* even of someone very wise, the senses can become so powerful that they just pick him up and throw him from the path. This is a warning given to all of us, particularly on the level of sex.

We do not have to belong to the monastic order to lead the spiritual life, and sex has a beautiful place in married relations, though even there with discrimination. But for people who indulge in sex in the wrong context, even though at the outset there may be some satisfaction, ultimately the relationship will be disrupted. If we ask any two people who have built their relationship on the physical level, they will say that in just a few months they could not bear each other. The tragedy is that after a short time they are again in the same relationship with someone else. If you ask them the same question again, they will say their new relationship also could not last even a few months. The senses are getting stronger and stronger, resistance is getting weaker and weaker, and one day such people will find that even if they want to, they will not be able to lead the spiritual life because of the turbulence of the mind. Sex is sacred; it has beauty and tenderness in the married relationship, where it brings two people closer and closer to become one. But on no account is it going to help us physically, psychologically, or spiritually to indulge this impulse as the mass media are trying to make us do.

We shall find that we give our best to each other when we put each other first; and when we do not put each other first, particularly in the married relationship, sex breeds jealousy. Shakespeare does not exaggerate when he talks about the "green-eyed monster" of jealousy, which is characteristic of sex on the physical level. Even when we do not suspect a trace of jealousy in ourselves, it may be clouding our eyes. I remember one of our friends who told me he could not take his girlfriend out on Telegraph Avenue because there were so many fellows there who wanted to deprive him of her. I got permission to accompany them one day, and as far as my rather bright eyes could see, nobody was looking at them. People were all engrossed in themselves or in their dinner. In his case, he was trying to build the relationship on the physical level, and as he could not avoid admitting that, I told him that jealousy is the nature of such a relationship.

Jealousy comes in only when we try to possess something for ourselves. It is good to admire beauty, but it is neither beautiful nor good if we want to take it home, put it on the mantle, and say, "You just stay there." When we see something beautiful, we begin to want it for ourselves. It may be a beautiful house, it may be a beautiful flower, it may be a beautiful dancer—we just want it. The Gita says by doing this we have lost all three. It is a very difficult secret to understand that when we do not want to possess another selfishly, he or she will always love us. It is when we do not want to possess, when we do not make demand after demand, that the relationship will last. Sri Krishna is giving us the secret of all relationships, not only between husband and wife, boyfriend and girlfriend, but between friend and friend, parents and children. Instead of trying to exact and demand, just give, and give more, and give still more. This is the way to keep love and respect; and it is something we have to learn the hard, hard way.

Unless we exercise vigilant control over the senses, we cannot put other people first. For example, if we let the palate run away with us, we will want to eat only what we like and may try to force others to eat what we like. If we do not restrain the senses, we may try to impose our self-will on those around us in all the little matters of daily living. I am sure that all of you will find, as I have, how delightful it can be to forget your own taste in eating what your wife, girlfriend, or mother wants you to eat. When you are not appreciating the taste very much, when it reminds you of gall and wormwood, try to smile, and you will see what real freedom means. Inside, the taste glands are conducting a funeral, but you just free yourself and smile. It begins with a half-paralyzed expression, but through repetition of the mantram the smile slowly pervades the whole face, until at last the eyes light up. We can train our senses with artistry by doing what will add to the joy of our parents, partner, children, and friends.

तानि सर्वाणि संयम्य युक्त आसीत मत्परः ।
वशे हि यस्येन्द्रियाणि तस्य प्रज्ञा प्रतिष्ठिता ॥ ६१॥

*61. But they live in wisdom who subdue them,*
*and keep their minds ever absorbed in Me.*

He is of unshakable wisdom and security who has subdued his senses and become completely absorbed in the Lord of Love, call him Krishna or Christ. The subjugation of the senses is enormously difficult when we keep telling ourselves, "I must subdue my senses; I must deny my body." On this impersonal path—the path of *neti neti,* 'not this, not this,' as the Upanishads put it—you are told you are not the body, you are not the senses, you are not the mind, you are not the intellect, you are not the ego. There are great mystics who have traveled this way to Self-realization, but it is hard to imagine ordinary people like ourselves climbing the Himālayas up such precipitous slopes.

One of the practical beauties of the Gita is that it is not negative in its presentation. The Gita approach, which I try to follow, is expressed here in the words *yukta āsīta matparah:* the Lord is in me, and I ask him, "Reveal yourself to me; unite me to yourself; make me the dust of your lotus feet." This is the positive approach, and I have seldom found it useful to keep on the negative path. Let us follow the positive way of asking the Lord to reveal himself to us in the depths of our consciousness, and of loving him in our parents, partner, children, and friends. This discipline of adding to the joy of those around us itself weakens the tyranny of the senses.

ध्यायतो विषयान्पुंसः सङ्गस्तेषूपजायते ।
सङ्गात्संजायते कामः कामात्क्रोधोऽभिजायते ॥६२॥
क्रोधाद्भवति संमोहः संमोहात्स्मृतिविभ्रमः ।
स्मृतिभ्रंशाद्बुद्धिनाशो बुद्धिनाशात्प्रणश्यति ॥६३॥

*62–63. When you keep thinking about sense objects, attachment comes. Attachment breeds desire, the lust of possession which, when thwarted, burns to anger. Anger clouds the judgment; you can no longer learn from past mistakes. Lost is the power to choose between the wise and the unwise, and your life is utter waste.*

In his autobiography, Gandhi narrates in moving language how these two verses, which he read for the first time in London, haunted him day in and day out and began to protect him from the dangers of life on the sensory level. Many times when I, too, have been tempted to follow the call of the senses, these words have rescued me from rushing headlong into torrential waters. I would suggest these two verses be used in meditation, particularly by people who want to subdue their senses, not to negate them but to use them as faithful servants in the service of others. The purpose of these verses is not negative; their purpose is to bring under our command the resources of love, wisdom, and selfless action which lie dormant within us all.

*Dhyāyato vishayān pumsah* means 'dwelling on sense objects.' To apply this to the modern context, we are dwelling on sense objects when we read books, for example, that are erotically charged, which means most of the books that come hot off the press today. Whenever I go into a bookstore now, I fail to find a section where Eros has not homesteaded. There is a tendency for all of us to be drawn into this kind of reading. Partly it is our conditioning, and partly it is our deep belief that we are the body, which leads us to think that by giving in to the senses we can win love, we can give love, we can become beautiful and fulfilled. It is good to select books in which there is not undue and distasteful description of what stimulates sexual desire. As a former student of both Sanskrit and English literature, I can say the most beautiful love scenes can be conveyed without a single sensate word. Last month we had the pleasure of seeing a movie by Satyajit Ray, the distinguished producer and director from Bengal, whose movies are well attended in this country. It was a powerful love story narrated from beginning to end without a kiss, without the two people ever throwing themselves into each other's arms, all the more powerful because it was so beautifully done with great restraint. It should not be too difficult for us to understand that power can be conveyed better by restraint than by taking the lid off. This is one of the great secrets of the classical tradition, where the enormous power that is contained within is suggested rather than explicitly described.

Books are a stage through which we pass, but we should slowly outgrow the need to draw upon other people's imagination and information, and especially upon the mass media, for our entertainment. Magazines particularly must be read with discrimination. When I am in the supermarket and take a look at the covers of the magazines on the shelves, every week there seems to be some new scandal, couched in such inconsiderate, unkind language that I often wonder why people even like to look at these articles. By not reading most magazines, we are not losing out on our education, though there are one or two we can select carefully and pass on to our friends.

My wife looks upon me as a well-informed critic of the movies, but I do not mind confessing that now and then I make a faux pas. Sometimes, after looking at the reviews, I come to the conclusion that I have found a peaceful movie. I think the scenes are going to be rather restrained, but before we know where we are, pandemonium has burst loose on the screen, and people are taking off their clothes on all sides. As far as the movies are concerned, I have now almost become resigned; and for those of you who want to share my secret, whenever this kind of disrobing begins I close my eyes and take a nap. The dangers of such movies are more serious than we sometimes think. We are still beginners on the spiritual path. We are still trying to bring the senses under control. The desires are all there, just hidden in a corner, waiting for their opportunity. When we see a voluptuous scene on the screen, we may not even notice it very carefully, or be conscious when we come home that it is this scene we see in our dream, meaning that it has gone into our deeper consciousness. The advertisers and movie makers know much better than we do how these stray, seductive, highly suggestive images get into our consciousness. Movies can be harmful if we do not have some kind of resistance, and one of the easiest ways to immunize oneself against the seductive powers of the movies is to learn to laugh, not with them, but at them.

*Sangas teshū 'pajāyate.* If we keep on reading about something, and seeing it, and hearing about it, even in the most self-controlled among us the seed will gradually germinate; and *sangāt samjāyate kāmah:* we will come to desire to have the experience ourselves. This is all underneath the surface level of consciousness, so we are often not even aware of what is going on until we suddenly find ourselves in a situation where we can gratify the desire.

Here the Gita does not talk about morality or ethics; it says what Patanjali also says: when we have a desire for a certain thing or experience, and fulfill that desire, the happiness we feel is due to having no craving for a little while. It is not because this craving has been satisfied, but because for just a little while there is a state of no craving. The Gita is in no way deprecating love and tenderness between man and woman in the legitimate context; it is merely trying to tell us that sensory desire makes us wrongly believe the object of desire can bring us satisfaction. It is our desire which gives quality to a relationship or a thing. In our own experience, where we have built a relationship on the sensory level, we must have asked the question: "Why is it that six months ago I thought I could go through ten incarnations with this person, and now I cannot go through ten weeks?" There is nothing wrong with us, nor is anything wrong with the other person. Our desire has exhausted itself.

It is the nature of sensory desire to come to an end very, very soon.

In most of us our desires are not under our control; but if, as the Upanishads say, we can get hold of our desires, we will get hold of our destiny. We can then direct our desires at will. The Katha Upanishad (1:3) uses a particularly vivid image:

> Know the Self as lord of the chariot,
> The body as the chariot indeed.
> Discrimination is the charioteer,
> And the mind the reins by which it governs.
> The senses, say the wise, are the horses;
> Selfish desires are the roads they travel.
> When we mistake the Self, the sages say,
> For the body, mind, and senses, it seems
> To enjoy pleasure and suffer sorrow.
> When a person lacks discrimination
> And leaves his mind undisciplined, his senses
> Run hither and thither like wild horses.
> But they obey the rein like trained horses
> When he has discrimination and his
> Mind is one-pointed. The man who lacks
> Discrimination, with little control
> Over his thoughts and far from pure, reaches
> Not the pure state of immortality
> But wanders from death to death, while he who
> Has discrimination, with a still mind
> And pure heart, reaches journey's end, never
> Again to fall into the jaws of death.
> With a discriminating intellect
> As charioteer and a trained mind as reins,
> He soon attains the supreme goal of life,
> To be united with the Lord of Love.

The more we indulge the senses, the less we get out of them, and the less we get out of them, the more we indulge them. Finally, we begin to get angry. This is the anger that bursts out between two people in a physical relationship, when they begin to quarrel and drag up the past. The physical desire has been exhausted, and now they just go on doing things which will bring the relationship to an end. When both parties become resentful, the most tragic stage in personal relationships is reached. Formerly, every little thing she did was so lovely that you could have gone on watching these innumerable acts of grace forever. Now the same thing begins to irk you. These were the things with which you used to be in love, about which you wrote minor poetry; why is it that now they only irritate you? When resentment begins to arise, even things not meant to be hostile are interpreted with hostility. The whole atmosphere of the home, of the relationship, becomes vitiated because the desire on the physical level has been exhausted.

When this kind of constant resentment and anger becomes established in our consciousness—it may be for any apparent reason outside—we begin to see what is not there. *Krodhād bhavati sammohah:* from anger arises delusion. We accuse people of things they have not dreamt of; we attack people for what they are not doing, and *sammohāt smritivibhramah:* we lose the capacity to learn from previous mistakes. All of us commit mistakes, and none of us need feel guilty about past errors if we have learned from them. The tragedy of this kind of anger is that the power of discrimination goes completely. Sri Krishna uses terms here which he very rarely uses, *smritibhramshād buddhināsho buddhināshāt pranashyati:* when a human being has lost all capacity to learn from the past, when he has lost all judgment, his life might as well be written off as a complete waste. Such a person, whatever else he may do in life, will be bringing misery upon himself as well as on those connected with him. He will leave this life having proved to be a burden, instead of being a contributor to the welfare of others.

Arjuna is now terrified because the Lord of Love does not talk in this way very often. These verses are meant to remind you and me that we cannot play the sensory game for long, saying, "Oh, we can always run away when it gets too hot." By restraining ourselves we do not lose joy; by indulging ourselves we lose all joy. By putting other people first, we do not lose joy; by putting ourselves first, we lose all joy. Many young people are under the impression that the only way to build a relationship is on the physical level. They are not aware that there is an alternative basis for relationships, which can grow in mutual understanding, love, and respect with the passage of time. The physical relationship promises what it cannot give, while the spiritual relationship gives and continues to give an abiding sense of joy all our life.

रागद्वेषवियुक्तैस्तु विषयानिन्द्रियैश्चरन् ।
आत्मवश्यैर्विधेयात्मा प्रसादमधिगच्छति ॥६४॥
प्रसादे सर्वदुःखानां हानिरस्योपजायते ।
प्रसन्नचेतसो ह्याशु बुद्धिः पर्यवतिष्ठते ॥६५॥

*64–65. But when you move amidst the world of sense, free from both attachment and aversion, there comes the peace in which all sorrows end, and you live in the wisdom of the Self.*

To go beyond suffering, to live in the full confidence that our life is meant for the service of others and that the Lord has given us ample resources to perform this service whatever the obstacles, we must shed all likes and dislikes. We cannot afford to say, "I like this; I dislike that. I like him; I dislike her." To try to translate this into neurological language, our nervous system is meant for two-way traffic. It should be able to move towards pain, if necessary, as well as towards pleasure. Now in the case of most of us, our nervous system will flow only one way, towards what we like. Most forms of allergy are a screaming protest from the nervous system: "You can't do this to me! I move in one direction only." If we are forced to go towards what we do not like, we get an ulcer in our stomach, a creeping sensation under the skin, and numbness of the fingers. Finally we faint, and then ask, "Do you blame me?" In order to grow up to our full beauty and maturity, we have to learn very often to go near what we have turned away from, to go with appreciation to the person we have always avoided. There is joy in this, and there is fulfillment in this, because we can do it for the sake of others—the mother for the child, the husband for the wife, the wife for the husband, and the friend for the friend. When the nervous system has been reconditioned for serving others, we will find ourselves free to enjoy what we do not like just as much as what we like. In the monastic order, I am told, they apply this kind of discipline with artistic perfection. If there is someone who has always been fond of books, out he goes into the garden, and if there is someone who is always after the potato bugs, in he goes to the library. The principle is to free ourselves.

We all can begin this discipline in many little ways in our daily life, particularly between parents and children, and husband and wife. We can fill the hours with freshness by putting the other person first. Whenever, for example, we go to a restaurant, it is good for the wife to give the menu to her husband and ask him to choose for her, or for the husband to ask the wife. In the early days the going may be hard, but if we can repeat the mantram and persist, we will find that gradually each person will be thinking only of what pleases the other. This exercise in the reduction of self-will can be done in all the little matters of daily life—hairstyle, books, movies, attitudes, and even opinions. I am very much in the prehistoric tradition. I have been charged with living five thousand years in the past, and I wouldn't disagree with this because, after all, my life is entirely based on the spiritual values proclaimed by the illumined sages of ancient India and the great mystics of the world. These values are timeless. They were completely valid five thousand years ago; they are completely valid today; and they will be completely valid five thousand years hence. Whatever unites people permanently is spiritual and heals individuals, families, and society. On the fundamental issues of life, a man and woman cannot help but see alike if they realize the unity underlying life. This is not losing one's personality but gaining it. All of us need to work towards realizing this unity in all our relationships.

The person who has gone beyond likes and dislikes, Sri Ramakrishna will say, is like an autumn leaf floating in the wind. It floats gently here when the wind blows here, it goes there when the wind blows there, and slowly it settles to the ground. On most occasions we can be pliable and ready to bend without any disloyalty to our ideals. People who will easily bend our way under normal circumstances can stand like a rock when a great crisis comes. Sometimes good things come to us, sometimes bad. We can learn from both; we have enough resources to meet any challenge that comes. This awareness does not denude life of joy, but enables us to accept the joy that comes, and also to face the sorrow that comes, with equanimity and resourcefulness.

नास्ति बुद्धिरयुक्तस्य न चायुक्तस्य भावना ।
न चाभावयतः शान्तिरशान्तस्य कुतः सुखम् ॥६६॥

*66. The disunited mind is far from wise; how can it meditate? How be at peace? When you know no peace, how can you know joy?*

Here there is no mention of religion, or of the spiritual life, or of God; Sri Krishna simply asks Arjuna what intelligence anyone has who is not united within. To bring this into a modern context, try to imagine an automobile whose four wheels want to go off in four different directions. This is actually what is happening to you and me. The senses are always running out towards stimulation; the mind runs out in the direction of agitation; the intellect goes in the direction of argumentation; and the Ātman just sits there watching and says, "We cannot do anything with this car. These people shouldn't be given their driver's license, and this particular car should be recalled." Meditation and the disciplines recommended by the great mystics of all religions are for putting the four wheels of our car back on the same road.

*Nā 'sti buddhir ayuktasya na cā 'yuktasya bhāvanā:* "If you are not united inside, with all your desires flowing towards one goal, you cannot get access to your deeper creative faculties." This is practical language. If you want to be a great painter, you do not try to be a sculptor, a financier, and a linguistic expert, saying, "Well, painting is one of the many things I am going to do." If you are going to paint, you paint. Then the Lord continues, *Na cā 'bhāvayatah shāntir:* "If there is no harmony inside, if there is no unity inside, how can you have peace?" This is something all of us can understand. If we are restless inside, if there is a war going on inside, wherever we go, no matter what abundance we live in, we will never be able to know security. Then, *Ashāntasya kutah sukham:* "When you have no peace in your heart, how can you know joy?" The purpose of meditation and spiritual disciplines is to lead us to joy. It is understandable if we are rather skeptical about this in the earlier stages. We may even be unable to associate joy with meditation. "Getting up early morning when it is more joyful to sleep? Eating less when it is more joyful to eat more? And putting other people first? Have you heard of a more ridiculous idea of joy?" These are not unnatural questions for us to ask. We may feel the discipline dull and dreary in the early years of our sādhana, but the goal of meditation is complete, abiding joy, releasing the great capacities for service which lie untouched in all of us.

Bhakti yoga, the path of devotion or selfless love, is the very best way for ordinary people like ourselves to move towards the total unification of consciousness that is the climax of meditation. People often ask me how to deepen the vein of devotion that is in all of us, and I reply that by unifying our desires and undergoing the disciplines of meditation, we can all become devoted to the Lord and aware of his presence in everyone around us.

The other day we saw a movie filmed on the Himālayas, and in one scene a group of pilgrims was crossing a deep ravine on a rope bridge. While on the bridge, which is swinging like a pendulum, everyone is saying *Rāma, Rāma, Rāma, Rāma* with as much devotion as he can muster. But as soon as the first step is taken on terra firma, it is likely to be *kāma, kāma, kāma, kāma.* When there is trouble and turmoil we are very responsive to the mantram; but as soon as the current turns, when our health is good, income is steady, and pleasures are all flowing smoothly, we forget the Lord.

When trouble and turmoil come, let us remember that it is the Lord's way of saying, "Don't forget Me." Let us be grateful when God sends us joy, because we all need joy. But let us also be grateful when he sends us sorrow—physical ailments, mental distress, financial breakdown—because these can enable us to turn inwards to remember him.

Sri Ramakrishna was fond of saying that our love of God should be as great as the love of a miser for his gold, the love of a mother for her child, and the love of a lover for the beloved, all combined. That is the kind of *bhakti* we should try to cultivate. Most of us have our infinite capacity for love dissipated into innumerable little channels, but we can all develop single-minded, concentrated devotion by putting the welfare of those around us first. Devotion in any relationship helps to unify consciousness, and in the modern world, people who find it too difficult to accept a divine incarnation with complete love and loyalty can all cultivate devotion, or selfless love, in personal relationships.

Many of us may not find it easy to choose a personal incarnation to whom we can surrender our entire devotion. My suggestion to such people is to let the personal incarnation choose them. Instead of shopping around the pantheon of incarnations, why not just say, "We are at your feet. We are pretty bad, and we are going to be an encumbrance. Now will someone who has mercy, and who doesn't mind having a stone around his neck, pick me up?" There are great mystics who say in complete self-surrender, "Will somebody please pick me up?" and that is all there is to it. Because they have so completely unified their love for the Lord, their travail is over within an instant. The Lord comes to them immediately.

In our repetition of the mantram, we are asking the Lord to come and help us out because we cannot lift ourselves up by ourselves. For those who have this simple faith, the time may come when they will receive an indication that the Lord is coming to say, "You are mine." This is grace. And when the Lord puts his mark on us, every samskāra picks up its bag and leaves. This experience of grace is not unlikely to come to most of us who are steadfast in their meditation and who, even though they have occasional lapses, are doing the very best they can.

इन्द्रियाणां हि चरतां यन्मनोऽनुविधीयते ।
तदस्य हरति प्रज्ञां वायुर्नावमिवाम्भसि ॥६७॥
तस्माद्यस्य महाबाहो निगृहीतानि सर्वशः ।
इन्द्रियाणीन्द्रियार्थेभ्यस्तस्य प्रज्ञा प्रतिष्ठिता ॥६८॥

67. *When you let your mind heed the Siren call of
the senses, they will carry away your better judgment
as storms drive a boat off its safe charted course to
certain doom.*
68. *Use all your power to set the senses free from
attachment and aversion alike, and live in the full
wisdom of the Self.*

These two verses are a comment upon the fate our modern civilization faces if we do not correct the sensate philosophy on which it
seems to be operating at present. Anyone who tries to follow the seductive call of the senses, which promise satisfaction, security, and
fulfillment, is likely to meet with disaster. The Lord therefore tells
us to train our senses, to turn them from turbulent masters into obedient servants. Without this period of discriminating sense restraint,
all of us risk the danger of rebellion and continuous riots inside.

These two verses are of direct application every day, from morning when we go to the breakfast table until night when we finish the
midnight snack. There is a close connection between letting the palate have its way and letting the mind have its way; Gandhi says that
the control of the palate is a valuable aid to the control of the mind.
Today the mass media subject us to so many skillful advertisements
which tickle the palate that even the most vigilant among us may
find themselves falling into their trap. We must consistently retrain
the palate by giving the body nourishing, temperate food, rather
than responding to the advertiser's slogans, which try to make us
eat things that are undesirable and unnourishing. Even during the
past ten years there has been an increase in concern about good nutrition. More and more dieticians and doctors are telling us how
necessary it is to restrain the palate in order to be physically healthy.
There is likely to be a certain initial resistance by the senses, which

are used to being pampered, but we can all change our food habits gradually to anything that we approve of. Here each person is at liberty to do a certain amount of experimentation. We need not be too harsh, nor should we be too lenient, in changing our food habits. The changeover, for example, from nonvegetarian to vegetarian food can be made gradually. In most textbooks on nutrition we find statements about what foods to avoid and what foods to rely on, and often the ones to be avoided are nonvegetarian, especially in the case of heart disease. Even if they do not advocate it consistently, nutritionists seem to be slowly coming to the conclusion that the vegetarian diet is good for physical as well as mental well-being.

Vegetarianism not only helps us to maintain our health on the optimum level but also has the spiritual purpose of deepening our awareness of the unity of life. I am fortunate in being born in a Hindu family that has been vegetarian probably for over a thousand years, but I am not a vegetarian because my ancestors were; I am a vegetarian because I have come to know that I form one unity with everything around me. As our spiritual awareness deepens, we will come to have great compassion for animals and will never want to be a party to their ill-treatment. Vegetarianism affirms the unity of all life.

या निशा सर्वभूतानां तस्यां जागर्ति संयमी ।
यस्यां जाग्रति भूतानि सा निशा पश्यतो मुनेः ॥६९॥

*69. Such a sage awakes to light in the night of all creatures. That which the world calls day is the night of ignorance to the wise.*

What is night to the vast majority of human beings is day to the illumined man; and what we call day is night to the mystic. The world of our ego is the world of sense data, and as long as we identify ourselves with the body, we move in the sense-world of *samsāra,* that which is moving all the time. As long as we live in the field of the senses, as long as we live in the sea of flux, none of us can escape change, which culminates in the great change called death.

As our meditation deepens, our view of even the external world

will change considerably. I do not see the world today as I used to
see it twenty years ago. I do not see people as I saw them twenty
years ago. Everything changes in an almost miraculous fashion.
Where we looked upon someone as a threat to us, we come to regard
him as a friend; we begin to see the unity underlying all life. This
change comes on so gradually that we are not even aware of it unless
we stop to compare how we saw life a few years ago with how we see
it today.

Most of us see life not as it is, but as we are. We look at life
through our own needs and prejudices, and the ultimate narrowing
of vision occurs when we look at everything as pertaining to ourself.
Most people look at life through a very narrow ego-slit. We should
never say we see life as it is, and never denounce the world as evil
and tempestuous, because we are looking at it through one tiny slit.
If we could ask Sri Ramana Maharshi or Sri Ramakrishna what
they see in the world, we would be heartened to hear them say they
see it whole. They do see the turbulence and violence, but for them
the world is a hospital where we are all being treated and made
whole. Ramana Maharshi, with his dry humor, said that the body is
the biggest disease of all; and Sri Ramakrishna told his disciples that
no one can be discharged from the hospital without being fully
cured. The Buddha also, in the Four Noble Truths, declares that in
the world we are all suffering from the same devastating disease,
*tanhā,* the fierce thirst of selfish desire, and to cure this disease he
gave us the regimen of the Eightfold Path.

All we need learn in life is to forget ourselves little by little by
not dwelling upon the dullest, dreariest subject on earth, "I." In order to widen the ego-slit, we put first the welfare of those with whom
we live as good friends or family, and realize the unity of life in that
circle. Someone once asked me if it is possible to realize the unity
of all life just by putting first a few people with whom he lived. I answered, "If you want to be the tennis champion of the world, do you
go and play against every tennis player in the world? You just go to
the central court at Wimbledon and beat the few there, and when
you get the cup, you have become champion." Even in a small circle
of good friends, if we can consistently try to put their welfare first,

this will enable us to widen the slit until finally there is no slit at all, and we see the whole panorama. This is what nirvāna means: removing the constriction that makes me see only what conduces to my own profit and pleasure, until I see all life as it is, as one.

आपूर्यमाणमचलप्रतिष्ठं
समुद्रमापः प्रविशन्ति यद्वत् ।
तद्वत्कामा यं प्रविशन्ति सर्वे
स शान्तिमाप्नोति न कामकामी ॥७०॥

*70. As the rivers flow into the ocean, but cannot make the vast ocean overflow, so flow the magic streams of the sense-world into the sea of peace that is the sage.*

The first word is *āpūryamāṇam,* 'ever full.' This is your nature and mine. Our idea, born of ignorance, that we will become full if we can make a lot of money or enjoy a little pleasure is absurd, because we are already full. Our account is full; we cannot add to it, nor can we take away from it. Within ourselves we have the biggest bank in the cosmos, but instead of going in to claim our legitimate account, we go to little banks asking for petty loans. As long as we live on the egocentric level, we will never suspect what fullness and security lie within ourselves. We will always have an emptiness inside that only Self-realization can take away.

The Compassionate Buddha tells his disciples that the egocentric life consists of *duhkha.* On one level, the word *duhkha* means 'sorrow.' As long as we live as separate fragments in a world of separate fragments, clashing against one another, we cannot but suffer. There is also another connotation to the word: *duh* means 'bad'; *kha* means 'hole.' The Buddha says there is a fathomless hole running through our consciousness. To fill this emptiness inside, we keep running to bring pail after pail of dollars and pour them in; but at the end of the day it is still *duhkha,* the fathomless hole. We pour in money, material possessions, pleasure, power, prestige, and it all goes down the fathomless drain. Once we begin to realize that nothing can fill this chasm, we will understand St. Augustine's cry:

"Lord, how can I ever find rest anywhere else when I am made to rest in thee?" Sri Krishna tells Arjuna, "Why waste your life going after things that pass away? You do not need them. You are already full because I am living in the depths of your consciousness. You have only to look within to realize Me."

The second word is *achalapratishtham*, 'established in motionlessness.' This is the complete stillness of Brahman, the complete motionlessness of the supreme Reality. In order to be established in the changeless, immutable Reality called God, we have to still the turbulent mind completely. If you want to see what your mind is like, go stand on a high parapet overlooking a rocky seacoast when there is a storm. The only creatures who enjoy this maelstrom are the sea lions. They float along with the waves, and when a giant one comes, they all jump up to ride on it with joy. But being made in the image of the Lord, and having been brought into the human context, our glory is to play in the sea that is still. The mind is often compared in Sanskrit to the sea, ever moving, ever rolling, ever restless; but even though there are turbulent waves on the surface, in the depths of our consciousness is the divine stillness which, through the grace of the Lord, we enter as our meditation deepens.

Ten years ago, when I used to talk about the still mind and transcendental wisdom, people would sometimes object: "But we are men of reason. Ours is an age of reason." I agree that if we could act as men of reason, there would be a good deal of satisfaction in it, but our mind is not used to rational thinking. Very few people have the capacity to concentrate completely on a given topic. In the morning, when you are brushing your teeth, try to keep your mind on the toothbrush for just two minutes; you will find the mind jumping about from one topic to another, all irrelevant, and each more disconnected than the last. Most of our tension, frustration, conflict, fatigue, and lack of will are due to the continuous working of the mind. And in people who are self-centered and capable of resentments, this constant, undisciplined activity of the mind can lead to a terrible drain on energy. When we have a resentment, *prāna*, or vital energy, is leaking out all the time, even in our dreams. This is why some people may get up in the morning after eight hours of sleep saying, "Why is it I am so tired?" In order to stop this continuous draining of vital energy that demoralizes and debilitates us, we have to learn to keep the mind still.

Meditation in the early stages is a discipline to slow down the mind, which is now traveling at breakneck speed, weaving from lane to lane and observing no signals, no regulations. If you are practicing meditation sincerely, systematically, and with sustained enthusiasm, there will be certain times when the mind becomes concentrated. Just for ten minutes there may be complete concentration on the second chapter of the Gita, and you feel as if you are getting control over a very powerful car. You are on U.S. 101, there is very little traffic, and you are able to travel fifty-four miles per hour without even turning the wheel or stepping on the brakes. Everything is under control. You go down one lane only; there are no turns, no merging traffic. When you can concentrate on one thought, there is no tension because there is no division; there is complete security because there is complete concentration. On the other hand, most of us are like the drivers we see in San Francisco during the Christmas rush. You have only to look at the tension on their faces to see how much effort is required; they seem to be trying to lift the car and throw it forward. This is what we are doing in life—taking all our weight upon ourselves and trying to push ourselves forward, when the Lord is behind us saying, "Why don't you let Me do it? I have many arms."

When we realize the complete fullness and complete stillness within us, it is an extremely satisfying experience, which, in the course of time as our meditation deepens, many of us may have. Just for a little while all the wires are disconnected, and there is no contact with the external world. The Buddha, using a negative term, calls it *shūnyatā,* the Void, where there is no friction, no disharmony, no separateness. The Hindu mystics describe this stillness as *pūrnatā,* complete fullness.

Even after we have attained deep spiritual awareness, however, occasional desires may still come into our minds. This may happen to all of us because we are encased in the body; we are corporeal beings functioning in a physically oriented world. But when we are aware spiritually, even if desires come, we will not identify ourselves with them or be upset by them. Desires will come into the mind just as rivers come into the vast sea, which remains full and established in stillness. As long as we are living on the separate level, putting ourselves first, when a canal brings in a little water there are huge waves and landslides, and banks are swept away. But when we begin to live in the depths of our being, realizing that all of us are one, however different we may appear, then even a big river like the Ganges, coming down from the Himālayas with the monsoon flood, will not disturb the sea of stillness within.

The last word of this verse is *kāmakāmī,* 'the desirer of desires.' One friend who is going to accompany us deep, deep into our meditation is kāma in the form of sexual desire. Even after many years of meditation, when we think we have at last parted from this companion, we will sit down to meditate one morning and there he will be, as friendly as ever. Kāma, which is personified in the Hindu tradition as Kāmadeva, has many names:

> *Madano manmatho mārah pradyumno mīnaketanah*
> *Kandarpo darpako 'nangah kāmah pancasharah smarah*

*Manmatha* is 'he who churns the mind': when Kāma comes with his cosmic churner, we cannot sit quiet; we cannot breathe; we cannot think. This is a very penetrating name, because sex is not just on the physical level. It is very much in the mind, and it is in the mind, not just the body, that we must learn to control this powerful force. *Māra* is 'the striker.' *Smara* is 'he who will not let you forget.' Once we have had a sexual experience, we just cannot forget it; such is the power of Kāma that no matter what we try to do, we cannot help dwelling on it. The only refuge we have at that time is Shiva—*Smarāri,* 'the enemy of Smara,' who enables us to forget and to recall our vital power. *Pancashara* is 'having five arrows.' When Kāma draws back his bow to the end of the world, aims at our heart, and begins to fire his arrows, we feel we are completely lost. Our refuge then is in the mantram.

When a strong desire is threatening to sweep us away, we grapple with it in morning meditation and still the mind a little. But the real challenge comes afterwards, during the rest of the day, in using the power released in meditation to meet the temptation. We still have the desire, but we turn against it. Whenever desires threaten to agitate us, we have an opportunity to remain calm and compassionate and repeat the mantram. This is the greatest challenge in life. Every time we push these desires back, we strengthen the will; and gradually we begin to realize that He who made the sea and sun, sky and moon, is within us, giving us the infinite power and immense energy to transform our desires. The control of sex is not the negation of it. Sex is closely connected with *kundalinī,* which is evolutionary energy, and when we learn to control this power instead of being controlled by it, all our creative abilities and capacities for selfless service are released.

विहाय कामान्यः सर्वान् पुमांश्चरति निःस्पृहः ।
निर्ममो निरहंकारः स शान्तिमधिगच्छति ॥ ७१॥

*71. They are forever free who break away from the ego-cage of 'I,' 'me,' and 'mine' to be united with the Lord of Love.*

In this verse the Lord gives us the secret of how to attain *shānti,* "the peace that passeth all understanding," that resolves all conflicts, fulfills all desires, and banishes all fear. In our consciousness there is a division, just a little split at first, that prevents our being completely loving and loyal. When we allow conflicts to rage within us, or disloyalty to separate us from others, the split grows wider and wider until finally it runs clear through our consciousness. Meditation is the process of healing this split so that the two parts become one indivisible unity. This is the purpose of meditation: to do away with the internal divisions of our heart and mind and to mend the external division that separates us from our family, community, and world.

If we are trying to unify our consciousness, we cannot afford to be disloyal to anyone. If we are disloyal to our parents, the same disloyalty will enter our relationship with our partner and our friends. Right in our home, in our early days, we can learn how to unify our fragmented love and loyalty. Otherwise, once we have left home and begun to deal with the problems of the world, disloyalty may begin to disrupt our relationships.

Disloyalty gave the Buddha serious problems, as it did Jesus the Christ. Peter was always promising Jesus, "I am completely loyal to you." But Jesus said, "Before the cock crows, you will deny me three times." Just as disloyalty breeds division, loyalty brings union. Every relationship is an opportunity to develop complete loyalty. When I suggest that the family context is the ideal situation in which to learn this art, I do not mean that we should all be married and have a dozen children. Where friends live together, or where people play or work together, there is a family. We all have somebody to put first, and if no friend is available, then we can always find an enemy. Someone may have said or done something harsh towards us. If we can bear with him, we are becoming loyal. If, instead of retaliating, we try to help him get over his problem, we are healing the division that splits his consciousness and ours too. As St. Francis reminds us, the man or woman who has not learned to forgive others has lost the greatest joy in life.

In the Hindu tradition, religious functions such as marriages and funerals always conclude with the words *Om shānti shānti shānti,* because everyone is destined for this peace which words cannot capture nor concepts convey. Every day the work you do in meditation is preparing you for *shānti.* You may have slept a little, digressed a little, or lost the passage at times; still your meditation is bringing you closer to the supreme fulfillment that is *shānti.* One day when you least expect it, your concentration will become complete. Then the mind quietly puts down a pillow and sleeps for just a few minutes. You look at the slumbering mind and say, "God bless you; may you never wake up." This is what the Buddhists call the state of no-mind. No-mind is a profound condition in which you know intuitively and directly, without the medium of the senses or the intellect. All mystics tell us this immediate knowledge far exceeds the limitations of the intellect.

It takes a long time to have even a preliminary experience of *shānti.* When you have this experience even for a few minutes, it is as if the factory of the mind has closed down completely. Everywhere there is a soothing stillness, a silent splendor. Only when you experience this state can you know how healing it is for the body, senses, mind, and intellect, and how bad it is for the ego. This is the only party who suffers. I have said more than once that I am not competent to perform a marriage or a funeral ceremony. But for the funeral of the ego you may call me any time, and I will come immediately. This is the job I love. When you have the ego lying on the funeral pyre, light the torch and give me the signal; I will set it on fire. *Shānti* is the supreme state of perfect peace and purity in which we become love itself, loving not only this or that person but all creation, for we have realized the unity underlying all life.

To be *nihspriha* is to be without sensory craving, without any desire for satisfaction from the outside. One by one, each of these desires has to be given up. This is why it takes a long, long time to attain spiritual awareness. If we had only five desires, it might take us just five weeks; but we have an almost endless number of desires, for the nature of the mind is to desire, to desire, to desire. Most of us seem to believe that if we could make a lot of money, or win prizes, or have our portrait unveiled in the city hall, we would be happy. I have even heard people insist that the day they made their first million, or the moment the curtain fell from their portrait, they were very happy. Patanjali is a wet blanket to such people when he explains what really happens on these occasions. He says we are happy because one desire has temporarily subsided, and there is not time for another desire to well up in our mind. The mind-factory is closed down for the weekend. Happiness comes when the mind is at rest. We can all attest that when one desire has been fulfilled, there is an interim period of peace before another desire rises. I do not deny that this temporary satisfaction can be very pleasant, but when we yield to one desire, the next one is usually stronger, and if we continue to give in to selfish desires, the interval between them will become shorter and shorter until there is hardly any respite at all.

A close relationship exists between the constant desire for things outside ourselves and the drain of vital energy. Window-shopping

is considered an inoffensive relaxation. Maybe it does not affect our
bank balance, but it does affect our vital wealth. When we look
at things and want to have them, or look at people and envy them,
vitality is ebbing out. To become *nihspriha* we must vigilantly ask,
"Should I go after this?" By asking this question in every situation,
we will gradually learn which things are really necessary and which
are only cumbersome.

Then Sri Krishna adds *nirmamo*. Just as the sense of 'I' can be
very painful and can cost us our best friendships, so can the desire
for 'mine.' In politics this is particularly true. War breaks out when
the concept of 'mine' becomes outrageously inflated. All of us can
be caught in mass estrangement. When Jesus says, "Blessed are the
peacemakers, for they shall be called the children of God," he is
telling us, as does Sri Krishna, that you and I can help bring friends,
communities, countries, and enemies together by the example of our
own personal lives.

*Nirmamo* should also remind us that the Lord gives us all the resources and life of the earth to care for as trustees. Sri Krishna is the
landlord and we are poor tenants. What we have done to his apartment no human landlord would tolerate. Just try to misuse the
apartment you are renting—fill it with smoke, pollute the water,
punch holes in the walls, smash the windows—and see how fast you
are evicted. The Lord, though, keeps on putting up with us. He
doesn't even collect his rent. The rent he expects from every one of
us is that we live for other people, and very few will pay so much.
We want to live for ourselves, and we expect him to subsidize our
selfishness and our self-will. Yet nothing on earth is ours; everything
is the Lord's. We have always assumed we could use as much air as
we like, as much water as we like, because there would be an unending supply. Now we know our resources are limited and must be
used carefully. When we abuse our environment, our water and air,
it is at the cost of future generations.

*Nirahamkāra* means free from self-will. I have just been reading
the life of St. Francis of Assisi, and I am captivated by the saint's
capacity to extinguish his self-will. Jesus says that he who wants to
find himself has first to lose himself, and the Sufi mystic Ansari of

Herat tells us in glorious language: "Know that when you learn to lose yourself, you will reach the Beloved. There is no other secret to be learnt, and more than this is not known to me."

In order to lose myself, I have to stop thinking about that most dreary topic, 'me.' When your spiritual awareness deepens, you will find what a monotonous, infernal bore the ego is, always wanting to be the cynosure of all eyes and the center of attention. As a matter of discipline, it is good to remain in the background. Sometimes I cannot help chuckling at the ways young people here in Berkeley try to attract attention. On one occasion I saw a truck drive past the campus carrying a piano at which a young fellow was sitting and playing away as the truck moved along. Naturally, everyone stopped and looked at the pianist, and his face beamed. There is a similar purpose behind dressing in unusual clothes. This is all right for a child, Sri Krishna tells us, but you and I do not want attention from those outside; we want to draw the attention of the Lord of Love who is within. The way to draw the Lord is to repeat the mantram. Keep on calling him, *Jesus, Jesus* or *Rāma, Rāma.* When we grow more secure, we shall see there is no need to search for security outside ourselves. We are all very important because the Lord lives in us. We need not daydream, "I wish I were like him; I wish I were like her." One of the nicest things anyone has said about me is, "He is very much at home with himself." When we are at home with ourselves, we are at home everywhere in the world. When we have found peace within ourselves, peace and love follow us wherever we go.

एषा ब्राह्मी स्थिति: पार्थ नैनां प्राप्य विमुह्यति ।
स्थित्वाऽस्यामन्तकालेऽपि ब्रह्मनिर्वाणमृच्छति ॥७२॥

*72. This is the supreme state. Attain to this, and*
*pass from death to immortality.*

When the ego dies, we come into eternal life. When in the climax of meditation called samādhi we break through the wrong identification with the body, senses, mind, and intellect, learning experientially that we are the Ātman, the Christ within, the Krishna within, we go beyond death and know our immortality. This promise of immortality is given us by mystics of all religions who have attained illumination. When Sri Ramana Maharshi talked about death, he was able to convey to those who were deeply responsive and devoted to him that death need not come to all. Sri Ramana Maharshi attained complete illumination when still a high-school boy. He was not Sri Ramana Maharshi then; he was just Venkataraman, a high school student trying to cut classes like everyone else. He had some difficult exercises to do in English grammar, and behaving as any schoolboy would, he did not go to school that day. Instead, he just lay down in his room and killed his ego. It was all done in half an hour's time. In the language of mysticism, what died during that thirty minutes was not Ramana Maharshi, but the separate, finite ego. This is nirvāna: the annihilation of the finite boundary of separateness in which we realize our true, immortal Self.

To throw a little light on this elusive spiritual phenomenon, we must look at what takes place in meditation. In meditation, over a long, long period of time, we learn to recall all our vital energy from the past and future. In samādhi the future vanishes, the past vanishes, and we live completely on the pinpoint of the moment. To live completely in the moment is to realize immortality, here and now. Mystics who have lived like this tell us that in the complete unification of consciousness we are released from time; we are delivered from time into eternity.

My spiritual teacher, my Grandmother, used to go every morning for many, many years to a sacred spring near our village. This spring is considered to have been sanctified by Rāma. Legends say that when he and Sītā were wandering through South India during their period of exile, Sītā became thirsty. She told her husband, "You have great love for me, so you must be able to give me a drink of cool water." There was no water in that place, so Rāma took an arrow and, sending it deep into the earth, caused a spring of sacred Ganges water to come up. Today the spring is a place of pilgrimage. On one side, roughly hewn in black stone, are the feet of Rāma. Just the feet alone are considered to be a beautiful, respectful way of representing an incarnation, and this humble image is in the best spiritual tradition. My simple Grandmother, after having her ceremonial bath, would stand looking at the rough, long, black feet in stone and repeat the mantram. She must have done this every morning for half a century, and when the time came for her to shed her body, according to my mother's own words, the last she said was, "I have caught Rāma by his feet."

This experience at the time of death is narrated of many mystics who have attained immortality. Until we experience a unification of consciousness and are released from the bondage of time, we cannot realize that it is not going to satisfy us to live a hundred or even a thousand years. Our need is to live forever.

इति सांख्ययोगो नाम द्वितीयोऽध्यायः ॥२॥

# CHAPTER THREE
## Selfless Service

अर्जुन उवाच
ज्यायसी चेत्कर्मणस्ते मता बुद्धिर्जनार्दन ।
तत्किं कर्मणि घोरे मां नियोजयसि केशव ॥१॥

ARJUNA:

*1. O Janārdana, you have said that knowledge is greater than action; why then do you ask me to wage this terrible war?*

Arjuna addresses Sri Krishna as *Janārdana*, 'he who stirs up the people,' because he is being aroused by the Lord's wisdom and love. But, like a worthy man of the world, he is not prepared to admit it. Instead he asks, like a modern man, "If you say that spiritual wisdom is the best path to Self-realization, then why do you ask me to fight against my passions and tyrannize over my senses? Just show me the path to spiritual wisdom and stop talking about discriminating restraint of the senses. Tell me about the spirit. As for the senses, I am content to believe you when you say I am not my senses. Let's leave the matter there."

Arjuna believes the paths of knowledge and action to be separate or even inconsistent. But there is no contradiction between these two paths. St. Francis will say that our knowledge is as deep as our action. There may be no connection between intellectual knowledge and the will, but spiritual wisdom always reveals itself in our actions.

व्यामिश्रेणेव वाक्येन बुद्धिं मोहयसीव मे ।
तदेकं वद निश्चित्य येन श्रेयोऽहमाप्नुयाम् ॥२॥

*2. Your advice seems inconsistent, O Keshava; give
me one path to follow to the supreme good.*

Arjuna is trying to judge with his intellect, which believes in clas-
sification. The intellect must divide and categorize. This does not
mean that we should not value the intellect, but we should realize
its limitations; it can see only the parts, not the whole. This tendency
of the intellect often leads to problems on the spiritual path. Many
people used to ask Sri Ramakrishna, "Is God personal or impersonal?" and he would say, very wisely, that He is both personal and
impersonal. Shankara[1] probably would say, on one occasion, "God
is both"; on another occasion, "He is neither."

Arjuna is thinking, "I wouldn't have believed it, Krishna, if
someone had told me you were not very consistent, but I see a contradiction, and in the Lord of Love this is not permissible." He says,
*Buddhim mohayasī 'va me:* "My head reels. Before I listened to
those last eighteen verses, I had some idea of who I was. Now I don't
know who you are or who I am." *Nishcitya:* "Think carefully. Don't
try to talk in a higher state of consciousness." Then, *Ekam vada:*
"Show me only one line of action. Be rigid." Arjuna wants one
single line of action, no eight steps on the path, no total way of life.
Otherwise, as you and I do, he complains that he will become more
and more bewildered.

This confusion, which many of us face as we start the spiritual
life, will be gradually overcome as through the practice of meditation we begin to develop a higher mode of knowing, called *prajñā*
in Sanskrit, which leaps beyond the duality of subject and object. In
meditation, as we grow from day to day, many of the problems we
now face will be transcended. As long as we are meditating sincerely, there may be no need even to try to understand the cause of our
difficulties, to analyze them, dwell on them, or discuss them. There

1. A mystic from Kerala, eighth century A.D. Foremost teacher of the
Vedānta school.

is no need because we are going to leave the slum where they live. After a few years of meditation, many of the physical and emotional problems in which we are caught will be left behind, although at present they are so oppressive they will not let us sleep at night. As we gradually detach ourselves from the ego, those terrific conflicts of the past will seem like Gilbert and Sullivan operas.

श्री भगवानुवाच
लोकेऽस्मिन्द्विविधा निष्ठा पुरा प्रोक्ता मयानघ।
ज्ञानयोगेन सांख्यानां कर्मयोगेन योगिनाम् ॥३॥

SRI KRISHNA:
*3. At the beginning of time I declared two paths for
the pure heart, the intuitive path of spiritual wisdom
and the active path of selfless service.*

Long ago, when life was simple, when the environment was pure, when there was little competition, the Lord revealed to man two paths to Self-realization. For people whose self-will and separateness were very small, who could discriminate between the real and the unreal, who had an awareness of the unity of all life, he revealed the path of spiritual wisdom, or *jnāna*. In those times, when people identified themselves very little with the body and ego, jnāna yoga, or the way of spiritual wisdom, was feasible. Jnāna is not an intellectual but an intuitive mode of knowing, which transcends the duality of subject and object. Arjuna, however, is a very active person, and for his type Sri Krishna recommends karma yoga, the path of selfless action. In our own age, when competition is rife, when we are so conditioned by the mass media, jnāna yoga is extremely difficult except for a rare spiritual genius like Sri Ramana Maharshi. Karma yoga, too, is difficult, but when we live in the midst of so much suffering, all of us must learn to act as selflessly as possible for the amelioration of the problems which face mankind.

This verse, like almost all verses in the Gita, can be applied to our daily life in the modern world if interpreted in relation to the spiritual life. Many mystics will say that for people who are extroverted, more meditation is necessary, and for people who are intro-verted, more work. This is an adjustment which we shall find useful even in our daily sādhana. There are days when we just do not want to work. Meditation is the greatest thing on earth! After two and a half hours, we don't want to get up: "Let us meditate for two more hours!" On days like this you really feel that meditation is the thing, that it is what you have to do all the time. But that is the day to get outside and start digging. When you feel highly contemplative, get a shovel and start digging. The urge to meditate is a good one, but it must be under your control. When you begin to work hard, attention is slowly turned outward, as it must be for every human being who wants to be healthy, happy, selfless, and spiritual. With vigorous exercise—particularly for the young, under no pressure, with no desire for profit or prestige—tensions are released. The senses turn outward, and you just want to keep on digging. The contemplative mood is gone, and now "shoveling, more shoveling, and still more shoveling" has become your slogan.

Just as some people are contemplative, there are others who are action-oriented all of the time. If they finish all of their work during the day and have a few free hours at night, they complain, "We keep awake at night. We will come to your place and do some typing." This is not free work when we cannot keep quiet, when we cannot lie down and go to sleep peacefully at night. Such work, Sri Krishna says, should be discouraged. For people who are working all the time, who work compulsively, who cannot drop their work when necessary, more meditation is called for.

When lethargy is coming, that is the time to get after work. When tamas is descending upon us, that is the time to be rajasic, and when rajas is driving us, that is the time not to go back into tamas, but to go forward into sattva. This requires a certain amount of self-knowledge and comparative freedom from the sway of likes and dislikes.

न कर्मणामनारम्भान्नैष्कर्म्यं पुरुषोऽश्नुते ।
न च संन्यसनादेव सिद्धिं समधिगच्छति ॥४॥
न हि कश्चित्क्षणमपि जातु तिष्ठत्यकर्मकृत् ।
कार्यते ह्यवशः कर्म सर्वः प्रकृतिजैर्गुणैः ॥५॥

*4. He who shirks action does not attain freedom,
nor does he gain perfection by abstaining from work.
5. Indeed, there is no one who rests for even an instant;
every creature is driven to action by his own nature.*

Here Sri Krishna makes a significant statement about the necessity
for hard work on the spiritual path. Though we give a good deal of
time every day to the practice of meditation and to the repetition of
the mantram, we still cannot abstain from work and expect to attain
the spiritual state. We have all come into the world to make a contribution, to pay off old debts which have accumulated during millions of years of evolution. No one among ordinary people like you
and me can abstain from hard work on the spiritual path. There will
come a time for all of us when work will fall away, but if I can make
a prediction, this is not likely to take place during the present century; so, during this century, let us make a virtue of necessity and be
cheerful about our work. This is the message of the Gita, that without work none of us is likely to go forward on the spiritual path.

An effective safeguard against erratic impulses, against uncon-
trolled wisps of consciousness floating in our mind, is to concentrate completely on the job we have to do. One of my simple obser-
vations has been that many of us have difficulties in dealing with
work we do not like because we cannot concentrate. When we have
a job to do which we dislike, most of us find our attention wandering. We become like children. Children will be looking at this glass
for a moment, then at this bell; after that there is nothing to look at
and they start crying. This is what often happens to us. When we get
a job that we do not like, we say that we are artists, that this job is
drudgery, that we require work challenging our creative talents.
This is often just a very euphemistic way of saying that the job is one
we don't like doing. I have seen that if we could only attend a little

more to work we dislike, it would become interesting. It is not in the nature of the job to be interesting or not; it is in the nature of the attention we give to it. Anything, when we can give it our full attention, becomes interesting. And anything, when we do not give it full attention, becomes uninteresting.

We should give our full attention to whatever we are doing. This is not easy. When we try to concentrate upon a given job, even for a short time, we will often find our attention flickering. And then the question comes: "Am I concentrating, or am I not concentrating?" If we are observing ourselves like this all the time, we have introduced another distraction to divide our consciousness. The capacity to give full attention grows with effort, and if we keep giving more and more effort in everything we do, we shall benefit even in our meditation. It is not only by meditating that we deepen our meditation; it is by working hard, giving our concentrated attention, and taking into account the needs of the body for recreation and rest. In this way we make rāja yoga, the path of meditation, and karma yoga, the path of selfless action, go together. This is Sri Krishna's advice to all of us: by throwing ourselves into energetic, selfless action, we shall be deepening our meditation as well as serving the Lord.

There is a widespread notion that the spiritual life is a passive one. But Gandhiji exploded this long-held superstition by showing that when we lead the spiritual life and remove all selfishness from ourselves, we are able to contribute to life in the fullest measure. Gandhi transformed almost every phase of life in India during his lifetime, and if I can make a prediction, the twentieth century may come to be known not as the nuclear age, but as the Gandhian age, because it is only by renouncing violence and working for others without any selfish motive that we can continue to survive as the human race.

*Naishkarmya,* or 'the state of worklessness,' is the state attained by great mystics like Sri Ramana Maharshi, who was physically with us in India until 1950. For anyone coming into his presence, he could swiftly resolve their dilemmas. In orthodox Hindu circles he is considered an *avatāra,* a divine incarnation. He was never involved in the world. He never committed any of the mistakes that even some of the greatest mystics have committed. Like Sri Rama-krishna, he was always pure, having attained illumination around the age of seventeen. When European writers would ask him whether it wasn't possible for him to lead a productive life, he just used to sit and chuckle because his life influenced not only South India, but the entire world. By just one person attaining this stature, finding himself in union with God, human evolution takes a step forward. And you and I, even without our knowledge, have bene-fited from the presence on earth of these great spiritual figures.

*Naishkarmya* is a glorious ideal whereby we help humanity by just sitting, and I can understand all of us being drawn by this ideal: we do not have to lift a finger; we just sit and everybody is helped. But now Lord Krishna points out that this state of worklessness, where action falls away and we become a living center of the divine spirit, is not reached by the path of inaction. It is not by abstaining from action, by refraining from work, by dropping out of society, by quitting school, by throwing up our hands in despair, that the state of *naishkarmya* is achieved.

When I say I have the softest corner in my heart for Arjuna, it is because he is so much like you and me. Now I imagine him asking just the question we would have asked. Arjuna begins, "Supposing, just for the sake of argument, hypothetically . . ."

Sri Krishna says, "Yes, you are talking about yourself. Go on."

"If I were to put on saffron robes, grow my hair very long, wear a rosary around my neck, and go from village to village singing hymns, eating where there is a meal, sleeping where there is a temple, wouldn't that also be a path to *naishkarmya?*"

Now Sri Krishna answers him, *Na ca samnyasanād eva siddhim samadhigacchati:* "Not through mere renunciation is perfection to be attained." Even if you retire to the Himālayas, find the most iso-lated, ice-ridden cave there, get in, put out a sign saying "There is nobody here," and live there for twelve years—even then you will not attain this state.

The Lord is emphasizing here that you and I have a debt to pay to the world. This concept of karma is personified in Sanskrit as

Chitragupta, the "hidden auditor" in every cell of the human system. The moment I think a selfish thought, every cell in my biological system has received a minus, and the moment I think a selfless thought about my parents, partner, children, friends, and even enemies, as to how I can contribute to their welfare, every cell of my being has received a plus sign. Chitragupta doesn't work an eighthour day, but all the twenty-four hours, because even in our sleep he has to keep on, mostly giving minuses. His supply of minus signs is a big pile. Only once in a way does he have to give a plus.

When we were on the Blue Mountain, I was invited to address the local club of Indian businessmen which met in a hotel called the Ritz. When my wife and I arrived, we found the members dressed in fine British suits and carrying attaché cases. Telephones were ringing all over the place, and everyone was running about. It was a tense business atmosphere. At the dinner we said we were vegetarians, and the majority of them, being successful business people, must have thought that vegetarian food wasn't strong enough to bring in high dividends, because they were asking us, "You mean even after wandering all over the West, you still stick to okra and eggplant?" So I told them I not only continued to be a vegetarian, but all my friends in the West had become complete vegetarians. At the end of my talk there was a question and answer period, and the secretary of the club, who was an Indian Christian, got up and said, "I presume that the law of karma is only applicable to people born into the Hindu or Buddhist traditions. May I take it we Christians are all exempted from this law?" I would be happy if he could have been exempted, but Jesus states the law of karma in precise terms, "As ye sow, so shall ye reap." If we have caused suffering to other people, we are going to reap suffering. If we have added to the happiness of others, we will receive happiness more and more. And Jesus adds: "With what measure you mete, it shall be measured to you again."

It is a terrifying thought for all of us that we have the choice of joy or sorrow, happiness or misery in our hands; and nobody is justified in saying, "My parents made me like this; my partner, children, and society made me like this," because we all reap what we sow. In whatever troubled circumstances we live, in whatever country, we all have one choice: shall we go after our own profit and pleasure, or shall we forget these and add to the happiness and welfare of those around us?

कर्मेन्द्रियाणि संयम्य य आस्ते मनसा स्मरन्।
इन्द्रियार्थान्विमूढात्मा मिथ्याचारः स उच्यते ॥६॥

*6. Whoever abstains from action while allowing the mind to dwell on sensual pleasure cannot be called a sincere spiritual aspirant.*

Last Sunday we spent an Indian day in Berkeley. We went to a classical music concert given by Ali Akbar Khan, India's greatest sarod player. Two days before the concert, I found my mind saying, "It certainly will be nice to listen to good Indian classical music." Even while I was walking on the beach my mind was trying to jump out of control, and I had to get blunt with it and tell it to keep quiet. This is controlling the mind, not letting it jump out of my grasp into the past or the future. Even when good things are likely to come, I do not anticipate them, and every time my mind jumps out to try and meet them, I bring it back by repeating the mantram in order to keep it in the present. Then, when the event takes place, my mind will be all there, completely concentrated.

Even though we refrain from eating a large pizza, even though we keep our eyes from spinning like ocular tops when we go to the beach, if we are not struggling to keep the mind from dwelling on these sense objects, then we are what Sri Krishna calls *mithyācāra,* 'hypocrites.' Particularly in the early days, the aspirant is expected to struggle as much as possible against the blandishment of the senses. It is not possible to be completely successful, but as long as we try our best to concentrate during meditation and to restrain the senses during the day, we are doing well. Of course, if we are yawning in meditation, we are not trying very hard; it is only by making a maximum effort that we develop the capacity to make greater effort.

Later on, when our meditation has been very good and we have really been concentrating, the Lord not infrequently tries to test us by placing us in a difficult situation. We get up from meditation confident that the mind has been stilled; we open the door and walk right into a booby trap. Such difficult situations enable us to verify the strength and validity of our meditation. As we can see from the life of every great mystic, it is when our capacities to govern our thoughts, to control our mind, and to unify our consciousness develop to an enormous degree that the tests, the problems we face, become more exacting. After all, a freshman is not asked to take the qualifying examination for the doctoral degree. When I was head of the department of English at my university in India, we had two examiners: the external examiner tried to see how much the student did not know, and the internal examiner, usually played by me, found out how much he did know. In meditation there will be all kinds of examinations by the external examiner, who is Kāma, but the internal examiner, the Lord of Love, is always there within us to help us show who we really are.

यस्त्विन्द्रियाणि मनसा नियम्यारभतेऽर्जुन ।
कर्मेन्द्रियैः कर्मयोगमसक्तः स विशिष्यते ॥७॥

*7. But they excel who control their senses through
their mind and use them for selfless service.*

This is a perfect description of Mahatma Gandhi. When Gandhi was in London, he made the discovery that taste lies in the mind. Whenever he discovered that something was good for the body, he would smack his lips over it and enjoy it as none of us can enjoy even the most delectable ice cream. In India we have a tree, called the neem tree, with the bitterest-tasting leaves imaginable. These leaves are said to have antiseptic value, and Gandhi, in a stroke of culinary genius, decided to make them into chutney. For him any discovery was translated immediately into action. He stripped the neem tree of a bagful of leaves and got his wife, Kasturbai, to grind them into a chutney; and it is said there was an unexpected exodus from the āshram when Gandhi started serving this bitter dish. It was in the bitterness of life we call grief that he used to find joy; he was at his best when taking on suffering to save other people. The same insight is given us in this verse. When we are involved in an unfortunate episode with our parents, partner, children, or friends, it is very bitter to pocket the resentment and try to behave affectionately. But doing this will benefit us like Gandhi's neem chutney. At first it will be quite bitter, but if we swallow it, it will act as a disinfectant to remove the virus of selfishness, anger, and fear from our hearts. By acting selflessly, no matter how painful it is, there will come a time when we can enjoy not only what is pleasant but what is unpleasant as well.

नियतं कुरु कर्म त्वं कर्म ज्यायो ह्यकर्मणः ।
शरीरयात्रापि च ते न प्रसिद्ध्येदकर्मणः ॥८॥

*8. You are obliged to act, Arjuna, even to maintain your body. Fulfill all your duties; action is better than inaction.*

Work is a necessity. Just imagine what would happen to people if they did not have the stimulus and release of daily work! That is why my Granny used to say, "When God gave you a mouth, he gave you two hands with which to feed the mouth." Instead of using our hands to manipulate others, or to attack our enemies, we should use them to sustain ourselves and others.

Eating, exercising, and all activities that keep the body healthy for serving others can be considered sacraments. The implication is that bodies which are overfed, overstimulated, and underexercised are not capable of learning to act selflessly. Good health is essential if we are to lead the spiritual life.

The Lord of Love gives Arjuna an axiom now: Action is better than inaction. Eons back in our evolution, when we were rocks, it was all right for us just to sit inactively; but in the human context, inaction is a violation of the basis of our existence. The Bible tells us we must earn our bread by the sweat of our brow. Hard physical work is good for us in the early stages of our sādhana, for it keeps us from dwelling on the body, a great cause of much of our tension. Work is a particularly effective tonic when it is performed without desire for profit, prestige, or power.

In order to practice the teaching contained in this verse, let us ask ourselves how much our daily work contributes to the welfare of our family and community. We are all given the choice in this life of acting for our own personal pleasure and profit, which will lead to ill will, frustration, and insecurity, or of acting for the benefit of others, which will lead to increasing health, security, and wisdom. If we lead a selfish life, by the time the body and senses wear out the story will have come to an end. If we lead a selfless life, our contribution becomes an eternal force, released into the stream of life, that will help in however small a way to elevate the consciousness of mankind. This is why people like Gandhi never die; his body was assassinated, but his spirit lives on in everyone who tries to be nonviolent.

यज्ञार्थात्कर्मणोऽन्यत्र लोकोऽयं कर्म बन्धनः ।
तदर्थं कर्म कौन्तेय मुक्तसङ्गः समाचर ॥९॥

*9. The world is imprisoned in selfish action, Kaunteya;*
*act selflessly, without any thought of personal profit.*

The Lord of Love continues in the same vein by telling Arjuna, *Loko 'yam karmabandhanah:* "The whole world is imprisoned in action." This may strike us as removed from the facts of life because we are all under the impression that when we are pursuing prestige, pleasure, and power we are really free agents. It never occurs to us that we are so driven we hardly have any liberty to lift even a finger to help somebody lying helpless by the roadside. We begin life with action that is motivated by selfish desire, for this is the stuff of which ego-centered life is made. But after a certain period of experimentation with money, material possessions, pleasure, and power, the Lord expects us to find out that these things are not the real goal of life.

This reminds me of the game of hide and seek called "Kooee" which we used to play in my village. We would scatter ourselves throughout my ancestral home in little rooms where people were not likely to look for us, and then, when everyone was well hidden, we would shout "Kooee." The person who was "it" would try to locate the call, which was very difficult because the house was large and full of echoes. "Kooee . . . kooee"—he would hear the voice from all sides and lose his sense of direction. Similarly, we hear the desire for pleasure or profit calling "kooee . . . kooee . . . kooee," and we think, "Maybe that voice is coming from under the floor." We tear up the floor, look all around under it, and discover nothing there after all. When we climb out, we hear the call again. This time we think, "Maybe it's above the ceiling," so we tear down the ceiling. We go on this way, trying to follow echoes, wasting time in endless searching until life is about to ebb out. This is applicable to almost all of us, because once we get caught in the sense game, in the profit game, in the power game, or in the prestige game, it can go on and on until it becomes an inescapable compulsion.

It is necessary for us to engage ourselves in selfless action, which we can learn to do over a long period of time. Sri Krishna refers to selfless action as *yajna*. There are many ways in which even the busiest people can serve the welfare of others. We can give our time, our money, our skill, our land. *Yajna* can take any form when we give to a worthy cause without expecting any return. To give in this spirit, Sri Krishna tells us, we must develop *muktasangah samācara,* the capacity not to get caught in any of our actions. When we get caught in our own job, our own interests, we lose our discrimination and forget the real purpose of life. One of the ways we get caught in our actions is by bringing our work home, from our job, our campus, or our factory. We do not have to put it in a briefcase to bring it home; we carefully store it in our minds where we can dwell on it all the time. The person who can drop his work in the evening and pick it up completely the following morning is the master of his work. This capacity comes after a long time of striving to concentrate on the job at hand.

It is true that most of us are good at doing the jobs we like, but a necessary part of the spiritual life is to be able to do the things we do not like. Life has a subtle way of ferreting out what we do not like and sticking it right under our nose, where we cannot ignore or escape it. One of the eloquent laws of life is that when you do not dislike anything, only the things you like come your way, whereas if you dislike a job and quit, the next job will be even worse. Just as Gandhiji says "Taste lies in the mind," I would say the taste for work lies in the mind. When you understand that doing a particular job will enable you to function in freedom in all matters, whether you like them or not, joy will slowly begin to rise in your heart. Then you will want to verify the truth of this timeless teaching in your own life by working in whatever way you can for the welfare of others. In this connection, Gandhi is an inspiring example, showing that when you begin a life of selfless service you really become secure, established in the center of your being, which is divine.

सहयज्ञाः प्रजाः सृष्ट्वा पुरोवाच प्रजापतिः ।
अनेन प्रसविष्यध्वमेष वोऽस्त्विष्टकामधुक् ॥१०॥

*10. At the time of creation the Lord gave humanity the path of selfless service and said: "Through selfless service you will always be fruitful and find the fulfillment of all your desires."*

In the Hindu scriptures there is a miraculous cow, called *Kāmadhenu,* that is said to grant all our desires. Here we have the term *kāmadhuk,* 'that which grants all our right desires.' Any boon not connected with our profit or pleasure that we ask for in order to carry out spiritual work, to add to the welfare of our society or to the peace of the world, will be given to us.

In this verse Sri Krishna says that the very principle behind the individual's growth lies in forgetting himself in living for the welfare of all. On this basis alone will we be granted peace, joy, beauty, and wisdom. Here the Gita urges us to regard our very lives as *yajna* by trying to act selflessly in all circumstances. When we talk about war, for example, we should include the guerilla strategies that go on in our homes. In this sense we can all claim ourselves as experts on warfare, because whenever we put ourselves first we are making war. But if we can learn to live for our family, our country, and our world, then there will be peace everywhere. So far, in thousands of years, we have verified this statement only negatively. In the last two thousand years there have been innumerable wars, and some statistician once calculated that every peace treaty has lasted, on the average, only two years. Peace treaties do not produce peace. Until we have peace in the home and on the street we cannot have peace in the world. Sri Krishna's language is thus applicable to political turmoil, to racial strife, and to domestic friction. In all of us there is a selfless motive and a selfish motive coming together in mortal combat most of the time. To establish peace in our hearts all we need to do is identify ourselves more and more each day with our selfless Self.

देवान्भावयतानेन ते देवा भावयन्तु वः ।
परस्परं भावयन्तः श्रेयः परमवाप्स्यथ ॥११॥

*11. Honor and cherish the devas as they honor
and cherish you; through this honor and love you will
attain the supreme good.*

Sri Krishna uses the significant spiritual word *deva,* 'divine being' or 'shining one.' Artists often represent the splendor of the sage and the saint by the symbol of the halo, but the selfish person has his distinguishing mark, too—a dark cloud. Just as the saint radiates light, the selfish man spreads darkness; just as the saint lights up the path of ordinary people, the selfish man makes confusion worse confounded.

In Sanskrit literature, when a man addresses a woman, he often uses the title *Devī.* This perfect form of address is used even today in orthodox communities in India. *Devī* is also an epithet for the Divine Mother. When we address a woman as Devī, she cannot afford to be angry; she has to be patient and forgiving, she has to endure and forbear, as this is the way a devī behaves. My Grandmother, even in her seventies, took our breath away by the glow of her skin, the gentleness of her eyes, and the resolute set of her mouth which said, "Self-willed people, be careful when you come near me."

Even some of my least spiritual uncles could not stay away from her. Everyone would gather around her because all were aware that here was beauty and femininity that time could not touch.

All of us are devas and devīs, and we reveal the divinity of our nature in the details of daily life by serving and loving one another. When a man and woman love and honor one another, the relationship will grow more beautiful with the passage of time. We can foster this type of relationship in many ways. In Kerala little girls look after their father, grandfather, brothers, and uncles. It is not just make-believe; they are actually learning to forget themselves by thinking about the needs of their menfolk. If I may say so, it is not easy to be looked after; it is a great art. To receive love gracefully and gratefully is one of the most difficult jobs in the world. But by trying harder each day to be loving towards those around us, we help everyone, including ourselves, to become devas and devīs.

इष्टान्भोगान्हि वो देवा दास्यन्ते यज्ञभाविताः ।
तैर्दत्तानप्रदायैभ्यो यो भुङ्क्ते स्तेन एव सः ॥१२॥

*12. When you engage in selfless service, all your desires are fulfilled by the devas. But anyone who enjoys the things given by the devas without offering selfless acts in return is a thief.*

The Lord declares he has sent us into this world to serve one another, and anyone who lives for pleasure, profit, power, or prestige is *stena,* 'a thief.' The greatest motive for action we can have is the awareness that the Lord has given us life, time, and energy to contribute to the welfare of those around us. Remember the words of St. Francis, "It is in giving that we receive." It is in always trying to receive that we lose everything, but when we give to those around us, we will have more and more to give.

यज्ञशिष्टाशिनः सन्तो मुच्यन्ते सर्वकिल्बिषैः ।
भुञ्जते ते त्वघं पापा ये पचन्त्यात्मकारणात् ॥१३॥

*13. The spiritually minded, who eat in the spirit of
service, are freed from all their sins; but the selfish,
who prepare food for their own satisfaction, eat sin.*

To eat to satisfy the palate, to crave for gourmet foods, to go to
restaurants just to taste exotic food, Srī Krishna says is wrong.
Food that we eat just to titillate the palate often disagrees with us,
while temperate, nourishing food, cooked and served with love and
eaten to strengthen our body and mind for serving others, is considered to be part of sādhana.

Eating good food is not a sin, but we should not dwell on it; we
should not let our mind wander in meditation from the words of St.
Francis to the cheese omelette we hope to have for breakfast. Even
too much talk about food amounts to dwelling on it. See that you
are eating nourishing, healthy food, and then forget about it. As
the Chinese mystic Huang Po puts it aptly: "Thus there is sensual
eating and wise eating. When the body composed of the four elements suffers the pangs of hunger and accordingly you provide it
with food, but without greed, that is called wise eating. On the
other hand, if you gluttonously delight in purity and flavor, you
are permitting the distinctions which arise from wrong thinking.
Merely seeking to gratify the organ of taste without realizing when
you have taken enough is called sensual eating."

What is important is what we do with the energy food gives us.
As Jesus told the Pharisees: "Not what goes into the mouth defiles
a man, but what comes out of the mouth, this defiles a man."
Of what use is it to procure hand-cultivated, organically grown
food when we act violently or use resentful language? If instead we
use our vitality to help other people, to wipe away their tears, our
eyes will become brighter and our life a source of strength to a
deeply troubled world.

अन्नाद्भवन्ति भूतानि पर्जन्यादन्नसंभवः ।
यज्ञाद्भवति पर्जन्यो यज्ञः कर्मसमुद्भवः ॥१४॥

*14. Living creatures are nourished by food, and food
is nourished by the rain; this rain is the water of life
that comes from selfless action, worship, and service.*

Food is one of our ubiquitous topics. Here Sri Krishna reminds us
that it is extremely important for us to eat the right kind of food, in
the right amount, at the right time, and in the right company. Translated into daily life, this means eating healthy, nutritious food, in
temperate quantities, that is prepared and served with love. It also
implies that eating together is a great sacrament, a time not for ac-
rimonious discussion but for a loving, peaceful atmosphere.

   This verse suggests the delicate relationships existing throughout
all nature. We know today from the work of ecologists that our actions can easily upset the balance of nature. In India vast forests
have been cut down, and now people are worrying about the lack
of rain. This reminds me of Gandhi, a skilled ecologist, who was so
careful about using resources that he would clip the blank margins
from newspapers and magazines for letter writing. I notice that little
children in America write two words on a sheet of paper and throw
it away, whereas Meera and Geetha, my two little nieces from India,
have been taught to start writing way up in the left corner of a piece
of paper and to fill the whole page down to the lower right corner.
We should teach children the habit of using all resources correctly.
By every economy we make in paper, we save a tree. In this connection, I would also say that many of the books written are only an
injury to trees. Isn't it Truman Capote who makes a pointed comment to the effect that many people who write are not writers but
typists? We can always save a tree by not purchasing books not
really necessary for our school work, our job, our wholesome entertainment, or our spiritual development.

   Many of the steps we must take to preserve our environment require us to change our habits, to transform our lives, and this is what

all of us can learn to do through the practice of meditation. The basis of ecological improvement is to turn what is selfish and violent in us into selflessness and compassion. We do not realize the power little people have. My Grandmother used to say that the elephant does not know its own size at all because it looks out at the world through tiny eyes, ridiculously small for its huge bulk. We, too, are much larger than we think, for the Lord lives in us. We cannot see ourselves as we really are, but if we could, we would say, "How big, how tremendous, how invincible!" Once we see who is within us, we are not afraid of any problem in the world – pollution, violence, or war. We can solve the transportation problem with our feet; we can solve the job problem with our own industries; we can change the present political framework by transforming ourselves. We shall find that everyone around us participates in the change we are able to bring about in our own lives. So whatever challenges confront us, whatever perils threaten to swallow us up, none of us need be despondent, for the Lord who is the source of all power, all wisdom, and all beauty is waiting to act through us.

कर्म ब्रह्मोद्भवं विद्धि ब्रह्माक्षरसमुद्भवम् ।
तस्मात्सर्वगतं ब्रह्म नित्यं यज्ञे प्रतिष्ठितम् ॥१५॥

*15. Arjuna, understand that every selfless act is*
*born from Brahman, the eternal, infinite Godhead,*
*and that he is present in every act of service.*

In order to be a brahmin, we do not need to wear a sacred thread or to undergo purification ceremonies. Whoever tries to know Brahman, the supreme Reality embedded within him or her, is a brahmin. Another name for the brahmin is *dvija,* 'twice-born.' You and I are born once and we die once, but the brahmin is born twice and does not die at all. His is a very enviable state. According to the tradition of *dvija,* we are born once at the hands of the doctor or midwife. This is our physical birth. But we can be born again, to the joy of the spirit, if we put our ego to death. Now we imagine that when all our selfishness and separateness die, when all the desires that torment our heart are burnt to ashes, there will be a terrible funeral pyre. Actually it is a jubilant procession with bands in the front, people singing *Hare Rāma,* and others strewing flowers all over our path. It is a day of great celebration for the whole world, because one such person putting the ego to death in himself has done the greatest service he can render to others. Whatever his life has been, it now becomes a constant source of support and inspiration and an unending reminder that this is the supreme state we have come into the world to attain. Meister Eckhart calls the second birth "a mighty upheaval"; to bring it about requires enormous endurance, immense patience, and the resolute dedication to overcome every obstacle on the path.

The desire and the capacity to eliminate our ego come through the grace of the Lord. You and I are really modest, humble people, and for a long time we cannot accept the idea that the Lord of Love could want poor, paltry us. To illustrate from my own life, many mornings I used to get up and say, "Is there anyone less suited for this high destiny than I am?" Finally, with utter humility, I accepted this boundless gift of the Lord's grace, and since then there has been a continuing spring of joy and love for him.

एवं प्रवर्तितं चक्रं नानुवर्तयतीह यः ।
अघायुरिन्द्रियारामो मोघं पार्थ स जीवति ॥१६॥

*16. All life turns on this law, O Pārtha; whoever
violates it, indulging his senses for his own pleasure
and ignoring the needs of others, has wasted his life.*

The Lord, our Creator, has written the law of selflessness into every one of our cells. This law is what the Buddha called *dharma.* The dharma of the human being is to turn anger into forgiveness and hatred into love. In practical, straightforward language, the mystics tell us that he who lives for himself dies, while he who lives for others lives completely and joyfully. It is all too easy to say, "An eye for an eye, and a tooth for a tooth." Retaliation requires very little courage, but making the mind calm and compassionate when it is seething with fury requires tremendous courage and endurance.

The more we can reduce our ego, or self-will, the more our real personality, the Ātman, can reveal all its beauty, wisdom, and love in our lives. Now we are all wearing a mask of separateness made from selfish desires for pleasure, profit, prestige, and power. To take off this mask of misery, we need only to call on the Lord and calm our mind with his Holy Name. By ceaselessly repeating the mantram when we feel a wave of anger or fear erupting in our consciousness, by using the power of the Holy Name to move closer to others when we want to go our own separate way, we will gradually pry off the ugly mask of the ego. Then we will know the boundless joy that springs from the loss of self-will.

Once when Sri Krishna was playing on his flute, Rādhā eyed it with jealous eyes and asked, "What has your flute done to enjoy the blessing of being held to your lips while you play upon it hour after hour?" In answer, Sri Krishna took the flute from his lips and turned it so Rādhā could see inside, saying, "Look, it's completely empty, so it is easy for me to fill it with the melody of my divine song." We, too, can become full of the Lord's infinite love and abiding joy when we empty ourselves of all that is selfish and separate.

यस्त्वात्मरतिरेव स्यादात्मतृप्तश्च मानव: ।
आत्मन्येव च संतुष्टस्तस्य कार्यं न विद्यते ॥१७॥
नैव तस्य कृतेनार्थो नाकृतेनेह कश्चन ।
न चास्य सर्वभूतेषु कश्चिदर्थव्यपाश्रय: ॥१८॥

*17–18. But they who have found the Ātman are always satisfied. They have found the source of joy and fulfillment, and no longer seek happiness from the external world. They have nothing to gain or lose by any action; neither people nor things can affect their security.*

As long as we have a hankering for personal profit or power, we cannot act freely. Gandhi is the perfect model for us to follow in this respect, for he was able to work fifteen hours a day without any trace of tension or fatigue. Imagine the responsibility he had for the lives of millions of people in his *satyāgraha* campaign, and for the state of peace or war between two countries. Yet because he had extinguished every desire for self-aggrandizement, he could always act in freedom. According to the Gita, all work motivated by selfish urges, no matter how subtle, is tainted. In order to follow in Gandhi's footsteps, we need to embark on the exhilarating discipline of putting others first without any thought of whether or not we are going to be recognized or rewarded.

As long as there is a desire for anything external to us, there is a vacuum in our consciousness. The person who thinks he will be happy if only he can get a million dollars is really claiming bankruptcy. The man who feels he will be happy if only he can become president of his country is really saying, "I am now completely vacant—an utter vacuum." Even in the daily activities of life, we cannot escape feeling we would be happy "if only. . . ." But when we desire happiness conditioned by the possession of anything or anybody, we are likely to manipulate people and to work unconsciously at the expense of even our dear ones. Thus we should heed well Sri Krishna's words: if you want to act in freedom, develop a sustained spiritual campaign to remove every vestige of self-will and separateness from your consciousness.

तस्मादसक्तः सततं कार्यं कर्म समाचर।
असक्तो ह्याचरन्कर्म परमाप्नोति पूरुषः ॥१९॥

*19. Strive constantly to serve the welfare of the world; by devotion to selfless work a man attains the supreme goal of life.*

Sri Krishna tells us, through Arjuna, to detach ourselves from our ego, to escape from the grip of our self-will so that we can act for the welfare of all around us. As we gain this freedom in action, we will begin, ever so gradually, to realize we are only an instrument of which the Lord is the operator. This truth, no matter how dimly perceived, gives tremendous motivation for removing every trace of selfishness in order to be as perfect an instrument as is within our power.

We like to think that we make big decisions and carry terrible responsibilities on our shoulders. Our shoulders are bent, our back gives us problems, and we are too tired to stand on our feet because of the weighty burdens we try to bear. Few of us realize there is somebody standing with arms outstretched, just waiting to carry our burdens for us.

In Kerala, the state in South India from which I come, there are stone parapets along the roadside the height of a man's head. When people need to rest from carrying heavy loads of rice or fruit on their heads, they stand next to the parapet and shift their load onto it. For us the Lord is the perennial parapet, standing at exactly the right height for each one of us. For those of us who are very selfish, he stands very tall to support an awesome load; for those of us who are average in selfishness, he stands about six feet high; and for the selfless, the parapet can hardly be seen because the burden is so light that almost no support is needed. Through the practice of meditation, we can gradually learn to shift our load into the Lord's mighty arms. By developing this blessed capacity, we will be able to face the greatest of challenges, terrifying even to national leaders, with ease and equanimity.

कर्मणैव हि संसिद्धिमास्थिता जनकादयः ।
लोकसंग्रहमेवापि संपश्यन्कर्तुमर्हसि ॥२०॥

*20. Keeping in mind the welfare of others, you*
*should work in their service. It was by such action*
*that Janaka attained perfection; others, too,*
*have followed this path.*

Janaka appears in the Brihadāranyaka Upanishad as a great king, and he is also renowned as the father of Sītā, wife of Rāma. Janaka attained complete illumination while reigning as king; he had a wife, a family, and a kingdom to attend to, and yet he remained an ideal lover of the Lord. We can be a perfect professor and lover of the Lord, a perfect nurse and lover of the Lord, or a perfect lawyer and lover of the Lord. But we cannot be a manufacturer of weapons and a lover of the Lord; it is not possible to work at the expense of others and progress greatly on the spiritual path.

The phrase *lokasamgraham* used in this verse is a famous one indicating the Lord sent us into the world to contribute to it. Whether we work on a large or a small scale does not matter, as long as we are doing the best within our power to make our parents, our partner, our children, our friends, and even our enemies happier. This means forgetting ourselves and reversing all the selfish inclinations we have followed. This going against what seems to be the grain of our nature is what makes the spiritual life seem so difficult. It is a hard thing to do, but by calling on the Lord, by repeating his Name, it is gradually possible to extinguish our self-will. When we start living for others, we come to life. All our deeper capacities flow into our hands; our security increases and our wisdom grows, as does our creative ability to solve the problems that confront the world. Living and acting selflessly, we will be constantly aware that all life is one—that all men are brothers, as Gandhi would say—and that throughout creation there is an underlying unity binding us all together.

Today was smoggy, so we sought fresh air and freedom from the hurly-burly of city life by going to the Marina. We walked on the pier for a long distance, and from beginning to end it was a very depressing spectacle. I will describe it in some detail because it is good for us to know how our preoccupation with pleasure can blind us and make us callous, almost brutal. It is good for us to know this so that we can begin to transform these responses into the more positive ones of compassion and sensitivity to the welfare of all living creatures.

The pier was crowded with hundreds of men, women, and children, all fishing. There were chairs, sleeping bags, and transistor radios all over the place contributing to the pandemonium. A man was sleeping, but he still had his fishing rod in hand. There were little children six and seven years old, beautiful boys and girls being taught to kill fish. When one little boy caught one, his father came up to him, patted him on the back, and congratulated him saying,

"Chip off the old block." A little girl came squealing, "Mommy, I've got another one." Parents were giving instructions to their children and friends to their friends. But to me the saddest sight of all was when the fish were landed. Still alive, they were dashed against the wooden plank, and the hooks torn away.

It is perhaps not fair to condemn or censure these people; we can only try to help them out of the situation by our own personal example. They were not really cruel, but insensitive. This can happen to all of us when we become preoccupied with our own pleasure and forget the unity underlying all life. When we were coming back from the end of the pier, we saw a big, broad, beautiful fish lying on the pier. As I don't know much about fish, I asked my wife about it, and she said it was a sea fish that probably doesn't often come close to shore. As I walked by, its eyes gazed at me in agony. It was almost telling me with its last breath, "Tell them about us."

We shouldn't say we or our children don't know about these things, for it is our duty in life to know about them. Ignorance of the law is not accepted as an excuse for crime. In the days of British rule, in an Indian court of law we couldn't say we didn't know Section XYZ of the Indian Penal Code by which we could be thrown into political prison. If we went to court and claimed we didn't know about this section, the British judge used to say, "Two months in solitary," and add some strong remarks. Similarly, when those little children fishing on the pier grow up, they cannot hide behind the shield of ignorance, for it is no shield at all. The law of karma is an impersonal, relentless force that doggedly follows everybody. The Buddha tells us, "You can try to find shelter in the skies, or in the bowels of the earth; the law of karma will come after you." Thus it is the duty of all parents to tell their children that all life is one. William Blake, who saw this unity of life, said:

> A robin red-breast in a cage
> Puts all heaven in a rage. . . .
> A dog starved at his master's gate
> Predicts the ruin of the State.

Even by putting a little robin into a cage, the cosmic order is vio-

lated; the law of karma is at work all the time in the smallest details
of life. Everything is closely interwoven, and even a little hook
causing pain in the smallest fish disturbs the consciousness of the
Lord.

It is our duty, particularly where children are concerned, to remind others, as my spiritual teacher, my Grandmother, reminded
me, that we must respect our kinship with all living creatures. This
can be conveyed in simple language like my Granny's. She used to
tell me, "Squirrels have grannies, and if you hurt a squirrel, it'll go
complain to its granny." I had never thought about animals like
that, and it really opened my eyes. Likewise our children can understand the simple story that little fish have grandmas and grandpas
to whom they run complaining and crying when we hurt them.

Although some biologists say that animals may not have any
consciousness or emotions, we have to agree that as yet we do not
know what animals do or do not feel. In fact, there may be some
other mode of expressing their pain with which we are not acquainted. Two days ago, when we were coming back from Ramagiri, the conversation turned to cows. Someone who had grown up
in Utah remarked, "We just leave them, even during the depths of
the winter, and they thrive in the snow." I would like to hear the
Utah cow's point of view. It may not know how to convey its feelings in the language with which we are accustomed, but if it could
talk, I have an idea that it may not corroborate the statement that
it is "thriving" in the snow. I have even come to suspect it is not
advisable for children to have dogs, because even to have a pet you
should have the capacity to put it first all of the time, and a little
child is not capable of doing this unless guided by the parents.

In India we have had cows for five thousand years. Cows have always been an important symbol in the rural economy. People count
their wealth in cows; instead of saying "We have four cars in our garage," we say "We have four cows in our cow shed." One of our
cows, called Shobha, had been born in our home on the Blue Mountain, and my mother and sister brought her up from the time she
was just a baby. She became a big cow and served us very well, giving us a lot of milk, curds, and butter, and then, like a human be-

ing, she became old, decrepit, and developed rheumatism. Some of our animal husbandry experts used to come and look at our cows and approve of them, but then they would tell my mother, "Why don't you sell that one? Let her go to the butcher."

My mother, who can get roused when we talk about her cows, said, "I have rheumatism just as that cow has, and do you think that I, too, should be discarded now that I am not able to serve people very well?"

We should try to practice this awareness of the unity of life in every relationship. Ten years ago, when I would go to restaurants where my eating habits caused consternation, I used to explain, "I'm a vegetarian." They would suggest fish: "You are a vegetarian; you will love fish." I used to add, "I do love fish; that's just why I don't eat them." This is the point of the Gita: you eat fish because you don't love them, and when you love something, you cannot eat it. Once we saw a French movie, which you couldn't say was influenced by the Hindu mystics, in which a little boy who had pet rabbits was served rabbit for dinner. He said, "I don't eat my buddies." This is the language of the Gita: "You don't eat your buddies." Cats, dogs, cows, and rabbits—these are all our buddies.

Another way we can look at our deep kinship with all living creatures is in terms of the long story of evolution. According to this, our friend Garry was a little orchid long, long ago; that is why he likes them so much. He loves orchids and grows them and looks after them because of this faint memory that gives him a sense of unity with the orchid. There is a similar explanation, according to the theory of reincarnation, that today on the pier I remembered in a very dim way the days when I used to splash about in the water; and I remembered the joy and the sparkle of it and identified myself with the fish as if it were really I swimming about. This is what spiritual awareness means. The pain inflicted on the fish is in me. It was not the fish out there on the pier who were suffering, as separate beings; it was I who was suffering in them. This is how spiritual awareness shows itself in us; we begin to suffer in everything that is subjected to suffering. Until we become aware of this unity underlying all life, all talk of spiritual awareness is just playing games.

यद्यदाचरति श्रेष्ठस्तत्तदेवेतरो जनः ।
स यत्प्रमाणं कुरुते लोकस्तदनुवर्तते ॥२१॥

*21. What the outstanding person does, others will
try to do. The standards such people create will be
followed by the whole world.*

The more gifted we are intellectually, spiritually, and even physically, the greater is our responsibility to contribute to life. Through
the practice of meditation our deeper resources will come into play,
and we will have to be increasingly careful about not writing or
speaking a word that adds to the agitation of others or tends to
separate friends, families, communities, races, or countries.

As householders we can begin to influence others beneficially
right in our own home, starting with our children. Our idea of setting an example is to improvise a domestic pulpit and preach to our
dear ones. I would say that all of us are preaching all the time
through our actions, our words, and our thoughts. Little ones are
ruthless observers. When I see a five-year-old watching me, I feel as
though Sherlock Holmes is on my track. I can almost hear him saying, "Elementary, Dr. Watson. I can see the inconsistency between
his word and deed quite clearly." The way to make our children patient and loving is to be that way ourselves.

There are innumerable opportunities every day to set a good example to others. I have been asking Meera and Geetha to take off
their muddy shoes outside so as not to bring dirt into the house.
They paid no heed to my request because they saw me walking inside wearing my shoes. So the next time we were going indoors together, I just sat on the steps, and without making any comments I
took off my clean shoes and placed them near the door. They sat
down next to me and followed my example. On the subject of patience, my pen disappears every day, and I used to show an unconscious trace of annoyance and ask, "Who has been taking my pen?"
Today when it was missing, however, I put on my best smile, looked
at Meera and Geetha, and asked, "Has anyone seen my pen?" One
of them brought it to me. Whether or not the pen was returned was

not so important as their knowing I am continually trying to be patient with them.

Those who have children can become masters of patience, endurance, and steadfastness, because children will test you at every turn. When we are provoked, most of us get agitated, and it is on these occasions we can repeat the mantram. By continually calling on the Lord, who is the source of strength within us, we can make our lives an inspiring example to all those who come in contact with us.

I have been reading, too, about the tragic tendency among young people to experiment with drugs and how easily it can lead to heroin addiction. Doctors are telling us that as parents we can help our children by not making them drug-conscious—by not depending on drugs to go to sleep, to change our moods, or to become more active. If we really love our children, we will give up smoking and drinking and the use of pep pills and tranquilizers. Our children will be strengthened if instead of drugs we use the most perfect tranquilizer we have, the name of the Lord.

न मे पार्थास्ति कर्तव्यं त्रिषु लोकेषु किंचन ।
नानवाप्तमवाप्तव्यं वर्त एव च कर्मणि ॥२२॥
यदि ह्यहं न वर्तेयं जातु कर्मण्यतन्द्रितः ।
मम वर्त्मानुवर्तन्ते मनुष्याः पार्थ सर्वशः ॥२३॥
उत्सीदेयुरिमे लोका न कुर्यां कर्म चेदहम् ।
संकरस्य च कर्ता स्यामुपहन्यामिमाः प्रजाः ॥२४॥

*22. O Pārtha, there is nothing in the three worlds for me to gain, nor is there anything I do not have. I continue to act, but am not driven by any need of my own.*
*23. If I ever refrained from this continuous work, everyone would immediately follow my example.*
*24. If I ever stopped working, I would be the cause of cosmic chaos, and finally of the destruction of this world and these people.*

In these verses Sri Krishna is telling us how he, from whom the cosmos comes, in whom the cosmos exists, and to whom it returns, works incessantly for our welfare. Yesterday we saw a big spider's web glistening in the light; it was perfectly woven and in the center sat a spider, having his siesta. The Upanishads tell us the Lord weaves the whole universe out of himself and sits in the midst of it, working hardest of all. It is difficult even to imagine the Lord's labor. In a period of decline and dissent over twenty-five hundred years ago, he came as the Compassionate Buddha to toil for our enlightenment. He shed his Buddha body and no sooner got home when a call came from the shores of Galilee: "Trouble brewing—come quickly." With hardly any rest, he went off again to look for suitable parents. He finally decided on Mary and Joseph, but there was no place in which to be born except a stable. With this humble birth the Lord came to us as Jesus and worked for us until his body was crucified. Then he went home only to hear another call of tribulation, this time from Arabia. He came again as an ordinary man who became united with Allah and gave us the Koran. Once again he returned home, but while he was recovering from the desert heat the call came for him to be born as Shankara in Kerala, then again in the nineteenth century as Sri Ramakrishna.

Our age, called *Kaliyuga* or the Age of Anger, demands a chain of incarnations, one after the other. If we really love the Lord, we should be able to say, "We do not want you to be so overworked. We'll be good; we'll meditate every day, repeat your name all the time, restrain our senses at every opportunity, and always put everybody else first." In India there is a festival called *Shivarātrī,* Shiva's Night, popular especially among devotees of Shiva. Shiva stays awake 364 nights of the year looking after us, but on this last night we tell him tenderly that we will be selfless so that he can rest in peace. If we truly love the Lord, our proof is not to cause him any problems by being self-willed. When the Lord does not have a dire need to come into the human context as an incarnation, it means that every one of us has become aware of him. Since the Lord has toiled so long for us, it is not unreasonable for us to try to follow his personal example of selfless living. When our own little tragedies are interfering with our capacity to contribute to the welfare of our family or friends, it is good to remind ourselves of how the Lord labors for everyone's benefit, no matter how distressing the context into which he is called.

Every time a great incarnation comes to us, even today, it is not to bring new truths or to establish a new religion. In fact, they do not come to teach us but to remind us of what we have forgotten—that we are neither our body nor our mind, neither our intellect nor our ego, but pure love, eternal and immutable. Any suffering inflicted on others is suffering inflicted on ourselves; any joy given to others is joy that will permeate our own consciousness.

सक्ताः कर्मण्यविद्वांसो यथा कुर्वन्ति भारत ।
कुर्याद्विद्वांस्तथासक्तश्चिकीर्षुर्लोकसंग्रहम् ॥२५॥

*25. The ignorant work for their own profit,*
*O Bhārata; the wise work for the welfare of others,*
*without thought for themselves.*

It is difficult to persuade people not to go after personal profit, pleasure, prestige, or power, because it is asking them to go against the conditioning to which they have been subjected. The word "rebel" is often misused by our modern mass media. It takes a tremendous amount of endurance and an enormous faith in the Lord within to rebel. Playing games with our appearance is not rebellion. Real rebellion is going against our selfish desires and sense cravings. One of the greatest rebels in the world, Jesus, tells us: "Love your enemies, bless them that curse you, do good to them that hate you." When the Buddha encourages us to seek nirvāna, he is raising the banner of real rebellion. He is asking us to blow out our self-will, to extinguish our limited, selfish personality. To help others understand the truth of rebellion, it is of little avail to put pressure on them. The best way of influencing others is to show by our personal example how the spiritual life adds to the unity of the family, the peace of the neighborhood, and the security of the country. Lord Krishna tells Arjuna, whom he calls *Bhārata,* the 'representative of India': "If you want to influence India, remove all that is selfish, all that is calculating, all that seeks self-aggrandizement in yourself, and you will help the whole country, from the Himālayas to Kanyakumārī."

I can testify to the incredible influence one little man, Gandhi, exercised over all of India. He lived in utter simplicity in a one-room hermitage, and yet he received everybody with the same love and respect, whether it happened to be a member of the British cabinet or a sweeper from Sevagram. When India became independent, the offices of president and prime minister were his for the asking; but he declined, saying that he wanted no reward, that he had worked for Indian independence in order to show the world how even the greatest of international problems can be solved nonviolently. On the night when all India celebrated independence, Gandhi went into prayer.

As the result of Gandhi's contribution, people are taking nonviolence seriously all over the world; fortunately, it has become an important force even on our campuses today. In our own lives, if we want to find the joy of living in peace, we have to establish peace first in our hearts and our homes. We start by cultivating perfect love between all the members of our family; then we extend this love to the members of our community, and by expanding our love ever so gradually, we finally bring the whole world into its embrace.

न बुद्धिभेदं जनयेदज्ञानां कर्मसङ्गिनाम् ।
जोषयेत्सर्वकर्माणि विद्वान्युक्तः समाचरन् ॥२६॥

*26. By abstaining from work you will confuse the ignorant, who are engrossed in their actions; perform all work selflessly, guided by compassion.*

This is a very simple verse, yet far-reaching in its application to our lives. Sri Krishna is telling Arjuna, "You are always influencing others, not only your dear ones but also your antagonists." On the one hand, when we hate our enemies, we are helping them hate us more; when we attack them, we are encouraging them to attack us back. On the other hand, when we forgive them, we are helping them forgive us, and when we move closer to them, we are drawing them closer to us.

Gandhi was always at his best with those who thought they were his mortal enemies. His favorite hymn, "Vaishnavajanito," reminds us in its refrain that he is a true lover of the Lord who returns love for hatred. All we need to do to love the Lord is love those that hate us and be compassionate with those who strike out against us. When we develop the capacity to love those whom we hate, we will be united with the Lord through his grace.

प्रकृतेः क्रियमाणानि गुणैः कर्माणि सर्वशः ।
अहंकारविमूढात्मा कर्ताहमिति मन्यते ॥२७॥

*27. All actions are performed by the gunas of prakriti; deluded by his identification with the ego, a man thinks, "I am the doer."*

*Prakriti* is the word used for anything that changes, anything that is impermanent, anything that is born and will die one day. The entire physical universe is within the realm of *prakriti.* The body is *prakriti,* which means that just as it was born one day, it will die one day. The Buddha, in one of his very tender moments, will tell those around him in reference to his body, "This house was assembled one day, and it has to be disassembled one day; what is there in this to grieve about?"

It is because we identify ourselves obsessively with the body that the very thought of dismantling the house fills us with terror. Last week, on our way to class from our home in Oakland, we saw a gracious old home which could have served a useful purpose for many decades. When we were passing by the next day it was gone. I could not help feeling a little sense of grief, because a beautiful home had been demolished. In this way we do feel a detached sense of loss when the house in which one of our dear ones lived has been dismantled. But if we can realize that we are not the house, but the dweller within it, we will lose our terrible fear of death.

The relationship between *prakriti,* the body, and *purusha,* our real Self, may be explained with the homely metaphor of old clothes (see Gita 2:22). This coat that I am wearing is still rather new, only five years old. At the end of ten years, which is its natural span of life, when I have to discard it, I quietly take it off, throw it into the give-away box, and put on a new one. When I throw away this old jacket, I am not going to say, "My heart is broken; my old jacket is gone." I will say, "Yes, it has served its useful purpose; now I will get a new one."

Another important word used in this verse is *guna,* which denotes the three ultimate constituents of *prakriti*. The first is sattva, or law; the second is rajas, or energy; the third is tamas, or inertia. In each of us there is a different combination of sattva, rajas, and tamas. No one is entirely free from sattva; there is no one who cannot be self-less. You will find some of the most objectionable characters suddenly becoming very selfless towards their pet parrot or raccoon. Everyone can suddenly reveal himself in innocence.

The second guna, rajas, is predominant in many of us in the modern world. It is energy, restlessness, desire. This energy and restlessness, when directed inward, can help us progress rapidly on the spiritual path.

The third factor is tamas, which is inertia or lethargy. "What does it matter? Let the world go"—this is the attitude of tamas. Such an attitude is the opposite of spiritual wisdom. Everything matters on the spiritual path; it is little things, when put together, that amount to a great change. We may feel that we are small people, but working together, we are tremendous. In the realization that each of us can make a definite contribution to the world about us, tamas disappears. Gandhi, inspired by the Gita, tells us that evil has no existence of its own. We support it; that is why it exists. His program of noncooperation was based on his conviction that evil would cease to exist if we would withdraw our support from it. This knowledge enables us to transform tamas into rajas, rajas into sattva, and finally to go beyond all three gunas.

Our real Self, the Ātman or *purusha,* exists outside the realm of change and the three gunas. It is ever pure, ever free. But, deluded by self-will, we remain unaware of the Ātman and identify ourselves

with the mind and body, which are subject to change. It is helpful,
even when we cannot realize it completely, to remind ourselves that
we are not the mind. It is the mind that is angry, it is the mind that
is afraid, it is the mind that is selfish, not our real Self. That is why
the Buddha says, "Take the mind and throw it out." It is very easy
to say this, but extremely difficult to do. Yesterday I saw a boy at the
āshram playing with a new toy. I asked him what he was playing
with, and he explained: "It's a yo-yo. You just can't get rid of the
thing!" This is the ego; you throw it anywhere and it will come back
to you. No amount of saying "I am going to throw this far away"
will eliminate the ego.

The surest way of reducing self-will is to begin to put the welfare
of those around us first, to love others more than we love ourselves.
We must not love only those who love us; we must learn to love our
enemies as well. It is good to forgive those who have offended us. As
St. Francis says, he who has not learned to forgive has lost the greatest source of joy in life. If, through the practice of meditation and the
repetition of the mantram, we can forgive others from the depths of
our being and transform our attitude towards them into selfless love,
we will immediately be able to forgive our own mistakes and drawbacks. The more we forgive others, the more the Lord, who is within, forgives us.

तत्त्वविनु महाबाहो गुणकर्मविभागयोः ।
गुणा गुणेषु वर्तन्त इति मत्वा न सज्जते ॥२८॥
प्रकृतेर्गुणसंमूढाः सज्जन्ते गुणकर्मसु ।
तानकृत्स्नविदो मन्दान्कृत्स्नविन्न विचालयेत् ॥२९॥

*28. But the illumined man or woman understands
the domain of the gunas and is not attached. Such
people know that the gunas interact with each other;
they do not claim to be the doer.*
*29. Those who are deluded by the operation of
the gunas become attached to the results of their
action. Those who understand these truths should
not unsettle the ignorant.*

The theory of the three gunas tells us about the nature of our desires. When we have desires which require urgent satisfaction, none of us, no matter what he tries to do, can divest himself of the belief that he is these desires. If only we could jump out of this little circle of desires and look at any one desire, we would realize that it is not ours at all, because our real nature is ever full. Our real nature, the Ātman, can admit of no desire, and when we say "I desire this," "I cannot be happy without this," we are making statements which are metaphorical. When I first arrived here from India, I was not used to automobiles. I have some acquaintance with them now, but the phrases that people use about automobiles used to strike me as rather puzzling. When I first heard someone saying, "I am out of gas," I did not understand that he was talking about his car. Most of our statements which begin with "I desire" are in this category. This is what Sri Krishna is sending deep into Arjuna's consciousness. When we say, "I desire money, material possessions, pleasure, power," Sri Krishna says we are the victim of our own language.

The Lord tells Arjuna that when the senses and sense objects see one another, they are just drawn to each other. You and I have no part in this; we are neutral. This is such a compassionate, humorous, and factual observation, and Arjuna is so enraptured by it, that he begins to understand that we actually do not participate in any selfish desire or sensory attraction. We wrongly identify ourselves with these desires because we have been conditioned to do so in our home, by our friends, and by the mass media.

Attraction and aversion are closely related; they are the extremes of a pendulum. We are tied to what we hate; we cannot help thinking about people we hate. Naturally we think about those whom we love, but we also dwell on those we hate. As long as we believe we are our desires, we have to be a party in the quarrel of attraction and aversion, very often on the wrong side. But as our mind becomes less and less agitated through the practice of meditation, we shall see, to our great surprise, that we are just spectators. Once we understand this, we are free from the clamor of the senses, and they can no longer drag us into their quarrel of attraction and aversion.

When the senses and sense objects draw each other, do not be afraid that you will be swept away. Your desires may look towering, but through the grace of the Lord of Love within, you can learn to master even the greatest of them. In trying to release yourself from your involvement in the attraction and repulsion between the senses and sense objects, it is necessary to be very vigilant for a long time. It is by yielding to small desires that you are drawn gradually into greater desires. Today, for example, we took our nieces to the circus, and when we went in, everyone had a carton of popcorn. Someone very unsophisticated—someone, say, from a village in India—seeing that everyone has a ticket in one hand and popcorn in the other, might actually think that you couldn't be admitted without popcorn. Our nieces had some, and to keep them company, I ate a little also. Then, after eating the popcorn, I got thirsty. I hadn't expected this. But the salesboys, who *had* expected it, were right there selling cold drinks; and later, outside, the cigarette merchant was waiting too.

In the second line of this verse, Sri Krishna is reminding us, through Arjuna, that we should not disturb people by preaching at them; it is much easier to influence others through our personal example. When Gandhi was observing his day of silence, someone once asked him for a message. He just wrote, "My life is my message." This is true of us also. We are always influencing those around us by our daily life, and when we try to lead the spiritual life, putting those around us first, we cannot help but win them over in the end.

मयि सर्वाणि कर्माणि संन्यस्याध्यात्मचेतसा ।
निराशीर्निर्ममो भूत्वा युध्यस्व विगतज्वरः ॥ ३०॥

*30. Completely absorbed in the Ātman, without expectations, and free from the fever of the ego, fight your self-will, performing all actions for my sake.*

You may remember in the first chapter where Arjuna, like you and me, says, "Why should I govern my passions, why should I reduce my self-will?" and refuses to fight. Sri Krishna now tells him, "You are not well now; you are suffering from the fever of self-will. But when your fever has subsided, get ready to fight. Do your very best: meditate regularly, try to restrain your senses, and put the welfare of those around you first." In other words, Sri Krishna reminds us, we are all likely to make mistakes on the spiritual path, and we can be overcome by regret. But rather than regretting our mistakes, it is much more useful to forget the past and keep marching forward with renewed enthusiasm.

Sri Ramakrishna often refers to the fever of the ego from which all of us suffer to some degree. In many of us it is only a little above normal—ninety-nine degrees. We get on very well in life; we are loved and respected. But when the temperature begins to rise above one hundred, we become more and more dangerous, not only to ourselves but to the family and community in which we dwell. When we suffer from this fever, we become blind to the needs of those around us and to the unity of life.

*Adhyātmacetasā* means completely absorbed in the Ātman. This complete absorption can happen to all of us as our meditation deepens through the grace of the Lord. We may be enabled to go through all of the last eighteen verses of the second chapter of the Gita, for example, without our mind wandering once, without falling asleep once. This indicates that we have reached a profound state of concentration in which there is unbroken continuity of meditation. When such a state is attained, those verses have become an integral part of our consciousness, and the proof of it will be seen in our life. When suffering comes, we are not agitated, because we are equal to it. All our compassion, which has been misspent on ourselves, now goes to the person who has caused us sorrow. When desires come, we do not identify ourselves with them; we are masters of our desires. If they are selfless, we welcome them; if they are selfish, we defy them with equal joy. We have gained freedom from selfish attachments, fear, and anger.

*Nirāshī* means having no expectations; it is only when you have expectations that you have disappointments, get frustrated, become insecure, and try to manipulate others. Here Sri Krishna is giving Arjuna very strong counsel. He says, "Whatever I give, accept it gratefully: say yes if it is joy, say yes if it is sorrow. Then you will be free." Gradually you will find that as you detach yourself from the results of your actions and stop worrying about results, you are able to concentrate better on your work. "If you want to give your best in any selfless service," the Lord says, "choose the right goal, use right means, and don't think about results; leave them to Me."

ये मे मतमिदं नित्यमनुतिष्ठन्ति मानवाः ।
श्रद्धावन्तोऽनसूयन्तो मुच्यन्ते तेऽपि कर्मभिः ॥ ३१॥

*31. Those who live in accordance with these*
*divine laws with an unwavering sense of purpose,*
*firmly established in faith, are released from karma.*

The teaching which Sri Krishna gives to Arjuna contains the divine laws of existence, which are inscribed deep in our consciousness, written in the very cells of every creature. It is because these laws are within us that we suffer so much when we try to break them. As someone wisely said, we cannot break God's laws; we can only break ourselves against them. Here the appeal of the Gita lies not in forcing us, saying *thou shalt* or *thou shalt not,* but in presenting us with two alternatives: one leading to abiding joy, unassailable security, and an enormous capacity for contributing to the welfare of others, and the other leading to sorrow, insecurity, and the suffering of those around us. The Lord tells Arjuna, "If you cannot shake yourself free from the fever of the ego, you will become a curse on the face of the earth. But if you can turn your back upon your own pleasure, profit, and prestige, and devote yourself to enriching your family, community, and world, you will become a great blessing to all."

Thus all of us have the choice, in whatever country we live, whatever position we occupy, to live for ourselves or to live for others. The choice is left entirely to us. If we live for others, we live in complete harmony with the laws of life, bringing joy to those around us and to ourselves. If we live only for ourselves, as most of us are conditioned to do, we will plunge ourselves and all those around us into misery.

With the words *mucyante te 'pi karmabhih,* "they also are released from karma," Sri Krishna makes a promise, a promise that
has been fulfilled in the lives of many who have surrendered to the
Lord. When we devote ourselves completely to the service of all,
our families' needs are provided for by the Lord, who knows how to
look after them better than we do. Sri Krishna tells Arjuna that if
he will throw himself wholeheartedly into the service of mankind,
he will be released from the responsibility of working for personal
needs; these become the Lord's responsibility.

When we dedicate our whole life unreservedly to the service of
humanity, the Lord will magnify all our faculties. In some amazing
way, even our sleep will be given us to serve others. As our meditation deepens, we will find that we need less sleep, less food, and
more opportunities for service. We will find that we must use the
tremendous forces placed in our hands. A family of two or three or
four will not satisfy us; we will want a whole continent for our family, as Gandhiji had. When Mrs. Gandhi was asked how many children she had, her reply was, "I have four, but my husband has four
hundred million." As meditation deepens and self-will becomes
less, we come to regard everyone as our own; if they have problems,
it is our privilege to live for helping them to solve those problems.
When at last we regard the entire world as our family, we will be
enabled to draw upon the vast reservoir of love and wisdom lying
unsuspected in all of us.

We should not mistakenly interpret Sri Krishna's declaration as
telling us to go serve others and neglect our own at home. It is not
that we learn to love our family less, but that we learn to love everyone equally well. It is a travesty of the spiritual life to think that
Gandhi did not love his family because he loved everybody else. His
capacity to love became so limitless that he was able to flood the
whole country and the whole world with it. Not only in India are his
teachings cherished; all over the world we are beginning to see what
a tremendous contribution this humble man has made to the welfare
of all. Gandhi loved mankind and showed us the way to regard all
countries with love, trying to understand the other person's needs
exactly as we understand our own.

Here again Arjuna is very much like us; the prospect of having his resources magnified is very appealing. He would like to have his creative intelligence and capacity to love increased; he knows that they are in need of magnification. The Lord understands what is going on in his mind and tells him:

ये त्वेतदभ्यसूयन्तो नानुतिष्ठन्ति मे मतम् ।
सर्वज्ञानविमूढांस्तान्विद्धि नष्टानचेतसः ॥३२॥

*32. Understand that those who violate these laws,
criticizing and complaining about fate, are utterly
deluded, and are the cause of their own suffering.*

Here Sri Krishna cautions Arjuna that if he chooses not to observe the Lord's spiritual laws, but lives for his own pleasure and profit, even the small capacities that he has will be reduced still further. Instead of being maximized, they will be minimized. We have only to look at people who live only for themselves to see how constricted their consciousness is, how easily they can be upset, and how people naturally avoid them. We cannot avoid making this choice between living for ourselves and living for others. If we try to serve others without turning our back on our own self-will, we will neither be able to serve others nor to help ourselves.

Ignorance and scepticism do not exempt us from the spiritual laws governing the world. Many people question the validity of these laws, and I remind them that whether we believe in them or not they apply equally to all of us. When I was speaking at the Kaiser Center in Oakland—not before a gathering of Hindu mystics but before hard-headed Kaiser businessmen—one of my friends there came up to me one day and told me in a very affectionate manner, "We like you, and we appreciate your talks, your enthusiasm, and your humor, but this law of karma isn't applicable to us. We do not believe in it as you do in India. We live west of Suez, and the law of karma stops at Port Said."

I just said, "All right, I'm going to the roof, and I'm going to wave my arms and fly over Lake Merritt."

He got terribly upset and said, "Why do you want to try that? Don't you know it will kill you?"

"Why should it kill me?"

"The law of gravity, man!"

So I said, "The law of gravity stops at Port Said; we in the East don't subscribe to it. After all, it was not given to us by a Hindu mystic but by a British scientist."

He came close to me, put his arm on my shoulder, and said, "My dear fellow, whether you believe in it or not, the law of gravity works."

Then I put my arm around him saying, "Whether you believe it or not, the law of karma works everywhere, every day, in everyone's life."

This should remind us to start going beyond the law of karma by subordinating our personal feelings and desires to the welfare of all those around us. There are people who claim they know nothing of these laws. They will tell you, "I am completely ignorant. I always thought that by living for myself I would become secure. I always thought that by dwelling upon myself I would enhance my personality. You shouldn't hold these things against me when I didn't know." Sri Krishna's reply to this is that all of us are expected to use our common sense in observing who is secure, who is at peace, who is able to contribute to the welfare of others.

When we make the choice to lead a selfless life, we are really being practical and using our common sense. One of Gandhiji's favorite hymns in his mother tongue says, "Lord, give me piety, give me devotion, but please don't deny me common sense." On the spiritual path there seems to be the mistaken belief in some minds that the less common sense we have, the more advanced we are on the path. If there is anybody terribly practical in life, it is the man of God. If there is anybody terribly impractical in life, it is the man of the world, because he spends his whole life in the pursuit of money, trying to follow a pattern of life that only fills him with insecurity.

सदृशं चेष्टते स्वस्याः प्रकृतेर्ज्ञानवानपि ।
प्रकृतिं यान्ति भूतानि निग्रहः किं करिष्यति ॥३३॥

*33. Even a wise man acts within the limitations of
his own nature. Every creature is subject to prakriti:
what is the use of repression?*

Even though all of us are governed by the indivisible unity that is
the divine principle of existence, on the surface level of life we are
all individuals, with special samskāras. Though we are all one at the
very source of life, no two of us are alike on the surface of it. This is
the marvel of life—that we should be so different outwardly, yet in
the deepest sense be one and indivisible.

In the Upanishads, there is a vivid description of how the one
reality, the Lord, became very lonesome. The Lord, being *advaita,*
'One without a second,' had no one to play with, and just like a little
boy he said, "I want boys and girls to play with, and animals and
birds. But there is no one in the world but Me, so whom can I ask to
be my playmate?" He began to meditate, and thought, "Why don't
I ask myself?" Then he divided himself into millions of creatures,
and when he looked around, he was surrounded by a big football
team. He said, "Now I want a big stadium to stage all these big
games. Let the world be my stadium." This is the coliseum of the
ego, and for the superficial observer, life is really like going to a big
game. Everyone looks different—different clothes, different things
to eat, different ways of cheering. But in this stadium it is the Lord
himself who is playing on both teams. The home team and the visiting team are part of a conspiracy, just pretending to play against
each other, to win or lose.

Once we begin to perceive the unity underlying all life, we will
have nothing but love and respect for everyone around us, beginning in our home and extending to the entire world. We have only
to look at the newspapers today, every page reporting violence and
conflict, to see that the vast majority have forgotten this unity. Sri
Krishna reminds all of us that in politics also we should never forget
that there is only One; what conduces to the welfare of all is inclu-

sive of the welfare of each one of us. There is no one in the world except the Lord disguised as many, but as long as we live for ourselves, pursuing our own private satisfaction and dwelling upon ourselves, we can never see this underlying unity. It is selfish people who see separateness everywhere because they look at life through their own selfishness, whereas the selfless person sees what is common to himself and others. Spiritual awareness is seeing this basic unity.

The one Lord within, who has disguised himself as many, is the soul or Self in man. This *purusha,* as it is called in Sanskrit, is what unites us all. *Prakriti* is what makes us appear separate. Our physical and mental being evolves according to the laws of *prakriti.* To use the language of Hindu mysticism, all of us have evolved through millions of lives to become man, but even among humans there are different degrees of evolution. From this point of view, the person who is excited by money has come into the human context just recently. He has been wandering in the jungle as a lion or tiger and has never seen money. They don't use currency in the jungle, so he has had no contact with money at all. When he comes into the human situation, he is fascinated by the dollar, the pound, the rupee, and the ruble, because they are all new. According to this theory, when he has been this way a number of times—has been to banks, bought shares, seen them going up and down, and been agitated—he slowly learns to look upon money as rather irrelevant. Then when he sees it he says, "This is just metal; it has no intrinsic value at all."

The process of learning is the same in the case of pleasure. People who have been through the sensory game a number of times do not get easily drawn into sensate stimulations. The compassion of this explanation can appeal to all of us, for it does not classify us as either good or bad. It is not good to sit in judgment on those who pursue ephemeral pleasure; in a little while they will find it fails to satisfy, because there is an innate need for a supreme purpose in every human being. We cannot live without a supreme purpose, and though we may mistakenly try to fulfill this purpose by building houses, or sailing boats, or painting pictures, we must eventually find that nothing finite will ever satisfy us. We can go to the moon; it is a great achievement, but after a while our eyes turn beyond to

Neptune. Wherever we go in space, wherever we go in time, we find limitations. Our need is for infinite joy, infinite love, infinite wisdom, and infinite capacity for service, and until this need is met, we can never, never rest peacefully. But from the very day we begin meditation, supplementing it by discriminating restraint of the senses and putting the welfare of those around us first, we have started after the infinite. We will find our very endeavor gives us joy.

We begin our journey towards the supreme goal of life from where we stand. All of us begin the spiritual ascent by accepting ourselves as we are. Just as it is good to be patient with others, it is equally necessary to be patient with ourselves. After all, when the desire to lead the spiritual life and live for others comes to us, we can be haunted by our past mistakes, by the amount of time and energy we have wasted in selfish pursuits. But the Lord of Love implies here that we must accept ourselves with all our strengths and weaknesses. Without this kind of great patience with ourselves, the precipitous ascent to the summit of human awareness is fraught with great danger. There are many obstacles on the spiritual path meant to strengthen us, and these cannot be overcome unless we have infinite patience with ourselves. When we are patient with others, we cannot help being patient with ourselves. As this verse indicates, each of us is individual, with his own special samskāras and qualities. We start now, where we are, with our partial love for money, partial love for pleasure, partial love for prestige, and a little love for the Lord.

Just as we all start our sādhana from a different point, as determined by our *prakriti,* we also set our own pace on the path. We should be careful that each person keep within his own stride. Christine and I are usually rather fast walkers, but when we go for a walk with our little nieces, Meera and Geetha, we shorten our stride, rest a little more on each foot, and make use of any excuse to look at a seagull or pick up a pebble. One of the necessities in spiritual counseling is to see that each person goes at the right pace. People who have spent their time in the pursuit of money and pleasure may sprain an ankle with a long stride and fast walk.

There are different types on the spiritual path. There are people capable of tremendous enthusiasm who suddenly turn over a new leaf. The man who slept until noon now starts getting up at three in the morning for meditation. The same enthusiasm he had for money or pleasure can be redirected towards the spiritual life. The highly enthusiastic person is already one-pointed and, because of his concentration, can easily take to the spiritual life. It is the butterfly, flitting from flower to flower, that will find it difficult to attain samādhi. Those who say, "What does it matter? Why go to school? Why take up a job?" will also question, "Why meditate? Why repeat the mantram?" People capable of throwing themselves heart and soul into any great endeavor, even though it may not be the most spiritual, will find themselves taking enthusiastically to the spiritual life when the time comes. It is good to have enthusiasm, not for many things but for one big passion, because this unifies the mind and increases concentration.

We do not have to wait until we have advanced on the path of evolution to turn our face to the Lord. There are many great sinners in the annals of mysticism who have turned to the Lord and become completely pure and perfect through his grace. In the ninth chapter there is a tremendous verse which has consoled millions of human beings who have committed many mistakes through ignorance. The Lord tells us: "A person may be very selfish, may have led a very reckless life, causing suffering to others as well as to himself, but when he turns his back upon himself and surrenders to Me, he becomes pure rapidly, and I lead him into the perfection which is my nature. Any person, whatever his past, when he gives Me all his heart, becomes free and is united with Me" (Gita 9:31–2).

All of us, no matter what our past has been, no matter what our present drawbacks are, can take to the spiritual life, and we will progress on the path at our own pace. It is not good to compare one person's progress with another's. This, as well as guidance in meditation, is very much a personal matter.

Last Saturday when we took my mother and nieces to Santa Rosa, we went to a big shopping center where we were able to treat the children to ice cream. The children then wanted to ride on the escalator, which they had never seen in India. My mother was very timorous about this, but I assured her that the art could be learned gradually. First Meera wanted to try. I stood by her side and told her to watch me and do as I did. We took the first step together, as I held her hand. When the time came for us to get off, I said, still holding her hand, "Now you do the same thing; take your foot off and put it on the floor, just as I do it." We came down the escalator in the same way. In this first experience she had been just doing what I was doing because she identifies herself easily with me. Even my mother was reassured. Then we made the same pilgrimage, but without holding hands. Now confident, she went up and came down by herself. This is very much the meditation experience too; for a long time we have to hold on to an experienced person.

Now, seeing Meera, who is older, doing this in three easy lessons, Geetha said, "I want to go up and down the escalator too, just like Meera." I took Geetha's hand, but as we stepped onto the escalator, it was as if I were holding her in the air. All her weight was on my arm, but she was under the impression that she was on her own.

Similarly in meditation there are a few people who have to be helped in this way without their ever becoming aware of it. A good teacher is one whose touch is so light that you can hardly feel it, whose muscles are so supple that he shows no effort at all. He just looks at you saying, "Yes, you are doing well; you are doing very well." Even a person who must be helped in this way will begin to learn, but he may not learn in three easy lessons. He may require six hard lessons. We should never ask ourselves why there is this difference between people. It is good to be content with the speed at which we are able to go because it is in accordance with our dharma.

इन्द्रियस्येन्द्रियस्यार्थे रागद्वेषौ व्यवस्थितौ ।
तयोर्न वशमागच्छेत्तौ ह्यस्य परिपन्थिनौ ॥३४॥

*34. The senses have been conditioned by attraction to the pleasant and aversion to the unpleasant. Do not be ruled by them; they are obstacles in your path.*

Two of the important words used in this verse are *indriya* and *indriyārtha*. *Indriya* denotes the sense organs, and *indriyārtha* the sense objects of which the external world is composed. In the relationship between these two, there exists *rāgadvesha*, 'attraction and aversion.' All of us are governed in a large measure by this tyrannical duality of likes and dislikes. We avoid something because we do not like it; we move away from people because we dislike them. We are tied not only to what we like but also to what we dislike. To give an extreme example, when we love someone, we are always thinking about that person, wanting to serve their welfare. Unfortunately, when we hate someone, we also think about the person all the time, about how to frustrate their welfare. It is the same emotional relationship.

In my mother tongue, there is a folksong about a boy who knows a good bit about girls. He tells his girl, "Love me or hate me, I don't care; I have got you. But don't ever become indifferent to me; then I have lost you." When someone says, "I hate you," don't give up— they are as entangled emotionally with you as they can ever be. When your girlfriend says this, do not slam the door and say, "I don't want to see you again." That is the time to close the door from inside and say, "I am not going to leave you at all."

I think it was Sai Baba, one of the spectacular mystics of modern India, who put this concept of likes and dislikes into epigrammatic words when he said that if you do not do what you like, then you can do what you want. As long as we are dominated by likes and dislikes —in our job, in our studies, in our friendships, in our food, in our recreation—we are just being compelled by our nervous system to move towards what we like and away from what we dislike.

A friend of ours who is a physicist made the keen observation that most of meditation is a reconditioning of the nervous system. As long as our nervous system works only one way, enabling us to run towards the pleasant and away from the unpleasant, it is considerably damaged. It is really meant for two-way traffic, the mystics tell us, and it is only because of our long conditioning that it has come to be so constricted, able to move only towards the pleasant. When it has been reconditioned through meditation, we can live in

freedom, choosing to do what is in the interests of others even though
it may be painful to us, may cause us mental and physical distress.

After the nervous system has been reconditioned, we will find
such joy in contributing to the welfare of others that we no longer
will fear moving towards the unpleasant and doing what previously
we did not like. Then we will find we have been psycho-allergic, to
use a modern term, towards certain people, partly because of the
distorting medium of our own prejudices and conditioning through
which we view the world. This veil which we throw over others can
magnify their faults and sometimes even attribute to them faults
which are really ours. For example, if we believe, as many people
do, that only the desire for money can motivate people deeply, we
will be suspicious even of a person who works without any thought
of personal profit. But when the nervous system has been reconditioned, we see life without likes and dislikes. The veil which we have
thrown over others is removed, and we come to have *samadrishti,* an
equal eye for all. Then we discover that all life is one—that underlying all our infinite variety there exists the indivisible unity, the divine principle of existence.

Sri Krishna is telling you and me, through Arjuna, that we should
try every day to calm the mind and not become agitated by likes and
dislikes. This is practical advice because very often in life we must
do many things we dislike. Every day we should do a few things we
do not like and try to do them with enthusiasm. Everyone begins
this with a certain amount of reluctance, but by welcoming jobs we
dislike, and doing them with concentration, we can learn to enjoy
them. It is often just the fear of having to face an unpleasant task
that makes us complain, saps our will, and finally makes us give up.
The will is strengthened greatly when we welcome jobs we dislike,
when we do first what we like least.

One of the most graceful ways of learning to juggle with our likes
and dislikes is to do things we dislike for those we love. For example,
at home, where kitchen chores are concerned, there are many things
which no one likes to do. But my mother, even at the age of almost
eighty, is able to take delight in preparing meals for us. Two days
ago, to celebrate the harvest festival of Kerala, she spent hours pre-

paring a delicious meal of the traditional dishes, without any feeling of being tired or under pressure, because of her desire to make a contribution to the health and happiness of all at Ramagiri.

Another way of overcoming dislikes in the matter of work is to give more attention when we are becoming bored with a particular job. I have known many students both in India and in America, and when they say something is "boring," what they usually mean is they are not interested in it. The simple cure for boredom is to give a little more attention, a little more concentration, and we will find the more concentration we give, the more interesting the subject becomes. But we are so perverse that when something bores us, we immediately begin thinking about something else. If we can only straighten ourselves up and give more concentration, we will find how good this discipline is for our intellectual development. Ultimately, we should be able to give our concentration to anything.

Today I was reading a brilliant paper by a friend of ours on biophysics. He appreciates our work and has visited us many times, so I thought it a token of my appreciation to give my complete concentration to this highly scientific essay. To my amazement, halfway I was beginning to understand it, and by the time I finished, I agreed with it. Even subjects with which we are not familiar can be understood and appreciated by giving them enough concentration.

It is only after we have freed our nervous system from the tyranny of likes and dislikes that we live in complete freedom and security. Every morning we will get up eager to continue our life of service, and every evening we will go to bed at peace in spite of the terrible problems with which the world is confronted, knowing that we have made a contribution, however small, to the solution of these problems.

श्रेयान्स्वधर्मो विगुणः परधर्मात्स्वनुष्ठितात् ।
स्वधर्मे निधनं श्रेयः परधर्मो भयावहः ॥३५॥

*35. It is better to strive in one's own dharma than
to succeed in the dharma of another: nothing is ever
lost in following one's own dharma, but competition
in another's dharma breeds fear and insecurity.*

The word used here is *dharma,* a word common to Hinduism and Buddhism. It comes from the root *dhri,* 'to support'; dharma is what supports us, keeps us together, prevents us from flying to pieces in the face of stress. Dharma is the central law of our being, which is to extinguish our separateness and attain Self-realization, to lose ourselves and be united with the Lord. In Buddhism this transformation is called nirvāna, the extinction of self-will in union with the infinite. Ansari of Herat, a great Sufi mystic, tells us, "Know that when you learn to lose yourself, you will reach the Beloved." And in the Gita (12:8), Sri Krishna says, "Still your mind in Me, still yourself in Me, and without doubt you shall be united with Me, Lord of Love, dwelling in your heart." This universal law is inscribed on every cell of our being, and the proof of it is that the more we live for others, the healthier our body becomes, the calmer our mind becomes, the clearer our intellect becomes, the deeper our love and wisdom become.

When *sva* is added to *dharma,* the word becomes *svadharma,* our own personal dharma. This is our present context, our present assets and liabilities. On the spiritual path, we start from where we stand by fulfilling our present responsibilities, on the campus, at the office, or in the home. This *svadharma* may change as our spiritual awareness deepens. Later on, as our capacities grow, our responsibilities and opportunities for service will become greater. What is the right occupation now may not be right later on, but as long as it is not at the expense of others, our job or profession can be made a part of our sādhana. We should be careful, however, to choose a career that is not at the expense of any living creature.

By using the word *svadharma* Sri Krishna is saying not to try to follow a profession because someone else is following it. It is much better for you to learn to know yourself, to know your assets and liabilities, to remember your training and follow the career which blends with your sādhana, than for you to compare yourself with others and do what they are doing. Try to exercise your own judgment instead of doing things because some movie star or baseball player does them. Why should I look like the Beatles? I look better when I am myself. Why should I drink something because some baseball player drinks it? I would drink it if the nutritionist Jean Mayer told me to.

It is a very enjoyable thing to be oneself, to stop acting. Only after considerable progress in meditation do we discover what consummate actors we are. Early morning we get up and start acting; we go to the office or to the campus and keep acting. It is because we are always on the stage, worrying if the audience is going to applaud or if anyone is going to throw rotten tomatoes, that tension builds up. But Sri Krishna says, "Be yourself completely; accept yourself completely."

The ability to know oneself and be oneself comes through a long period of discipline. One of the mistakes young people often make is thinking, "I am going to be spontaneous. Tomorrow morning when I get up I am just going to be myself." It is only after we have unlearned many of our old habits and freed ourselves from the tyranny of likes and dislikes that we are truly spontaneous. Then we will find that when we are at home with ourselves we are at home with everyone else.

अर्जुन उवाच
अथ केन प्रयुक्तोऽयं पापं चरति पूरुषः ।
अनिच्छन्नपि वार्ष्णेय बलादिव नियोजितः ॥३६॥

ARJUNA:

*36. What is the force that binds us to selfish deeds, Vārshneya? What power moves us, despite our desire to act for the good of all?*

Arjuna, like all of us, has a great desire to lead a selfless life, but has great difficulties in implementing his desire. In this question, which is so human, so personal, that it is easy to appreciate how much Arjuna represents every one of us, Arjuna addresses Sri Krishna as *Vārshneya.* Sri Krishna was born in the Vrishni community as an *avatāra,* an incarnation; and just as Sri Krishna calls Arjuna *Kaunteya,* 'son of Kuntī,' Arjuna here returns the compliment. This is the give-and-take of good friends. Arjuna is asking this question of Sri Krishna partly as his spiritual teacher and partly as his good friend, who will not be offended, who will not misunderstand, and who will not hold anything against him.

Arjuna is saying, "I want to lead the right life; I want to enter into a state of abiding joy, and I do not want to be a plaything of circumstances. I want to do what is good for every creature in the world, but what force prevents me from carrying out these high ideals? What makes me fall over and over again? What makes me go after my personal profit and personal pleasure?"

Sri Krishna will answer Arjuna in the concluding words of the third chapter. Try to imagine Sri Krishna now as I do, as looking at Arjuna and almost saying, "So you think you are the only one who has this problem?" It is in this bantering, loving, divine tone that Sri Krishna reveals what causes the great ordeal for all of us on the spiritual path.

श्री भगवानुवाच
काम एष क्रोध एष रजोगुणसमुद्भवः ।
महाशनो महापाप्मा विद्ध्येनमिह वैरिणम् ॥३७॥

SRI KRISHNA:
*37. It is selfish desire and anger, arising from the guna of rajas; these are the appetites and deeds which threaten a person in this life.*

The Lord says that our greatest enemies, waiting to bring about our downfall, are *kāma* and *krodha*. *Kāma* is selfish desire, or self-will. It drives us to impose our will on all around us, to satisfy our selfish desires even at the expense of others, to feel that it is *our* family, *our* friends, *our* country alone that deserve consideration. *Kāma* shows itself in many ways: in physical cravings, greed for money, and lust for power and prestige. This drive for personal satisfaction is inevitably connected with *krodha,* or anger, because when we are driven in this way there is always the possibility of being frustrated by obstacles, of being challenged by others. The same urges which we have for personal satisfaction, others have too; therefore friction arises.

In my mother tongue, when someone is very angry, he will say,

"Hum!" In the village you will often hear this exclamation. You can see mothers shaking their finger and saying *hum!* Sometimes even a little boy can imitate his mother and reply *hum!* in exactly the same tone. It was my Grandmother who taught me that this *hum!* is very often an expression of violated self-will, and because of her teaching, when I hear *hum!* it reminds me of the Sanskrit word *aham,* which means 'I.' When I say *hum!* to you it really means, "Do you know who I am? I am I." There can still be peace if you do not challenge me, but you too are likely to reply, *"Hum! I too am I."* Just as this problem of ahamkāra, or self-will, exists between individuals, it exists among nations as well. The same language of anger that is used by one nation is used by the other when national self-will is frustrated.

Even though we have good intentions, once our ego is opposed, our self-will is challenged. Once our personal desires are flouted, our mind becomes agitated, and the moment our mind is agitated, our judgment becomes clouded. With the very best intentions, we may impose our self-will on our partner. With the desire of cementing the relationship, we say, "Why don't you do what I want you to do?" Our partner, also with the very same intentions of cementing the relationship, says, "Why don't *you* do what *I* want you to?" Once this clash comes about, both minds become agitated, and both, with the desire of strengthening the partnership, do everything possible to disrupt it. At that time, even though propelled by anger, we should try not to give in to it, but to maintain our attitude of love and respect for the person who has opposed us.

This morning it was so hot that we weren't able to have our long walk in Oakland, so we went to the San Francisco beach. Looking down from Cliff House at the great array of surfers—whom I enjoy watching because they remind me so much of what takes place in meditation—we noticed many of the surfers were beginners, dhārana people. There were also a few more experienced ones, the dhyāna people. There were no samādhi people. It was very interesting to watch these two categories. The beginner would wade into the water, wait for a big wave, and when it came, he would try to stand up. Then not only would he be thrown down, but the surfboard would fly up like a toy in the air. But not even the most timid would immediately put his surfboard on his head and go home. They just came back and got into the water again.

This is the real secret of the spiritual life. When the passions, which can tower over the tidal waves of the Pacific, come and ask us, like the waves, "Would you like to play a game with us?" we must be ready to control them and ride them just as we ride a wave. To me this surfing is a game between the waves and the surfboard. It isn't a hostile encounter; it's a very friendly game where the waves are telling the surfboard, "You bring your rider along. I'll throw you both up in the air. Why don't you try me? You can learn to ride on me, but first I am going to make both of you fly in the air like toys."

The other surfers we saw were more skillful, more resolute, more secure. They were not content with the white waters, but would go into what Ramakrishna calls the black waters, far away from the shore, where the waves were getting very high. Today we saw two or three people getting the right timing and "shooting the tube" so fast that we were amazed a person could learn such a skill. In governing our passions, it is the same story. It is a game in which the passions dare us, "Would you like to come? We are three: fear, anger, and greed. You are only one." To this the really adventurous person will say, "You are three, I am one, so this is the right game for me. I am going to fall. I am going to drink a lot of sea water. But one day I will ride on you." When we bring this determination to our sādhana, the great day will soon come when, through the grace of the Lord, we will be able to harness the power of anger, fear, and greed and use it in contributing to the welfare of others. An angry man is allowing power to rise against him and enslave him, but when he learns to control these tremendous sources of power, he can use them to meet the most formidable challenges of the day and to make his greatest contribution to those around him.

In daily living, even though we advance fairly well in meditation and are able to use the mantram most of the time, we will all have to face circumstances in which the senses will be strongly tempted. The Bible tells us that even Jesus was not free from these great temptations, and the Buddhist scriptures record for us the Buddha's struggle with Māra, the tempter. When sense cravings and self-will propel us, when we find ourselves almost helpless, the example of Jesus and the Buddha inspires us to turn against these powerful drives and learn to control them. The duel with the senses can be so satisfying, so thrilling, that no victory in worldly life can compare with it. And gradually, as we free ourselves from the tyranny of these selfish desires in our actions, they will subside from the mind also.

धूमेनात्रियते वह्निर्यथादर्शो मलेन च ।
यथोल्बेनावृतो गर्भस्तथा तेनेदमावृतम् ॥३८॥

*38. Just as a fire is covered by smoke and a mirror*
*is obscured by dust, just as the embryo rests deep with-*
*in the womb, knowledge is hidden by selfish desire.*

Just as a great pall of smoke obscures the fire blazing underneath, just so the pall of desire—selfish, self-willed, separate—hides the blazing fire of power, the blazing light of divinity, that shines forever in the depths of our consciousness.

Just as a mirror is covered by dust, so is knowledge of the Ātman hidden by *kāma*. Sri Krishna is telling Arjuna that if you try to use a mirror clouded by dust, you will not be able to see yourself at all. Just so, if you indulge your senses all of the time, exercising no discrimination in what you eat, what you read, what you say, and what you think about, you will not be able to see your real Self at all. You will see only the body, not the dweller within, only the house, not the resident. In order to see yourself as you are—as beautiful, wise, loving, universal—you must rise above physical consciousness. You can put this into practice every day by asking yourself, "In what ways can I guard myself against being trapped in body consciousness?" Once you ask this question, you see that everywhere there is a choice. Let the bakery put all kinds of cakes in the window; you will say, "I don't want to get trapped in them." Let the stores advertise the latest fashions; you will say, "I don't want to get trapped here." It is these right choices which will gradually enable you to rise above physical consciousness.

Sri Krishna goes on to use the simile of the embryo, well protected and hidden in the mother's womb. With these three similes, the Lord reminds us that the Ātman is always within us. The Lord is always present, call him Krishna, Christ, the Buddha, or Allah, but it is we who bring all kinds of covers to hide his glory. Wherever we go we bring home some cover to conceal the Lord, and it will take a lot of recycling to get rid of all these envelopes. Sri Krishna is telling Arjuna, "We don't want all of this. Instead of bringing more covers home, start removing them; instead of adding to your burden of envelopes, begin to remove them one by one." The moment we begin to restrain our senses diligently and practice other spiritual disciplines, we shall see that envelope after envelope—or as the Sufis say, veil after veil—falls away until we at last see the Beloved, who is the Lord, in the depths of our own consciousness.

आवृतं ज्ञानमेतेन ज्ञानिनो नित्यवैरिणा ।
कामरूपेण कौन्तेय दुष्पूरेणानलेन च ॥३९॥

*39. Knowledge is hidden, Kaunteya, by this unquenchable fire for self-satisfaction, the inveterate enemy of the wise.*

Arjuna has asked Sri Krishna a very personal question, which could be asked by any one of us when we make mistakes in spite of the fact that we know they are mistakes. "What makes me do these things? I know this is not the way to joy and security, but there seems to be some compulsion in me to make these mistakes." And Sri Krishna, who has infinite love for you and me, answers Arjuna by saying that this compulsion is *kāma,* the worst enemy we have on the face of the earth. If we try to look at life through this perspective, we shall see how conflicts cannot help arising when a nation, group, or individual keeps its eyes only on its own development, ignoring the needs and rights of others. The Buddha calls this compulsion by a very homely name: *tanhā,* the fierce thirst that demands to be quenched at any cost, if necessary by robbing other people of their water.

Take, for example, the question of money. The mystics do not say that money is bad; money is just metal or paper, which is amoral. It is the love of money that is bad. The Gita says that to be able to use anything wisely we must not be attached to it. Gandhiji, whose material possessions were worth only two dollars at the time of his death, handled millions and millions of rupees. Because he had no personal attachment, no selfish craving to accumulate money, he was able to use it very wisely to benefit millions of helpless people in India.

Not only in the accumulation of money, but in the accumulation of every material thing, we are likely to get caught unless we have the capacity for detachment. We know people, for example, who give much of their love to their wardrobe. I have seen one of those wardrobes—countless pairs of shoes to match the colors of the season, and numberless dresses and hats. I could not see how that lady would have any time for meditation, and when I was told she didn't meditate, I said, "No wonder." I have seen very well-dressed women, both here and in India, having a small, select wardrobe that freed them from spending hours weighing the pros and cons of particular colors and hemlines. They have a small closet where they can walk in and come out well dressed without becoming prey to the whims and fancies of some fashion expert in Europe. Even to wear clothes well, we must be detached. To keep our hair in the best condition, we have to be detached; otherwise we are likely to be caught in fads and fancies.

Arjuna must now be completely overwhelmed. I can imagine his agreeing, "Without detachment, you can't do anything in life." And here, as elsewhere, when Sri Krishna throws a flood of light on something in his life, I imagine Arjuna saying "That's right!" just as you and I would say it.

In this verse Sri Krishna uses the very strong word *kāma* which, in general, means keeping our eyes only on what will serve our personal ends, what will satisfy our needs to the exclusion of the rights and needs of others. Unfortunately, there is no human being who, once he develops this sense of 'I and mine' by dwelling upon himself, can remain sensitive to the needs of others. Once we get caught in money, everywhere we go there is a dollar sign painted on our pupils. Everywhere we see money. We see a beautiful landscape and instead of wanting to write a poem about it, or paint a picture of it, or just enjoy it, we say, "If it could only be subdivided, developed, and rented out, it would bring in millions of dollars for us." This is just what is now happening in some of the most beautiful areas of our state of California.

Sri Krishna's teaching can be translated into practice every day by remembering that everything belongs to the Lord. The basis of all ecology is the awareness that the whole world belongs to the Lord. We are just transients or, if you prefer, guests who refuse to move out. The Lord doesn't expect any rent; he doesn't expect any cleaning deposit. All that he asks is that we please don't tear up the curtains, don't cut up the carpets, don't pull away the pillars, and keep the house reasonably tidy, which is the least any landlord will ask of us.

Even this body doesn't belong to us, but has been given to us to serve others; therefore, we cannot afford to do whatever we like with it, to give it cigarettes, alcohol, drugs, or too much food. The body is really like a rented car. As we come into the cosmos, we line up and say, "I would like to have a body." We specify the color and the horsepower, and the Lord, whose models are infinite, says, "You've got it." He trusts us; we look so honest and conscientious that he doesn't take any deposit; he doesn't even ask for references. But when we return it at the end of the journey, there is no battery, there are only two wheels, there is only one windshield wiper, and the hood is missing. To understand this, one doesn't have to be very philosophical; one can be very practical. Ordinary courtesy requires that when someone has very graciously lent us a body, we should use it for a good purpose and return it in good condition.

When we talk about the use of tobacco, alcohol, and drugs, it is not just a personal matter; the owner also has a say in it. The Lord has given this body to us on trust, and we shouldn't betray his trust under any circumstances. In the early days, when our selfish desires and sense cravings may not be very strong, we may say, "We will take it out for a small detour on a rough road. After all, it is only a couple of miles. We will come back and not go there again." Once we have taken our car on a detour of a couple of miles, the next time we want to take it three miles, four miles, and finally, taking it further and further from the main road, we don't know how to get back.

In yielding to most compulsions, like drugs, this is unfortunately what happens. No one wants to be a victim; no one wants to lose his liberty. But we know from many, many incidents every day in the Bay Area alone that there comes a time when in order to maintain, for example, a heroin habit, people rob and even kill.

This is the application of the simple word *kāma*. The Lord warns Arjuna never to lose his vigilance against the blandishments of the desire for selfish satisfaction, whether it is the craving of the senses or the urge to enforce self-will on those around. Little by little, Sri Krishna says, this will become his fiercest enemy; any time he yields to a selfish desire, he is actually strengthening his enemy.

इन्द्रियाणि मनो बुद्धिरस्याधिष्ठानमुच्यते ।
एतैर्विमोहयत्येष ज्ञानमावृत्य देहिनम् ॥४०॥

*40. Selfish desire is said to be found in the senses, mind, and intellect, misleading them and burying the understanding in delusion.*

Sri Krishna now tells us where Kāma lives. Just as a wealthy person may have a house in London, a manor in Yorkshire, and a villa in the south of France, similarly Kāma has three houses—*indriya, manas,* and *buddhi.* His favorite house is *indriya,* the five senses, where he is usually to be found. He spends most of the year in the eye, in the ear, and of course on the palate. If we want to see Kāma, we do not have to look very far at mealtime to see which is his favorite room.

Kāma's second home is *manas,* the mind, where he lives during the turbulent periods. Though the word *kāma* is usually applied on the sensory level, and especially to sexual desire, it can also refer to the lust for power, which is one of the most terrible urges in the human being. By the side of the lust for power, the cravings of the palate are insignificant. The control of the palate is not a serious problem. Yielding to the senses does not usually harm others. It is the lust for power that in our modern age is responsible for so much misery all over the world. In order to guard ourselves against competition and turmoil, whether in international politics or in the home, we must remember the needs of those around us and forget our personal needs for power and prestige.

*Buddhi,* the intellect, is Kāma's third home. Even though we usually do not associate the intellect with selfish desire, we cannot help agreeing with Sri Krishna if we examine many of the books published today. Good books are rare, and to have a really good library, a few shelves are all we need. When I was still on my campus in India, I was convinced, like many professors, that if the Lord was to be found anywhere, it was in the lower stacks of the library. But now—just as when I go into a big department store, I can say, "How many things I don't need! How many expensive suits I don't want!"—when I enter a big library I say, "What tomes I don't have to read again! What folios I will never open!" This feeling of freedom will come to all of us when we realize, in the depths of our meditation, that all wisdom lies within.

Even to use the intellect wisely, we must be detached from it. The communication gap between the older and younger generations is caused mostly by our identifying ourselves with our opinions. We all can render a great service by listening to opposing opinions without agitation, discourtesy, or violence, and by offering our opinions not as nonnegotiable demands but as calm, courteous statements. Gandhi could listen to opposing views with concentration, calmness, and respect, which would enable his opponent to ask for his views also. Gandhi showed the world that we can state our case well in simple, gentle, and respectful language. It is the person with a weak argument who tries to rely on violent or obscene language.

When most of us say "True! Absolutely right!" the translation is "Just what I think!" At my university in India, I would emphasize to my classes not to make marginal comments in library books. On one occasion I found, in delicate feminine handwriting, "How true!"

As I recognized the handwriting, I went to the girl, sat by her and said, "My dear, what do you mean by 'How true!'" Immediately she said, "This is exactly what I think."

Even though we may use courteous phrases like "apparently" or "to the best of my knowledge," underneath we are saying our statements are completely, irrevocably true. If we really mean "to the best of my knowledge"—or as I like to say, "to the best of my ignorance"—there would be no agitation. Today I read a penetrating anecdote from the meditation notebook of a student in our university extension class. She and her husband were having a heated discussion. When the situation was almost out of control, she said, "My course instructor says we are not arguing about opinions or philosophies; we are just trying to impose our self-will on each other." Even in a moment of heat, when patience is wearing thin, it is good to remind ourselves that it is not a philosophical dispute, it is not a question of principles; it is just your self-will against mine. If we can remember this, we will be more courteous, more lenient, and not condemn views different from ours or use violence to express our disapproval.

When the senses have come under our control and Kāma has been evicted from his first home, he moves with all his luggage to the mind, his second line of defense. Evict him there too, and you will find him in the intellect, where he is so strongly barricaded he can be thrown out only with great difficulty.

तस्मात्त्वमिन्द्रियाण्यादौ नियम्य भरतर्षभ ।
पाप्मानं प्रजहि ह्येनं ज्ञानविज्ञाननाशनम् ॥४१॥

*41. Fight with all your strength, O Bhārata;*
*controlling your senses, attack your enemy directly,*
*who is the destroyer of knowledge and realization.*

We begin our conquest of Kāma by controlling the senses, especially the palate, which is very much like training a puppy. Today, as we were walking around Lake Merritt, we saw an Alsatian being trained by a lady who was tugging at his leash, giving him angry looks, and using strong language. Knowing something about the dog's point of view, I told my wife that I had easily trained my own dogs just by loving them, being patient with them, and giving them my appreciation when they obeyed. When we went to the circus some time ago, we saw a group of dogs who were really in love with their trainer, a girl. After every performance they would leap into her arms, and she hugged them and talked baby language to them. Even the really big dogs would act like little pups, playing up to her. In this way, little by little, we can train the senses if we have a deep desire to bring them under control and a sense of artistry that prevents us from being too austere or over-indulgent.

Sri Krishna tells us through Arjuna to put to death this greed for personal pleasure, profit, prestige, and power. It is our worst enemy, which prevents us from living in joy and security and attaining spiritual wisdom.

In the *Rāmāyana,* this enemy is personified as Rāvana, the ten-headed one. Rāma, the desire for selfless service, and Rāvana, the desire for selfish satisfaction, both exist within us. When Rāma faces Rāvana on the battlefield, he must sever all ten heads of his enemy at once, which is how we must slay the selfish 'I,' the only barrier between us and the Lord. In our own daily life we begin the conquest of Rāvana by keeping the happiness of those around us first and ours last.

इन्द्रियाणि पराण्याहुरिन्द्रियेभ्यः परं मनः ।
मनसस्तु परा बुद्धिर्यो बुद्धेः परतस्तु सः ॥४२॥

*42. The senses are said to be higher than the body, the mind higher than the senses; above the mind is the intellect, and above the intellect is the Ātman.*

Here we have a simple hierarchy of the various members composing the human individual. We not only have a family at home; each of us is himself a family, whose members are the body, senses, mind, and intellect, who seldom pay any respect to the advice of the head, the Ātman. Sometimes in meditation the Ātman says, "Boys, let's all get together and think one thought on the Lord." Immediately the body goes to sleep; that is his way of meditation. He says, "This is good for me. In this I find security," and the Ātman really doesn't know what to do. Then the palate says, "I am going out for a quick one." The mind begins to re-enact a quarrel which everyone else has forgotten, saying, "I don't want to live in the present; I want to re-enact a drama that took place five years ago in which my girlfriend gave me my hat." The intellect, supposedly the most cultured member of the group, says, "Nobody listens to my opinions." Finally the Ātman says, "I guess we'd better wait for another incarnation to get these boys together," and we just throw up our hands.

We can become united within only by training these rebels to act in harmony with the Ātman through a total discipline based on the practice of meditation. We train the body by giving it the right exercise and food. The senses are trained through discriminating restraint. The Gita will tell us that we can poison ourselves not only through our mouth, but through our eyes and ears. In this respect, we can do our children a great service by guiding them in the movies they go to, the television programs they watch, and the books they read. We should remember that children do not know what to read and what not to read. It is the duty of the parents to educate their tastes gradually by giving them the right books and then, when they are older, leaving them to make their own choice.

Just as the body and senses can be trained and made to act in harmony with the Ātman, the mind and intellect can also be trained. We train the mind by learning to transform negative emotions into positive ones, ill will into goodwill, hatred into love. To train the intellect, we must learn to be detached from our opinions. Even to have sound intellectual knowledge, we have to be, in a certain measure, detached from the intellect. In using the word "objective," a favorite term in academic circles, we should remember that we cannot be objective as long as we identify ourselves with our opinions.

It is good to respect the opinions of the opposite camp and of the older generation. One day our children are going to look upon our opinions as rather old-fogyish. When we are looking upon ourselves as the avant garde, the spearhead of radicalism and revolution, we should remember that our grandchildren one day are going to point us out with "Here comes the rear guard, bringing up reaction." Often those who are fanatically attached to their opinions come with the passage of time to be just as fanatically attached to the opposite views. One could write a comedy, if it were not so macabre, about how radicals become reactionaries in their old age. But if we can have respect for opposing opinions now, later on also, whatever time or circumstance may bring, we will have the same tolerance. Even in the evening of our life, we will be able to listen to the views of our grandchildren and say, "There is something in what you say."

No problem is insoluble if we are prepared to sit down and listen affectionately and respectfully to what the other person has to say. This is true not only in the home and on the campus but in areas of international friction as well. As Winston Churchill put it, "It is better to jaw, jaw, jaw than war, war, war." In communicating with the enemy, Gandhi was really at his best. There was a very important political figure in India who opposed every move Gandhi made. It was said that he had a problem for every solution that Gandhiji brought forth, but even with him, Gandhi was loving, respectful, yet completely clear in elucidating his own point of view.

एवं बुद्धेः परं बुद्ध्वा संस्तभ्यात्मानमात्मना ।
जहि शत्रुं महाबाहो कामरूपं दुरासदम् ॥४३॥

*43. Thus, knowing that which is supreme, let the Ātman rule the ego; use your mighty arms to slay the fierce enemy that is selfish desire.*

If all our faculties do not listen completely to the Ātman, there is division, conflict, and despair; there can never be joy. Meditation is a practical discipline for bringing under control these rebels who try to destroy the unity of the individual. Drawing upon the power released in meditation, we can train the body, senses, mind, and intellect to work in perfect harmony, until we finally go beyond these to realize the Ātman within.

This transformation requires enormous perseverance and, as Gandhiji would point out, the infinite patience of a person trying to empty the sea with a cup. But even here people differ, especially at the outset. There are a few rare people in every country, every age, who require only a minimum of work to make themselves selfless. These people are like our meditation hall, called Shānti, which is solid and well built. When we first moved to the āshram, it required only reroofing to make it suitable for our use. For the vast majority of us, however, the appropriate simile is the men's dormitory. There we had to rebuild the foundations completely. It required an enormous amount of work, a good deal of equipment, and a lot of thinking on the part of the authorities before they could give their approval. Most of us have to change completely the foundations of our lives, which are at present based upon the belief that by following personal profit, pleasure, and prestige we can build a personality that is beautiful and loving.

In the deeper stages of meditation, we make the salutary discovery that the ego is a crashing bore. We all know how unpleasant it can be to associate with people who dwell upon themselves. Nobody wants our selfishness, including us. Do not try to show your ego to anybody; no one wants to look at it. Do not talk about it; nobody wants to hear about it. Whatever our past may have been, if we can dissolve the ego, we shall find this is all we need to do to become radiantly beautiful, perennially wise, and tireless in our service of those around us.

The Lord concludes the third chapter with this resounding verse, in which he tells Arjuna: "Slay all that is selfish in you. Extinguish your ego completely." This is exactly what the word *nirvāna* means: *nir,* 'out'; *vāna,* 'to blow.' Blow out all that is selfish in you, extinguish all that is separate in you, and you will realize the Ātman, the indivisible unity of all life.

इति कर्मयोगो नाम तृतीयोऽध्यायः ॥३॥

## CHAPTER FOUR
# *Wisdom in Action*

श्री भगवानुवाच
इमं विवस्वते योगं प्रोक्तवानहमव्ययम् ।
विवस्वान्मनवे प्राह मनुरिक्ष्वाकवेऽब्रवीत् ॥१॥

SRI KRISHNA:
*1. I told this eternal secret to Vivasvat. Vivasvat
instructed Manu, and Manu instructed Ikshvāku.*

This verse is very much in the traditional scriptural style, almost
like the Old Testament narratives where A begat B, B begat C, C
begat D. But we should not get bored; they will tell us in their own
way what finally happened.

When Sri Krishna says, "I told this eternal secret to Vivasvat,"
he means that he inspired Vivasvat to start meditating, to restrain
the senses, to put other people first, and to discover the Lord within.
Vivasvat, having traveled this way, instructed Manu in meditation
and the allied disciplines, and he too discovered the Lord within
himself. Manu immediately ran after another man, called Ikshvāku,
and instructed him to meditate and attain Self-realization also.

Almost all religions emphasize the precious truth of God's grace.
In some inscrutable way, there comes a time when the grace of the
Lord touches us. When this happens, as Meister Eckhart says, we
thrash about like a fish caught by the fisherman's hook. The hook
has entered the flesh of the fish, and though it may thrash and jump
about, trying to get free, the hook only enters deeper and deeper.

We do not want to be released out of the prison we have come to love. But even though the grace of the Lord may have touched us, we cannot expect him to do all of the work. In order to progress on the spiritual path, we must have the grace of our own mind as well. We must make the right choices. As my Granny would say, "Even if the Lord grants you grace, the temple priest may still stand in your way."

Grace can come like the explosion of a bomb in our consciousness and often is followed by a period of turmoil and turbulence. Nothing seems to satisfy us. Money, material possessions, and prestige no longer satisfy us. The old palate-blandishments now taste insipid. We say that peach ice cream is not as good as it used to be; maybe the secret of making peach ice cream has been lost. So we try spumoni, but that proves to be even worse than peach.

Along with dissatisfaction comes utter restlessness. We cannot sit still; we cannot sleep in peace. This is the call from the Lord within to sit down and start meditating. Restlessness is power rising, which can be harnessed to turn us inwards to the practice of meditation.

एवं परम्पराप्राप्तमिमं राजर्षयो विदुः ।
स कालेनेह महता योगो नष्टः परंतप ॥२॥

*2. Thus, O Arjuna, eminent sages received knowledge of yoga in a continuous tradition. But through time the practice of yoga was lost in the world.*

The word used here is *parampara,* which means from one person to another, from one generation to another, very often in the family line. Even today, in the Indian musical tradition, there are ancient families who, instead of bequeathing land or wealth to their children, bequeath a love for music. A few miles away from my little village in India there was a family like this. A boy from that home was in my high school. While we had our lunch under a mango tree he would sing devotional songs, and we would all stop eating to listen to him. When we would ask him, "How did you learn to sing?" he would say, "You don't have to learn to sing. I was just born singing." In this tradition, the parents grant the legacy of musical consciousness to the children, and the son and daughter glory in carrying on the tradition of the parents to greater heights.

In the mystical tradition, if even one person takes to meditation and tries to lead the spiritual life, he is establishing a *parampara*. After many years, someone in the family or an old friend, even someone who was sceptical in the beginning, may be inspired to meditate. Sometimes these *paramparas* may come to a temporary stop. The son becomes a potter, the daughter becomes a Shakespeare critic; the tradition goes down a blind alley and appears to stop there. But it is never lost for long, as we can see in the case of India, which has been blessed with an unbroken continuity of sages and saints. This spiritual tradition has sustained her civilization for more than five thousand years, even though her history is sorrowfully marred by invasion after invasion. Whenever India began to look away from her supreme goal, there has always arisen a great spiritual teacher, like Ramakrishna, Ramana Maharshi, or Mahatma Gandhi, to restore her sense of direction.

But today, if travelers go to India, it is difficult for them to see traces of this tradition. The cities are like cities everywhere—turbulent, often violent, driven by material pursuits. Some people who go to India in search of the spiritual life, idealizing the country, imagine that as soon as they board Air India and put the safety belt on, the pilot and air hostess will begin chanting the mantram. They expect, upon landing at the Madras airport, to see people seated in meditation in the lobby. Unprepared for the appalling poverty and superstition they find almost everywhere, they want to run back to the airport and get the first flight to the West. But on the way back they may find someone like Ramana Maharshi sitting quietly under a banyan tree, fully enlightened, aware that all life is one. Immediately, they tear up their round-trip ticket and decide to settle down in his āshram.

In the following verses, the Lord reassures us that even though humanity seems to lose its way now and then, a great spiritual figure will arise at the appropriate time to remind us that it is not in the accumulation of money, prestige, and power but in living for others that we discover and fulfill the supreme goal of life.

स एवायं मया तेऽद्य योगः प्रोक्तः पुरातनः ।
भक्तोऽसि मे सखा चेति रहस्यं ह्येतदुत्तमम् ॥३॥

*3. The secret of these teachings is profound. I have
explained them to you today because you are my
friend and devotee.*

Arjuna likes to be called Krishna's friend, as we saw recently in
the excellent Kerala Kalamandalam performance of *Kirātārjunī-
yam,* "Arjuna and the Kirāta." In this Kathakali drama there is a
scene where Arjuna is tested by Shiva, who is disguised as a rough
forester. Shiva taunts him by asking the Indian equivalent of "Who
do you think you are?"

Arjuna answers, "I come from a very ancient, noble family, the
Pāndavas."

Shiva says, "Never heard of them." That doesn't upset Arjuna
too much; he goes on talking about himself, his family, his kingdom. To everything Shiva says, "Never heard of it." Finally, Shiva
says, "Can't you even tell me one little thing about yourself that
might impress me?"

Arjuna, very proudly drawing himself up, says, "I have a friend.
Guess who!"

"You tell me."

"Krishna!"

Arjuna expects his opponent to be completely overwhelmed, but
instead Shiva just laughs and tests Arjuna by saying, "That butter-
stealing, flute-playing cowherd who calls himself a divine incarnation?" Then, all of his love for Sri Krishna aroused, Arjuna pounces
on Shiva, who is delighted with Arjuna's devotion.

Now Lord Krishna reassures Arjuna of his love and says, "It is
true that the spiritual tradition seems to come to a stop now and
then, but I am going to whisper in your ears and give you personal
instruction as to how you can discover Me in your consciousness. I
am doing this especially for you because you love Me so much."
This is the same emphasis on love that we find in the words of Jesus:
"Thou shalt love the Lord thy God with all thy heart, and with all

thy soul, and with all thy mind, and with all thy strength." When
we love those around us with all our heart by putting their welfare
first, even though it is not easy for us, we are loving the Lord.

अर्जुन उवाच
अपरं भवतो जन्म परं जन्म विवस्वतः ।
कथमेतद्विजानीयां त्वमादौ प्रोक्तवानिति ॥४॥

ARJUNA:
*4. You were born much after Vivasvat; he was born
long ago. Why do you say that you taught this yoga
in the beginning?*

"Krishna," says Arjuna, "you and I are about the same age, but
you are telling me that you have guided the meditation of spiritual
aspirants in ancient times. I find this difficult to grasp. Perhaps my
imagination is limited, but it looks to me as if you were not there.
Why are you telling me of events that took place thousands of years
before you were born in Mathurā?" This is not asked critically,
but Arjuna is historically oriented, just as you and I are, and would
like to have a rational explanation.

श्री भगवानुवाच
बहूनि मे व्यतीतानि जन्मानि तव चार्जुन ।
तान्यहं वेद सर्वाणि न त्वं वेत्थ परंतप ॥५॥

SRI KRISHNA:
*5. You and I have passed through many births,
Arjuna. You have forgotten, Parantapa, but I
remember them all.*

Now I imagine the Lord of Love as smiling, *prahasann iva,* and
looking at Arjuna with great love; we should picture Sri Krishna
now not as a forbidding spiritual figure, beetle-browed, with pursed
lips, but as a playful, loving, and rather mischievous cowherd from
Vrindāvana. He tells Arjuna, "This is going to be a bit of a shock

to you, but this is not the first time you have been on earth. You have been here many times before."

It is not necessary to believe in reincarnation in order to lead the spiritual life. Whether we believe in one life or in many, we can all meditate, restrain our senses, and put others first. There is even a little danger in blindly accepting reincarnation. It may breed resignation and apathy if interpreted wrongly. The urgency of a task can be forgotten when we know we are going to come this way again. There is a story about a Hindu aspirant who was learning the headstand. He tried a few times but lost his balance and fell down. Then he gave up, saying, "I can always learn to do it the next time I come this way."

Reincarnation is something like going back to school again. The other day, one of our friends, a professor on the Berkeley campus, was taken by his wife to get "back-to-school" clothes, and I told him that all of us have back-to-school clothes already—this body of ours. Until we are able to put our parents, partner, children, friends, and enemies first, we will have to come back to school. After a long semester, one hundred years, we are asked for our progress report, and we say, "We have dropped out. We haven't taken the finals. We still love ourselves." Whoever is in charge, whether it is Jesus the Christ, the Buddha, or Sri Krishna, will say very compassionately, "You had better register for the next semester." In the Tibetan tradition, *Bardo* is the name given to the place where we wait between terms. The semester break may sometimes last a few hundred years while we wait for the right context. Someone who has dropped out this semester may come back a thousand years later and run into old classmates who ask, "What have you been doing the last nine hundred years?" "Oh, just waiting in Bardo," comes the reply. "Just couldn't get readmitted."

The purpose of life is to finish our schooling by eliminating all that is selfish and separate in us. And when the degrees are awarded at commencement, our real parent, seated right in front, sometimes looking like Sri Krishna, sometimes like the Compassionate Buddha or Jesus the Christ, will proudly say that we have really graduated at last.

While Sri Krishna explains to Arjuna that he has been here many times, Arjuna thinks to himself, "My memory is a blank. I just don't remember anything at all." He is too polite to say, "I never have been here before. Why do you try to put all of these ideas into my head?"

The Lord says, "You have just forgotten. I too have been this way before, but I remember because I have maintained the continuity of my existence which is the Ātman."

As long as we believe we are the body, we cannot escape a disruption of consciousness at the time of death. But if we can rise above physical consciousness and discover for ourselves that we are not the perishable body but the imperishable Self, there can be no break in our awareness of the infinite continuity of existence. As Jalalu'l-Din Rumi has said:

> I was a mineral, and arose a plant.
> I died as a plant, and became a beast.
> I died as a beast, and evolved into a man.
> Why should I fear that I will lose by dying?
> Once again I shall die as man to join
> The holy company of angels. But I must
> Soar above them too. "Everything must die
> Save His Face." When I have died as an angel,
> I shall be that which is beyond the mind's grasp.
> Let me die to myself, for the ego's death
> Declares, "To Him we return."

This is the unanimous testimony of the great mystics of what the practice of meditation can lead to in the supreme climax called samādhi.

अजोऽपि सन्नव्ययात्मा भूतानामीश्वरोऽपि सन् ।
प्रकृतिं स्वामधिष्ठाय संभवाम्यात्ममायया ॥६॥
यदा यदा हि धर्मस्य ग्लानिर्भवति भारत ।
अभ्युत्थानमधर्मस्य तदात्मानं सृजाम्यहम् ॥७॥

*6. My true being is unborn and changeless. I am
the Lord who dwells in every creature. Through the
power of my own Māyā, I manifest myself in a
finite form.*
*7. Whenever dharma declines, O Bhārata, and the
purpose of life is forgotten, I manifest myself.*

The Lord of Love, even though immortal and infinite, comes as a
divine incarnation in times of great crisis to rescue mankind from
disaster. The Lord, who is enthroned in all hearts, comes to life in a
blessed individual in every country, every age, to bring humanity
back to the spiritual path.

Dharma, the central law of our being, is to live for others, to love
others more than we love ourselves. The proof of this law is that the
more we dwell upon ourselves, the more insecure we become. It is
only when we forget ourselves in the welfare of those around us that
we can live in abiding joy and unshaken security. Jesus puts this into
immortal words when he says, "Bless them that curse you; do good
to them that hate you." By doing so we will help not only them, but
ourselves also.

In any conflict, it is absurd to retaliate. It only adds to the chaos
and makes conflict more violent. Never in the history of human
relations has any problem been solved except through greater love,
endurance, and forgiveness on the part of some person. Between
parents and children, husband and wife, friend and friend, the central law of the relationship is putting the other person first.

Even in international relations, in order to establish peace on
earth and goodwill among men, Gandhi has shown that nonviolence
is the only way. At the beginning of the twentieth century, if anything looked eternal, it was the British Empire. When I was in high
school, one of our geography teacher's favorite tests was to have us

color the Empire with our red crayon, and a good part of the world was red. Most of us took the Empire for granted and thought all we could do was accept it and learn to live with it. But Gandhi, as ordinary as you and I, received the touch of grace.

Gandhi's school life was quite normal. He played truant and postponed projects just like you and me; and when he went to London to fulfill his family's desire that he become a little pillar of the Empire, his early days there were just as ordinary. One of the most delightful pictures that we have of Gandhiji, the future ascetic, is in his striped suit, frock coat, and top hat. He carried a silver-headed cane and wore those indescribable relics of fashion, spats. He was growing up just like any other young fellow, wanting to be the mirror of fashion. He even tried to learn to play the violin and to dance the foxtrot. But already the light was being lit inside, entirely without his knowledge. The perennial spring of grace was beginning to open up inside, and when it finally reached the surface, it produced such power that one whole nation was able to free itself from foreign domination without firing a single shot. This measures the power locked up inside the consciousness of man; because this divine explosion took place in the deepest consciousness of one little man in faraway India, those days of imperialism and colonialism are ended.

In the early days of mystical transformation, people may not take it very seriously. They are likely to think, "He is always playacting. This is just another role that he has assumed. He is a born actor, but he will get tired of this mystic's role soon." Gandhiji said that in the early days he was supposed to be either an imposter, a madman, or a fool. And in Sri Ramana Maharshi's village, I can imagine them saying, "At seventeen what can you expect? This is just another of his games. He thinks he is illumined, that he has attained nirvikalpa samādhi, but one of these days he will snap out of it and go back to his old crowd again." It is during this period, when we have to face criticism and scepticism, that we learn to remain patient and unperturbed, sure that the source of all security is within.

It takes a few years for ordinary people like us to come to accept that the greatest blessing has fallen upon us without our deserving it. We can never get over the amazement of it. We are so frail, so petty, so full of weaknesses, yet in spite of all this, He whose love and power know no bounds has in his infinite mercy chosen us. For a long time, we think there must have been some mistake. Only after years of observing the daily growth in security, the increasing capacity to think of others, do we come to accept that, for no reason we can give, the mystic's mantle has fallen upon us. Afterwards, this wonderment continues all the time. There was a mystic in India who used to sit on the bank of the river, look at his reflection in the flowing waters from morning to evening, and say, "How wonderful! How miraculous!" Once he was asked by the people passing by, "Whom are you describing, Blessed One?" The simple mystic became very shy and very embarrassed, but replied, "Myself." Even in our dreams, we may come to hear the voice of Sri Krishna or Jesus the Christ saying, "My beloved." And when we have reluctantly, humbly accepted this, there is no earthly circumstance that can ever affect our security. Once this mystical transformation has begun to take place, even though we may be small people, each one of us can make a significant contribution to world peace. If we can establish peace in our hearts, return love for hatred, and live for the welfare of our family and community, we have changed the world picture. In this way, many small candles can light up the night of selfishness that threatens us.

परित्राणाय साधूनां विनाशाय च दुष्कृताम् ।
धर्मसंस्थापनार्थाय संभवामि युगे युगे ॥८॥

*8. I am born in every age to protect the good, to destroy evil, and to re-establish dharma.*

In age after age, when violence increases, there comes a time when Mother Earth says, "I cannot bear any more; I am filled with grief seeing the way my children are raising their hands against each other." To this cry, the Lord responds by coming to inspire and protect those who turn to him, who live in harmony with the law of unity, and who contribute to the joy of others. He comes to protect such people from the heavy odds ranged against them, to defeat violence, and to eliminate selfishness.

These words may be interpreted on several levels. First is the divine incarnation, called *avatāra* in Sanskrit, of which Sri Krishna, the Compassionate Buddha, and Jesus the Christ are supreme examples. These mighty spiritual figures come, in answer to Mother Earth's plea, to rescue the world from the morass of selfishness and violence in which it gets caught now and then.

There is another level also on which this incarnation can take place, as in the case of Mahatma Gandhi, who was completely transformed by the grace of the Lord. Gandhi, whose stature became like the Himālayas, changed the direction of human evolution by showing us through his life that nonviolence is the only way, that love is no longer a luxury, but a dire necessity. Hate and perish or love and prosper is the choice placed before us in the great crisis of human civilization facing the modern world. So even though spiritual giants like Mahatma Gandhi are not in the same category as Jesus or the Buddha, who were never involved in life, they do achieve great victories for the human spirit over selfishness.

On the third level, the ordinary level which I call the blessed anonymous level, every one of us has this choice: shall I prepare for the divine incarnation to take place in my consciousness by abolishing every vestige of selfishness and separateness in my heart, and thus contribute to the progress of humanity, or shall I, by foolishly running after my own profit and pleasure, handicap humanity to the extent that it is in my power?

Sri Ramakrishna, in one of his inimitable images, says that a great incarnation is like a mighty ship that takes many thousands across the sea. *Avatāras* like Jesus or the Buddha are like mighty liners that ply the seven seas, but you and I can be little boats, or at least canoes. In Tamil there is a word which has passed into English, *kattumaram: kattu* is 'to tie,' *maram* is 'wood,' so *catamaran* means tying a few planks together and floating on the sea. We may not have the Ātman-power to propel a big ship, but we can improvise—pick up a few pieces of driftwood, tie them together, and get into the sea. We may be able to take at least our family with us across the sea of life.

It is up to you and me to keep our doors open, to put up a little sign outside, "Ready for receiving an incarnation." But the hall inside must not be cluttered up. It must be completely empty of attachments to one's opinions and self-will. If we can empty our house and put up the little board outside, the Lord will come, pick it up, and say, "I am here."

Even ordinary people like ourselves can gradually blossom into mahātmas. *Maha* is 'great,' and *Ātma* is 'Self.' You and I are imprisoned in our little self. We just don't like being free; we like thinking about ourselves, always on the lookout to see if others are denying us things to which we are entitled. The mahātmā is the Great Self, the person who says "You and I are one," and who lives in accordance with this oneness which is the divine principle of existence.

Even the desire to empty ourselves—to turn our back on our own pleasure and profit and to contribute to the happiness of others—is the result of divine grace. The desire to go against desires is one of the surest signs of grace. When desires come which formerly used to pick us up by the scruff of the neck and throw us from here across the Bay, we will now want to resist—not with weeping and sobbing but with a fierce joy, a sense of exultation.

But there is also the old momentum which now and then drives us to cling to some strong, secret selfish attachment. While we are progressing, resisting old desires, suddenly we see a little ego-hold. Immediately we cling to it. And this is the finest sign of grace: the Lord takes out his holy hammer and gives such a well-aimed, direct hit on the knuckles that we let go. Do not think that this happens only to you and me. Some of the greatest mystics have said, "How much you must love us, Lord! How many times you have hit us! If you had cared less, you would have given just one hit and said, 'All right, he is a free man; he can choose.'" The great mystic will even say with joy, "Every time my thoughts stray from you, hit me hard. Take your hammer back as far as you can and bring it down hard." All sorrow is lost when we can say this; everything becomes joy.

जन्म कर्म च मे दिव्यमेवं यो वेत्ति तत्त्वतः ।
त्यक्त्वा देहं पुनर्जन्म नैतिमामेति सोऽर्जुन ॥९॥

*9 He who knows Me as his own divine Self,*
*as the Operator in him, breaks through the belief*
*that he is the body and is not born separate again.*
*Such a one is united with Me, O Arjuna.*

He who has known the divine birth of the Lord within himself, and
who knows the Lord to be the operator and himself the instrument,
will never again fall into the superstition that he is the body, neither
in this life nor thereafter.

We are so enmeshed in identification with our body that it is beyond our wildest imagination even for a split second to see what we
will be without our body. It is a very merciful provision of sādhana
that it takes many years to get over the age-old, race-old fallacy that
we are the body. If out of a playful sense of mischief the Lord were
to deprive us of our body-consciousness during meditation tonight,
if kundalinī were to burst into a cataclysmic explosion and send us
fathoms deep into our consciousness, we would not be able even to
get up from our chair. So for practical purposes, there may be some
disadvantages in instant illumination. To be able to function in life
after realizing the indivisible unity, Sri Ramakrishna says delight-
fully that we need to keep the "ripe ego," in which we still know
that we have parents, partners, and children. But this selfless little
ego does not get trapped in its role. It knows it is acting in a play,
performing with complete artistry.

We should do everything possible to reduce identification with
the body. This can be done in many ways: by not allowing the palate to dictate what we should eat, by eating what is nourishing for
the body, and by getting plenty of physical exercise.

Body-identification is perhaps the greatest superstition ever to
trouble the world. That the sun goes around the earth is a small superstition. That the sun sinks in the sea and has his bath in its waters,
as an old poem in my mother tongue puts it, is a very small superstition that does no one any harm. But this superstition that we are

the body immediately leads to disastrous consequences. When we talk about people being different, races being different, we are really referring to the body. Separateness and insecurity are at their worst in people who are excessively body-conscious.

Sometimes there is the misunderstanding that in talking about rising above physical consciousness I am striking a note of stoicism. But it is the person who is least body-conscious who feels most deeply the departure of dear friends. If I may draw upon a personal example, yesterday I received a letter from my village informing me that one of my old friends in India passed away last week. I know he cannot die. I know that he is eternal because he is the Ātman. But at the same time I so humanly remember his body, his little ways, that even in my sleep last night I was troubled. My friend's cousin, whom I also knew in India, said in his letter yesterday, "Whatever the scriptures may say, it is terrible to bear the departure of somebody who has grown up with you and lived with you." Rising above physical consciousness does not mean losing my sense of endearment and love for the Lord disguised in my own family and friends.

वीतरागभयक्रोधा मन्मया मामुपाश्रिताः ।
बहवो ज्ञानतपसा पूता मद्भावमागताः ॥१०॥

*10. Delivered from selfish attachment, fear,
and anger, filled with Me, surrendering themselves
to Me, purified in the fire of my being, many have
reached the state of unity in Me.*

*Vītarāgabhayakrodha:* "Be without selfish attachment, fear, or anger." The Lord says, "Throw these three away. They are your worst enemies, trapping you in the cycle of birth, death, sorrow, and despair. Every day, do everything possible to get over selfish attachment to people and to things. Do everything possible to get over being the victim of fear and anger. Surmount these obstacles." In this the practice of meditation can be of enormous help. In the very depths of your meditation, when you are no longer aware of the body, when concentration is complete, you can free yourself from selfish attachments to money, to material possessions, and to people, whom you may try to manipulate because of lack of detachment from your own ego.

Pain often accompanies the development of detachment. If as a child I have not been told no by my parents, then when I become an adult, I will not be able to take no from anyone at all. In relationships with children, love often expresses itself in the capacity to say no when necessary.

The other day we went to Santa Rosa to buy shoes for our little nieces, Meera and Geetha. While Christine was buying the shoes, with my mother smiling approval, I noticed a very loving mother with a girl about nine years old, who had probably been spoiled by always being allowed to have her own way. To everything that the salesgirl brought she said, "I don't want it. It looks ugly. I am not going to wear it." Within ten minutes the mother was at the end of her tether. She was a loving mother, but she had lost control of the situation.

So the application of this verse comes even in small things. We should not allow children to keep demanding what they want; we should exercise our good judgment and fill their needs but not spoil them by yielding to their likes and dislikes all the time. It is better to cross our child a little, and give him or her the shoes and clothes we think best, rather than let the child go on saying "No, no, no." It is not a matter of clothes; it is a matter of self-will. If we cannot say no to our children when necessary, we will actually be teaching them to have more self-will.

In every relationship, the cultivation of detachment is painful, because we must go against our self-will, opinions, and pleasures. Even in our most intimate personal relationships, it must be admitted that often there is this taint of trying to bend others to our will, of expecting others to conform to our image of what they should be. This is often what disrupts personal relationships between older and younger people.

I must say with infinite gratitude to my Grandmother, who had never heard of educational psychology, that after I left high school she began actively to help me rebel against some of the ideas with which I had been brought up. This was marvelous spiritual psychology, because when my spiritual teacher encouraged me to rebel against constricting ideas, it was no longer rebellion.

Without detachment, it is very hard for parents to go against their own self-will, their ways and upbringing, even though they know that their children are living in a different world and are exposed to a different climate. Only when we are detached in good measure from our own ego can we encourage our children to follow their own dharma, to grow to their full stature in their own way, by saying, "We will support you as long as you turn your back on what is selfish and self-willed." Young people can respond tremendously to this capacity on the part of the older people to put their children first.

If only I can extinguish all that is selfish in me, erase every desire for personal profit, personal pleasure, personal prestige, and personal power, which is often at the expense of others, then the Lord will be free to fill me with his own love, his own wisdom, his own beauty. This is the significance of the word *manmayā,* 'filled with Me.'

In the classical Krishna tradition, this is expressed in a very loving manner in a story about Sri Krishna and Rādhā. Rādhā is a lovely girl who represents the human heart, longing for the Lord. Sri Krishna is always represented as playing on the flute. One of his names is *Venugopāla,* the divine flute-player, who is always playing his magic melody to rouse us from sleep, to make us come alive. Rādhā is head over heels in love with Krishna. This is just what you and I are wanting all the time, though we don't know it: to be united with him, which means to be united with our Self, to be always embracing him who is our real Self. Rādhā looks at Sri Krishna with great jealousy in her eyes, and Sri Krishna says, "Honey, what's the matter? Why are your eyes so green with jealousy?"

Rādhā answers, "Look at that flute; your lips are always resting on it. When will your lips rest on mine like that always?"

And Sri Krishna, very mischievously, takes the bamboo flute from his lips and shows it to Rādhā, saying, "See! It is empty, so I can fill it with music. You are so full of yourself, dwelling upon yourself all the time, that I cannot send in even one breath."

*Mām upāshritāh:* "Depend completely on the Lord within." Once when we went to the park, we saw a big circular area in which there were a number of little electrically run cars. Children would get into them, and at the appointed signal, the cars would all go around. Then the little children would call out to their mother and father, "Look! We are driving all by ourselves!"

All we have to do on the spiritual path is to surrender completely to the Lord within, to identify ourselves completely with him. He is the perfect driver. But instead we keep doing all sorts of things without really going anywhere at all—stepping on the brake, accelerating, and honking the horn, which we are really good at. We just keep honking, making the loudest noise possible. The Lord within says, "Why don't you let me drive the car? You just keep quiet. You can sit by my side, but don't give me instructions about where to go or what speed to use. Just trust me completely."

One of the names of the Lord is *Pārthasārathi. Pārtha* means 'son of Prithā,' which is a name for Arjuna; *sārathi* means 'he who drives the chariot.' The Lord is Arjuna's charioteer and can be ours also. He comes to us and says, "I am such a good driver, let me be your chauffeur. You don't have to give me anything; you don't have to pay my salary; you don't even have to repair your car. Just give me the keys; that's all I want. Come and sit down, be quiet, and keep repeating my Name."

This does not mean that we should not take necessary precautions. Just because we are leading the spiritual life, we cannot afford to take traffic risks. We should not be under the impression that because the Lord is in us we can drive against the red light. If we were to ask Sri Krishna, "How do we show our faith in you during rush-hour traffic?" he would say, "It's very simple. Don't try to travel during rush-hour traffic. If you have to, check your car carefully and don't ask the driver questions or get him entangled in arguments." We show our respect for the Lord by taking every reasonable precaution and then saying, "I have done all that I can; now look after me."

*Madbhāvam āgatāh:* "He enters into my being." As you drive out the love of material things from your heart, overcome selfish attachment to people, and free yourself of fear and anger, the Lord says, "I will fill you with love for everyone, love in which there is not the slightest trace of selfish desire for pleasure or prestige. And I will release the deeper resources in you to translate that love into selfless service."

ये यथा मां प्रपद्यन्ते तांस्तथैव भजाम्यहम् ।
मम वर्त्मानुवर्तन्ते मनुष्याः पार्थ सर्वशः ॥११॥

*11. As men approach Me, so do I receive them.*
*All paths lead to Me, O Arjuna.*

In medieval India there was a mystic called Kabir, who was claimed both by the Hindus and by the Muslims. Actually he was neither, because once he had experienced the unitive state, no names could confine him. One of his beautiful poems begins with the lines:

> Where are you searching for me, friend?
> Look! Here am I right within you.
> Not in temple, nor in mosque,
> Not in Kaaba, nor Kailas,
> But here right within you am I.

Tragically enough, in the history of religious institutions, there sometimes has been a gradual forgetfulness of the central teaching of the founder, and an increase in emphasis on dogmas, doctrines, and rituals which are not of primary importance. This preoccupation with superficial matters makes us forget that all religions are founded upon the same mystical experience of the indivisible unity that is the Divine Ground of existence.

In this verse, one of the most marvelous in the Gita, the Lord says, with his infinite love, that it does not matter what religion you profess. Be a Christian. Be a Jew. Be a Buddhist. Be a Hindu, Muslim, or Zoroastrian. The important point is to follow faithfully what the Lord reveals through your particular scripture with all your heart and all your mind and all your strength and all your spirit, and you will become united with the Lord of Love. This verse is perhaps the most superb exposition of the reality of all religions, the reality of all divine incarnations. Here, once and for all, the equality of all religions is emphasized, and we are told that we do not have to change our cultural context or leave the country, religion, or society in which we were born to attain the supreme goal of life and become united with the Lord.

The change that the Lord wants is a change of heart in which we turn our back upon all that is self-willed and separate in us. When the time comes for us to enter the portals of heaven, we are not going to be asked to show our membership card, not even of the Blue Mountain Center. The Lord is not going to ask us to which religion we belong, which church we attended, or who is our favorite padre. What he is going to ask us is, "Do you love Me in all those around you? Have you put Me first in those around you?" And the only answer we have to make is that, to the extent possible for us, we have been trying our best to submerge our own petty personality in the general joy and welfare of our family, community, and world.

काङ्क्षन्तः कर्मणां सिद्धिं यजन्त इह देवताः ।
क्षिप्रं हि मानुषे लोके सिद्धिर्भवति कर्मजा ॥१२॥

*12. Those who desire the pleasures of this world,*
*which are born of action, are really praying for them*
*through their desires. For by action in the world*
*the fulfillment of these desires is quickly obtained.*

In this verse, the Lord lets us in on a big secret—that every desire is a prayer. When a person keeps on thinking, "I want money," even though he may call himself an atheist, even though he may wear a button saying, "I don't believe in God," he is really saying to the Lord, who is within him, "Please give me money." In this sense, the stock exchange is a temple. Everyone arrives early in the morning to perform the ritual. In the āshram, we meditate only one or two hours a day, but they meditate on money from morning until night, going through all kinds of altered states of consciousness with the advance of the bulls and the bears.

One of the cogent ways of looking upon the smoker, too, is as a religious man. In many oriental religious traditions the worshipper will come stand in front of the shrine, take a sandalwood incense stick, light it, put it in place gently, and pray. And the smoker, too, performs his ritual. He takes out his little packet and ceremoniously strikes the match. He does not just take the match and strike it: there is a way of balancing it and lighting it very artistically; otherwise it is not right. It is not just lighting the cigarette and putting it between his lips. There is a traditional way, sanctified by centuries, which must be followed. The way the smoker really prays is: "Lady Nicotine, if I find favor in your eyes, give me cancer. And if I am not found worthy of that, please don't deny me emphysema."

In everything we do, whenever we desire, we are praying to ourselves, and if our desire becomes deep enough, it will give us the will and show us the way in which we can fulfill it. For example, there is the desire for fame, which Ben Jonson called the "fruit that dead men eat." How many millions of people keep praying for fame! Even among our own ordinary friends, there are likely to be a few with the innate desire for attention. Right from the time that they are three or four, children can develop this desire. The little boy who has learned a nursery rhyme — "Humpty Dumpty had a great fall" — must recite it in front of his grandfather, his grandmother, and anybody else who is prepared to listen. As our self-knowledge begins to improve, it is very interesting to see in what ways we try to draw attention. In innumerable little acts, from morning until evening, the main motive seems to be to draw attention, prop ourselves up, and make ourselves secure. Sri Krishna will say, "Why do you want to draw attention? You are completely secure, because I am here all the time." Even a temporary awareness that the Lord of Love is always present within us will immediately free us from this deleterious habit of doing things to draw attention.

It is very easy to become famous. But one of the paradoxes of fame is that people who have longed for fame and striven for many years to become famous, to have their picture on the cover page of weekly magazines, after achieving fame come to envy anonymous people like us. It is so good not to be known. It is so refreshing to be anonymous, to live on the blessed anonymous level. Nobody recognizes us, nobody bothers us, everybody ignores us. Well-known figures from all over the world will say how much they deplore publicity. But if I may say so, if we do not want publicity, nobody is going to give it to us. There is no difficulty in remaining obscure, which is the ideal condition for leading the spiritual life.

It is very easy to make money. It is very easy to become famous. If we can unify our desires, even for a finite goal, we can attain it; but once all of our desires are unified, we will find that nothing finite can ever satisfy us.

In the Upanishads, there is a glorious passage that is one of the central principles of mysticism. It sums up the secret of all life: "You are what your deep, driving desire is. As your deep, driving desire is, so is your will. As your will is, so is your deed. As your deed is, so is your destiny." All of us are capable of immense desires, but our capacity to desire and love is unfortunately cut up into innumerable little desires for profit, power, pleasure, and prestige. It is possible, through the dynamic discipline of meditation, to recall our innumerable detrimental desires from the wasteful channels into which they have flowed. And when we recall our desires from the restaurant, from the bank, from our wardrobe, and from all the petty little channels which consume our vital wealth, they all merge into one huge, all-consuming desire that can never be satisfied with anything finite. It is only those who live on the superficial level who can be satisfied by money, material possessions, pleasure, or fame. There is no point in blaming them. They live on the superficial level, and their mouth is very small, just a little parrot beak. Put one cherry in, and they are satisfied. But as our meditation deepens, our capacity to desire grows greater, and as a Hindi proverb says, you cannot satisfy the hunger of a camel by putting a mustard seed in its mouth.

Our capacity to desire is infinite when all of our desires are unified. Nothing finite can ever really satisfy the immense desires of a human being. St. Augustine—who used to paint Carthage red and knew what he was talking about—would say, "Lord, how can I ever find peace anywhere else when I am made to rest in thee?" This is written in every cell of our being, and paraphrasing it in applying it to modern times, I would say, "When you and I are made to find our joy in the Lord, how can we find it in LSD, in money, in food, in clothes?"

Once when Christine and I were going for our walk, we saw a little girl playing a game I hadn't seen since we left India. She was making mud pies. I was so delighted on seeing a little girl making mud pies, just as they do in all the villages of Kerala, that I watched her for some time and, just to make conversation, asked her, "What are these?"

"Oh," she said, "mud pies"—adding, just as her mother would, "but I don't make them as well as I used to."

I said, "Will you please let me have a few to eat?"

She looked at me and said, "They're horrible! You shouldn't eat mud pies. If you're hungry, you should go home and ask your mother or wife to give you lunch."

Unfortunately, what most of us are trying to do in life is eat mud pies.

The Lord says, "Don't waste your love on money; that love is meant for Me. Don't waste your love on your own petty pleasure and profit. This is misusing the capacity for love that I have given you to find Me present in everyone, everywhere." The Lord has given us all a wide margin for experimenting with our desires. It requires a certain amount of juggling with the senses to find out they will not bring us abiding joy, but it becomes very tragic when we keep on juggling all our lives: first three balls, then four, then five, until finally we are the expert, juggling with sixteen balls while riding on a horse.

Over and over again, the Gita will say that this is not a moral issue at all; it is an engineering issue. Sri Krishna has given each of us a certain amount of fuel to undertake the long journey to the goal of life. The Lord is not miserly, either, so with all the responsibility of love, he gives us a few extra gallons for making a few detours. If he were an efficiency-minded fuel manager, he would say, "This is all you need, not one drop more." But he loves us so much that he says, "I know the quirks of your mind, and I have given you some extra fuel." He knows that before setting out on our trans-

Atlantic flight we will want to go to Milpitas or Walnut Creek once or twice, just to see what is going on. And as long as we make a few trips and find out that there is nothing doing in Milpitas, the Lord is satisfied, and life has served its purpose. But tragedy strikes when we use all of our great total of fuel in just making little local flights, going around and around in the same old circle, so that when the time comes to try the flight across the Atlantic, we find we do not have any gas. This is what may happen to all of us if we postpone the spiritual search too long.

चातुर्वर्ण्यं मया सृष्टं गुणकर्मविभागशः ।
तस्य कर्तारमपि मां विद्ध्यकर्तारमव्ययम् ॥१३॥

*13. The distinctions of caste, guna, and karma have come from Me. Understanding that I am their cause, realize that I am changeless and beyond all action.*

The perennial philosophy in the Hindu tradition interprets the cosmos in terms of three gunas—sattva, rajas, and tamas. *Sattva* means law, *rajas* means energy, and *tamas* means inertia. According to this theory of the gunas, there may be surface differences between all of us, even though at bottom we are one.

If you look at the five fingers of your hand, Booker T. Washington used to say, they all look different. Even the names are different. The thumb will say, "Don't call me finger. I am Mr. Thumb." And another will say, "Don't just call me finger. I am Little Finger." Another says, "I point. I am the Index Finger." The vision of people who are living on the physical level, going by physical appearance, living just for the moment, is only on the fingers. They see everything as separate. But as Booker T. Washington put it, if you look below at the palm, you will see there is only one.

It is only on the surface of life that we all look different and feel separate, only on the surface that sometimes, in order to bring about our own satisfaction, we clash with those around us. But if we can only deepen our awareness through the practice of meditation and direct our vision deep below, we shall begin to see that, as

Meher Baba has said, "You and I are not 'we'; you and I are One."

The lowest guna is tamas, the state of inertia. This is a state familiar to all of us. When duties call for us to act, we feel inclined to say, "What does it matter? Why not drop out of society? Why not live in my ivory tower, the world forgetting, by the world forgotten?" One of the interesting characteristics of our time is the belief that by dropping out of society and turning our back upon the world, we can become aware of the indivisible unity of all life. But the Bhagavad Gita says emphatically that this is not the path for us to follow, and the language it uses is to the point: it is all right for a rock not to act, it is all right for a stone just to sit, but you and I as human beings have to respond to the challenges of the day and make a contribution in our own way to the solution of its problems. In one of the strong verses of the Gita (3:12), Sri Krishna says the person who refrains from action and drops out of life, when there are such terrible problems pressing upon us, is *stena,* a thief. The Gita is a call to selfless action, not action just for feathering our own nest but for contributing to the greatest extent possible to the welfare of our family, community, and world.

On the campus, the application of this verse is not to procrastinate, not to postpone last quarter's project until next quarter. This only makes the problem worse. When we try to postpone we are making tamas more established instead of transforming it into rajas. When I was a professor at my university in India, during finals time all the usual symptoms that I see in Berkeley used to break out there, too. But there was one additional thing that I used to see in the Hindu temples, particularly in the villages. Many students who had seldom been to the temple would feel a sudden spurt of devotion on the eve of the finals. They would ask the Lord for his blessing and break coconuts in front of Lord Ganesha, who is called "the remover of obstacles." The faculty used to say that when the price of coconuts has gone up, it means that finals have begun. And when the price of coconuts went down, I knew that finals were over and that students were not going to the temple any more. When she saw students going to the temple on the eve of finals, my Grandmother used to remind me that not even the Lord would help those who postponed and did not study. She would say that it is good to go to the temple to show our faith in the Lord, but he expects us to study well all the same.

Whenever there is a tendency to postpone, it is good to get down to work immediately whether it is at our job, on the campus, or in the home. When there is something not very pleasant to be done, do it immediately. The pleasant things can wait a little, but the unpleasant things should be done immediately.

Here the practical hint I would give is that when you feel lethargic, unequal to the tasks that are incumbent upon you, go for a good, long walk repeating the mantram. This can change your attitude in less than an hour's time. It is the initial leap that you have to make. You just have to press hard on the arms of your chair and leap like a mustang. The initial leap should give you the momentum to go for a long, fast walk, and once the blood has started spinning in your veins, the lungs have started going strongly, and the rhythm of the mantram has started echoing in your consciousness, in an hour's time your attitudes change. There is no longer what you thought was a permanent resistance to work, no longer the diffidence in yourself. Even to prepare for the most important occasion, I would suggest a good, long walk repeating the mantram.

The body is meant for motion, but in our modern way of life, we have almost begun to forget this. In the morning we move about from the bedroom to the dining room where we sit. Then we go into the garage, get into the car, and sit until we reach our office, where we sit again at our desk. We come back in the evening and sit in front of the bridge table or television set. It is helpful to remember that the heart is not what the poets represent it to be—a delicate, brittle instrument. It is a sturdy old pump, and it has an immense capacity to keep itself well, to keep itself strong, provided we obey the simple, sensible rules of good health: eat moderately, eat only what is nourishing, eat only when hungry, keep walking whenever there is the chance, and keep repeating the name of the Lord whenever there is agitation, fear, anxiety, or conflict. If we observe these simple rules, we shall see in our own life how easy it is to be well.

The way to transform tamas into rajas is through activity. Then slowly we have to transform rajas into sattva; we must begin to direct all of our energies to the selfless service of those around us. We can harness our energy and restlessness and direct it to the supreme goal. Whenever we feel restless, that is the time not to run away, but to sit down, meditate, and sink down into the depths of our own consciousness.

The third stage, sattva, is known by its characteristics of serenity, tranquility, and detachment, which all of us need, particularly today in our troubled times. In sattva we work arduously but not for our own personal aggrandizement. Even in sattva, however, we still believe that we are the doer; therefore we are still involved in the fruits of action. It is not enough if we attain the sattvic level, because the supreme purpose of life according to the scriptures of all religions is to realize the Lord of Love who is present in everyone. The person who has become aware of the Lord is said to have gone beyond the three gunas. He has realized the unchanging reality, the indivisible unity which underlies the world of change. In every religion there are those who have gone beyond the three gunas, like Jesus the Christ, the Buddha, or, in our own times, Mahatma Gandhi, who is an inspiring example of one who transcended the limitations of space, time, and causality to become the perfect instrument of the Lord.

Applying the categories of the gunas to human evolution, the Gita says that the least evolved are the apathetic who do not act at all. Higher are those who act, even though part selfishly. Higher than they are those who act selflessly, but the highest are those who have realized the indivisible unity of all life, who have seen the Lord within all. This spiritual evolution is the original basis of what is called the caste system in India. But though in ancient times a man could move from one caste to another depending upon his personal merits, the system became rigid so that a man's caste was determined only by birth, not by merit. In modern times the caste system in India became a great source of suffering and exploitation to all of us. It was a crying evil which Mahatma Gandhi tackled with his indomitable weapon of nonviolence, so that today the system is dying out in the cruel form it had gradually acquired over the centuries.

In the early days, one of the questions that I had to face often on the platform was, "What about the caste system?" I would ask in turn, "Where?" Every country has its own caste system wherever there is exploitation or discrimination, whether because of nationality, religion, property, race, color, education, or sex. There is one kind of caste system in India, another kind in Europe, a third in America, and a fourth in Africa; everywhere there is a caste system as long as we do not treat all those around us with complete love and respect, knowing the Lord is present in everyone.

न मां कर्माणि लिम्पन्ति न मे कर्मफले स्पृहा ।
इति मां योऽभिजानाति कर्मभिर्न स बध्यते ॥१४॥

*14. Actions do not cling to Me because I am not attached to their results. He who understands this and practices it lives in freedom.*

In this verse, Sri Krishna, the Lord of Love present in all hearts, gives us the secret of selfless action, called karma yoga. Anyone, according to Sri Krishna, who pursues personal pleasure and profit, anyone who indulges in action for money, for material possessions, power, or prestige, is a prisoner in action.

This is a marvelous concept which most of us cannot even grasp, because we live in the prison of the ego, compelled and driven into action for the sake of money, material possessions, power, and pleasure. As long as we continue to act while propelled by these personal motives of self-interest, we are not free agents but robots, automata being pushed from behind by forces out of our control. We can live selfishly, doing as much as we like and working very hard, but we know from the Gita that this action will only imprison us more and more. There may come a time, later in life, when the walls of this prison have become so high we cannot climb over them at all.

As long as we are living only for ourselves, to make a little money or to acquire a little prestige, we cannot have access to the deeper resources within us. On this point, my Grandmother would sum up the message of the Gita in a few simple words. She would say that Sri Krishna gives me two ways to live. One is for myself, and when I live for myself I wither away and die. The other is to live for those around me, no matter how painful it may be at the outset, and to widen the circle more and more until it at last embraces all creation. With this path, the more I live for others the more resources will come into my hands.

A few days ago, on the way to San Francisco, we saw the new arrangement at the tollgate of the Bay Bridge. The traffic was particularly heavy, bumper to bumper, but there was one lane marked Exact Change where you keep your change ready, throw it in the basket, and shoot through. There is a rare kind of person who has this kind of ego. It is just little and crumpled up from living for his parents, partner, children, family, community, country, and world. He has always been thinking about others and never about himself, so his ego is tiny like a peanut. In life he goes through the Exact Change line, throws his ego into the basket, and shoots through. The others come with their egos on trucks—sometimes huge trucks with two trailers, which are so large that they have to wait for all the other trucks in front to pass through first.

On the spiritual path, we have one choice, whether we live in a rich or a poor family, whether we are ignorant or learned, whether we are healthy or ailing: shall we go after what pleases us, or shall we go after what promises to bring the increasing happiness of all those around us? When we work under the compulsion of self-will, we are preventing the Lord from using us as instruments of his work. But if we let the Lord act through us and realize that he is the operator, we go beyond the law of karma, no longer to be bound by actions.

एवं ज्ञात्वा कृतं कर्म पूर्वैरपि मुमुक्षुभिः ।
कुरु कर्मैव तस्मात्त्वं पूर्वैः पूर्वतरं कृतम् ॥१५॥

*15. Knowing this truth and desiring liberation, the spiritual aspirants of ancient times engaged in action. Perform action in the manner of those ancient sages.*

Sri Krishna now tells Arjuna about *mumukshu*, which means 'he who is very eager to have awareness of the indivisible unity of life.' It is this eagerness to know for ourselves, in our own consciousness, that parents and children are one, husband and wife are one, boyfriend and girlfriend are one, friend and friend are one, and even friend and enemy are one, that will deepen our meditation, strengthen our willpower, and enable us to turn our back upon what is petty and selfish in all of us. Whenever people have deeply desired liberation, whenever they have wanted to realize the Lord of Love who is ever present in all creatures, they have always learned to act selflessly, to live for others, and to turn their back upon whatever selfish satisfaction they may have wanted in their earlier days.

Whatever mistakes you may have committed in the past, once you turn your back upon personal profit and pleasure and set your eyes on the shining goal, then the past begins to fall away from you. Thus, Sri Krishna adds, you, too, have the latent, seldom-suspected capacity within yourself to change yourself completely, to become *mumukshu*. It is this divine unpredictability which is the mark of the mystic, and in everyone there is this capacity. Through the practice of meditation, one of the most delightful pastimes you develop is the capacity to change your habits at will. You can take tea and become a tea addict, like Dr. Johnson, for a few months, and when your body is beginning to clamor for tea in the morning, you can just give it a cup of coffee. There is no "Et tu, Brute?" Then you give it coffee for a number of weeks, and when the body has forgotten tea and has become addicted to coffee, you give it Sanka. This is how you win the freedom of the body.

The Gita will say, in marvelous language, even good habits are ties. First you get rid of bad habits by developing good habits. You cannot get rid of bad habits by saying "Go, go, go"; you get rid of bad habits by bringing in good habits which will force them out, and you don't have to push because there won't be any room to put their sleeping bag down. And then, the giants of all religions say, even the good habits have to go, because any habit is a form of rigid conditioning; any habit keeps you from freedom.

My wife and I used to go around Lake Merritt every day when

we were in Oakland. We had been used to going around clockwise, and you know the feet; they almost get automatic: you get there and they immediately turn in the same direction. So one day I just turned in the opposite direction instead. Even in little things you can experience this thrill of liberating yourself from your habits. When you want to sit in a very comfortable chair, go and sit down in a very uncomfortable one. This is how you free yourself.

A friend of ours, who is much more daring than I am, once went into an ice cream parlor and said, "What is the worst kind of ice cream you have?"

The proprietor answered, "Licorice."

"Bring a bowlful, please."

The proprietor gasped. "You're sure? One spoonful may be enough."

She said, "Please bring a bowlful of licorice ice cream, and leave it to me."

She disposed of every vestige of it, and when she asked for the bill, the proprietor looked at her with awe and said, "It's on the house."

This is one of the secrets the mystics tell us: when you free yourself from the tyranny of likes and dislikes, you can enjoy everything. With freedom from the tyranny of likes and dislikes comes freedom from allergy, which has become the bane of millions. Allergy is often a protest by the nervous system: "I have strong likes and strong dislikes; don't try to trifle with me." This is allergy. Gradually you can so free your nervous system that you can juggle with your likes and dislikes, which means you have gone beyond the law of duality where things are divided into pleasure and pain, success and defeat, birth and death. It is freedom from the tyranny of pain and pleasure, likes and dislikes, that will eventually give us the strength to realize *moksha,* or the indivisible unity of life, in our own consciousness.

किं कर्म किमकर्मेति कवयोऽप्यत्र मोहिताः ।
तत्ते कर्म प्रवक्ष्यामि यज्ज्ञात्वा मोक्ष्यसेऽशुभात् ॥१६॥

*16. What is action and what is inaction? This
question has confused the greatest sages. I will give
you the secret of action, with which you can free
yourself from bondage.*

Here Sri Krishna comforts Arjuna by telling him that he needn't
think badly of himself because he lacks discrimination. Even some
of the great sages lacked discrimination when they started on the
spiritual path. Arjuna says, "Wait! Great sages? Maybe one day I
too will become a great sage!" And he is consoled by the way that
Sri Krishna says that even the *kavis,* the great sages, were sometimes
confused about action and inaction.

Then Sri Krishna adds, "I will give you practical hints which will
enable you to cultivate this discrimination. And"—to put his advice in the modern idiom—"remember, *yaj jnātvā mokshyase 'shu-
bhāt:* these words are not only for your diary. They are not to be put
on buttons or on stickers for the back of your chariot. They are to be
practiced. You have to carry them into your daily life, even though
it may be unpleasant or even distressing."

कर्मणो ह्यपि बोद्धव्यं बोद्धव्यं च विकर्मणः ।
अकर्मणश्च बोद्धव्यं गहना कर्मणो गतिः ॥१७॥

*17. You must understand what is action, what
actions should be avoided, and what is inaction. For
the true nature of action is difficult to grasp.*

Sri Krishna, the Lord of Love present in all hearts, tells us how best
we can use our life to alleviate the many woes to which the world
has become subject during the course of the centuries. In understanding this secret of karma yoga, or selfless action, the word
*karma* has to be understood not only as meaning deeds, but also
words and thoughts. Even words are actions, and we all know from

the advertising world the power of the word. Those word wizards who coin slogans which can even come with us into our sleep are, to use Aldous Huxley's words, "the most influential of popular moralists and philosophers." Some of these advertising slogans are the surest proof of the negative power of words. If anyone doubts the efficacy of the mantram, let him observe the power of the advertising slogan.

Even thinking is a subtle form of action. Sigmund Freud has said that thought is action in rehearsal. When we are thinking angry thoughts against somebody, we actually are throwing abstract rocks at them. Sometimes I think a rock does not hurt so much as a harsh thought. We know how long people to whom we have unfortunately shown anger can suffer because of resentment and hostility. And we, too, suffer because we are violating the fundamental law of the unity of life.

People who think selfish thoughts can really show us that, as the mystics say, thinking is action. Living in a place where people are always thinking about their selfish satisfactions is living in an atmosphere worse than smog. The worst kind of smog is ego smog, and we have only to live with very egocentric people to know how deleterious it is. When we associate with agitated people, we come home so agitated that we cannot sit and have our dinner; we cannot go to sleep in peace. We cannot understand: in the afternoon we were feeling so placid and so composed; what happened to make us so agitated? Then we suddenly see: we went out with that fellow. We can all testify to this. When we are with agitated people, if we are not fairly calm within ourselves, naturally we participate in their agitation.

Conversely, in a very beautiful manner, when we are agitated, when we want to express our agitation by agitating a few more around us, we may go by mistake to the house of a serene person. Quietly established in himself, he comes out and says, "You want to agitate me? Come in." We go right in and start agitating, recapitulating what wrongs the world has done to us, how we have always been innocent. But halfway we begin to say that maybe sometimes we do make mistakes, maybe sometimes we do provoke people. Our host is still not saying anything. He is just looking with shining eyes of love and understanding, and by the time the interview ends, we have become calm. We come out and don't know what has happened to our agitation. "Is it the meal I had that may have corrected my agitation?" It takes a long time to understand that when we associate with people we also participate in their mental states. In Sanskrit there is a very good saying, *Samsargād doshagunam bhavati:* "By association we can become good and selfless, and by association we can become bad and selfish."

Let us remember that we cannot avoid action by staying at home. Even if we tie ourselves up in a chair and take a vow not to move for the whole day, we are acting inside, and thoughts can be action in a very subtle form. In order to be entirely free in our action, the mystics say, thought has to be controlled at its origin. The Buddha has said in the Dhammapada that all we are is the result of what we have thought. The thoughts that germinate in the depths of our consciousness slowly drive us into action. Action, therefore, begins at the level of thinking, and the purpose of meditation is to control action at the source.

*Vikarma* is action which is prohibited to us because it inflicts suffering on others. *Vikarma* is wrong action. Any action which is born of anger, fear, or greed is *vikarma*. The Gita will say that any action that is propelled by anger is likely to bring sorrow not only to those against whom the action is directed, but also to the doer. When we are angry, most of us are prompted to action. Immediately tamas is transformed into rajas. Even the most phlegmatic person, when roused to anger, will leap up and start acting right and left, bringing suffering on everyone around.

In order to act wisely, we have to be free from anger, free from hostility, free from resentment. Unfortunately, even in the efforts being made to banish violence from our midst, I sometimes see an element of resentment and hatred. In order to counter violence, we should not get violent at all. We can deal effectively with violence by being persuasive, courteous, and considerate, and yet very, very firm. Gentleness and friendly persuasion can be effective with all human beings. The moment I get angry, you are going to get more angry; and when you get more angry, I am going to get most angry. This is what happens when we meet anger with anger. We move further and further apart; and two people who stood only two yards apart at the outset, by the time the peace negotiations are finished, have moved two hundred yards apart. Jesus has said that it is by bearing with people who provoke us, by blessing those who curse us, by doing good to those who hate us, that we can win them over. My humble conviction is that there is no human being who lacks this capacity to love and respond to love, because the Lord lives in all of us.

Just as action born of anger leads to disaster, so do actions done out of fear and greed. When we do things out of fear, we are likely to be far off the mark. When we do things out of the third propelling force, greed, this too leads to disaster. Actions motivated by these three do not benefit anyone.

The third term used is *akarma,* 'inaction.' When we empty ourselves of all selfishness and realize that the Lord within is the operator, all action falls away. We do not act; the Lord acts through us. Whenever Gandhi was asked how he was able to free India from the political domination of the greatest empire the world has known without firing a shot, he would reply that all he did was empty himself of his selfishness and separateness to become a humble instrument in the hands of the Lord.

This is the real meaning of inaction, but we do not achieve this state by merely refusing to act. There is a tremendous need for action in all of us ordinary human beings. The choice that we have is: shall we act under the compulsion of self-will, bringing about our own downfall and the downfall of others, or shall we act as an instrument of the Lord, contributing to the welfare of our family, community, country, and world?

कर्मण्यकर्म यः पश्येदकर्मणि च कर्म यः ।
स बुद्धिमान्मनुष्येषु स युक्तः कृत्स्नकर्मकृत् ॥१८॥

*18. They who see action where there is inaction,
and inaction where there is action, live in wisdom.
Their consciousness is unified, and their every act is
done with complete awareness.*

Here Sri Krishna says a strange thing to Arjuna: "When a person
becomes united with Me, when he becomes an instrument in my
hands, then even though he acts, he does not act." The person who
has surrendered himself to the Lord does not act; the Lord acts
through him.

This reminds me of when we held weekly meetings on the University of California campus in Berkeley. Curious things used to
take place on campus in those days. One day, as I was leaving the
meditation meeting, I saw a group of demonstrators being hauled
away by the police. They would struggle for a while and then suddenly go limp. Then there was no struggle, no effort, and evidently
no resistance at all. This was very protective, and I saw what effect it
had on the people who were dragging those students away. It took
away all their animosity, for what is the use of dragging a person
who doesn't object to being dragged? In this verse Sri Krishna tells
Arjuna, "When the ego tries to drag you away, go limp." When spiritual awareness increases, you can act from morning to night with
great power and in the evening come back so fresh, so vital, and so
light on your feet that you say, "Oh, I am not tired. I haven't been
acting; I've just been going limp."

For me, Gandhi is the perfect example of the statement that a
person filled with the love of God, practicing the presence of God,
never acts at all. Once when I went to Gandhiji's āshram, as I
walked about in the neighborhood of his little cottage, I saw the unending stream of political leaders from Britain and India who came
to him throughout the day. I was wondering how he was able to bear
the pressure of these significant interviews which would change the
relations of two great countries, and in the evening, I expected to see

a tired, irascible, very impatient man coming out. Instead I saw a smiling figure who looked as if he had been playing bingo with children all day. I could not believe my eyes, because I was used to the idea that if we work eight hours we should be tense and ready to be irritated by anybody who tries to be nice to us. But he was completely untouched by his action.

Every day in our work, as long as it is not at the expense of others, we can learn to avoid tension and pressure when attending to the most challenging tasks that life may bring us. For most of us, tension has become a badge of action. In fact, we usually expect someone who has engaged in intense action during the day to complain about his ulcer. Tension need not accompany action; we can act free from any tension, any movement in the mind, any ripple of consciousness. Once Gandhi was asked by Western friends, "Mr. Gandhi, you have been working fifteen hours a day for fifty years for these helpless millions of India. Why don't you take a long holiday?" Gandhi replied, "I am always on holiday."

When a person has made himself an instrument in the hands of the Lord as Gandhi did, then Sri Krishna says, "He is not acting at all. I act through him." In the Gita this is called "inaction in action." Conversely there are people who say they want to drop out of society and go away from the world. Such people, even if they try to keep quiet in the midst of the woods, are still active. All of us are active everywhere, and all of us influence our environment everywhere. A parent is influencing his children by his attitudes and by his ways, even if he does not look after them. Even when we refuse to act, Sri Krishna maintains, we influence people by our apathy.

The practice of meditation demands intense action. Without energetic, intense, selfless action, the practice of meditation can become quite dangerous, and we can become caught inside. To the orthodox Hindu the working out of bad karma through good karma is an essential part of spiritual progress. As long as we have a heavy load of unfavorable karma on our back, it will not be possible for us to wake up when we plunge into the depths of the unconscious. In some of the most profound stages of meditation, when we have touched the floor of consciousness, we are like a diver who has gone fathoms deep to stand on the sea bed. Similar to the tremendous pressures bearing down on him is the pressure that bears down on the person who reaches the unconscious in meditation. When we reach the depths of the unconscious, we naturally become completely unconscious, but we must learn to become conscious at that time. Now to give a little preview of this magnificent climax of meditation, when we are standing there with this vast sea of consciousness pressing down upon us, instead of being frightened or paralyzed, or becoming completely unconscious, we must be able to repeat the mantram in the depths of our unconscious. If we can do this, we are worthy of becoming aware of the Lord.

यस्य सर्वे समारम्भाः कामसंकल्पवर्जिताः ।
ज्ञानाग्निदग्धकर्माणं तमाहुः पण्डितं बुधाः ॥१९॥

*19. The awakened sages call a man wise when all*
*his undertakings are free from anxiety about results;*
*all his selfish desires have been consumed in the fire*
*of knowledge.*

The Gita is an imperative call to action in which the Lord insists that none of us can afford to lie here inactive while the world burns in turmoil and violence. If each one of us makes the maximum contribution that lies within his power to conquer violence, we would see the reign of peace, of goodwill, and of love. It is natural for the vast majority of us, as we look around the world and see the conflagration threatening to engulf us, to throw up our hands in despair and say, "What can I do?" "But," Sri Krishna will ask, "what is it that you cannot do?"

If we realize that in the depths of our consciousness dwells the Lord of Love, who is infinite love, infinite wisdom, and infinite capacity for selfless service, none of us would ever feel despondent or defeated. The feeling of being inadequate to the call made by life upon us, the Gita says precisely, is caused by our anxiety about results. We get involved in the results. We want to say, "See what I have accomplished." We want posterity to turn the pages of history to see how many are devoted to our exploits. The secret of all action, as embodied by Mahatma Gandhi in his own masterly personal life, is to select a selfless goal—it does not matter how big or impossible—and do everything we can, in the face of challenges, difficulties, or persecution, to move towards that goal. It may not be possible for one person to achieve his goal, but his work will be continued and supplemented, becoming larger and larger until it reaches fulfillment.

The word used here is *budhāh,* 'those who are awake.' These awakened ones would not say that you and I are acting. They would say we are only chasing our tail, going round and round in ineffective action, wasting our time and energy. Only the man who turns his back upon his own self-will and dedicates all his energy, time, resources, everything to the Lord in the service of Him in everyone around, is truly wise.

If we look at the so-called great achievements of people who have made their name in history, we will find the motive often may have been ambition, or prestige, or the lust for power. The Gita says such people do not really make a lasting contribution to the world. This is particularly true of the lust for power, which is perhaps the most corrupting of all lusts. As Lord Acton once said, "Power tends to corrupt and absolute power corrupts absolutely." When we go after personal power, in the early days we might really want to make a contribution to our country and to world peace, but as power begins to intoxicate us, all these honest motives recede until finally we want power for the sake of power, for imposing our self-will on everyone around.

Sometimes after dinner at Ramagiri we talk about current issues, and the other day we were having a discussion about the concept of leadership in modern politics. I pointed out that the concept of leadership placed before us by Gandhi is that of the leader who turns his back upon personal power, who seeks not to enjoy the perquisites of office, and who thinks not of his image or of what posterity will read about him in history books. We all know how many times the occupants of office do things simply for ensuring victory in the next election. In India, too, it was not uncommon for us to see leaders coming on the platform to harangue us about what they were going to do for our benefit, what they were going to do for our progress, only to ensure their personal re-election. The concept that Gandhiji placed before the whole world is that the best leader is one who is not interested in himself, but only in making his maximum contribution to the welfare of the people and the world. I give Mahatma Gandhi as an unvarying example of a great leader in politics who has worked for his people and his country without any thought of profit, prestige, or power.

People like Mahatma Gandhi, according to Sri Krishna, are those whose selfish desires, whose personal motives of profit, prestige, and power, have been consumed to ashes in the fire of knowledge. Sri Krishna, very compassionately, is saying that those who aim for office or anything else only for themselves are ignorant. They are ignorant of the most basic truth, that you and I are one.

त्यक्त्वा कर्मफलासङ्गं नित्यतृप्तो निराश्रयः ।
कर्मण्यभिप्रवृत्तोऽपि नैव किंचित्करोति सः ॥२०॥

*20. The wise man, ever satisfied, has abandoned all external supports. His security is unaffected by the results of his action; even while acting he is only an instrument.*

When you have directed your life towards a selfless goal, then *Tyaktvā karmaphalāsangam:* "Do not get entangled in the result." In order to undertake the great work for peace that is dear to all of us, we should have an adequate sense of detachment from the results of our work. If we are going to get agitated every time there is a rebuff, every time there is a reverse, we ourselves will become violent. As we all know, sometimes even the demonstrators against violence become violent. In the words of the Compassionate Buddha: *Hatred does not cease by hatred at any time. Hatred ceases by love. This is an unalterable law.* Similarly, we can say today: "Violence will not cease by violence. Violence ceases by nonviolence. This is an unalterable law." In order to win over opposition, to bring people together, we have to be serene and compassionate, whatever the vicissitudes of life may bring us. Mahatma Gandhi was at his best when seemingly defeated. He used to say it was from prison that he struck his hardest bargains. Most of us look upon defeat and reverses as weakening us; but in karma yoga, every time we are defeated we seem to go deeper into our consciousness to bring out greater resources. When we think we have been defeated, when we come home and tell our family that we have been beaten, Sri Krishna may say, "In my book I say the guy is doing well." In order to grow, in order to strengthen our muscles, we need opposition.

Defeat is found very often in the lives of selfless people as an opening into opportunity. The Gita says that when you follow the spiritual path, living for others, very often there come to you increased challenges, increased threats, to make you go deeper and deeper into your consciousness. If there were no difficulties, you would only be skimming on the surface of life. Gandhiji, in a rare statement in which he gave himself away, said, "I love storms." It is a thrill to be in the midst of a storm when you are keeping the welfare of those around you first, when the lightning is playing about your eyes, and thunder is crashing in your ears. When everything is against you, you feel so sure that the Lord is within you that you have only to put your hand out and say, "Hold me; my morale is sinking." It is not that Gandhiji was not afraid. He could get as afraid as you and I do under the pressure of circumstances, but he always knew how to say, "Please take my hand. See, it's trembling." And Sri Krishna loves trembling fingers when they are stretched towards him. He does not like those who proudly say, "Feel my hand. How steady it is!" When you surrender to him—when you say, "By myself I am so weak, so incapable of facing opposition, but with the Lord supporting me, what opposition is there that I will not face?"—then he comes to help you.

*Nityatripta* means 'always satisfied.' When we are engaged in a great struggle, for example against violence, one day we will gain a small victory. Then we want to celebrate, sing and dance, and get very elated. But on the following day there may come defeat, and on that evening there will be wailing and gnashing of teeth. Here Sri

Krishna says, "What kind of equanimity are you observing? When there is victory, you should go about quietly repeating my Name and at night peacefully fall asleep. There is nothing to be elated about. And when there is a reverse, why gnash your teeth? It's not good for them. At that time, too, repeat my Name and in the evening go to bed and fall asleep in the mantram."

Every movement in the mind is insecurity. Every movement of the mind, whether it is caused by ambition, anger, fear, lust, or any other agitation, alienates us from our real nature. This is why the Bible says, "Be still, and know that I am God." When the mind is still, we have gone beyond the mind. In meditation we try to still the mind, which is a very difficult thing to do. We may have been meditating for half an hour, and the mind is fairly calm. "Well, the mind is still," we think. "I don't have to concentrate now." We relax our vigilance and immediately pandemonium bursts loose.

At no time should we allow the mind to be agitated. Agitation of the mind prevents us from releasing our deeper resources for creative action. *Nityatripta* also conveys the idea, given elsewhere in the Gita, that in order to be united with the Lord, in order to discover the indivisible unity of life, the mind has to be serene and waveless. In the Gita (12:17) Krishna says the person who never gets excited is very dear to him. This word "exciting," that has become part and parcel of our advertising paraphernalia, is a very dangerous word, because its other side is "depressing." We usually see only the facade. But whenever we see excitement, we should say, "Turn your back. Let me see what is written on it: *d-e-p-r-e-s-s-i-o-n.*" This is the lettering on the back of excitement. If we could have excitement without depression, I would recommend it for everybody, but so far no one has ever succeeded in separating the two, and according to the Gita this separation is not likely to be effected, not even by our best psychologists or technologists.

When John F. Kennedy was being installed as president, and all of us were looking forward eagerly to what he had to say, I remember a journalist going up and asking him, "Mr. President, you must be greatly excited today." It was a very mature reply, in the Gita tradition, that he gave: "Excited, no. Very interested." This is the mature attitude. After all, one is likely to be very interested when one is moving into the White House. This mature equanimity that all of us can learn to have is not lack of interest. It is the mystic who is interested in everything. There is a photograph of Gandhiji looking through a microscope, and I do not think even Louis Pasteur could have had that expression of concentration. Gandhi was interested in everything, but not excited by anything at all.

When you and I have a tendency to get excited, especially when good things happen, that is the time to go out for a walk, repeating the mantram. When your ship comes home, when you see it moving up to the pier, don't stand there clapping wildly. Get off the pier and go for a long walk repeating *Rāma, Rāma, Rāma* or *Jesus, Jesus, Jesus*. Otherwise, if you keep on saying, "My ship has come home! My ship has come home!" before you know where you are, you will not be on the pier; you will be floating about on cloud number nine. It is all right riding on cloud nine, but the next day you will be skin diving. Sri Krishna tells Arjuna, "I am not asking you to avoid excitement. But when depression comes, as it must, don't ask, 'Why did this happen to me?'"

In order to understand the powerlessness of the intellect, talk to people who are just going into a depression. If we ask people who have some self-knowledge, "Why do you look like that? Why are your eyes so glassy? Why are you so indrawn? And why can't I hear some of those old chuckles?" they will reply, "We are going into a depression."

And I have often suggested, "You have a bright intellect. Say 'I am not going into a depression,' and pull yourself out."

"It doesn't work," is their answer.

At that time, go for a tearing walk, burning up the sidewalk. Walk as fast as you can, repeating the mantram, and see what just one hour of walking repeating *Rāma, Rāma, Rāma* can do. When you come back, you may even have forgotten what you were depressed about. This is a comment on the powerlessness of the intellect as compared to the immense power of the Holy Name.

The next objective is even more severe: *nirāshraya,* 'without any support.' In order to be the instrument of the Lord, we must let go of all supports other than the Lord himself. Now we are prepared to let our right hand go free, provided we can hold on with our left. We all are trying to hold on to something. If it is not money, it is food, or cigarettes, or alcohol. Others try to draw support and security from prestige and power. This is the human condition. We have to hold on to something, and the Lord says, "Why don't you hold on to Me? I am right inside you. You don't have to walk miles in the rain. You don't have to go searching for anything. You don't have to work hard to make money. Just hold on to Me and say, 'Let me be firm.'" The Lord says to all of us through Arjuna, "Let go of all your supports. Throw yourself at my feet, and I will protect you."

Almost all of us will call to the Lord, "Hold me, help me," but at the same time we continue to hold on to external supports. My Grandmother drove this home to me when we went together to see a ballet in Kathakali based on a very moving episode in the *Mahābhārata*. Draupadī, Arjuna's wife, is being stripped of her clothes in front of a large number of courtiers by a revengeful enemy of her husband. Draupadī, whose honor is being violated, cries aloud, "Krishna, Krishna, Krishna, protect me!"

Then, on another part of the stage, Sri Krishna is seen quietly seated playing on his flute. Sri Krishna's queen gets very angry at her lord and says, "What kind of god are you? Here is your devotee, a loving, beautiful woman, being stripped naked in front of a hundred jeering enemies, and you are seated here, playing on your flute. Have you no love in your heart?"

Sri Krishna takes the flute from his lips very leisurely and pointing with it says, "Look." Krishna's queen looks down from their heavenly vantage point and sees that Draupadī is holding on to her sari with one hand while she stretches the other up towards the Lord in supplication. For a while Sri Krishna and his queen both look at Draupadī, until suddenly she lets go of her sari and joins both hands in prayer. It is a very thrilling moment, and when the whole gathering of courtiers gasps with terrible suspense, Sri Krishna sends down an unending sari. My Grandmother, even though she must have seen this scene enacted many times, was so thrilled that she said, "Go on! Keep pulling the sari. Let us see you exhaust it!" And the more the enemy pulled, the more sari there was.

On the spiritual path we are likely to say to the Lord, "We know you are the citadel of security, Lord, but we would prefer to keep 25 percent in shares, 25 percent in currency, and 50 percent in you." We shall find that it is this reservation, this looking backward, that keeps us from making rapid progress on the spiritual path. Never has anyone succeeded in seeing the Lord except by surrendering completely to him.

The person who is the same in victory and defeat, who is always loyal to the goal, come obstacle, come ordeal, and who does not depend upon any external support, does not act at all; the Lord acts through him. The Lord will act through us if we will only empty ourselves of all self-will, of all separateness. This is what we do when we truly love. When a husband loves his wife more than himself, or a wife loves her husband more than herself, this is what they are doing; they are emptying themselves of themselves. This can be done in every relationship, and every one of us has the opportunity to empty himself of his selfishness in his relationship with his parents, partner, and friends. Someone once asked me, "Supposing there is someone who doesn't have any of these?" I said, "How about enemies? Who is there who doesn't have enemies?" It is possible for everyone, through unremitting endeavor and the practice of meditation, to empty himself of all that is selfish, self-willed, and separate, so that he can make a great contribution to the amelioration of the lamentable conditions that exist in the world today.

निराशीर्यतचित्तात्मा त्यक्तसर्वपरिग्रहः ।
शारीरं केवलं कर्म कुर्वन्नाप्नोति किल्बिषम् ॥२१॥

*21. Free from expectations and all sense of possession, with mind and body firmly controlled by the Self, such a one does not incur sin by the performance of physical action.*

To be free in action, to make his greatest contribution to the welfare of society, Sri Krishna tells Arjuna *nirāshī:* he should have no expectations. It is a difficult concept for us to understand, because we think that if we do not have expectations, we will have no motive for action. But as long as we are expecting something, life can hold us hostage. Quiet reflection can bring home the profound wisdom of these words: if you want to go through life free, do not expect anything.

Sri Krishna says, "Do not go about begging of life, 'Give me this; give me that.' Then you are bound. Say instead, 'I don't want anything, Lord. If you want to give me defeat, I am not afraid. If you want to give me victory, I won't object.'" This is the stature that the human being can reach by becoming aware of the Lord of Love within. He can function with complete freedom, not dependent on what comes to him in the way of success or defeat.

We have only to examine ourselves to see what a catalog of expectations we have in life. Accordingly, "disappointed" is one of the most frequently used words in our vocabulary. Almost every day there is some disappointment because, as the Gita implies, expectation and disappointment go together. In very loving language, Sri Krishna tells us through Arjuna, "I don't want you to be beggars. You are my children, inheritors of all my wisdom, love, and beauty. There is no need for you to go about hankering for success or apprehensive of defeat." When we take up a task which contributes to at least one person's welfare—without asking, "Will this bring me promotion? Will this send my image down in history as a great man? Will this bring me that prize, or this profit?"—then we work without anxiety. To work in this way, without expectation, it is necessary to have complete faith in the Lord of Love within, who always sends us what is good for our spiritual development.

If we are to work and live in freedom, our body and mind must listen to us. When we sit down in meditation we are slowly teaching the body and mind to listen to us implicitly, to obey even our gentle hints. In the early days of meditation it is likely that the body will go to sleep. This is its idea of security. In order to train our body to keep awake in the deeper stages of meditation, every time we get sleepy we must draw away from our back support, sit up straight, and make the maximum effort possible to keep awake. For everybody at some time there is the problem of drowsiness. As concentration deepens, as the words of the inspirational passage begin to go slowly, the neuromuscular system relaxes. To see this happening during meditation we have only to look at the faces of people who have been tense; slowly they start smiling and the lips begin to open in beatitude. It pains me to say that this is the time when we should jut our chin forward and sit sternly erect.

As for the mind, for everyone the path of meditation begins with a wealth of distractions, because we have always let the mind have its own way. The Compassionate Buddha used to remark that there is nothing so disobedient as an undisciplined mind. When we do not want to think about something, the mind will say, "That's exactly what I am going to think about, and you can't do anything about it." None of us like harboring resentful thoughts, and we all have known times when hostile thoughts have kept boiling in our minds and we have tried to tell the mind, "This is not good for me." But the mind says, "It's good for *me!* It may not be good for you, but I like resentment. I like agitation, because that's what makes me come to life."

For a long, long time in meditation the main effort is in disciplining the mind, in bringing it back whenever it wanders away, in keeping it on the words of the passage in spite of all its attempts to get away from them. This is drastic and very dull discipline, but it will pay the richest dividends in the long run. Even if you sit for an hour in meditation doing nothing but bringing your mind back to the passage sixty times in sixty minutes, you have made progress on the spiritual path. Every time the mind runs out, you run after it, pick it up from the restaurant, or the bank, or the movie theater, and bring it back. Then, the moment you are not looking, the mind has run out again. You again run after it and bring it back. It is just like following a little child. For some years in meditation there is a real test of your patience. There are no thrills. There are no visions. There is no rapture. There is just plain tedium. If your desire for the Lord is great, you will put up with all this cheerfully, but if you are meditating just because, for example, the Beatles did it, your enthusiasm will not last long.

In the next word, *tyaktasarvaparigraha,* the Lord says, "You must not own anything. I am the owner. Don't try to put your tag 'mine' on anything. Don't ever say 'This is my exclusive property.'" We own nothing because the Lord is the owner. He is the landlord; we are just transients. Here the practical application is that only when we are detached from things can we use them wisely. The man who is fond of money cannot use it wisely. Often rich people unfortunately use money to their own detriment, because they do not know how to use it for their own and others' benefit. This does not mean we should give away everything. Sri Krishna is saying we should not be attached to our wealth and material possessions. It is possible for a millionaire to be completely detached in his villa in the south of France, while it is possible for a poor man to be attached to his shack with violent egoism. It is the attitude that matters here.

In the final stages of meditation, we become very eager to unify our love, to give everything to the Lord and be united with him. As Sri Ramakrishna puts it, when our boat is nearing the harbor we want to reach the harbor so soon, we are so eager to be in our home, that we start picking up everything and throwing it overboard to lighten the boat. We start throwing away all of the excess baggage that we have hoarded down the years. Then our eagerness becomes so great that we may start throwing away the anchor and the sails. This is where we have to be discriminating. The spiritual life does not require us to give up reasonable comfort and the necessities of life. If we live in poverty, without having enough food, instead of meditating on the Lord we will be meditating on food. It is luxury and the hoarding of things because of selfish attachment that we must give up.

Such a person—who has no expectations, who is prepared for weal or woe, who has no selfish attachments to things or people, who does not even look upon his body as his own, but as an instrument given him by the Lord with which to serve humanity—such a person does not act. The Lord acts through him. Sri Krishna almost implies, "Even when he raises his arm, it is not he who does it; it is I." When he does anything, it is from the deepest level of his consciousness where the Lord dwells all the time. Instead of acting on the surface level of life, he allows the Lord to act through him from the deepest level. Then there is no tension, no fatigue, no fear, and there is immense creative activity which enables him to give his very best even in the most adverse circumstances.

यदृच्छालाभसंतुष्टो द्वन्द्वातीतो विमत्सरः ।
समः सिद्धावसिद्धौ च कृत्वापि न निबध्यते ॥२२॥

*22. They live in freedom who have gone beyond
the dualities of life, and who never compete. They
are alike in success and failure and content with
whatever comes to them.*

The nature of life is to bring us sunshine and shadow, pleasure and pain, success and failure, praise and censure. Wherever we live, in the West or in the East, on the campus or in the bazaar, this inescapable duality of life will always be around us. It shows our pathetic condition that almost every one of us hopes that one day we will be able to isolate pleasure from pain. This is one of the everlasting projects of humanity. It may not have been done by anybody in history, but I am going to do this one day in my lab; and when I have isolated the pleasure bacillus, I will be free. There are others who would like to isolate praise. Most of us appreciate praise, but it is disastrous to become dependent on it. If we are going to allow our security to be bolstered up by the praise, appreciation, and applause of others, we are done for. I have even heard about a well-known movie star who goes to sleep at night with an applause record playing. This is going to make him more and more insecure.

Under no circumstances should we be agitated if someone ignores us. I for one cannot find enough words for the advantages of being ignored. Nobody recognizes me—how good it is! I can walk anywhere in freedom, for nobody thinks I am anybody—how good it is! I always say that if I could write a play I would call it "A Place to

Be Nobody," which means that I do not want any attention from others, I do not want any appreciation from others, I do not want any support from others, because I have the source of all appreciation, support, and security within me. In life there are occasions when we are ignored and sometimes forgotten. That is the time for us to remind ourselves, "Oh, I am forgotten, very good! Nobody attends to me—excellent! Why should I need anybody's attention?" This is the attitude of the real mystic, who is content because he is complete. We have a standing invitation from the Lord within, who says, "Any time you feel like it, you can make yourself free. Come to me. I have a banquet spread for you with ambrosia, the nectar that gives everlasting life."

These attitudes can be cultivated skillfully. When I see the kind of feats performed in the circus, I know they must have required enormous endeavor. Most of us have seen two trapeze artists swinging over and under each other across the tent to exchange trapezes in midair; you don't just go on the trapeze one day and say, "I am going to jump from one to another." It is the same kind of practice, the same kind of skill, that people develop who win tennis championships. You do not go to Wimbledon on the first day you play tennis; you keep practicing, you develop your skills, and one day you will be at Wimbledon playing on the central court. It is the same on the spiritual path. These are attitudes that all of us can develop; even those of us who are the most sensitive to praise and appreciation can learn to be so secure within ourselves that the word *rejected* can be expelled from our dictionary. The one person who will never reject us is the Lord, and that is enough to make up for all the rejections we may have to undergo at the hands of everyone else.

One of the central ideas of the Gita is that as long as you look at life through the spectacles of pain and pleasure, success and failure, praise and censure, you will never see life whole. One of the fatal flaws of the intellect is that it can thrive only in the land of duality. You take the intellect from the sea of duality and throw it on the land of unity, and it dies. It says, "You mean, I can't divide, I can't categorize, I can't classify things? I'm done for." When Sri Ramana Maharshi used to tell people to go beyond pleasure and pain, they would ask, "Do you mean be indifferent?" His answer would be, "When you go beyond pleasure and pain, you reach abiding joy."

Pleasure is something that comes and goes; joy is something that abides, and it is this state of abiding joy for which the mantram *Rāma* stands. We enter into this state when we gradually go beyond the duality of pleasure and pain, success and defeat, praise and censure.

The next word is *vimatsara:* "Do not compete." It is a strong word, and a concept which is alien to us today. We have come to believe it is only when we compete that we can give our best. I think there are other ways in which we can be inspired to give our best, and one is by reminding ourselves that when we contribute to the welfare of our family, our community, our country, and our world, we are actually serving the Lord. If we want to be aware of the Lord, if we want to be united with the Lord, we must contribute as much as we can to the happiness of those around us, turning our back upon our own petty pleasures and profit when necessary.

This word *vimatsara* also touches upon the harmful way in which most of us tend to compare ourselves with others. This, too, has become so common today that in order to esteem myself, I should always be able to say, "I am better than he, so I am good." We have a distinguished American spiritual teacher in India, nearing his hundredth year now, who took the Sanskrit name *Atulānanda.* It is a lovely name which means 'one who does not compare people.' As our spiritual awareness grows, we will know that the Lord is present in everyone and that there is a uniqueness about everyone. The truly spiritual person never tries to compare himself with others, or others among themselves. I have never been able to understand the origin of this phrase "keeping up with the Joneses." It does not matter very much whether we keep up with Tom Jones or anybody else; what is important is for us to keep up with the Lord by serving him in everyone around us. Even here, as long as we compete with each other and compare one with another, a certain amount of envy is inescapable. There is a girl in Kālidāsa's[1] play *Shakuntalā* who has a

1. A well-known poet and dramatist of India in the fourth century A.D.

very beautiful name: *Anasūyā,* 'she who is free from jealousy.' This is a very rare type, an ideal we can all try to imitate by not competing among ourselves or comparing ourselves to others around us, remembering that all of us have complete worth and value because the Lord is present in us all the time.

*Samah siddhāv asiddhau ca. Siddha* is success; *asiddha* is failure. Sri Krishna again repeats these important words, saying, "If you want to love Me, you must remain alike in success and failure." In my humble observation it is not so very difficult to remain calm in failure. It is much more difficult to remain calm in success, which goes straight to the head. Those who have made money, who have become famous, for example, sometimes drop their old acquaintances and move out of their old area. In the spiritual tradition, it is when you become famous that you go to your old area and say to your old friends, "Now you can all bask in my success. We have grown up together, and you have taught me so many things that I owe my upbringing to you." This is the kind of reverse perspective we can all try to follow. The higher we rise the more we should remember those who are less fortunate. Whether people recognize us, or praise us, or drop us, or even denounce us, there is no need for us to lose our calmness, our security, and our awareness that the Lord is within us all the time.

गतसङ्गस्य मुक्तस्य ज्ञानावस्थितचेतसः ।
यज्ञायाचरतः कर्म समग्रं प्रविलीयते ॥२३॥

*23. Those without attachment to the ego are free; their minds are purified by the knowledge that all life is one. They perform all work freely, in the spirit of service.*

Here Sri Krishna gives us the word *gatasanga,* 'he who is free from attachment to his own ego.' All of us have immense resources of love, most of which swirl around our own ego. As long as we are in love with our own ego, dwelling upon ourselves, dreaming about ourselves, it will not be possible for us to love our family or our community. In meditation, we gradually release this swirling whirlpool into channels of fruitful service which flow towards others. The more we think about ourselves, the less we can love others; the less we think about ourselves, the more we are able to love others. When the great day comes when I forget that most monotonous subject in the world, myself, on that day I am free to love everybody.

We all can enter into this state of abiding love by working at it every day, particularly in our domestic relationships, where we have the greatest opportunities for forgetting ourselves. It is absurd to talk about leading the spiritual life when we do not try to put the welfare of our family first. This is the training ground, and though the training is not easy at all, it can be accomplished by all of us with the repetition of the mantram. When irritations or conflicts occur—as they are bound to occur between two people who are brought up differently, who are conditioned differently, who have been exposed to different cultural influences in their early days—do not try to move further away; do not say, "I am not going to talk to you; I don't want to see you." That is the time to say, "I am going to get closer to you, and I am going to try to put your welfare first." This is the challenge of friction; even friction can have spiritual value. The Bhagavad Gita throws a flood of light on how the unfavorable circumstances in our life can be utilized. If we do not utilize them, we are failing to take advantage of the great opportunities that come to us for removing friction, for banishing conflict, and for moving closer to the Lord in everyone around us.

The next word is one of Sri Krishna's favorites: *muktasya. Mukta* means free. Sri Krishna asks, "Don't you want to live in freedom?" When somebody is angry at you, and you are angry at that person, you are not living in freedom; you are living in bondage. You are only doing what the other person is making you do.

I used to get amazed at my Granny, my spiritual teacher, when she would tell me that when I retaliate, when I move away from people, when I get estranged, I am only dancing to a tune anybody can play. I was a little puppet, she said, whose wires were being pulled by some of my high school classmates whom I disliked. If I want to be free, all that I have to co, whatever others may do, is try to stand calm, move closer, and give them greater love and greater respect. In my own small personal experience, when people get angry and cause trouble in personal relationships, I have found they are often crying out, "Help me to move closer to you." We all have such experiences. Every one of us can do something in his own home, in his own life, to apply these precious words of the Lord to enable him to live in freedom.

We should remember that "freedom" here implies not only my own freedom, but also the freedom of all around me, in which I find my freedom. According to the Gita, it is not possible to find freedom by one's own self; it is not possible for X, Y, or Z alone to become free and lead a free life. Freedom is indivisible, and in order for me to be free, I have to help others to be free. When we use the word "freedom," what we usually mean is that as long as I am free, it does not matter whether or not you are free. What does matter is that I should be free, my community should be free, my country should be free. The Gita implies that this concept is preposterous; all life is one, and it is only in this total freedom that I can enjoy freedom.

The most challenging effort of freeing ourselves by helping those around us to become free begins, as usual, in the family. I have been reading a good deal lately about the family becoming obsolete. This is the fantasy of those who do not understand the value of the family in training us to learn to find our freedom by living for the freedom of all those around us. The family is really a free university. We are now familiar with free universities; we find them in Palo Alto and Berkeley. Everywhere now people are trying to establish free universities. I would say this is carrying coal to Newcastle. We all have a free university at home, where we really get our finest education in freedom. If we do not learn that the freedom of the family is the freedom of the individual members of the family, we are likely to be misfits in life for a long, long time. I would have no hesitation in saying a good son or daughter makes a good husband or wife, a good father or mother, and a good citizen. We can all start acting on this concept of freedom right in our own family, which does not mean Papa, Mama, Junior, and Janie, but all the members, including grandparents, uncles and aunts, and country cousins. The family can include our dearest friends and those who participate closely in all our endeavors.

To begin the spiritual life, which will enable us to become free, we need not play a part on a gigantic scale. Mogul art, one of the great periods of artistic achievement in India, often is in miniature. The artist concentrated on very small areas, on little things, and worked with such tenderness and precision that only somebody who understands art will be able to see all the love and labor that has gone into it. Family living is like Mogul art, worked in miniature. The canvas is so small, and the skill required is so great, that most of us really do not evaluate the vast potentialities of family life which can enable us all to find our freedom.

My wife and I can draw a little parallel from our own life at Ramagiri with my mother and the children. We usually keep one day in the week for outings, and last Sunday, a beautiful, balmy day, we took them to Santa Rosa. On the way, I was seated with Meera on one side and Geetha on the other, and they were asking me all kinds of questions to which it is very easy to say, "Keep quiet." From an adult viewpoint, most of their questions were juvenile. But that is exactly what children are—juvenile people who are asking me juvenile questions that are just right for them. In fact, if they had asked me some adult question, I would have said, "Keep quiet." All the time I was trying to remember what most of us older people forget: that every child has a point of view. They have their outlook on the world, their way of looking at life, which makes them ask these questions, and for them, these are matters of vital importance. They wanted to know, for example, why *Texaco* and *Mexico* should be spelled differently, why *Texaco* should be spelled with an *a* and *Mexico* with an *i*. To this you just do not say, "They are not the same."

I had my arms around both of them. They had those high rainboots on, so every now and then I would get a kick from both sides, and it hurt. They are children, active and lively, and they sometimes kick. They do not intend to kick others, but my legs happened to be in the way so they got hit. In all these little details, we have to remind ourselves, "These children are not really kicking me; they are kicking their heels in the air, and my legs happen to be in the way." I had to repeat the mantram, *Rāma Rāma,* to keep smiling. It is in these little things that we learn how to be loving. In order to love, to find our freedom, we do not have to go to the Himālayas or the Sierras. We just go to Santa Rosa in one of those little VW bugs, where we are so constricted that every kick is amplified.

When we got to Santa Rosa, we had to walk slowly because my mother is nearing her eightieth year. But the children wanted to run. We were in a crowded shopping center, where it is not proper for a sedate professor to be running about. But they were saying, "Uncle, we want you to run; to run is fun." I did not say that a pompous professor like me should not be running; it would take away from my pomp. Instead I said, "I don't care what people say; I'll run with you," and I started to make a good dash for it. I thought I was going to meet with appreciation, but little Geetha came up to me and said, "You are not supposed to step on the lines." There was no "Thank you," there was no "Well done," so I had to do it all over again. This is the way you show love for children.

We usually conclude our visit to Santa Rosa by dropping in at an ice cream parlor. Little Geetha has just learned to read, and she was looking at the big board and asking, "What are all those flavors?"

I said, "There are many there."

She tried to read a few, and then she said, "What is that long word I can't read?"

I said, "Pistachio."

"That's my flavor." So she got that, double dip, and Meera got butter brickle. They wanted to nurse their ice cream cones all the way back to Ramagiri. I was in the back seat again with both of them on either side, and such is their love for each other that every now and then they would exchange licks across my lap. It was dripping all along. I do not like suits being spoiled by pistachio and butter-brickle drips, and my first impulse was to say, "Stop dripping all over me." Instead, I again tried to look at the situation from their point of view. For them it is not clothes that are important; it is their ice cream. I could see they were cone-conscious, and so I let them drip all the way home.

My mother, watching all this, was very happy that I still have not forgotten how to be tender to my own family. I learned how to be tender from my mother and from my Grandmother, because they were able to show great tenderness to me. It is in this way that we find our freedom, by being tender and unselfish and putting up with innumerable discomforts for the sake of adding to the joy of the members of our family, and then gradually extending our love to include our friends, our community, our country, and our world.

Finally we come to *jnānāvasthitacetas,* 'he whose mind has been purified by the knowledge that all life is one.' When we begin to realize the unity of life in all our personal relationships, our mind becomes purified.

ब्रह्मार्पणं ब्रह्म हविर्ब्रह्माग्नौ ब्रह्मणा हुतम् ।
ब्रह्मैव तेन गन्तव्यं ब्रह्मकर्मसमाधिना ॥२४॥

*24. The process of offering is Brahman; that which
is offered is Brahman. Brahman offers the sacrifice in
the fire of Brahman. Brahman is attained by the man
who sees Brahman in every action.*

This is an image taken from an ancient form of ritualistic worship in the orthodox Hindu tradition. In this ritual, called *yajna,* or sacrifice, the sacrificial fire is lighted and butter is poured as an oblation into the fire which represents the Lord. When we live for others in peace, in love, and in wisdom, our life becomes divine, and everything we do becomes an offering unto the Lord.

दैवमेवापरे यज्ञं योगिनः पर्युपासते ।
ब्रह्माग्नावपरे यज्ञं यज्ञेनैवोपजुह्वति ॥२५॥

*25. Some aspirants perform sacrifices to the gods.
Others offer selfless service as sacrifice in the fire of
Brahman.*

There are many ways in which you can make your offering unto the Lord. It is not what you give to the Lord, but the love with which you give that makes your sacrifice acceptable to him. The greatest gift you can give the Lord is yourself, and in order to do this, you must eliminate all your self-will and banish all violence from your life. Let me assure you that when you make this supreme offering to the Lord, it is not the Lord who is getting the bargain. He is not a good businessman. If at any time the Lord says he is prepared to receive you, do not make any terms. Agree on the spot, and he will never desert you.

श्रोत्रादीनीन्द्रयाण्यन्ये सयमाग्निषु जुह्वति ।
शब्दादीन्विषयानन्य इन्द्रियाग्निषु जुह्वति ॥२६॥

*26. Some renounce all enjoyment of the senses and sacrifice them in the fire of sense restraint. Others partake of sense objects, offering them in service through the fire of the senses.*

Here Sri Krishna is distinguishing between two different approaches to the spiritual life. One is the ascetic way, followed by members of the monastic order, and the other is the middle path of moderation to be followed by those of us who live in the world.

We should respect members of the monastic order in all religions because they have turned their backs upon the world in order to lead the spiritual life. While we were in India, we had the privilege of knowing a Hindu monk who had been the head of a great monastery in the Himālayas for many years. He retired from this office in his later years to lead a completely contemplative life. There is nothing in the world to tempt him. His eyes are always fixed on the supreme goal, and he therefore feels no conflicts. He does not envy the man of the world's freedom to go to a movie or drop in at an ice cream parlor; in fact, he probably feels compassion for those of us who still respond to the call of these little delights. For him, these are wrong, but for those of us who live in the world, who follow the householder's path to spiritual awareness, these little pleasures are not wrong. To live the monastic life and turn our back upon the world, and, in a sense, negate our senses and the world, is only one approach to the spiritual life. This path is suitable for a very rare type of person, and we should never deprecate those who follow it. But there is another approach to the spiritual life which is just as challenging, and more suited for the vast majority of us living in the modern world. On this path we live in the world and yet are not of it. For me, this kind of spiritual life is very satisfying. We live in the bosom of our family, as integral members of our society, and yet never forget that the Lord is enthroned in the hearts of all. We live in the midst of life and find our fulfillment not by negating the senses, but by harnessing them in the selfless service of others. Instead of going on fasts, for example, I try to eat good, wholesome food in temperate quantities, not for the satisfaction of my palate, but to strengthen the body so that I can help carry the burdens of those around me. If my body is not strong, I cannot contribute to the welfare of society, and I cannot give the best account of myself in life. Instead of fasting, therefore, I suggest eating moderately. Fasting may not be as easy as feasting, but after a while it is not too different. Both are extremes. It is not hard to go the extreme way, but what is really difficult is neither to fast nor to feast, but to be moderate in everything we do. This is what the Buddha called *Madhyamārga*, the Middle Path—the ideal path for the householder. It requires great artistry and vigilance. Instead of negating the body and senses, we train them to be instruments of selfless service. We harness our physical, mental, and intellectual capacities not to make money or achieve power or fame for ourselves, but to use these faculties with great detachment to make our contribution to life.

सर्वाणीन्द्रियकर्माणि प्राणकर्माणि चापरे ।
आत्मसंयमयोगाग्नौ जुह्वति ज्ञानदीपिते ॥ २७॥
द्रव्ययज्ञास्तपोयज्ञा योगयज्ञास्तथापरे ।
स्वाध्यायज्ञानयज्ञाश्च यतयः संशितव्रताः ॥ २८॥

27. *Some offer the workings of the senses and the vital forces through the fire of self-control, kindled in the path of knowledge.*

*28. Some offer wealth, and some offer sense restraint
and suffering. Some take vows and offer knowledge
and study of the scriptures; and some make the
offering of meditation.*

This word *yajna*, 'offering,' means that everything we do should be
for the welfare of all those around us. There are different ways in
which people make contributions in the Lord's service, and one is
through wealth. Money is not evil; it is love of money that is evil.
The scriptures always emphasize that it is the Lord alone who is to
be loved; everything else is to be used.

We can look to Mahatma Gandhi to see how *yajna* can be applied
in life. His material possessions were worth only two dollars at the
time of his death, yet some of his best friends were very successful
businessmen. He had a group of multimillionaires around him, and
he was often criticized severely for being so close to them. But Gandhi would say that the Lord was present in them also. We should
never forget that the Lord is present not only in the poor but in the
wealthy too, not only in the ignorant but in the learned too.

When Gandhi was on a fast, distinguished doctors from various
parts of the country would come to examine him, sometimes to get
on the front page of the newspapers, and Gandhiji, who was aware
of their motives, would allow himself to be examined carefully and
then say, "My fee is twenty-five rupees." All his faculties, all his
skills, everything was used to raise money for his work. Among the
women of the villages of India, he was particularly successful.
There is a saying in India that a man's best bank is his wife's neck,
and most well-to-do Indian wives have a lot of jewelry, which is
considered to be a good investment. Gandhi would tell these
women, "Your beauty does not depend on diamonds; your beauty
comes from inside. You should reveal this beauty by putting the
welfare of your family, your community, and your country first."
Then he would ask them all, even the little girls, to take off their
gold bangles, and almost everybody present would respond immediately to his call. As long as there are poor people in the world, as
long as there are people who are deprived and handicapped in the

world, if we are sensitive, we will not load ourselves with unnecessary adornment. Again, this is not a plea for poverty but a plea for contented, simple living, in which all the legitimate needs of the body are satisfied. We can use our money, whether we have a lot of it or not, to contribute to selfless work that is aimed at the welfare of all.

Another way of making an offering to the Lord is *tapoyajna.* The word *tapas* has a number of related meanings: suffering, the practice of sense restraint, and heat. In deepening meditation a sense of rising heat, which is the rise of kundalinī, is not unusual. On such occasions, have as much physical exercise as you can. Hard physical labor is the very best use of this rising heat, which becomes an offering unto the Lord when it is given for selfless service.

Now comes the word *yogayajna,* 'the offering of meditation.' People who meditate for long hours in the morning and evening are not doing so for selfish ends. It is a misunderstanding to think that people who meditate are seeking only their own salvation or illumination. What they are seeking is the removal of their selfishness and separateness. Every person who meditates rightly is doing so for all of us. In a home where there is one person, say the granddaughter, meditating regularly, even if the rest of the family does not see eye-to-eye with her, they will share in the spiritual bonus, because she is going to be secure, selfless, and able to put the welfare of those around her first. All of us benefit by living with someone who does not live for himself or herself. We do not need to examine all the pros and cons; we have only to live with such a person, and by some unwritten law, our hearts and our respect gradually go out to him. In an unguarded moment we may say, "I wish I could be like him."

Once a student from the University at Berkeley came to me at our meditation class and said, "I have a roommate who used to be a pain in the neck for a long time. Now I kind of like him, and I'm even beginning to wish I could be like him. I want to see what is happening here to turn him from a person I disliked into a person I want to be like." My comment was, "That's about the best description of meditation I have ever heard."

So if in your home people refer to your meditation by saying, "Oh, he is still out on that Indian trip," do not get agitated or try to defend yourself. There is no need to defend yourself; when you are meditating you have got a good defense lawyer in the Lord, who not only knows the law but wrote it. At first it is only natural that people will have misgivings about your moving away from the normal ways of life. But if you can show by your life that you are becoming less selfish, less self-willed, and increasingly able to love others, it is only a matter of time before everybody will benefit from your meditation.

In order to live the spiritual life, therefore, we can all follow this concept of *yajna,* which means we should give some of our time, our talent, our resources, our wealth, our skill, and our love to everyone around us. The more we give to those around us, the more we shall have to give. It is not the person who has much who is rich; it is the person who gives much. In other words, Srí Krishna is telling us through Arjuna that there are many, many ways in which we can worship the Lord who is in every one of us.

अपाने जुह्वति प्राणं प्राणेऽपानं तथापरे ।
प्राणापानगती रुद्ध्वा प्राणायामपरायणाः ॥ २९ ॥

*29. Some offer the forces of vitality, regulating*
*their inhalation and exhalation, and thus gain control*
*over these forces.*

The word used here is *prāna,* which has a number of meanings. Most generally it means vitality, or to use a colloquialism, that which makes us tick. *Prāna* can also be translated as our immense capacity to desire, which is closely related to our capacity to love.

Another meaning of the word *prāna* is breath. In certain schools of meditation breathing exercises are prescribed to control the mind. I lose no opportunity to caution everyone not to take to these breathing exercises, because they can be dangerous. This is especially the case in our modern times, as our way of life is so artificial, so divorced from the natural rhythm of life, and these exercises require pure living conditions, which are rarely found anywhere these days. Such exercises must be done under the close supervision of a teacher who is thoroughly familiar with all the turns and twists we may come across on this particular path. Some of the occult exercises are so powerful that they can split a personality in two.

The very best practice for improving the breathing rhythm is to go for a long, hard, fast walk repeating *Jesus, Jesus, Jesus* or *Rāma, Rāma, Rāma.* The rhythm of breathing, coupled with the rhythm of the footstep, will blend with the rhythm of the mantram to calm the mind. In the deeper stages of meditation, as our concentration increases, breathing can become so slow that it can drop from sixteen times per minute to eight. Do not pay any attention to this; the more attention you pay to the breathing rhythm, the more difficult it is for it to slow down. When you are meditating sincerely, the great day will come when breathing is suspended for two or three minutes. At the time, you may not be aware of it at all. But afterwards you feel such relaxation in the nervous system, such a quiet knowledge that things are going well on your spiritual path, that you will long more and more to recapture this spell when breathing has been momentarily suspended.

People who are very forgiving, who do not easily get agitated by dwelling upon themselves and can return goodwill for ill will, love for hatred, usually have long breathing rhythms. The agitated, resentful person, who is ready to take offense any time at anything, is the one who breathes fast and irregularly. Any provocation can throw his breathing out of gear. This disruption cannot help but affect physical well-being, and in many forms of physical illness, emotional stress is very much responsible. For example, asthma and many more serious ailments are often emotional in origin. As our meditation deepens, our concentration increases, and our breathing rhythm slows down, we shall find the answer to many of our physical problems. In order to facilitate this slowing of the breathing rhythm, it is helpful to have regular walks every day repeating the mantram.

अपरे नियताहाराः प्राणान्प्राणेषु जुह्वति ।
सर्वेऽप्येते यज्ञविदो यज्ञक्षपितकल्मषाः ॥३०॥

*30. Some offer the forces of vitality through restraint
of their senses. All these understand the meaning of
service and will be cleansed of their impurities.*

The purification of the body is an essential step on the spiritual
path. If we want to discover our real identity, to realize that all life
is one and live in harmony with this unity, we must have a body that
is healthy and strong, one which will never fail in the selfless service
of others. This gives us a deep motive for exercising discriminating
restraint over the senses. For example, we should not eat things
simply because they look or taste good. The proper function of food
is to have food value, and we should take care to eat only what is
nourishing. It is not good to dwell on food, either. The gourmet
who is constantly looking for new ways to stimulate the palate will
become more and more trapped on the physical level. After we
have taken reasonable care to see that we get the right food, served
with love, we should then forget about it and leave it to the digestive
system to do the rest. There is no need to talk about it; there is no
need to ask, "When are we going to have another meal like this?"
In this way, instead of being used by the senses and wasting our vital capacity on petty sensory pleasures, we must train the senses to
be obedient servants. In recalling our desires from the wasteful sensory channels into which they are now flowing, we unify our capacity to desire. Then we can direct this unified love and energy towards the supreme goal.

यज्ञशिष्टामृतभुजो यान्ति ब्रह्म सनातनम् ।
नायं लोकोऽस्त्ययज्ञस्य कुतोऽन्यः कुरुसत्तम ॥३१॥

*31. True sustenance is in service, and through it
a man or woman reaches the eternal Brahman. But
those who do not seek to serve are without a home
in this world. How can they be at home in any
world to come, Arjuna?*

It is in making others happy that we find our happiness, and it is in serving others that we become fulfilled. If we pursue only our own private satisfaction, even in this world we are likely to be completely frustrated and insecure. In other words, even if we do not meditate, even if we do not follow the spiritual path, we cannot help finding that when we forget ourselves we are happy, and when we dwell upon ourselves we are miserable. The egocentric person is not only cut off from the mystical experience; he is also unable to enjoy the world. The selfless person enjoys life to the fullest, because he is always free.

एवं बहुविधा यज्ञा वितता ब्रह्मणो मुखे ।
कर्मजान्विद्धि तान्सर्वानेवं ज्ञात्वा विमोक्ष्यसे ॥३२॥
श्रेयान्द्रव्यमयाद्यज्ञाज्ज्ञानयज्ञः परंतप ।
सर्वं कर्माखिलं पार्थ ज्ञाने परिसमाप्यते ॥३३॥

*32. These offerings are born of work, and each guides man along a path to Brahman. Understanding this, you will attain liberation.*
*33. The offering of wisdom is better than any material offering, Arjuna. For the goal of all work is spiritual wisdom.*

The concept of *yajna* is now brought to its consummation. The Lord says that it is good to give our money, material possessions, time, and energy to a worthy cause that seeks the general welfare. It is good for us to give, if necessary by reducing our style of living to simple comfort. This does not mean that we must sacrifice minimum comforts, but most of us can work long and hard enough to be able to give part of our time and earnings to a great cause. To be able to work for others without thought of a paycheck can bring joy to everyone. As long as we have been working just for pay, calculating how much we are making per hour, we cannot realize that working for a selfless cause can give more satisfaction than the pay envelope we bring home. This does not mean that we must give up our jobs; all of us have to maintain ourselves and our families. But over and above this it is necessary for all of us, in our own interest and in the interest of the general welfare, to give part of our time, talent, and money to a selfless cause.

But even though all these offerings are very important, the Lord will not be fully content with only these gifts. The greatest sacrifice is *jñānayajna*, the offering of wisdom. The greatest gift we can give the Lord is the sharing of spiritual wisdom with others. Helping others to find the Lord of Love hidden in their own heart is the greatest *yajna*. The Lord says here, "I want you to be united with Me, to realize that I live in every living thing, that all life is one."

All actions must eventually lead us to this knowledge of the unity of life. Even the mistakes we make will force us gradually, through increasing suffering, to go forward on the spiritual path. The Lord does not want us to suffer, but suffering is the only way he can keep us from going further and further away from him. We can all save ourselves a great deal of pain by the simple method of learning to respect other people's needs more than our own. We may ask, "How do I know other people's needs? I am not psychology-oriented. I am not a very good observer." The Buddha's answer to this is simple: "What hurts you hurts others." We do not have to read books about other people's needs. We do not have to go to the university or read Sanskrit or study Pānini's[2] grammar. All we must do is remember that what hurts us hurts our father, what pains us pains our mother, what annoys us annoys our children, and what irritates us irritates our friends. All the psychology we need to know is contained in this: "Others and I are one." We can understand everybody's needs just by looking at our own, and we can realize the unity underlying all life by resolving: "Even if I have to inconvenience myself, even if I have to lead an uncomfortable life, may I be given the strength, wisdom, and humility never to contribute to the suffering of anyone on earth." This is the supreme *yajna* which the Lord asks everyone to make.

2. Fourth-century B.C. grammarian who constructed a complete description of the Sanskrit language; author of the primary text on Sanskrit grammar.

तद्विद्धि प्रणिपातेन परिप्रश्नेन सेवया ।
उपदेक्ष्यन्ति ते ज्ञानं ज्ञानिनस्तत्त्वदर्शिनः ॥३४॥

*34. You should approach someone who has
realized the purpose of life, and question him with
reverence and devotion. He will instruct you in
this wisdom.*

In this and the following verses, Sri Krishna uses the word *jnāna*
again and again. *Jnāna* means 'knowing' in the sense in which
Socrates used it, that is, knowing oneself. We all have an amusing
idea of knowledge. We can answer any question about Shakespeare,
about Milton, or even about *Beowulf,* but if someone asks us who
we are, we say, "How do I know?" This is the strange paradox that
all the great spiritual teachers point out: what is the use of knowing
everything else on earth if we don't know who the knower is? We
are born, we go to school, we get married, beget children, buy and
sell, and pass away without knowing who we are. It is an appalling
commentary on our concept of knowledge. In knowing ourselves
we fulfill the supreme purpose of life; when we know ourselves, we
know all life is one, and we have the desire and the will to live in
harmony with this knowledge.

Spiritual awareness is really not taught; it is caught. This is a
beautiful way of saying that when we love someone who lives without any thought of his own personal satisfaction, who devotes all
his energy, love, and wisdom to help those around him find wisdom,
we absorb, through our deep love for him, something of his spiritual
awareness. Constant association with people who are spiritually advanced supports us by a process of absorption.

In English poetry, Edmund Spenser, the author of the *Faerie
Queene,* is often called the poet's poet because he has inspired so
many poets. I sometimes feel tempted to call Sri Ramana Maharshi
the saint's saint because he has inspired so many saints. That is the
kind of saint who takes my breath away. It is said also of Mahatma
Gandhi that his glory lay in transforming little people into heroes.
We go into the presence of a great mystic, look at him, listen to him,

open our hearts to him, and even those of us who are clay are transmuted into gold.

The small quantity of spiritual awareness that has come to me is through my deep love for my Grandmother, my spiritual teacher, who, without knowing how to read or write, is the most educated person I have ever known.

When I was a student at college, every weekend some students would have a holiday by going boating; but my idea of a holiday was to make for my village, about fifty miles from the college, to be reunited with my Grandmother. It became quite a standing joke on the campus; everyone would say, "He has gone to see his Grandmother." Slowly, however, they began to see, even in this simple gesture, how intensely I yearned to be with her, and how intensely I felt the deprivation of being away from her. I used to go by train to the little town close to my village. On one Saturday morning I didn't have a penny, but I had to go. I had such faith that I went to the railway station where the train was waiting. The guard of the train was watching me rather curiously because I looked so wistful. He asked me where I was going, and I said, "I want to go and see my Granny." He suppressed a smile and told the driver that there was a boy who wanted to go and see his Granny. Then he asked, "Where does your Granny live?"

"Near Palghat."

"Have you got a ticket?"

"That's the problem. I don't have any money."

Touched, he said, "Hop into my compartment. Don't tell anybody. Don't put it in your college magazine or I'll lose my job. Just jump in here." And he told the driver, "We have to take him to see his Granny."

There was such love in my eyes and such eagerness that even a railway guard, who sometimes can be pretty tough, was prepared to go out of his way and put me into his compartment. He let me out at Palghat and said, "Now run!"

From Palghat to my village it was seven miles of beautiful road with big trees on either side, sometimes with monkeys swinging from them. I used to enjoy walking along it, but more than the monkeys, and more than the trees, and more than the brooks, what gave me joy was the knowledge that every step would bring me closer to my Granny. At that time I didn't know she was my spiritual teacher; she was just my Grandmother. When I arrived home, she would hold my hands and look and look at me; she didn't need words. The first question she would ask me was, "What did you learn this week?" This gave me just the opportunity I had been waiting for. I would put my hands behind my back and say, "Now, Granny, listen carefully. This week the professor who teaches me logic has taught me what a syllogism is." She used to gasp with admiration. "Syllogism!" Then, like most scholars, I would indulge in academic jargon to my heart's content. Today I use very simple language; my standard is that what I say must be completely understandable to the garbage collector as well as the graduate student. If I were to consult some of my old academic colleagues on this, they would say I have become simplistic. I really thought my Granny was simplistic, though I didn't dare call her so. With the childlike simplicity of the spiritual woman, she would say, "Now, son, give me an example of this great learning that you have absorbed." So I would quote my logic professor and say, "All men are mortal. I am a man. Therefore, *ergo*, I am mortal." She just laughed and laughed and said, "I pay all this money so that you can learn this trash?" Then this unlettered, untutored woman stated the syllogism perfectly: "All men, all creatures, are immortal because the Lord lives in them. I am a creature. Therefore I am immortal."

The secret of absorbing such spiritual wisdom is to open our hearts wide and give all our love to our spiritual teacher, who symbolizes our Ātman for the present. When I would run home to see my Granny, I did not know I had an Ātman. Now that I look back I see that my Grandmother was my Ātman. That is why I loved her; she was my real 'me,' my perfect 'me,' my pure 'me.' I didn't know this intellectually, but deep inside, from the very depths of my heart, a little voice was saying, "That's you." This is what happens to us when we see a great saint like Sri Ramana Maharshi. People whose hearts are not open, who have the window of their consciousness bolted and barred, look and see only a dapper, brown little man in a dhoti. But those whose hearts have opened, who are searching for the answer to the riddle of life and have flung the doors of their consciousness wide open, have only to see Sri Ramana Maharshi seated quietly before them to hear that little voice within them say in its sweet tones, "That's you." Beautiful hymns have been composed to Sri Ramana Maharshi, great singers and poets have described his beauty. But he will quietly say, "There is no Ramana Maharshi here. There is nobody here. It's all empty. I am just an empty keyhole." You apply your eye closely and look through this empty keyhole, and in the dim distance, you see the immense glory of the Lord flaming up against the background of the cosmos.

It is by this process of osmosis that spiritual awareness really comes to all of us. Books can never give spiritual awareness; it is only by seeing someone who has become united with the Lord through His grace that ordinary people like you and me can learn to discover our real Self.

यज्ज्ञात्वा न पुनर्मोहमेवं यास्यसि पाण्डव ।
येन भूतान्यशेषेण द्रक्ष्यस्यात्मन्यथो मयि ॥३५॥

*35. Arjuna, having attained this wisdom you will never again be deluded. You will see yourself in all creatures, and all creatures in Me.*

Once we wake up through the grace of the Lord from the long, lurid dream of multiplicity and separateness into the indivisible unity that pervades all life, we will never fall asleep again. Once we have awakened into this higher state of consciousness in which we see all as coming from God, subsisting in God, and returning to God, we cannot fall back again into the old dream of separateness. This is a significant verse because some people—great writers and artists, for example—have had an occasional flash in which they see the unity behind life for just a moment. Although they treasure the memory of this experience, they fall asleep again; they are caught again in the dream. Just as among dreams there are a few significant ones which strengthen us inwardly, so in this waking dream we may have an occasional insight into Reality, but we have no control over these experiences. Waking up permanently into a higher level of consciousness comes as the result of sustained sādhana. We can become established in the unitive state only through long and systematic discipline. These occasional flashes of mystical experience are only indications of a latent capacity which must be cultivated through the practice of meditation and ancillary disciplines if we are finally to wake up completely, never to fall asleep or dream again.

The word *moha,* 'delusion,' is used by Sri Krishna to tell us we are under a kind of hypnotic spell. We are all running after what we have been hypnotized to believe we want. We are told to go after money, and we start looking for money everywhere. We don't want to know who we are because we are only looking for money. Some people even seem to have a dollar sign printed on their pupils; wherever they look they see possibilities for making money. They see a beautiful landscape and say, "Ah, what a nice subdivision this would make." They go to a mountain top and see it as a good place for a motel. The same applies to pleasure. We are told to give our senses free rein by the mass media. The senses are wild horses that we can train to respond to the slightest move of our fingers. But if we do not train them, if we leave these wild horses to themselves, they will not know where to go; they will plunge headlong across moor and mountain, into morass and quagmire. We should never follow the siren call of sense-pleasures which seems to tell us, "We will give you joy; we will give you security; we will give you fulfillment." These promises are phantoms that will lead us further and further away from joy, from security, and from fulfillment.

As we progress on the spiritual path and awake from the confusion of separateness and self-will, we will begin to see the unity of life. We will begin to see the Lord in all. Even to be able to love a dog, we have to be spiritual. It is not enough if we buy a dog, get a collar, and call him Fido. The other day we saw a beautiful Newfoundland retriever in a car. He looked exactly like a small bear, occupying the whole front seat. The family who owned the dog must have been traveling throughout the night, because I could see from the bleary eyes of the dog that he hadn't slept. His eyes re-

minded me of a scholar who has been poring over his books through
the night; if he had been a human being he might have said, "I
didn't have a wink of sleep; I was up all night writing a paper on the
tragedies of Shakespeare." Instead he was trying to jump out of the
car. I understand dogs very well, because I love them very much. I
patted him and tried to clean his eyes a little, and he almost told me,
"You know, I don't like being cooped up in automobiles. One
whole night I've been traveling. All I want is to jump out and run
and run and run." His eyes kept saying, "Run, run, run," and in
one moment he gave a leap and was out of the car. People thought
he was a bear, and they were all running helter-skelter when his
master, who would say he loves dogs, came and issued an order,
"Get in!" He expected the dog to stand up and salute. The poor dog
was trying to say, "All I want is a long, long run on the beach. Take
me for a run, and then put me back in the car." But there was one
little boy we saw who really loved his dog. The dog was running on
the beach wherever he wanted, and the boy was telling the dog,
"I will follow you wherever you want to go." The dog darted into
the water, and the boy followed him into the water; then the dog
jumped out of the water and onto a rock, and the boy followed him
onto the rock. The boy was putting the dog first.

In every relationship this is the secret of love. If I love you it
means only one thing: that your happiness is more important to me
than my own. This kind of love will give me the wisdom, the sensitiveness, and the will to conduct myself selflessly.

अपि चेदसि पापेभ्यः सर्वेभ्यः पापकृत्तमः ।
सर्वं ज्ञानप्लवेनैव वृजिनं संतरिष्यसि ॥३६॥

*36. Even if you were the most sinful of all sinners,
you could cross beyond all sin by the raft of spiritual
wisdom.*

Spiritual wisdom, or *jnāna,* which is developed through the practice
of meditation, can do what nothing else can do; it is a boat that can
take you across the stormy, treacherous sea of life. Sri Krishna says

this *jnāna* enables you to pick up two planks, discrimination and dispassion, tie them together, sit on them, and paddle with your hands until you reach the other shore of abiding joy, peace, and love.

The Compassionate Buddha was very fond of representing himself as a boatman offering to take us to the other shore that is nirvāna. We usually tell ourselves he is misleading us; we like to be on this shore quarreling, manipulating, and being separate. The thought of going across to the other shore, where there are no quarrels, makes us wonder what we would do there.

Sri Krishna too says, in a magnificent verse in the invocation to the Bhagavad Gita, that he is *kaivartakah keshavah,* the boatman who will ferry us across the river of life to the other shore. We, however, prefer this shore. We don't want to begin the journey towards peace and security; the mind keeps us on this shore visiting different ports here and there. In almost every port we have a love: food, money, clothes, all kinds of exotic things to add to our collection. But in moving away from this coast to the other, we must throw all these attachments overboard.

The grace of the Lord is like a wind that is blowing all the time, but it is our responsibility to get rid of our excess luggage and set the sail correctly. For a long, long time in meditation we are merely bailing out the boat and throwing things overboard. Everybody has an antique shop right in his basement: over the years we have collected all sorts of things, this one because it was on sale, that one because we couldn't resist it. Some of the great mystics started, as you and I did, by throwing out things they had become tired of. This is how renunciation begins, by getting rid of things to which we are not very attached. If I have two sets of the *Encyclopaedia Britannica,* I can give you one. We shouldn't blame ourselves for beginning this way, for renunciation grows slowly with renunciation.

The second stage is harder; then we begin to throw away some of the things to which we are attached. There is a tussle, an inner conflict; to throw or not to throw is the question, but out it goes. But in the final stages, when we see the lights on the other shore, when we see Jesus walking about, the Buddha meditating, and Sri Krishna playing on the flute, all we want is to get where the action is. At that time, even selfish people like you and me, who have committed many mistakes in their ignorance, want to get there so fast that they take hold of everything—their glasses, the shirt on their back, even the sail and rudder—and start throwing it all overboard. The spiritual teacher will say at that time, "Don't throw your glasses away; you won't be able to see Sri Krishna!" In the final stages, the great difficulty is to persuade people to keep a few things, to keep their body fit and their intellect active to serve the Lord.

After reaching the other shore, to come back and take other people in your boat seems heartbreaking. When you have reached the shore of bliss and then come back, you see wars, famines, pestilence, and selfishness. You come back, as the Bible puts it, to the "valley of the shadow of death," which takes a lot of renunciation. Sri Ramakrishna uses language which no other mystic has ever used to describe this. He calls it a soccer match. India is a poor country, and many of the fellows who really want to see a soccer match do not have the money to buy a ticket. But they have acrobatic skills, so they say to their friends, "Let's stand on each other's shoulders and have the fellow on the top, who can see over the bamboo fence, describe the game kick for kick, pass for pass, goal for goal." With great effort, one of them finally gets to the top and sees the game. The whole team is playing as one; each team is putting the other one first. Who can lose? He gets so excited and so drawn in that he forgets his friends and throws himself over the fence. But a great mystic like Sri Ramakrishna, even though he sees the game and wants to jump in, thinks of all the poor people outside in life, so caught up in strife, so utterly miserable, and he denies himself the game. He jumps backwards, goes and gets us, and stands on the bottom so that we can get up on his shoulders and watch the game too. This is what Jesus is doing, what the Buddha is doing, standing and allowing anyone who wants to climb upon their shoulders and see the game. Great saints like Sri Ramakrishna, Sri Ramana Maharshi, St. Francis of Assisi, Meister Eckhart, and St. John of the Cross have come and told us what the game is like. The Gita now asks us, "Don't you too want to see this game where all become one, and to understand the game of *līlā,* the divine play called life?"

यथैधांसि समिद्धोऽग्निर्भस्मसात्कुरुतेऽर्जुन ।
ज्ञानाग्निः सर्वकर्माणि भस्मसात्कुरुते तथा ॥३७॥
न हि ज्ञानेन सदृशं पवित्रमिह विद्यते ।
तत्स्वयं योगसंसिद्धः कालेनात्मनि विन्दति ॥३८॥

*37. O Arjuna, even as the heat of a fire reduces wood to ashes, the fire of knowledge turns to ashes all selfish attachment to work.*
*38. Nothing in this world purifies like spiritual wisdom. It is the perfection achieved in time through the path of yoga, the path which leads to the Self within.*

Sri Krishna says that even if in the past we have lived selfishly, often trying to snatch our happiness at the expense of others, *jnāna* or spiritual wisdom will reduce our big funeral pyre of unfavorable karma to ashes. Do not be despondent over the past. Do not let it become oppressive. All the past, with all its mistakes, will fall away from us if we turn our eyes to the Lord with a one-pointed mind and travel untiringly towards the spiritual goal. This is the Lord's promise given to us by the Gita.

In order to develop *jnāna,* I know of no other discipline than the practice of meditation. In all religions, meditation—sometimes called contemplation or interior prayer—is emphasized by the great mystics as the path, the ladder of love, leading to the Lord. There are many allied disciplines, too, that accompany the practice of meditation, such as the discriminating restraint of the senses and the constant attempt to put the welfare of those around us first. One of the remarkable developments in meditation is that even if we take to meditation without any desire to practice these related disciplines, after a while we will be drawn to them. I used to have a friend who was allergic to my talk on vegetarianism. In an attempt to initiate me into the delights of eating my fellow creatures, he actually took me for dinner to a number of restaurants. He was meditating regularly, but every time I would talk about not wanting to eat my friends, he would say, "This doesn't apply to me. I am going to show you that it is possible to progress in meditation without changes in diet." I didn't argue with him, which disappointed him; but after a year of meditation, he began to have a distaste for nonvegetarian food.

If we are practicing meditation regularly with sustained enthusiasm, this development is likely to take place. As meditation dispels the delusion of separateness, we become more and more conscious of a sense of fellowship with all creatures. The other day, while going to the beach, I was delighted to see the young lambs, some black-faced, some white-faced, running about on the green hills just like children. When we got to the beach, I enjoyed watching the sea gulls and those little creatures that I love so much, the sandpipers, who are like the imp Ariel in Shakespeare's *Tempest*. They go up to the very edge of the water, and when a wave rolls in, they come running back on their thin little legs. We also saw three deer, a mother and two fawns, which had come down onto the beach. The people living nearby must have been very good to these deer for them to have such confidence; they were playing about, sure that the people loved them and wouldn't harm them in any way.

As meditation deepens, our spiritual awareness should show itself in the capacity to understand the point of view of other creatures. Ecology is beginning to teach us that even in our relationships with plants and trees, we must be careful lest we exploit them thoughtlessly. Mahatma Gandhi was so aware of this relationship that he did not even like flowers to be plucked. He said a flower is most beautiful when it is on the bush. In India we have a hoary custom of garlanding people with heavy strings of flowers. Gandhi was constantly subjected to this garlanding, but when he became aware of his kinship with plants and trees, he told everyone that he would accept only garlands of homespun yarn made by the person offering the garland. This considerably reduced garlanding.

But while it is good to be friendly with trees and animals, it is most important to be friendly with human beings. It is most of all in our human relationships that we realize the unity of life. Trees don't talk back. Animals don't say, "Now you listen to me." This give-and-take is the joy of the human situation. Wherever we go and say, "Now you listen to me," the other person will say, "You first listen to me." Where we find the you-first-listen-to-me attitude, there is the opportunity for patience. If there weren't impatient people around us, how would we learn patience? I once asked my Grand-mother, my spiritual teacher, why there should be people to scold me, criticize me, attack me. Her reply was, "How else can you learn patience?" Left to ourselves we find it quite pleasant to say "Quiet!" and prevent others from talking. People who are not used to hear-ing no can become insufferable. When we purify ourselves by learn-ing to be patient, by learning to forbear, we come at last to see the Lord hidden in our own and everyone's heart.

श्रद्धावाँल्लभते ज्ञानं तत्परः संयतेन्द्रियः ।
ज्ञानं लब्ध्वा परां शान्तिमचिरेणाधिगच्छति ॥ ३९॥
अज्ञश्चाश्रद्दधानश्च संशयात्मा विनश्यति ।
नायं लोकोऽस्ति न परो न सुखं संशयात्मनः ॥ ४०॥

*39. The man or woman who has spiritual wisdom*
*as the highest goal, whose faith is deep and who*
*restrains the senses, attains that wisdom quickly and*
*enters into perfect peace.*
*40. But the ignorant, who are indecisive and without*
*faith, waste their life. They can never be happy in*
*this world or any other.*

If I haven't come to have faith in the Lord within, who is my real Self, how can I be secure? How can I be at peace? How can I live for others or be loved by others? Here "faith," or *shraddhā* in San-skrit, does not mean mere blind faith, but a deep belief based on personal experience. When we lead the spiritual life, we will begin to see an inner power guiding and protecting us in even the most difficult situations. When we experience this over and over again,

we come to have a deep faith or *shraddhā* in the Lord within. It is
not enough if we have blind faith in spiritual ideals, based on the
testimony of the scriptures or sages. We must realize these truths for
ourselves, in our own life and consciousness. As the Buddha was
fond of saying, the spiritual teacher only points the way; we must
do our own traveling. The personal experience of others may plant
the seed of *shraddhā* in our hearts, inspiring us to lead the spiritual
life, but *shraddhā* can develop fully only if we experience these
truths for ourselves.

While in South Africa, Gandhi made many friends among the
people of the Christian community. One of these acquaintances
tried to convert Gandhi to Christianity by assuring him that if he
only had faith in Jesus he would be saved in spite of all his sins.
Gandhi replied, "I do not seek redemption from the consequences
of my sin. I seek to be redeemed from sin itself, or rather from the
very thought of sin."

Without using the words *religion* or *Lord,* we can comment on
this verse by recalling the famous inquiry of Sri Ramana Maharshi,
*Who am I?* The whole purpose of spiritual discipline is to discover
who we are. In the supreme climax of meditation called samādhi, I
discover that there is no separate me, no separate you, that all of us
are governed by the underlying unity that is divine. On making this
discovery, the rest of our life becomes an earnest endeavor to live in
harmony with this unity, never inflicting suffering upon any creature but contributing to the best of our capacity to the progress of
those around us.

Sri Krishna emphasizes that until and unless we come to have at
least a dim awareness of the Lord within—which is what he calls
*shraddhā,* faith in oneself, faith in the unity of life, faith that the
Lord is present in all—it is not possible to live in peace. Violence, in
whatever form we see it, is a negation of this central unity. Any attempt at violence can only move people further and further apart.
In every home and community there are likely to be occasional differences, occasions when someone may make a mistake. But the
home or community can be held together if we believe in this underlying unity and act upon it.

योगसंन्यस्तकर्माणं ज्ञानसंछिन्नसंशयम् ।
आत्मवन्तं न कर्माणि निबध्नन्ति धनंजय ॥४१॥

*41. O Dhananjaya, the man or woman who is*
*established in the Self, who has renounced selfish*
*attachments in work and cut through doubts*
*with spiritual wisdom, acts in freedom.*

It is only after we have dehypnotized ourselves from the enticements
of money and the blandishments of pleasure that we find how good
it is to work when there is no paycheck coming. It is so soothing to
work hard for the welfare of those around us without a mercenary
motive that we forget all our tensions and frustrations. Some of us
may contribute our time; for others it may be energy or skills. For
still others it may be material possessions, or expert advice. But it is
incumbent upon everyone to devote part of his or her resources to
the welfare of others without any thought of personal profit or
prestige.

Whatever we contribute to the welfare of others without a
thought for our own profit or advancement is an offering made unto
the Lord. On a poignant occasion, Jesus took his disciples to task by
saying: "I was thirsty, and you gave me no drink; I was a stranger,
and you took me not in; naked, and you clothed me not; sick, and
in prison, and you visited me not."

And the disciples perhaps answered him, "We never saw you
hungry; we never had any occasion to quench your thirst."

Then Jesus really hit hard in answer: "Inasmuch as you did it
not to one of the least of these, you did it not to me."

When people agitate us, it is often their way of asking for help.
Anger is often a cry for help, and when we immediately get angry in
return, we are actually pushing away a person who is half paralyzed.
When someone is angry, the very best help we can render him or
her is to be patient. The first time we do this the other person may
actually take advantage of it, thinking, "Here is somebody who is
very patient. I want a suitable outlet for my anger, and here is a
godsend, just waiting for me to let him have it." But we cannot im-

prove the situation by returning anger for anger. This does not
mean that we simply let the other person have his way, but that we
patiently help him to see that his anger and self-will are not only
harmful to others but to himself as well.

तस्मादज्ञानसंभूतं हृत्स्थं ज्ञानासिनात्मनः ।
छित्त्वैनं संशयं योगमातिष्ठोत्तिष्ठ भारत ॥४२॥

*42. O Bhārata, out through this doubt in your
heart with the sword of spiritual wisdom. Arise; take
up the path of yoga!*

Yoga is neither belief, nor dogma, nor metaphysics, nor philosophy.
It is a method of union, a way of uniting all that is divided in our
consciousness, uniting all life into the Divine Ground which is one.
Yoga has very little to do with physical postures; the correct word
for them is *āsana*. We find all kinds of misuses of the word *yoga* in
newspapers, magazines, and books, but in the Hindu scriptures
*yoga* refers to the method, the spiritual disciplines, used to unify our
consciousness so that we can come to love the Lord within.

Sri Krishna gives us a secret useful in daily life when he says we
should be free from doubts. Most of us are plagued by doubts:
"Does she love me? Sometimes I think so, but maybe she doesn't."
She is also thinking the same thing. My Grandmother had a severe
statement to make about this kind of misgiving. She would say that
we doubt whether others love us because our own love is divided.
Wherever we have some reservation or division within ourselves,
we look at others through it and immediately say, "He isn't loving
me enough." The whole secret of love is not to ask how much others
love us but to keep on loving—as St. Francis would say, more than
we can. The more we try to love, the more we will be able to love.
The passage of time should enrich our love: the person who loves
at sixteen should be able to love much more at thirty. It is possible
for all of us to deepen our capacity to love by constantly trying to
put the welfare of those around us first, until we are finally able to
love the Lord in everyone around us.

When we begin to practice meditation, too, it is not unnatural for us to have some doubts and misgivings about the timeless truths of the spiritual life. We all accept the infallibility of physical laws, but when it comes to spiritual laws we are not quite sure. We all believe in the law of gravity, but we sometimes ignore the law of karma. The spiritual teacher does not say that physical laws do not work; he says that spiritual laws, however, are also valid. The charge of fanaticism should really be leveled at the worldly person, because it is he who says, "Only the physical world is real. I only believe in what I see with my eyes, hear with my ears." But we have the personal testimony of those who have rebuilt their lives on these timeless truths that they are not only real, but accessible to all. Gandhi, who practiced complete nonviolence in thought, word, and deed, said, "I have not the shadow of a doubt that any man or woman can achieve what I have, if he or she would make the same effort and cultivate the same hope and faith." Gandhi, who always claimed he had no more than ordinary capacities, is proof that these spiritual laws do work, and that by obeying them we can transform our character and consciousness. Gandhi belongs to our own century and faced many of the problems we ourselves are facing today, and even though physically dead, he still continues to give new direction to our civilization.

Even when we do come to believe in the validity of spiritual laws, we may still doubt our capacity to reach the goal by following all the drastic disciplines of meditation and sādhana. It is natural that this doubt continue to haunt us for a long time, but as we go deeper and deeper into our consciousness through the practice of meditation, this doubt also will disappear when our desires are completely unified. What is most urgent is that we start now without allowing our purpose to be weakened by doubts and misgivings, and follow with resolute enthusiasm the path recommended by the Gita.

Sri Ramakrishna used to say that if you repeat *Gita, Gita, Gita* it becomes *tagi, tagi, tagi,* which means 'one who has renounced.' The Gita does not ask us to renounce our family or the world, but to renounce our self-will and separateness, which are the only barriers between us and the Lord of Love enshrined in our hearts. The

English word "renounce" strikes a cold note, but the Sanskrit word *tyāga* implies a positive, joyful act in which we find fulfillment. In the words of Jesus, we have to lose ourselves to find ourselves.

When Gandhi was asked to sum up the secret of his life in three words, he quoted the opening of the Īshā Upanishad: *Tena tyaktena bhunjithah,* "Renounce and enjoy." Only when we renounce all selfish attachment, he meant, can we really enjoy anything in life. I would go farther and say, "Renounce and rejoice." When we renounce our petty, finite ego in living for the welfare of all, we find infinite joy. In self-naughting we gain the joy of self-mastery and the limitless capacity to love others more than we love ourselves.

We can practice this in the midst of our own family if we try to keep the happiness of our parents, partner, children, and friends first in our consciousness, and our own happiness last. The going may be rough, but gradually we will gain the love and respect of everyone in our family and community. In time all those who come in contact with us will benefit by our sādhana and our selfless living.

इति ज्ञानकर्मसंन्यासयोगो नाम चतुर्थोऽध्यायः ॥४॥

# CHAPTER FIVE

# Renounce and Rejoice

अर्जुन उवाच
संन्यासं कर्मणां कृष्ण पुनर्योगं च शंससि ।
यच्छ्रेय एतयोरेकं तन्मे ब्रूहि सुनिश्चितम् ॥१॥

ARJUNA:

*1. O Krishna, you have recommended both the
path of selfless action and also sannyāsa, the path
of renunciation of action. Tell me definitely
which is better.*

In the last chapter, Sri Krishna was talking to Arjuna about *san-nyāsa,* renunciation of action, and karma yoga, performance of action. In particular, he was telling Arjuna that it is by karma yoga, through hard, intense, selfless performance of action, that we reach the unitive state where by our very presence we help those around us and even influence our environment.

Arjuna now shows how representative he is of all of us in his tendency to classify everything into this or that. We can imagine Sri Krishna listening to him with a friendly smile in the same way that we listen to our little children at home when they ask questions which amuse us. For example, the other day little Geetha asked me whether she could tie the laces of my shoes. When I said yes, she asked, "Tight, loose, or medium?" For a first-grader I thought she was commanding a wealthy vocabulary. She is right in the Arjuna line of thinking, but while he talks only about two classes, she had three.

This need to categorize is a characteristic of the intellect; it must divide everything into two. One has to be either good or bad according to the intellect. However, there isn't any person who falls into such categories. Most of us are sometimes good, sometimes bad, and at other times both. Just as there is no human being who cannot show signs of utter selflessness, there is no one among the majority of us who also cannot show signs of utter selfishness.

श्री भगवानुवाच
संन्यासः कर्मयोगश्च निःश्रेयसकरावुभौ ।
तयोस्तु कर्मसंन्यासात्कर्मयोगो विशिष्यते ॥२॥

SRI KRISHNA:

*2. Both renunciation of action and performance of action lead to the supreme goal. But the path of action is better than renunciation.*

It is difficult for us to understand those rare creatures in the history of mysticism who help people around them by their very presence. Sri Ramana Maharshi was one of these. Sometimes when people came to him for help, he would sit reading the newspaper. This is not our usual conception of action: somebody sits rustling his newspaper and helps people. But many who were sore in spirit, or insecure and resentful, having knocked on all other doors, have gone into Sri Ramana Maharshi's presence as a last resort, sat and looked at him, and come out with their burden relieved, with their heart strengthened and their spirit soaring.

A distinguished philosopher once went to Ramana Maharshi's āshram with his pocket bulging with a long series of questions. He wondered whether the sage would have time to answer all his questions in detail. With utter simplicity, not very characteristic of a distinguished philosopher, he tells us how he went in and looked at Sri Ramana Maharshi, kept on looking at him, and found that none of his questions were necessary. This is the best way to answer questions—by making them unnecessary. Remember, too, the story of Jesus; troubled people had only to touch the hem of his garment, and they would find an upsurge of security and strength within.

This is an experience even you and I can have when we go into the presence of someone who has attained the supreme state. When we are with such people, by some strange means of communication they send some of their strength, love, and wisdom into our hearts.

A Westerner once asked Sri Ramana Maharshi why he wasn't leading a productive life. Sri Ramana Maharshi just chuckled. As far as I know, he is one of the few productive figures the world has produced. Because he was always meditating on the unity of life, everyone belonging to the human species has received an unearned bonus. Gandhiji, however, gives us another ideal: that of helping through selfless action. Sri Ramana Maharshi's way of helping is as effective as Mahatma Gandhi's, and both have a legitimate, important place on the spiritual path. It is the same whether we try to help through selfless action or selfless inaction; the whole world will receive the benefit of our contribution.

Arjuna, however, is an intellectually oriented person given to action, and he doesn't understand that there is a place for both selfless action and renunciation of action. Confused, he asks Sri Krishna which path is better: "Now, think clearly, and don't be vague. Can't you put these two ways in the balance and tell me which is faster, safer, and easier? That's the only language I can understand."

Sri Krishna, so loving, so patient, begins from Arjuna's point of view. He says, "It's true. I have placed renunciation of action before you as a great ideal, and I have also placed intense selfless action before you as a great ideal. But since you have an intellectual need for comparison, and an inescapable tendency to weigh one thing against the other, I am prepared to concede that selfless action is better for you than renunciation of action." At present we are not ready to renounce action. Even if we try not to act, even if we take a vow not to act, we will be forced into action. If there is no action physically, action still continues to go on all the time in the mind. The choice, therefore, for you and me is: shall we act selflessly for the benefit of all, or shall we act selfishly for our own personal aggrandizement? Meister Eckhart advises us in glorious words: "To be right, a person must do one of two things; either he must learn to have God in his work and hold fast to him there, or he must give up his work altogether. Since, however, man cannot live without activities that are both human and various, we must learn to keep God in everything we do, and whatever the job or place, keep on with him, letting nothing stand in our way."

In the practice of meditation, particularly as concentration increases, you should see to it that you engage yourself in intense, selfless action during the day. You should ask yourself if you have plenty of opportunity to be with other people. Suppose you have been meditating for a number of years alone in the forest, away from the hurly-burly of life. When you come back to the city and somebody pushes you aside on the sidewalk, not all your meditation in the forest is going to make you smile sweetly and say, "Forgive me for having been in your way." This capacity comes through regular meditation, and by walking on sidewalks where people push and are pushed about. Then you learn that if somebody pushes you, he may be just looking in the shop window and not seeing you. It is only by being with people who are irascible, sometimes because of you, that the angles and corners of your personality are slowly smoothed out. You, of course, are never short-tempered, but you sometimes run into people who are short-tempered, who do not easily understand your point of view. The answer here is to repeat the mantram, become patient, listen respectfully to the other's point of view, and be even more persuasive in presenting your position.

The world has become so difficult, so violent, that no one today can afford to keep quiet. No one can afford to drop out of society or fail to make a contribution. Each one of us can change the whole world by changing himself a little. When, instead of reacting violently, I renounce all violence in action, in word, in thought, and in my relationships with everybody else, I have actually changed my environment. When I can show others love instead of hatred, goodwill instead of ill will, respect instead of criticism, I not only change myself but also those who come in contact with me. In everything I do, every day, I am affecting my environment either favorably or unfavorably. To make this influence completely beneficial, and to enable it to reach as many people as possible, hard, intense, selfless action is a necessity.

In meditation we are going deep into ourselves, into the utter solitude that is within. As a counterbalance to this, it is necessary to be with people: to laugh with them, to sing with them, and to enjoy the healthy activities of life. It is not a luxury on the spiritual path to have hard work, or to have the company of spiritually oriented people; these are necessary for our spiritual development.

ज्ञेयः स नित्यसंन्यासी यो न द्वेष्टि न काङ्क्षति ।
निर्द्वन्द्वो हि महाबाहो सुखं बन्धात्प्रमुच्यते ॥ ३ ॥

*3. Those who have attained perfect renunciation*
*are free from any sense of duality; they are unaffected*
*by likes and dislikes, Arjuna, and are free from the*
*bondage of self-will.*

*Sannyāsī,* 'one who has renounced,' usually refers to a monk who has retired from the world to a monastic order to seek the supreme goal of life. *Sannyāsa* is often misunderstood as renunciation of the world, but for the vast majority of ordinary people like you and me, when the Lord asks us to renounce, he is not asking us to renounce the world. He is asking us to renounce our ego, our self-will, our separateness, which is the main obstacle to spiritual development.

In a story from the spiritual lore of India, the jackfruit is used to bring out the meaning of renunciation or detachment. The jackfruit is a big, burly fruit that grows plentifully in Kerala and Bengal. In Kerala, when we want to know if a household is well-to-do, we ask, "Do they have a lot of jackfruit and mango trees in their back yard?" A back yard groaning with jackfruit and mangoes is the equivalent of a land flowing with milk and honey. None of the jackfruit is wasted; the thorny skin is a delicacy for the cows, the pods are a delicacy for us, and the seeds are used in curry. People in some other parts of India, however, are not usually acquainted with the jackfruit. In Kerala a mischievous boy may ask a guest to eat a piece of it, and after the guest has eaten the fruit and enjoyed it thoroughly, the boy starts asking him all sorts of questions: where he comes from, what his name is, and where he went to school.

When the guest tries to speak he cannot articulate his words, because the jackfruit has a very thick, gluey juice, like cement, and his lips have become glued together. But in Kerala, before we eat the jackfruit, we smear our hands and lips with coconut oil. Then, if I had been the guest, I could have finished eating and started in, "To be or not to be, that is the question"; and I would have been able to continue with the whole soliloquy of Hamlet because the coconut oil would have prevented my lips from being glued together. Sri Ramakrishna in a magnificent simile says that we cannot love God, we cannot put others first or forget ourselves in the welfare of all those around us, because our heart is glued so that not a drop of love can come out of it. Love circulates inside, wanting to flow out; but there is not a pinprick of a hole that is not completely glued up by the fruit of the ego, which is much bigger than the biggest jackfruit to be seen in Kerala. If we want to release our capacity to love all those around us and find the joy of selfless living as members of our family, our community, our society, then we should apply the oil of renunciation and dispassion so that we will not get stuck in the glue of the ego.

It is most important to remember that all of us have this inborn capacity to love. We don't have to go to India or any other place to learn to love. Love is right within us; what prevents us from letting it flow outward to everyone around us, flooding our home and our community with happiness, is the glue of the ego which is so sticky that it hinders any attempt to love.

What is the evidence that we are detaching ourselves from our ego, that we are making our mind serene, that we are going beyond separateness? The word Sri Krishna uses is *nirdvandva:* 'without duality,' free from the pairs of opposites. As long as we see life divided into good and bad, right and wrong, success and defeat, birth and death, as long as we groan under the tyranny of likes and dislikes, always seeking the pleasant and avoiding the unpleasant, so long will our mind be like a sea that is agitated all the time.

Yesterday I happened to remember something my Grandmother did that shows how she could change her likes and dislikes at will. Many years ago, in our village, one of my uncles wanted to marry into a family which his family did not approve of on very legitimate grounds. Seldom in our village did any marriage take place without both families agreeing, and my uncle's choice caused a good deal of agitation. My Granny, who was quite fond of my uncle, told him, "This choice of yours is making all your people unhappy. Tomorrow your wife has got to come and meet them, and she is not going to be happy when they are unhappy." She tried all kinds of persuasive ways to get my uncle to choose another girl and let the girl choose another man, but it was springtime, and all of her persuasion fell on deaf ears. They married, even though everybody in his family showed their disapproval. On the very day when the marriage took place, when all the others were sulking, my Grandmother dropped all her opposition and disapproval and went up to them saying, "You are both meant for each other." She had tried her level best to dissuade my uncle in the interests of the whole family, but when she saw that they wanted each other so much, she immediately dropped her opposition. This is how freedom comes, even in attitudes. There are times when we feel that we should oppose a certain course of action, but when we find there is another side to it, a better side, we should be able to drop our opposition immediately. There are few people capable of this, but through the practice of meditation, we can all develop this capacity to change our likes and dislikes at will.

How to go beyond likes and dislikes in everyday living is an immediate problem. For those of us who are living with our families and friends, and who have wide contacts, I think reducing self-will and going beyond likes and dislikes is an easy job because of the many opportunities we receive for putting others first. Arjuna has four brothers, and Sri Krishna reminds him that five brothers all living together should have ample opportunity for overcoming likes and dislikes. In our own case, therefore, it is good to put the needs of those around us first in matters like food, recreation, and of course comforts and conveniences. We can find opportunities even in little things. We want to go to one movie and our friend wants to go to another. His may be more likely to suit both of us, but we have read all about our movie: the stars are our favorites, and the music is by someone we like. There are all sorts of ways we can support our arguments, but all we have to say is, "I would very much enjoy going to this movie, but I'd rather go with you to the other movie which you will enjoy." This is an excellent spiritual discipline.

सांख्ययोगौ पृथग्बालाः प्रवदन्ति न पण्डिताः ।
एकमप्यास्थितः सम्यगुभयोर्विन्दते फलम् ॥ ४ ॥

*4 Children say that knowledge and action are different, but the wise see them as the same. The person who is established in one path will attain the rewards of both.*

Sri Krishna is making a statement here about people who think that knowledge and action are different. People who talk about wisdom but are not able to translate it into their daily life are children, says Sri Krishna. If we have spiritual wisdom, it has to show itself in our daily living. There is no condemnation in this; the Lord, very compassionately, looks upon us as not fully grown up when we talk about the spiritual life yet yield to our self-will, have difficulties in our personal relationships, and are unable to exercise reasonable government over our senses.

St. Francis of Assisi expressed this same truth when he said that our knowledge is as deep as our action. In the Upanishads, the sages make a useful distinction between two kinds of knowledge. One, called *apara,* is intellectual knowledge, which is useful for living in the world and manipulating our physical environment but is of little help in transforming our character, conduct, and consciousness. The other, called *para,* is spiritual wisdom. This spiritual wisdom is directly connected with the will, and shines radiantly through our every action.

Intellectual knowledge is unfortunately not readily transformed into everyday action. Take, for example, smoking. We have such alarming evidence of the causal connection between smoking and cancer, yet there are millions of educated people, quite aware of this connection, who still continue to smoke because they cannot give it up. Even in hospitals we see many of the patients, who have come to be cured, smoking while sitting in the waiting room. I, for one, do not understand why cigarettes are sold in hospitals. This is the contradiction between intellectual knowledge and action. Intellectual knowledge, *apara,* does not seep into and transform the deeper recesses of our consciousness.

Contrasted with *apara* is *para,* spiritual wisdom. As our meditation deepens, we can ask the Lord, who is our real Self, "Let this craving fall away from me," and it falls away. This is the miracle of meditation. When we have gone sufficiently deep, many old cravings fall away without any violence done to ourselves; as our desires become unified, they are withdrawn from lesser cravings.

All of us would like to be more loving, but we cannot love those around us more until we have learned to withdraw our love from material things. The victim of money, who is always thinking about money, is not capable of loving his family, his friends, or anyone else. The person who is on drugs is not capable of giving his complete love and loyalty to another. Every little desire for pleasure or power diminishes our capacity to love. Desire is the raw material of love.

The mind is really an endless series of desires. To desire, to desire, to desire—this is the nature of the mind. In our attempt to recall our love from all the wasteful channels into which we have allowed it to go, and to still the continual waves of desire agitating our consciousness, the intellect is of no avail at all. Whether it is the frantic pursuit of money, material possessions, pleasure, power, or drugs, the problem is the same: we are caught in these cravings as long as we do not have access to our deeper resources. In meditation we develop the spiritual wisdom and the strength of will to recall our desires little by little. Our desires are like untrained puppies; they will run down any blind alley we pass. We may be walking down Telegraph Avenue; they see a blind alley and immediately they're off and we don't know how to call them back. In meditation, we can actually train our desires by telling them, "When we are on the Avenue, we keep on the Avenue. We don't go down side streets."

Little, little desires, thousands of them—for this dress, for that car, for this candy, for that prize—by themselves weigh only a little, but when put together, they amount to a large sum. All these little desires, every day, drain our vital capacity to love.

To quote the bank advertisement, "It all adds up": a few pennies here, a few pennies there, collected every day. While we were living on the Blue Mountain in India, we noticed that our local bank there had a very homely arrangement for collecting funds from the villagers. Poor villagers have very little to save, only a few copper pennies at most. To encourage them to deposit even these few pennies every day, the bank employed a boy who would go into the village to their homes, collect their few coppers, and enter the total in their account. In meditation it is the same: when the Lord comes, we can say, "We are no great mystic, but a few times today we have tried to be patient. A few times today we have tried to put our family first. A few times today we have resisted some little craving for personal satisfaction." And the Lord will say, "Give me your coppers." This is how most of us are going to lead the spiritual life for a long time. It's mostly in coppers. But in these innumerable little acts of selflessness lies spiritual growth, which over a long period can transform every one of us into a loving and spiritual person.

When we meditate on an inspirational passage, repeating it every day in the depths of our consciousness, we will find that it releases our inner resources of spiritual wisdom. When, for example, we meditate on the Prayer of St. Francis of Assisi, "It is in giving that we receive; it is in pardoning that we are pardoned," we find in our daily relationships that we are not getting angry any more, that we are not being resentful, that we are beginning to forgive and forget. This transformation of character, conduct, and consciousness comes naturally to us when we begin to draw upon the power released in meditation.

यत्सांख्यैः प्राप्यते स्थानं तद्योगैरपि गम्यते ।
एकं सांख्यं च योगं च यः पश्यति स पश्यति ॥५॥
संन्यासस्तु महाबाहो दुःखमाप्तुमयोगतः ।
योगयुक्तो मुनिर्ब्रह्म नचिरेणाधिगच्छति ॥६॥

*5. The goal of wisdom and the goal of service are
the same. If a man fails to see that knowledge and
action are one, he is blind.*
*6. Perfect renunciation is difficult to attain without
performing action. But the wise, who follow the
path of selfless service, quickly reach Brahman.*

The search for transcendental wisdom through negation of the
world, and the path of karma yoga or a life of selfless action in the
world, are both based on the practice of meditation, and both lead
ultimately to the same goal. But Sri Krishna points out that the path
of karma yoga is the easier of the two. Renunciation of the world,
or rather of our selfish attachment to the world, is impossible for
the vast majority of us without first practicing the disciplines of selfless action and meditation. Often we hear people, particularly the
young, saying they want to lead the spiritual life and, therefore,
have dropped out of school, quit their job, moved away from their
family, and are living in the woods. They hope this will enable them
to pursue their spiritual goal in peace. But the only barrier between
the Lord and ourselves is our self-will, called *ahamkāra* in Sanskrit.
There is no other barrier, and the whole purpose of spiritual living
is somehow to break through this barrier, which can assume gigantic proportions in our modern world. To eliminate our self-will, we
need the salutary context of our family, our friends, our campus,
and our society. Friends and family are not always easy to be with,
but they give us the much-needed opportunity for rubbing off the
angles and corners of our self-will little by little, in the innumerable
acts of give-and-take in everyday life.

When we were living on the Blue Mountain in India, we ran into
a young fellow from the Northwest who used to come to our place
now and then and had become very fond of us. He had led a very

lonely life: if ever there was a lone spiritual wolf, it was he. He used to avoid people completely, staying in lonely places so as not to come in contact with them. Sometimes he would twit me affectionately for always being with people, and would invite me to go on long walks to see the trees and hills. But even though I admire a beautiful landscape, I pleaded guilty to the charge of being more fond of people than of trees. I didn't try to argue with him when he praised the virtue of solitude, but one day a suitable opportunity presented itself, and I explained my point of view.

He was fond of talking about "flower power" and about being able naturally to love everybody. One day he was working in the garden in the midst of the flowers with the gardener's son, who was given to fist power. There was some altercation between them, and the gardener's son, being a simple boy, took a spade and threatened our young friend, who retaliated by threatening him with the hoe. Someone separated them before they could do each other any harm, and our young friend came to us so agitated that his hands were trembling. His teeth were clenched and he was bursting with fury. Instead of arguing with him, I asked him to join us at dinner. It is difficult to be furious when eating, and this gave him a little time to cool down. After he had finished his dinner, I said, "What happened to all your flower language? What happened to all your love? Why didn't you show him the universal love that you are capable of?"

He didn't know what to answer. He said, "You tell me what happened."

I said, "You are not used to people. You have never had the opportunity of living together with people who provoke you. You haven't learned to grit your teeth, repeat the mantram, stand firm, and move closer to people when they provoke you. It takes a man to do this. To be angry, to take a spade and hit the other person—that is not worthy of a human being."

He said, "How do you learn to do this?"

"Oh," I said, "by living with people like you!"

Even for a deeply spiritual person, selfless action is necessary for a long, long time. Today our troubled world is clamoring for action from each of us to help resolve the dilemmas with which it is faced. The Gita must be interpreted in accordance with the times in which we live, and in our age, we all must make a contribution to the world. It is not the time for us to "do our own thing"; it is the time to make selfless action a part of our spiritual way. Any person who tries to drop out of life, to turn his back upon society, is depriving the world of the contribution he can make. Without being the president of the country or the prime minister, even in our own small life, in our home, with our neighbors, on our campus, in our town, all of us can make a real contribution to peace by not being violent under any circumstances and learning to live in harmony even with those who may cause trouble to us.

Even if there is one person in the home who is really selfless, he or she—usually she—helps everyone else in becoming selfless. I never tire of pointing out that the noblest role of the woman is to be the selfless support of all the men around her, whether as a mother or wife, as a sister or niece. Through my simple eyes, any home is beautiful where there is a woman looking with love at all those around her, forgetting her own self-will and separateness in supporting those around her. Even though a home may have carpets from Bokhara, candelabra from Italy, and all the conveniences of modern civilization, if the woman is not selfless, I do not see beauty in the home.

Meditation and selfless action go hand in hand. When we try to live more for others than for ourselves, this will deepen our meditation. When we deepen our meditation, more and more energy will be released with which we can help others.

योगयुक्तो विशुद्धात्मा विजितात्मा जितेन्द्रियः ।
सर्वभूतात्मभूतात्मा कुर्वन्नपि न लिप्यते ॥७॥
नैव किंचित्करोमीति युक्तो मन्येत तत्त्ववित् ।
पश्यञ्शृण्वन्स्पृशञ्जिघ्रन्नश्नन्गच्छन्स्वपञ्श्वसन् ॥८॥
प्रलपन्विसृजन्गृह्णन्नुन्मिषन्निमिषन्नपि ।
इन्द्रियाणीन्द्रियार्थेषु वर्तन्त इति धारयन् ॥९॥

*7. Those who follow the path of service, who have completely purified themselves and conquered the senses and self-will, who see the Self in all creatures, are untouched by any action they may perform.*
*8–9. The person whose consciousness is unified thinks, "I am always the instrument." He is aware of this truth even while seeing or hearing, touching or smelling; eating, moving about, or sleeping; breathing or speaking, letting go or holding on, even opening or closing the eyes. He understands that these are the movements of the senses among sense objects.*

In our villages in Kerala, bags of rice, water jars, and other heavy burdens are often carried on the head. Villagers will walk long distances to market with their produce balanced on their heads. After carrying a bag of rice for many miles, when the villager wants to rest, he finds it difficult to sit down, take the burden from his head, and then, after resting, put it back on his head and get up again. So by the side of the rugged country roads they have constructed stone parapets, called *athāni* in my mother tongue, which are about the height of a man. When I have been carrying a heavy burden for a few miles, I come to a stone parapet, and all I have to do is move close to the *athāni*, nod my head, and the bag of rice will slide onto the wall. I can lie down and rest peacefully, and when I have refreshed myself, I can go back to the slab, give the bundle a little push, and balance it on my head again.

Vallathol Narayana Menon, a Malayali poet who was a Hindu,

but who was deeply in love with Jesus as a divine incarnation, wrote a poem about Mary Magdalene in which he uses this image of the *athāni*. In this beautiful poem in my mother tongue, with the title "Magdalana Mariyam," Jesus tells Mary: "Why do you carry the load of your guilt, the burden of your sins on your head? I am here, like the stone parapet. Don't stand far away. Come close to me; keep your head right near me, and when you nod your head, I am ready to take your burden."

This is an experience that will come to all of us when we lead the spiritual life and are prepared to live for others around us. Sometimes our problems will be greater, sometimes the challenges will be immense, but the Lord will always say from within, "I am the stone parapet. I am your support. Shift your burden to Me." My spiritual teacher, my Grandmother, who had more than her share of problems—partly because she had me on her hands—was never oppressed by her burden nor trapped in action and the results of action. When she had a great problem facing her, all that she had to do was close her eyes, surrender herself to the Lord, and then come back to us with wisdom, love, and the skill to help me or the family solve the problem.

The God-filled person, who is an instrument in the hands of the Lord, doesn't get discouraged or fatigued. He is so completely identified with the Ātman, so sure that the Lord is the operator, that he does not get entangled at all in the interplay of senses and sense objects, in which all of us are caught when we live for ourselves. His every action is done with utter detachment, as an offering to the Lord. Even when he eats, it is not for the sake of satisfying the palate; it is for the sake of serving the Lord. When we eat nourishing food as an offering unto the Lord, it strengthens the body, the mind, and the intellect. Similarly, we can keep our body strong and healthy with exercise so that it can be used for many years in selfless service.

We have another opportunity to move closer to the Lord when we go to sleep repeating the Holy Name. Between the last waking moment and the first moment of sleep there is an arrow's entry into the depths of our subconscious, into which the name of the Lord, whether it is *Jesus* or *Rāma,* can enter if we keep repeating it as we go to sleep. It takes some effort and perseverance, but when we have learned to fall asleep in the mantram, throughout the night the healing process continues in our sleep, and we wake up refreshed in body, mind, and spirit.

Every activity of ours should be performed as a service to the Lord if we are to become completely united with him. No harsh word, no sarcastic crack, no resentful look should come from us. We can see how demanding the Lord is: even the opening and closing of our eyes should be done with love. In all our little acts, we should come to feel that we are an instrument of the Lord. My Grandmother used to say that even in our dreams we should not have resentful thoughts or hostile attitudes toward anybody. We can come to have such mastery over our consciousness that even in our sleep we reach the state where nothing but love and the awareness of unity pervades us.

ब्रह्मण्याधाय कर्माणि सङ्गं त्यक्त्वा करोति यः ।
लिप्यते न स पापेन पद्मपत्रमिवाम्भसा ॥१०॥

*10. Those who have surrendered all selfish*
*attachments in work to the Lord are like the leaf*
*of a lotus floating clean and dry in water. Sin*
*cannot touch them.*

The lotus is a favorite flower in the Sanskrit scriptures, both Hindu and Buddhist. *Pankaja,* 'born in the mud,' is one of the Sanskrit names for this flower which grows abundantly in the pools and lakes of India. Born in the mud and dirt at the bottom of the pool, the lotus grows up through the water, rises above its surface, and blossoms towards the sun. The leaf of the lotus, which floats on the surface of the water, is a large one. In the villages, it is often used as a plate because it is waterproof; you can pour water on it and the water will not soak through the leaf but will just run off. Similarly, when we surrender ourselves to the Lord and become his instruments for carrying on selfless service, even though difficulties are sure to come to us, they will not cling to us; we will be able to face challenges without fatigue, tension, or diffidence.

कायेन मनसा बुद्ध्या केवलैरिन्द्रियैरपि ।
योगिनः कर्म कुर्वन्ति सङ्गं त्यक्त्वात्मशुद्धये ॥११॥
युक्तः कर्मफलं त्यक्त्वा शान्तिमाप्नोति नैष्ठिकीम् ।
अयुक्तः कामकारेण फले सक्तो निबध्यते ॥१२॥

*11. Those who follow the path of service renounce*
*their selfish attachments, and work with body, senses,*
*and mind for the sake of self-purification.*
*12. The man whose consciousness is unified abandons*
*all attachment to the results of actions and attains*
*supreme peace. But the man whose desires are*
*fragmented, and who is selfishly attached to the*
*results of his work, is bound in all he does.*

All of us begin the spiritual life with mixed motives. Perhaps we
perceive dimly that selfless action is a sure way of removing the barrier between ourselves and the Lord, and we want to contribute to
the welfare of those around us; but at the same time, we are concerned with ensuring our own private advantage. It takes quite a
while for most of us to become fully aware that our welfare is included in the welfare of all and to realize that when we are working
for everybody, we are also ensuring our own well-being.

To imagine that we are going to learn the secret of selfless action
in a few months, or even years, is being a little optimistic. Even sincere philanthropists, who do a lot of good for the world, are sometimes motivated by personal drives. I, for one, do not think it possible for anyone to become completely selfless in action without the
practice of meditation. It is rather easy to think that we are living
for others and contributing to their welfare, but very often we may
not even know what the needs of others are. In order to become
aware of the needs of those around us, to become sensitive to the
difficulties they face, we must minimize our obsession with ourselves. This requires the discipline of meditation, which enables us
gradually to reduce self-will and preoccupation with our private
needs.

It is all right for a child to be very aware of its needs and unaware of the needs of others, but for grown-up people like you and me to be conscious only of our wants and blind to those of others puts us back in the nursery. Sometimes I think that whether or not we have children, the nursery is an essential component of the modern home. When we are designing our house we shouldn't forget to include a nursery, into which we can crawl whenever we lose our adulthood and maturity and begin to brood upon ourselves. On such occasions we can simply crawl into the kiddie corral and put up a little sign, "Spoil me or spank me." Even brilliant intellectuals and people who are very effective in action sometimes crawl into their kiddie corral and do not know how to come out at all. For this reason, I would question whether it is possible to lead the spiritual life without being able to draw from a deeper source of power the energy we need to reduce our self-will. Meditation is the method we can use to reach these inner resources which are hidden deep in our consciousness. It is the bridge from the individual to the universal, from the ephemeral to the eternal, from the human to the divine.

We all have to begin the spiritual life with action that is partly egoistic, partly egoless, and none of us need be discouraged when we find, in the early days of our sādhana, that there is some motive of enlightened self-interest driving us on to action. Without this motive in the beginning, action may be difficult. But even though we may act partly for selfish reasons, we must make sure our action is not at the expense of other people. Any occupation harmful to others is not right occupation. Take, for example, the field of advertising. Though advertising of cigarettes has gone off television, we can see the increased vehemence of the advertiser's campaign on all the roadsides. Not content with billboards, the companies are giving out sample cigarettes on the streets. The other evening, coming back from San Francisco, we were grieved to see young girls distributing free cigarettes. Just imagine the cupidity of the human being: when people walking by were offered attractive cartons of cigarettes by these nicely dressed girls, they would turn and go out of their way to take them. Even though these girls are not doing this with any ill will, even though it may be just a job to them, they are going to acquire a certain load of karma because they are actually tempting people to get cancer. They are selling cancer to the people around them. Every day we have to ask ourselves how much of our life and work is for the welfare of mankind. If it is to the detriment of anyone, it does not matter how much money we are making, or how much power the job is bringing us; it is much better to live and die in poverty than to continue working at such a job.

When we are driven by the motive for personal profit, continually working for money, power, and prestige, anxiety takes a heavy toll on the nervous system. It is not work that tires us, but profit-motivated work: always doing work we like and avoiding work we dislike. It is the preoccupation with results that makes us tense and deprives us of sleep. When we are enmeshed in the results, anxious whether we will fail or win, our very anxiety exhausts us. For the majority of us, uncertainty is worse than disaster. Disaster comes to us only rarely; worry depletes us often. We never know whether we are going to get a brick or a bouquet. If we knew for certain it would be a brick, there would be no anxiety. We would just say, "Throw it and be done with it." For the person who has become aware of the Lord, however, it is all the same whether it is brick or bouquet, praise or censure, success or defeat. These will neither intoxicate him nor discourage him. When we can say, "Whatever disasters come, we will not be afraid because the Lord is within us," then this resoluteness and faith will enable us to work in complete security, free from tension, agitation, and fear of defeat. The person who works with this attitude is always at peace, always secure, because he is not anxious about the results of his action.

सर्वकर्माणि मनसा संन्यस्यास्ते सुखं वशी ।
नवद्वारे पुरे देही नैव कुर्वन्न कारयन् ॥१३॥

*13. Those who are self-controlled, who through discrimination have renounced attachment in all their deeds, live content in the city of nine gates. They are not driven to act, nor do they involve others in action.*

If you want to enjoy life, you have to renounce, not the world, but your ego. If you really want to have a merry time, all you need do is take out your ego and hide it where nobody will be able to find it. Unfortunately, the ego usually does not want to be thrown away; every time you try to throw it away it will come back to you.

No amount of trying to throw it away, no amount of resolving to be completely selfless from this moment on, is going to rid us of this unwanted ego-burden. Only by gradually learning to think about others, to love others more than we love ourselves and serve them rather than our own self-interest, can we finally get rid of the ego. By some strange magic, the more we love others, the wider we extend the circle of our love, the less the ego seems to like us; and one day, when we forget ourselves entirely, it disappears. Then we are free of it once and for all.

In the second line of the verse, there is the dryly humorous description of the body as the little town with nine gates. Our eyes are two wide-open gates through which sights are marching in procession. Our ears are two gates where sounds are coming through in long, long queues. Most of us are firmly convinced that we are the body; we are not aware that the body is just the little city in which we dwell. Because we identify others as well as ourselves with the body, we go through life without ever really seeing those around us. We do not even really get to know our own dear ones. Even after years of marriage, we have never seen our partner. Living with the members of our family all our life, we pass out of this world without even having seen them as they really are: as the Ātman, the pure, perfect dweller within the body.

न कर्तृत्वं न कर्माणि लोकस्य सृजति प्रभुः ।
न कर्मफलसंयोगं स्वभावस्तु प्रवर्तते ॥१४॥
नादत्ते कस्यचित्पापं न चैव सुकृतं विभुः ।
अज्ञानेनावृतं ज्ञानं तेन मुह्यन्ति जन्तवः ॥१५॥

*14. Neither self-will, nor actions, nor the union of action and result comes from the Lord of this world. They arise from ignorance of our own nature.*

*15. The Lord does not partake in the good and evil
deeds of any person. When wisdom is obscured by
ignorance, a person's judgment is clouded.*

Though we may have committed many mistakes in life, as most of
us do in our ignorance, the Lord will never desert us. Sri Krishna is
telling us with great simplicity: "I love everyone because I am in everyone. How can I hate anyone, even though he commits mistakes,
when I am in that person?" We often forget in dealing with people
who have gone astray that the Lord continues to dwell in them even
though they have made mistake after mistake. It is a great art to be
able to resist wrongdoing without withdrawing our love from the
wrongdoer. To be able to love someone very deeply and yet resist
firmly the wrong he may be doing us in his ignorance is one of the
most important arts we can learn in life. No one can resist for long
when we use the spiritual technique of embracing him with all our
love while still resisting what is selfish in him. Under no circumstances should we condemn a person even if he is being selfish and
self-willed. It serves no purpose to attack such people. The only
thing to do is to love and respect them because the Lord is present
in them, and to resist them nonviolently, bearing patiently whatever
suffering they may be inflicting upon us in their ignorance.

Mistakes are a natural part of growing up, and there is no need
to brood over the sins of the past. The purpose of making a mistake
is to learn not to make that mistake again. As my Grandmother
used to tell the young girls in my ancestral home when they began
to work in the kitchen, we can all expect to do a little spilling and
burning in order to learn to cook. Even though we have a certain
margin for error, the sooner we can learn from our mistakes, the
less suffering we will have to undergo in life. Mistakes are inevitably followed by consequences. The consequences of a mistake may
last for many years, and in making a major decision, many of us are
prone to overcalculate the satisfaction we are going to get out of it
and overlook the suffering involved for ourselves as well as others.
We often forget that the action we are contemplating contains the
seed of its result. We try to connect wrong means with right ends,

which will never work. Right ends are included in right means; wrong ends are included naturally in wrong means.

ज्ञानेन तु तदज्ञानं येषां नाशितमात्मनः ।
तेषामादित्यवज्ज्ञानं प्रकाशयति तत्परम् ॥ १६ ॥
तद्बुद्धयस्तदात्मानस्तन्निष्ठास्तत्परायणाः ।
गच्छन्त्यपुनरावृत्तिं ज्ञाननिर्धूतकल्मषाः ॥ १७ ॥

*16. But ignorance is destroyed by knowledge of the Self within. The light of this knowledge shines like the sunrise; it reveals the supreme Brahman.*
*17. The person who has cast off all sin through this knowledge, whose mind is absorbed in the Lord, and who is completely established in the Lord as his one goal and refuge, is never born again.*

When our self-will dies completely, when our separateness is extinguished completely, then we see the splendor of the Lord.

Yesterday we had a triune celebration at Ramagiri. It was Easter, the wedding reception of our dear friends Steve and Debbie, and also the Kerala New Year. I had forgotten all about New Year, so I was a little surprised when I came out of our room after meditation on Sunday morning and found our two little nieces waiting on either side of the door. I had my red knit cap on. They said, "Close your eyes, uncle." I closed my eyes like an obedient uncle, and they pulled the wool over them. Taking my hands, they led me into their room and had me sit down. Then they asked, "Would you like to see the Lord?"

"Very much," I replied.

"Then open your eyes!"

I did, and found myself looking into a mirror all beautifully decorated with fruits and flowers. The face I saw was my own.

This is the Kerala tradition, in which all members of the family are led to a mirror and reminded that the face they see there is the Lord's. Once this tradition has seeped into our consciousness, it is enough for a woman in the home—mother, sister, wife, or niece—

just to say in a very loving voice when we are getting angry: "Don't you remember where you saw the Lord on New Year's Day?" I have seen angry people breaking out in angelic smiles when they heard this. It is a beautiful thing to remind someone when he is angry that he is really trying to prevent the Lord within him from looking out through his eyes.

In order to see the Lord within we must do what the Bible commands us: "Be still and know that I am God." This supreme state is stillness of the body, mind, intellect, and, of course, the ego. In the Katha Upanishad the King of Death tells his disciple that when all these have been stilled, that is the highest state, in which he will find the Lord in his own heart and in the heart of everyone around him.

We cannot attain this state as long as we are searching for fulfillment without. It is difficult for us to understand that we are always out, always going on a trip somewhere. Today, when we were coming back from Ramagiri, we saw an unusually large number of hitchhikers with all kinds of sign boards. They have now started making changes on these little placards: formerly it was just "LA" or "SF," but today we saw one board which read, "Chicago—sister's wedding." I thought this was a personal way of getting the message across, something that touches all of us. After all, we have to give him a lift if he is going to attend his sister's wedding. Then there was a very quiet sign, "East, please." To me this also was rather personal. Another sign, probably by an Eskimo, just read "North." Now, if you ever find me with a placard by the roadside, it will read "In." This is what we do in meditation; we try to recall all our wandering energies back to the original source which is our home.

विद्याविनयसंपन्ने ब्राह्मणे गवि हस्तिनि ।
शुनि चैव श्वपाके च पण्डिताः समदर्शिनः ॥१८॥

*18. Those who possess this wisdom have equal love*
*for all. They see the same Self in a spiritual aspirant*
*and an outcaste, in an elephant, a cow, and a dog.*

In the one beautiful word *samadarshin*—'looking upon all equally,' having equal love for all—the Lord tells us the mark of those who live in God. The person who lives in God will love and respect all, without ever deprecating anybody because he or she is of a different religion, country, race, culture, or sex. Once we have realized the unity of all life, we will be incapable of feeling that we are superior to another, no matter what surface differences there appear to be.

In developing the capacity to love and respect all, we must go beyond superficial gestures. We must learn to be understanding and sympathetic to all. It is easy to appear cosmopolitan, to seem well disposed to all, but deep inside there still may be a tacit sense of superiority—the feeling that our culture, our country, our religion, or our race is greater than someone else's. Some of the books, for example, that are published about different countries by respected scholars are attempts, whether conscious or unconscious, to deprecate other countries and other cultures simply because they are foreign.

One of the deep causes of agitation in India during the British regime was the quiet pervasion of all levels of society with the attitude that British culture was superior. The worst thing about foreign domination is that it can gradually undermine the self-reliance and self-respect of a nation. Because of these far-reaching consequences of long periods of foreign misrule, it is not surprising that most of the Asian and African countries which have endured colonial governments have a kind of national neurosis. Western nations which have not had the misfortune of being dominated by a foreign power must bear with these nations of Asia and Africa, remembering that because they have been mercilessly exploited, they have the constant suspicion that they are likely to be exploited again.

As Mahatma Gandhi has pointed out, imperialism damages not only the ruled, but the rulers also. Even young Englishmen—often university graduates from Oxford or Cambridge—who came to India with high ideals and the desire to serve would in the course of a decade or so slowly become arrogant and come to believe that they belonged to a superior race, culture, and country. In recalling the dark days of foreign rule, however, we should not forget that many British people tried to make amends during the freedom struggle by joining Mahatma Gandhi to help him in his work. Today there are many British people who have settled down in India as citizens and who love the country as much as they loved England.

We begin the practice of equal love and respect for all right in our home. We need not be afraid or agitated if there are people with different opinions living in the same home. What makes us afraid of opinions opposed to ours, often causing the so-called generation gap, is the tendency to identify ourselves and others with opinions. Just because you happen to be one color and I happen to be another does not mean that we are different; we are just wearing different-colored jackets. Similarly with opinions: even if our opinions differ, this is no reason for us not to love and respect one another. Even though there may be differences of opinion between them, each generation can greatly enrich the life of the home. There is a contribution that older people can make with their experience of life, for which there is no substitute. Similarly, young people make a contribution to the home with their vitality and freshness. Children also can add to the life of the home with their innocence; they remind us of the words of Jesus: "Suffer the little children to come unto me, and forbid them not: for of such is the kingdom of God. Verily I say unto you, whosoever shall not receive the kingdom of God as a little child, he shall not enter therein."

In this verse Sri Krishna also refers to animals. We should show love and respect even to animals because the Lord is in them also. I need hardly say how much animals respond to a person who really loves them. Because they understand in some way that we have great love for them, that we are trying to realize the unity that makes us all one, more and more creatures are now coming to Ramagiri. I remember how nervous the jackrabbits were when we first moved to Ramagiri. As soon as we saw a jackrabbit, he would go sit behind a bush and say, "I am a bush." I used to reply, "If you believe that, all right. I won't look at you if you don't want me to." Then I would go away. They had probably been chased and were afraid. But our people at Ramagiri are extremely loving and particularly solicitous of the welfare of the creatures which live there, and one year has changed the atmosphere of the place considerably. So yesterday, when I saw a jackrabbit and immediately said, "That's a bush," he didn't try to hide. In fact, he might have heard me—jack-rabbits have very long ears—because he turned around, came back close to the path, and started performing.

इहैव तैर्जितः सर्गो येषां साम्ये स्थितं मनः ।
निर्दोषं हि समं ब्रह्म तस्माङ्ब्रह्मणि ते स्थिताः ॥१९॥

*19. Such people have conquered separate existence. Their minds are even and reflect the unity and per-fection of Brahman.*

In order to look with an equal eye of love and respect on all, whether they conduct themselves selfishly or selflessly towards us, we must have the capacity to keep our mind even at all times. In the Gita, Sri Krishna defines the unitive state as evenness of mind (2: 48). Now what usually happens to most of us is just the opposite of even-mindedness. As soon as someone pleases us, we begin to get exhilarated; when someone does what we want, there is an auto-matic sense of satisfaction. On the other hand, when someone says no to us, we immediately get dejected. This constant fluctuation of the mind takes away from our capacity to deal with everyday diffi-culties. To deal successfully with a difficult situation, all that is usu-ally required is that we preserve our equilibrium and not get agi-tated. When someone is flying into a rage, it is very easy for us to get angry in return, which can only change things for the worse. Arith-metic tells us there are now two people in a rage. The question is, how has the situation been improved by doubling the number of people in a rage?

When we are getting agitated and angry, the best thing we can do to maintain our equilibrium is to go out for a long, brisk walk re-peating the mantram in our mind. In the early days, after going around the block, we will want to come back because we have thought of a sparkling repartee which in our normal state of con-sciousness we wouldn't have been able to think of. When we want to come back, knowing what satisfaction our ego is going to get by making one more crack, that is the time to propel ourselves onwards saying the mantram. It is painful, because we have such good things to hit with. It seems a sorry waste. But after we have kept walking for an hour and the rhythm of the footstep, mantram, and breathing has calmed the mind, we will remember some of the nice things about the other person. When we were upset, it was unmitigated evil that we saw embodied before us. But it takes only an hour's walk, with the repetition of the mantram, to know that the evil is mitigated. If we can control our anger a few times this way, we will be able to remember when someone provokes us that even though he is angry now, when he comes back to normal he will be good, kind, and loving.

When we are burning with anger, we often conclude that this burning is going to last forever. But if we could quench the flames of anger consuming us and remember that in a little while we will have forgotten our anger, none of us would go to the extreme of moving away from people, which we now often try to do. Moving away is the worst thing to do in case of differences. Alienation deprives both parties of becoming aware of the unity in that relationship, and it weakens both. By strengthening the other person, in contrast, we are also strengthening ourselves. Living in peace and harmony with people who are agitated is one of the greatest services we can render them. Everyone is prepared to move away from people who are troubled, who are angry or afraid, but when troubled people find one person who can bear with them and support them, and at the same time guide them by his personal conduct, they respond beautifully with greater love and respect. It is the capacity to bear with people, whatever they do, which is the secret of love.

न प्रहृष्येत्प्रियं प्राप्य नोद्विजेत्प्राप्य चाप्रियम् ।
स्थिरबुद्धिरसंमूढो ब्रह्मविद्ब्रह्मणि स्थितः ॥२०॥

*20. They are not elated by good fortune or depressed by bad. With mind established in Brahman, they are free from delusion.*

The rare person who is able to receive good fortune without getting excited and bad fortune without getting depressed, who is able to treat those who are good to him with love and those who are not good to him with love, will never be deluded by the seeming multiplicity of life. When the mind gets agitated, we do not see life as it is, as one. The scriptures say that it is the constant agitation going on in our mind that deludes us into believing that you and I are separate.

The question we may ask is, "If we are to have neither pleasure nor pain in life, are we not likely to become insensitive to the joy of life?" The Gita says this doubt arises from the wrong assumption that in life there is only pleasure and pain and nothing else. One of the fatal weaknesses of the intellect is that it must always cut things up into two classes—everything must be either this or that. Because of this intellectual trap, we may find it difficult to understand that the person who has gone beyond both pleasure and pain lives in abiding joy. The Gita is telling us to go beyond pleasure and pain so that we may come into our legacy, which is the state of continuous joy and security.

To enter this state of abiding joy we must be very vigilant in the early years of our sādhana and often say no to pleasure while welcoming pain with a smile. In this way the nervous system can be reconditioned. Because of the conditioning we have received through the long travail of evolution, we are always looking for what is pleasant in life and trying to run away from what is not pleasant. This is the reaction that has now become inscribed on the nervous system: to the pleasant it says "Good, good," and to the painful, "Bad, bad." The Gita does not say we should not go after pleasure. When I first heard this from my Grandmother, I really took to the Gita immediately, but I wasn't expecting what she said next: "The Gita doesn't say not to go after pleasure; it says that when you go after pleasure you are also going after pain." It is not possible for most of us to accept this. There is always the distant hope in every one of us that while no other human being has ever succeeded in isolating pleasure, *we* are going to achieve this magnificent feat and live in a state of pleasure always.

For a long time, sādhana is a reconditioning of the nervous system to accept a temporary disappointment, if necessary, when it is for our permanent well-being. Sometimes on the spiritual path, when we want to eat a particular dainty that appeals to us, or when we want to eat a little more than is necessary, we can't help feeling a little tug at the heart as we walk out of the restaurant. We cannot help thinking that we could as well have stayed on at the table and had five more minutes of pleasure, forgetting that it would probably be followed by five hours of stomachache at night. The right time to get up from the meal is when we want just a little more. This is real artistry, real gourmet judgment: when we find that everything is so good that we would like to have one more helping, we get up and come out.

We should learn this art not only with food, but in all aspects of daily life. Even in personal relationships, when we call on a person or are at a party, we shouldn't linger until we reach the dregs of the cup. When the party is really bubbling and everyone is saying, "You are the life and soul of the party. Why don't you stay on?"—that is the time to leave in good dignity. If we can do this, we are living in freedom. To be able to break up the party at its zenith, before the downward curve begins, we must not get caught in it. In everything, we must have the freedom to drop what we are doing at will. We may not get the little pleasures that we have been going after, but we shall gradually find ourselves in the permanent state of joy which is indicated by the mantram *Rāma*.

बाह्यस्पर्शेष्वसक्तात्मा विन्दत्यात्मनि यत्सुखम् ।
स ब्रह्मयोगयुक्तात्मा सुखमक्षयमश्नुते ॥२१॥

*21. Not dependent upon any external support,*
*they have realized the joy of spiritual awareness.*
*With their consciousness unified through the practice*
*of meditation, they live in abiding joy.*

When the mind has become even, when we can retain our equanimity in pleasure and pain, friendship and enmity, treating everyone with equal love and respect, we truly have realized the Lord who is enthroned in every heart. Then our love will be given to all those around us without any expectation of return. This is the mark of true love. As the Catholic mystic St. Bernard puts it, "Love seeks no cause beyond itself and no fruit; it is its own fruit, its own enjoyment. I love because I love; I love in order that I may love." The moment we say, "I love you because I want something from you," it is no longer love; it is a contract.

When we are able to love all those around us and to live only for their welfare, we will find that all our support comes from within. It is when we are expecting something from the other person in return that we are leaning on him for our support, but when we do not expect anything in return, and love with all our heart, we are free. We are not dependent upon any external support but derive our support from the Lord within. When we discover that the Lord of Love is ever within us, we have entered into the state of joy and security which Jesus calls the kingdom of heaven within.

This joy and security that knows no end can never come to any person who is dependent upon external circumstances and external stimuli for his satisfaction. It is when you become dependent entirely on the Lord within, who is the source of all joy and security, that you become free; and until you have this freedom in some measure, you will not be able to use even material resources wisely. In order to use money or any material resources wisely, you must have no attachments to them. Otherwise you will get caught in them, as can happen when, for example, you start going after money. I often tease a friend who works with the media by saying that one day we hope to make a movie called *Leave the Money and Run*. "Take the money and run," as the real title goes, and you run into despair. Leave the money and run, and you run into fulfillment. In order to use any material possession wisely, whether it is a house, a car, or a guitar, you must not be attached to it. When you are greatly attached to a guitar, for example, the guitar will say at the time your term paper is due, "Now is the time for you to strum on me," and instead of writing your paper you will have to play your guitar.

If we are to enter into a state of unending joy, Sri Krishna says, on the one hand we should not be dependent on any external cir-

cumstances for our happiness, and on the other, we should be meditating regularly with complete concentration on the Lord who is
within us. For a long time, until we break through the surface layers
of consciousness, meditation is nothing but arduous discipline. But
once we enter the depths of our consciousness, we shall begin to
sense the deep peace that is called *shānti* in Sanskrit. When the tensions of the nervous system are relaxed, there is such profound
peace inside that even the body turns over like a little cat and basks
in this new-found joy.

ये हि संस्पर्शजा भोगा दुःखयोनय एव ते ।
आद्यन्तवन्तः कौन्तेय न तेषु रमते बुधः ॥२२॥

*22. Pleasures conceived in the world of the senses*
*have a beginning and an end and give birth to misery,*
*Kaunteya. The wise do not look for happiness in them.*

He or she is not wise who goes after any pleasure which has a beginning and an end. Our need is for joy that knows neither beginning
nor end, for the eternal joy called *Rāma* in Sanskrit. No lasting joy,
no lasting security can be ours if we pursue finite things, things that
pass away.

A little pleasure will satisfy us as long as we are living on the surface level of consciousness, but when we break through to the
deeper recesses of our consciousness, our capacity for joy is unlimited. If we just keep throwing little pleasures inside, they will be
completely lost in that vast space that is the world within. People
with access to deeper consciousness, with deeper states of awareness
open to them, will not take seriously the blandishments of material
possessions, because they know that these cannot satisfy them.

It takes a long time for most of us to learn that pleasure is not
permanent. If we go to the beach on days when the sea is stormy,
we sometimes find big footballs of foam and froth. We are tempted
to pick them up and say, "Why not bring these home to play soccer
with?" They look very round and inviting, but if we pick up a big
foam bubble in the hope of keeping it permanently, by the time we

get it home, it has vanished. This is the way pleasure slips through our fingers: when we are almost sure we have got it right here in our palm, it vanishes.

In the early years of our life, it is permissible to have the attitude that pleasure is something we can have always. But the Gita warns us to learn as quickly as we can that pleasure is impermanent. It is like the bubble that is blown away, dissolving immediately. The sooner we are able to learn this lesson in life, the less suffering we will be forced to undergo. The Gita is not talking only about the situation as it existed in India twenty-five hundred years ago, but about contemporary problems. What it says will always be found valid, because wherever we live, our fundamental need is to find within ourselves the Lord of Love who is the source of all joy and security.

The timelessness of the Gita was brought home to me today as I was reading an article about a recent convention of psychologists in San Francisco. One of the major concerns of the psychologists and medical doctors attending the conference is the increase in the use of "legal psychoactive" drugs, such as tranquilizers. Many patients who do not have an organic illness go to their doctors because of emotional problems and are given drugs which will calm them, help them sleep better, or stimulate them. As these psychologists point out, this chemical therapy is based partly on the assumption that we should all be in a state of continuous pleasure, untroubled by stress. The consequences of taking these drugs are far-reaching, and dependence upon them actually takes away from the capacity to deal with the problems of life. Also, dependence upon drugs by the older generation can influence their children to seek instant happiness through the more powerful mind-altering drugs.

शक्रोतीहैव यः सोढुं प्राक्शरीरविमोक्षणात् ।
कामक्रोधोद्भवं वेगं स युक्तः स सुखी नरः ॥२३॥
योऽन्तःसुखोऽन्तरारामस्तथान्तर्ज्योतिरेव यः ।
स योगी ब्रह्मनिर्वाणं ब्रह्मभूतोऽधिगच्छति ॥२४॥

*23. Those who overcome the impulse of lust and anger which arises in the body are made whole and live in joy.*

*24. They find their joy, their rest, and their light completely within themselves. They live in freedom and become united with the Lord.*

This is the same truth conveyed by Jesus when he tells us the kingdom of heaven is within. He is warning us not to roam the outer world looking for security. We can only find security by entering the world within, and then we shall find we can function with complete freedom in the outer world.

लभन्ते ब्रह्मनिर्वाणमृषयः क्षीणकल्मषाः ।
छिन्नद्वैधा यतात्मानः सर्वभूतहिते रताः ॥२५॥

*25. With all their conflicts healed and all their sins removed, the holy sages work for the good of all beings, and attain the nirvāna of Brahman.*

In this verse, the word *nirvāna* is used to indicate the goal towards which, according to the founders of the great religions of the world, all creation is moving. The mystics are not theorizing when they declare that the supreme goal of life is to become aware of the indivisible unity that is the Divine Ground of existence. They are drawing upon their own personal experience in which they have realized that all life is one.

The source of all sorrow lies in trying to resist our evolution towards this goal by maintaining our own separateness. It does not take much depth of observation, even for ordinary people like us, to discover that the person who does not merge his welfare into that of the family is usually very insecure, and so is the family in which he lives. If, for example, husband and wife try to compete with each other and maintain their separateness, they make themselves miserable, their children miserable, and even their locality miserable. In contrast, if we look at people who are secure, loved, and respected wherever they go, we usually find that they are able to base their action on an awareness that the interests of those around them are more important than their own individual interests. When I forget myself in the joy of those around me, I am fulfilling myself. It is when I try to maintain my separateness that I become more and more insecure, because my innate need, my deep, driving need, is to realize my oneness with all life.

This concept of the unity of all life is not peculiar to the mystics. Even the progress of science has brought us today very close to discovering that the welfare of the whole world is necessary if all of us are to live in peace and goodwill. The science of ecology has its basis in the spiritual truth that all life is one. We are now beginning to discover that there is a close relationship not only between human beings and animals, but among trees, land, water, and air as well, and that we cannot try to promote our own interests at the expense of even the trees. Nirvāna, therefore, is not a concept applicable only to ancient India. It is a concept which thoughtful people all over the world are beginning to appreciate.

In Hinduism and Buddhism, where reincarnation is a working proposition and not just a philosophical theory, and the law of karma is taken to be as infallible as the law of gravity, the whole responsibility of my development is thrown on my own shoulders. I have sometimes been asked whether the law of karma makes people fatalistic. It is just the opposite. The law of karma says that no matter what context I find myself in, it is neither my parents, nor my science teacher, nor the mailman, but I alone who have brought myself into this state because of my past actions. Instead of trapping me in a fatalistic snare, this gives me freedom. Because I alone have brought myself into my present condition, I myself, by working hard and striving earnestly, can reach the supreme state which is nirvāna.

Until we reach the unitive state, however, we have to continue to come back, life after life, to this world of separateness. In the Tibetan Book of the Dead, there is a sensible, scientific, and dryly humorous presentation of exactly what takes place in the process of rebirth. According to this description, there is a period between two lives where we wait in a place called Bardo, which is very much like a big, crowded bus depot. Between one life and another, we have to sit and wait to get the right context for rebirth. If I have been lacking in respect to my parents, I have to be born into a situation where my children will show me the same lack of respect. This is the law. We can't blame Sri Krishna and complain, "Why do you make me the father of children who don't respect me?" Whatever we have given with one hand we must receive with the other. I have to get a son who drops out of college, a daughter who goes to Europe and spends the rest of her life skiing, and another daughter who goes to Mexico and learns to make pottery. It is not an easy combination to get: a Mexican potter, a Swiss ski buff, and a university dropout. Not many homes have this unusual combination. India is ruled out; Africa is ruled out. We slowly come to ask, "What is that state within two hours of snow, university, and Mexico?" By elimination comes the answer, "California!"

Bardo is a kind of cosmic waiting room where, after they have shed the body, people just sit, as we sit at a bus depot. Some time ago we went to a big bus depot in Oakland. There were buses leaving for many different places, and people of all kinds seated on the benches waiting to hear their particular bus called. A disembodied voice calls out over the loudspeaker, "Reno Special leaving at Gate 9." Not everybody jumps up when the man announces the Reno bus; it is only those with the gambling samskāra who immediately jump up and tell the others, "Stick with me; I've got a system." This small group, who have bought their special Reno packet that contains fare, room, and gambling tokens, queue up and get on the bus. Similarly, in Bardo, those with anger samskāras have a special bus; they will be born into times which are propitious for bringing their samskāras into play. In the Hindu scriptures, our own age is called *Kaliyuga,* the Age of Anger. Everybody is angry about something or other, against somebody or other, and in such an age, it is not difficult to get a suitable context for the anger samskāra.

Often I remind our young people to show particular consideration for their parents' weaknesses because often the children suffer from the same weaknesses. Usually, the very defect we suffer from annoys us when we see it in another person. For this reason we should bear with older people, with our parents, and with others who suffer from our own infirmities. It is by supporting such people in moments of stress that we can use even unfavorable samskāras to make greater progress on the spiritual path.

The practice of meditation has been described marvelously as taking our evolution into our own hands. Instead of waiting for the forces of evolution to buffet us for the next million years and make us selfless, we say, "Let me try during this very life to take my destiny in my hands and, by working at my life day in and day out, remove every particle of selfishness from my consciousness so that I may become aware of the unity of life." There is a rare creature who catches fire when presented with this goal, and he will give everything he has to the pursuit of it. Patanjali says that it is this enthusiastic, hardworking person who will attain the goal. Success in meditation comes not to those whose horoscope is right or who live in the perfect place and era, but to those who grit their teeth and work at it all the time. We need not be born under Capricorn, or live in the Golden Age, to attain the supreme goal. In any age, any context, we can, through the practice of meditation, realize the unity of life and fulfill the goal of human evolution. No matter what context we find ourselves in, what samskāras we labor under, or what our horoscope may read, we can always redirect our lives to the goal, because our Ātman, or real personality, is eternal, immutable, and infinite.

कामक्रोधवियुक्तानां यतीनां यतचेतसाम् ।
अभितो ब्रह्मनिर्वाणं वर्तते विदितात्मनाम् ॥२६॥

*26. Those who have broken out of the bondage of selfish desire and anger through constant effort, who*

*have gained complete control over their minds and*
*realized the Self, are forever established in the*
*nirvāna of Brahman.*

Sri Krishna uses the word *brahmanirvāna* to refer to that supreme
goal which Jesus calls "the kingdom of heaven within." In order to
reach this state, there are two obstacles which must be overcome.
The first is selfish desire, which drives me to seek my own personal
profit, prestige, and power, if necessary at the expense of those
around me. The Buddha calls this *tanhā,* the fierce thirst which con-
sumes me and drives me often to be at loggerheads with all those
around me. The second obstacle is anger. Wherever there is the
fierce thirst for separateness, for selfish satisfaction, there is bound
to be anger. *Kāma* and *krodha,* selfish desire and anger, go together,
because when I have a fierce thirst for my personal aggrandizement,
and you have a fierce thirst for your personal aggrandizement, it is
inevitable that we will clash.

In most estrangements, not only individual but even international, there is this question of my interests against your interests,
my prosperity against your prosperity. Prosperity is one and indivisible. Peace is one and indivisible. We are being told more and more
by thoughtful leaders all over the world that peace is necessary for
the whole world, that it is impossible to have war in one corner of
the world and maintain peace elsewhere. It is impossible, too, to
have real prosperity in one country and starvation in another. If we
start a fire in the kitchen, it is only a matter of time before it will
spread to the bedroom and finally to the entire home. The central
truth of the Gita, that all life is one, is applicable not only to ancient
India; this truth is being rediscovered here and now, and if we do
not act upon it, it is at our peril.

To overcome selfish desires and anger, we have to begin to be
more loving in our own home. It is here that the seeds of war begin
to grow. In a home where there is friction, where there is the clash
of separateness, there is a little war going on. It may not be the
Thirty Years War or the World War of 1914–18, but it is a war
nonetheless. It breaks out at breakfast. There may be a truce at

lunch, but guerilla warfare can rage quietly in the kitchen, and again battle lines are drawn at dinner. Sometimes, even though there may not be an actual outbreak of hostility, there is a kind of cold war carried on. War is born in the minds of men: first it comes to our hearts, then to our homes, then to our community, and finally to our world. This is the nature of war. We have only to observe the little state of warfare in homes to see the appropriateness of the Gita's message that war rages fundamentally in the hearts of men, between what is selfish and what is selfless, impure and pure, demonic and divine. When the Gita talks about warfare, it is the war that rages in the human breast, and in this battle, all of us have the choice to identify ourselves either with the forces of light or with the forces of darkness. This is the choice that everyone has, in whatever country, community, or context he may live.

स्पर्शान्कृत्वा बहिर्बाह्यांश्चक्षुश्चैवान्तरे भ्रुवोः ।
प्राणापानौ समौ कृत्वा नासाभ्यन्तरचारिणौ ॥२७॥
यतेन्द्रियमनोबुद्धिर्मुनिर्मोक्षपरायणः ।
विगतेच्छाभयक्रोधो यः सदा मुक्त एव सः ॥२८॥

*27–28. Having closed their eyes in meditation and focused their attention on the center of spiritual consciousness, their breathing becomes even. The wise man or woman among these, who has controlled body, senses, and mind, who is dedicated to the attainment of liberation and has gone beyond selfish desire, fear, and anger, lives in freedom.*

These two verses describe the state of samādhi insofar as it can be expressed in words. Sri Krishna uses the word *mukta,* 'free,' to describe the person who has attained the supreme state of samādhi. He or she alone lives in freedom who has reached this unitive state, in which he or she knows that all life is one and has the will and wisdom to live in harmony with it. In order to live in complete freedom, which is the goal of the spiritual life, we should not be dependent upon any external object for our security, joy, and fulfillment. This is not a plea for poverty, which can be debilitating and degrading. It is a plea for being free from selfish attachments to our environment. This is the state of complete freedom that we enter in samā-dhi, the climax of meditation, when the windows of the senses close completely as a result of long spiritual discipline.

There is also a reference here to what happens to the eyes in deepening meditation. As our mind becomes quieter and our security begins to increase, the eyes become still, bright, and beautiful. It is an amazing commentary on our modern civilization that if we go to almost any store we will find a special section devoted to aids for eye-beautification, with a long row of all kinds of little bottles and brushes containing things to put around the eyes. When I first came to this country I wasn't used to these things, and whenever I saw those false eyelashes, Christine had to remind me not to stare. One day when I was riding on the cable car in San Francisco, I saw sitting in front of me a very attractive girl with some bluish stuff around her eyes. When I came home, I told Christine that I had met an awfully pretty girl with some kind of eye ailment which had made her eyelids blue. Christine said, "Don't be silly. That's a beauty aid." I am told that it takes quite a long time to apply all these cosmetics. This is the time that might be used for the practice of meditation.

Beauty comes into the eyes from within. We have only to look at a mother looking at her child to see how gloriously beautiful her eyes become when she loves. Or look at a husband and wife who live together in love and harmony; what beauty comes into their eyes! Even when long-lost friends meet at a class reunion, beauty leaps out from within through their eyes. All of us have beautiful eyes. But our eyes lose their beauty when we become angry, brood upon ourselves, nurse grievances, and become violent. The quiet mind, the heart full of love and forgiveness, lights up the eyes and reveals the beauty of the Lord through them.

In the practice of meditation, when we are deeply concentrated on the inspirational passage we are using, the pupils of the eyes will look a little upward. When concentration deepens, the eyes turn towards what is called the center of Christ-consciousness in the

Christian tradition. This is usually referred to as the third eye in Hindu and Buddhist mysticism. Even in the early days of our meditation, when we are concentrating intensely, there is a sense of movement in this spot, which is considered the seat of spiritual awareness.

Another change which takes place in deepening meditation is the slowing down of the breathing rhythm. According to the great mystics, especially in Hinduism and Buddhism, the breathing rhythm is closely connected with the rhythm of the mind. We know, for example, that as we are getting angry, the rhythm of the mind changes; and as the mind changes, there are a number of corresponding changes that take place in the body. Usually when we are angry our breathing becomes stertorous. My advice here is not to go in for any occult breathing exercises, which are fraught with danger. The best breathing exercise is to go for a long, fast walk repeating the mantram in our mind. This is the natural, effective way of regulating the breathing rhythm.

भोक्तारं यज्ञतपसां सर्वलोकमहेश्वरम् ।
सुहृदं सर्वभूतानां ज्ञात्वा मां शान्तिमृच्छति ॥२९॥

*29. Those who know Me as the friend of all creatures, the Lord of the universe, the source and end of all paths, attain eternal peace.*

With body, mind, and intellect under control, with all selfish desire, anger, and fear eliminated from consciousness, the human being attains the supreme goal of life, which is to become aware of God, from whom we come, in whom we subsist, and to whom we return. In this supreme state, we see in our own heart of hearts the Lord of Love, whether we call him Christ, Krishna, Shiva, or Buddha, and become united with him here and now in this very life.

इति संन्यासयोगो नाम पञ्चमोऽध्यायः ॥५॥

# CHAPTER SIX

# The Practice of Meditation

श्री भगवानुवाच
अनाश्रितः कर्मफलं कार्यं कर्म करोति यः ।
स संन्यासी च योगी च न निरग्निर्न चाक्रियः ॥१॥

SRI KRISHNA:

*1. Not those who lack energy or refrain from action,
but those who work without expectation of reward
have attained the goal of meditation and made
true renunciation.*

The Gita gives us three paths to illumination: karma yoga, the path
of selfless action, jnāna yoga, the path of spiritual wisdom, and
bhakti yoga, the path of love and devotion. All three are based upon
the practice of meditation.

Karma yoga appeals easily to people who are energetic and enter-
prising, but energy and effort are not enough. There must be no
thought of feathering our own nest, or of earning profit and prestige, for the moment these thoughts come in, our action is no longer
karma yoga. This is what makes karma yoga so difficult, why it
takes a giant like Mahatma Gandhi to practice it to perfection. But
even though we do not have the stature of Gandhi, we cannot afford
to wait until we are completely selfless to act, because that day is a
long way off. We can begin karma yoga now, and through the practice of meditation, over a long period of time, we can gradually
eliminate all our selfish motives. So for the vast majority of us, the
practice of karma yoga has to be based on meditation.

Jnāna yoga is even more difficult; it is like climbing a ninety-
degree precipice. Without meditation no *jnāna,* or spiritual wisdom,

will come to any of us. *Jnāna* does not refer to intellectual effort but to leaping beyond the duality of subject and object, going beyond the finite intellect into the intuitive mode of knowing—a capacity which is characteristic of a great spiritual genius like Meister Eckhart, and present to some degree even in a great scientific genius like Albert Einstein. For most of us, however, the path of love or *bhakti* is the safest, the swiftest, and the sweetest.

This word "love" is easy to read and write, but very difficult to put into practice. The basis of all loving relationships is the capacity to put each other's happiness first. Sometimes it is distressing to try to make another's happiness more important than our own; yet when we keep at it, there comes a fierce exhilaration. We can go to bed knowing that we have grown a tenth of an inch that day; and one tenth of an inch every day will make us tall by the time the year is out. Spiritual awareness grows little by little; it is sometimes easy to make a spectacular, dramatic gesture, but it is very difficult to bear incessant pinpricks patiently. Life is a permanent state of pinpricks that come in the form of likes and dislikes. Through constant patience and the practice of meditation, we learn to bear these pinpricks until finally we can overcome them joyfully, without effort.

We call our age materialistic, but I notice there is a refreshing change in the younger generation, which has a good deal of detachment from material goods and money. But if detachment is going to be complete, we also have to become detached from our self-will, which often expresses itself in our opinions. People will give away their money, clothes, and gifts, but the one thing they do not know how to give away is their opinions. If we were to stand on a busy street corner tomorrow and distribute our opinions free to anybody who would come and take them, everyone would just ignore us. Nobody wants our opinions because everyone wants to keep his own. One of our strongest drives is to impose our will on others, yet we can never understand why anyone should want to impose his self-will on us. In personal relationships, love expresses itself in accepting the other person's ways, particularly if they are better than our own.

To have harmonious personal relationships, the practice of meditation is necessary to keep the mind from getting agitated when someone goes against our grain. When we live together in intimate personal relationships, we have to expect a little bruising, a little spraining, and a little bumping, which are all part of life. Those who do not live together, who have not learned to accept the give-and-take of life, are forfeiting one of its fundamental joys: that of being a large family, in which we recognize the unity of life that is divine. In any home, whether with our family or with our friends, living together can multiply the joy of all, for the source of joy is in putting more and more people's welfare before our own. When we follow the path of integrated yoga, there is a place for selfless action, a place for knowledge, and a special place for love. But all these are governed by meditation, which we should practice every morning and every evening.

यं संन्यासमिति प्राहुर्योगं तं विद्धि पाण्डव ।
न ह्यसंन्यस्तसंकल्पो योगी भवति कश्चन ॥२॥

*2. Therefore, Arjuna, understand that renunciation and the performance of selfless service are the same. Those who cannot renounce attachment to the results of their work are far from the path.*

The expectation of getting money, prizes, prestige, or power, the idle imagination of rewards or results, is called *sankalpa* in Sanskrit. My Grandmother, who was as good as Aesop, used to tell a story which conveyed to me the idea of *sankalpa* better than great scholars have been able to do. In her simple manner, she would describe a village girl of about ten, walking home gracefully with a pot full of milk on her head. Under the spell of *sankalpa,* the little girl begins to daydream: "I am going to sell all my milk for five rupees, and with the money I'll get a dancing dress and real anklets with bells." Then she dreams of how she will be able to dance; and carried away, she starts dancing. The pot falls and the milk spills. This is what we do every day, only we say, "When my novel has gone into its sixth edition, and the movie rights have been bought, I am going to buy a yacht and a villa on the Mediterranean." People are given to this kind of imagining in all kinds of terms: money, pleasure, fame, and worst of all, power.

As long as we are subject to *sankalpa*, we are imprisoned in our selfish ways of thinking, and have no access to the deeper capacities in our consciousness that clamor to be used. There is no more effective way to rid the mind of *sankalpa* than the practice of meditation. Every time we meditate we free the mind a little more by not allowing it to wander off on a trail of fancy or vague associations. I am the first to admit that bringing the mind back over and over again to the words of the Prayer of St. Francis is dull, dreary work, but over a period of time this effort will free us from the oppressive memories of past events and the expectations of future actions. One of the signs that we are coming closer to this freedom is an increase in our vitality, energy, and capacity for selfless work. The more we work for others, stretching out our arms to embrace all those around us, the stronger our arms will grow.

आरुरुक्षोर्मुनेर्योगं कर्म कारणमुच्यते ।
योगारूढस्य तस्यैव शमः कारणमुच्यते ॥३॥

*3. For aspirants who wish to climb the mountain
of spiritual awareness, the path is selfless work. For
those who have attained the summit of union with
the Lord, the path is stillness and peace.*

Now Sri Krishna uses an image from mountain climbing, a sport that requires great endurance and skill. He compares two types: one is *ārurukshu,* someone who wants to climb the mountain of spiritual awareness; the other is *yogārūdha,* the adept who has already made it to the top. In order to climb the Himālayas within us, we have to train ourselves, little by little, every day. Sir Edmund Hillary, who climbed Mount Everest for the first time, did not just stand at the bottom, take one leap, and land on top of the Himālayas. He practiced climbing mountains for a long time to learn all the required skills; and for you and me to climb the spiritual mountain, we too have to strengthen our muscles over a long, long period of time.

When those of you who lead the householder's life are asked what you are doing, you can say, "Learning to climb a mountain." You are getting your training experience in the heart of your family. In mountain climbing, you tie yourself to others with ropes so that if somebody slips you do not say, "Have you hit the ground?" or "Good riddance"; you try to prevent that person from falling by hauling him up and saving him. Similarly in living with family or friends, if somebody slips you do not say, "Aha! Served him right," or "You've been asking for that for a long time." Instead you pull him up. Even if he has offended you, do not tell him, "Remember what you did last week? You'd better just stay there on the floor." If you do not like him, it is good for both of you if you can pull him up and support him. A person whom others have abandoned, who is looking at you through his own selfishness, expects you to walk away and wash your hands of him. At first he does not believe you are coming to help him, but when you support him, help him walk, and then give him something to get home with, he begins to think about what you have done; and on the way home he begins to like and finally love you.

There is no other way to deal with people who are difficult, who make mistakes. Demonstrating violently against them only makes the situation worse by making everyone blind with fury. This is where the practice of meditation is invaluable: when we are surrounded by people who cause us harm, we can help them by being patient and loving and returning good for their evil. To work like this for those whom we do not like, especially when we are involved in a tense emotional situation, is hard work. But when we work wholeheartedly in the service of others without thought of profit or prestige, we are using karma yoga every day as a mighty ladder to climb safely and steadily on the spiritual path. For a long, long time we will be aware only of the distress and the difficulty of always trying to turn our back upon ourselves; but after a period of years, when we think we have been stagnating all the time, we turn the corner and suddenly the goal is in view. We are no longer in the foothills; we are near Lhasa, the capital of Tibet, high among the clouds. We can see the Ganges flowing down, we can see views of some of the peaks, and we cannot help but thrill with exultation.

After we have reached the top of the spiritual Mount Everest, *shama,* perfect peace, becomes our ladder. This stillness of the ego means that we have become infinite love; that all our agitation has died down, all our anger, fear, greed, malice, and envy have died down, and there is a vast ocean of love flowing in our consciousness. This is what we discover after many years of assiduous effort. When our ego is completely eliminated and we have become all love, we no longer work; the Lord works through us. Our work then is to be the still center in the eye of the storm of the world which rages all about us.

यदा हि नेन्द्रियार्थेषु न कर्मस्वनुषज्जते ।
सर्वसंकल्पसंन्यासी  योगारूढस्तदोच्यते ॥४॥

*4. When a man has freed himself from attachment*
*to the results of work, and from desires for*
*the enjoyment of sense objects, he ascends to*
*the unitive state.*

Here we have a perfect picture of the person who has climbed to the summit of human consciousness, who sees the complete unity of all life and has the wisdom, the will, and the energy to live in harmony with it. The Buddha calls such a person one who has attained nir-vāna—that is, one who has broken out of the prison of selfishness, self-will, and separateness in which most of us spend our whole life.

The person who has become established in the Lord within him-self cannot be pushed about by selfish cravings, which can over-whelm even the most cultured and humanitarian among us if we let ourselves be drawn by prestige, fame, and power. Entirely indepen-dent of the external world for his support, the man who has attained the unitive state lives in abiding joy and security. As long as we lean on anything outside ourselves for support, we are going to be inse-cure. Most of us try to find support by leaning on all sorts of things —gold, books, learning, sensory stimulation—and if these things are taken away, we fall over. To the extent that we are dependent on these external supports, we grow weaker and more liable to upsets and misfortune.

Our sole support is really the Lord within. In a magnificent verse at the end of the Gita (18:66) Sri Krishna tells us not to cling to anything outside ourselves, but to cast aside all other supports and embrace only the Lord of Love who is within us all. Then we shall be free. It is a strange paradox that when we surrender everything to the Lord, we receive everything: when we depend entirely on the Lord, we become independent. In meditation we slowly learn to depend more and more on the Lord by increasing our concentration on the words of the inspirational piece. When the mind tries to slip out to the movie theater or the ice cream parlor and we bring it back to the words of St. Francis or the Gita, we are gently dislodging external supports and turning our eyes to the Lord.

उद्धरेदात्मनात्मानं नात्मानमवसादयेत् ।
आत्मैव ह्यात्मनो बन्धुरात्मैव रिपुरात्मनः ॥५॥

*5. A man should reshape himself through the power of the will. He should never let himself be degraded by self-will. The will is the only friend of the Self, and the will is the only enemy of the Self.*

No one can help us grow up, no one can help us become beautiful, except ourselves. We cannot expect anyone on the face of the earth to do the work necessary for our own enlightenment. Great teachers only show the way; we have to travel it, and the first step we can take is to accept responsibility for the position in which we find ourselves today and not try to leave it at the door of our parents, our partner, our children, or our society. By accepting this responsibility we immediately gain the certainty that if we brought ourselves into this morass, then we have the power to pull ourselves out completely, reshape ourselves, and become perfect.

The seed of perfection is within all of us. Meister Eckhart, in his inimitable way, tells us that as apple seeds grow into apple trees and pear seeds into pear trees, so the God-seed within us will grow into a mighty God-tree if it is watered, weeded, and protected. In India, the price of seeds goes up during the rainy season because that is the right time for planting. Because the seeds are expensive, the foolish farmer says, "I think I'll wait until there is a fifty percent reduction in the price of seeds. During the summer months you can pick up two packets of seed for the price of one." But at that time, when there is not a drop of water in the ground, nothing is likely to grow. Similarly, the right time for leading the spiritual life is now. When my Grandmother used to ask me when I was going to do a certain good deed, I would say, "One of these days, Granny." She would immediately retort in my mother tongue, "One of these days is none of these days." Most of us have a tendency to put things off until the right moment, the auspicious day, when everything is right. There are people who throw away jobs or move to a new home just because what they have now doesn't feel right. I would suggest a little less concern with feeling right and more with doing things now. If you want to lead the spiritual life, the time to start is immediately, and not one minute later. We have a venerable Hindu friend who says, in frightening language, "Don't postpone the spiritual life until tomorrow. How do you know you will be here tomorrow?"

Whatever mistakes we have committed, whatever difficulties we have, all that we have to do is leave aside all supports and trust the Lord completely, because he is right within us. In trusting the Lord, we are trusting our real Self; in putting our life under his guidance, we are letting our life be governed by the wisest part of our consciousness. Ultimately we have only one friend in the world: the Ātman, the Lord within, who is our real Self. He is telling us all the time, "I will forgive you whatever you have done, provided you now try to remove all selfishness from your heart and your life. I'll support you despite all the mistakes of the past, if you will now start to live for your family and your community. And I will bring you into your full beauty and wisdom if you will meditate on me and remember that I am present in every creature that lives on the face of the earth."

बन्धुरात्मात्मनस्तस्य येनात्मैवात्मना जितः ।
अनात्मनस्तु शत्रुत्वे वर्तेतात्मैव शत्रुवत् ॥६॥

*6. To those who have conquered themselves, the
will is a friend. But it is the enemy of those who have
not found the Self within them.*

We all have within us that curious pair, Dr. Jekyll and Mr. Hyde.
That is, we all have a pure, perfect, divine Self, side by side with a
hobgoblin with cloven feet and wagging tail who tries to make us
believe that he is our real Self. This hobgoblin is called by many
names. When Jalalu'l-Din Rumi, the great medieval Sufi saint,
would talk to his disciples about the devil, they used to retort in
their sophistication: "Devil? Devil? Never heard of him! We don't
believe in him." And Jalalu'l-Din Rumi replied, "You never heard
of him? Just turn your ear inward and listen to some of your
thoughts. 'I hate him. Drop dead.' That's the voice of the devil." We
don't have to go outside ourselves if we want to meet Mr. Mephistopheles. We have only to ask for an appointment, and he will tell
us to come any time—to walk right in, sit down, and make ourselves
at home. This is the selfish part of us, the monstrously ugly part of
us. When we hate, when we carry resentments, when we refuse to
forgive or become violent in our home, on the street, or on the campus, we are telling Mephistopheles that we look upon him as our
leader and will do whatever he wants.

Side by side with this hobgoblin is our pure, divine Self. One of
the beautiful names for this Self in Arabic is *al-Rahīm,* 'the Merciful.' The beauty of forgiveness, compassion, and love is that they
heal all the wounds within us, leaving not even a scar. Where there is
no forgiveness, not only are there scars; there are festering wounds
which sap our vitality. Remember the words of the Buddha in the
Dhammapada: "Hatred does not cease by hatred at any time;
hatred ceases by love. This is an unalterable law." He did not say it
is advisable to love, or it is recommended; he said it is an unalterable law: breaking it, we break ourselves; obeying it, we fulfill ourselves.

To learn to return love for hatred, all of us have to struggle for a long, long time. Learning any skill takes considerable effort, and we should not be surprised that learning to be selfless is the result of many, many years of difficult, exhilarating labor. Our niece Geetha has taken about a year to graduate from reading in that odd alphabet called ITA to the kind of books you and I read. When she came to us a year ago, she knew only a few words of English. Then she started going to school and saying *b-u-k* spells *book,* which really puzzled me. I would look this word up in the dictionary and say, "I don't think *buk* is English." She would say, "Uncle, it's that thing you're looking at—*buk.*" "Oh," I said, "that's *b-o-o-k.*" Now she too is beginning to read *book,* and there is such joy in the achievement. This morning, while Christine and I were meditating, a little slip of paper was passed underneath the door with a message written by Geetha, consisting of five words, every one of them lovingly misspelled: *Anti, ples pik ar dreses;* "Aunty, please pick our dresses." We were so overjoyed that we didn't see spelling peculiarities; we said, "How beautiful—she is able to communicate," which we often forget is the purpose of language.

In communicating with the Lord, for a long time we are going to say "ples Lord," and he is not going to consult the great mystics in heaven and say, "Poor English!" Instead he will say, "This person has turned to me and wants my help." In other words, we are not going to be perfect for a long, long time. We are going to have lapses, outbursts of temper, and difficulties, but as long as we keep trying our very best, the Lord is more than happy to receive our offering.

जितात्मनः प्रशान्तस्य परमात्मा समाहितः ।
शीतोष्णसुखदुःखेषु तथा मानापमानयोः ॥ ७ ॥

*7. The supreme Reality stands revealed in the consciousness of those who have conquered themselves. They live in peace, alike in cold and heat, pleasure and pain, praise and blame.*

To grow up we all need to learn to maintain an even mind in pain and pleasure, joy and sorrow, and we will find that keeping our balance, no matter how difficult the challenges we face, leads to security, cheerfulness, and the permanent happiness that is Rāma. In our world we are slowly forgetting that, as Meher Baba puts it, "Cheerfulness is a divine virtue." We go on a bus and see eyes that are glazed and faces that have no expression at all. It is as if some kind of arctic weather is blowing inside us all: our emotions are beginning to freeze; glaciers are forming, and icebergs are looming up everywhere. We are feeling less and less for others and less for ourselves as well. The impersonality of our modern urban society has become so frightening that people are trying to form smaller groups, smaller societies, where they can know and serve one another. It is a source of unending delight to all of us at Ramagiri to live as members of a large family, loving one another, working hard, and always being cheerful.

There are times when it is difficult to smile, but that is the perfect time to learn. When you are already happy, there is no effort in trying to smile. But when things are slowly beginning to look a little blue, when morale is sagging at the edges and people around you are beginning to irritate you, that is the time to start smiling. In the very act of smiling there seems to be some secret switch that is turned on, and somewhere inside a little fountain of joy begins to play.

Yogananda Paramahamsa has a beautiful suggestion for thawing the arctic state of our feelings; it is for all of us to become smile millionaires. This is the kind of millionaire that everyone can be, because everywhere we go we can always smile. Wherever you find someone seated alone, not knowing what to do, feeling utterly desolate, just smile at him. Almost everyone will thaw immediately and smile back. When you have been smiling at people in the park, at meter-maids passing by, at the mailman, and at schoolchildren, one day when you go to the mirror you will find smiling has become a habit. Your mouth has forgotten to droop at the corners; you try your best to scowl but you have lost the ability. Depression, unsociability, and lack of goodwill are beginning to get erased from your consciousness.

Every smile can be beautiful when we repeat the mantram, because gradually the mantram brings the smile into our eyes. We start smiling with our lips and end up smiling with our eyes as well. Once we have learned to do this we can never really be angry again. It is good to be with people who have smiling eyes—we do not even have to talk to them because communication is going on all the time at a deeper level.

ज्ञानविज्ञानतृप्तात्मा कूटस्थो विजितेन्द्रियः ।
युक्त इत्युच्यते योगी समलोष्टाश्मकाञ्चनः ॥ ८ ॥

*8. They are completely fulfilled by the knowledge and wisdom of the Self. Having conquered their senses, unmoved by opposition, they have climbed to the summit of human consciousness. To such a person a clod of dirt, a stone, and gold are the same.*

It is good to remember that gold is not valuable by itself; it is valuable because there is so little of it. If sand were found only in small quantities, people would treasure it in their safe-deposit boxes; they would buy sand certificates, on important occasions they would exchange a little sand, and they would have the expression "as good as sand." It shows how gullible we are and how little sense of value we have. What really gives value to anything is its usefulness in serving others. Our body draws its value from its usefulness in serving others, and our life draws its value not from the money we make, or the prizes we win, or the power we wield over others, but from the service we give every day to add a little bit more to the happiness of our family and our community. There is no better epitaph than "He lived for others," and this is all that the Lord asks us to do in order to move closer to him day by day.

The word *kūtastha,* 'established on the summit,' describes the man or woman who has learned the supreme skill of life, who has climbed the slopes of the Himālayas within to stand unshaken at the summit of human consciousness, no matter what storms rage about him or her. Not all the forces in the universe can shake one who is established in the Lord, the supreme protector. Gandhi's life is a perfect example of how one man who is established in himself can stand against all violence and yet be neither afraid nor alone.

There is a story in the *Mahābhārata* in which Duryodhana, the leader of the forces of selfishness, and Arjuna, the leader of the forces of selflessness, go to Sri Krishna to ask for help. Like a good Hindu god, Sri Krishna was having his siesta. There was one chair, a throne, near his head. Duryodhana, who always saw himself as the sun around which other planets should move, came in first and seated himself comfortably in his host's chair with the complete arrogance of the inflated ego. Sri Krishna, who was not really sleeping, opened his eyes slightly and thought, "That's where I thought you would sit." Then Arjuna came in and, seeing the lotus feet of the Lord, sat on the floor with his head at Sri Krishna's feet. When Sri Krishna opened his eyes, he naturally first saw the man sitting at his feet, and he asked Arjuna what he wanted. Arjuna, showing great love for his enemies, said, "There is somebody in the chair behind you who came before me. Give him what he wants first." Sri Krishna was greatly touched by Arjuna's putting Duryodhana first even on this special occasion, so he said, "I have two things to offer. To one of you I can give armies, navies, and any devastating weapon you want. To the other I will give myself."

Duryodhana made a note of this and said, "This is what I've been looking for. Throw in nuclear weapons as well and we'll be invincible."

Sri Krishna said, "You can have everything you want, but I won't come with it."

"Oh, that doesn't matter," Duryodhana said. "As long as we have a powerful arsenal, who can beat us?"

Then Sri Krishna asked Arjuna what he wanted, and Arjuna replied, "I don't want weapons; I want you to be with me and nothing else."

So Sri Krishna went with Arjuna, and to Duryodhana went all the forces of violence which finally destroyed him and his family. And in our lives, when we follow Arjuna's example and seek to become united with the Lord of Love within, no amount of violence can shake us.

सुहृन्मित्रार्युदासीनमध्यस्थद्वेष्यबन्धुषु ।
साधुष्वपि च पापेषु समबुद्धिर्विशिष्यते ॥९॥

*9. They are equally kind to relative, enemy, and
a friend; to someone who supports them, someone
who is indifferent or neutral, and even someone hateful. Through the ability to give love and respect to
all, they rise to great heights.*

One of the secrets of victorious living is found in the word *sama-
buddhi,* 'having an equal attitude towards all,' which tells us to live
in harmony with the law of life, to realize that all of us come from
God, exist in God, and return to God. In the supreme climax of
meditation called samādhi, we see the Lord in everyone, because
we see the indivisible unity which is the divine principle of existence.

To everyone, it is necessary to behave with respect: to those who
help us, to those who hinder us, to those who talk nicely to us, to
those who do not talk to us at all. This is the secret of perfect human
relations. Showing respect to our parents, to our friends, and to our
enemies not only helps us; it helps them as well. Even if others are
not entirely worthy of our respect, when we show respect to them,
they begin to rise up to it. If we can keep faith in even the most self-
willed person, if we can put our trust in him and expect him to
grow, gradually he will try to deserve our respect. We do not have
to worry about how the other person will behave towards us, and
we do not need to think constantly in terms of reciprocity: "You
take the first step; let me see how long it is, and then I'll take the
next—not one inch shorter or longer." Here my actions are dependent on the other person, and when we act in this way, our steps get
smaller and smaller until we do not move at all. In all our relationships, our primary concern should be how best to give our love and
respect. When we try in this way to give every possible service without any thought of return or remuneration, others respond deeply
and reveal what is divine within them also.

The code of behavior that many so-called civilized people observe is stimulus and response: you love me, I'll love you; you hate

me, I'll hate you in return. But through the practice of meditation, when we begin to mold ourselves in the image of an inspiring incarnation like Sri Krishna, Jesus the Christ, or the Compassionate Buddha, we will find, to our great delight, that we are no longer dependent on how others conduct themselves towards us. This is real freedom. Now we are far from free; we are always wondering how the other person is going to react. We have all kinds of defenses—moats, drawbridges, walls, and then several trapdoors—which prevent us from acting with natural grace. But when we find the exhilarating freedom in which we are able to give our very best without getting caught up in others' reactions, others' attitudes, we find that those around us begin to benefit from our freedom. Those who come into close contact with us will start to lower their defenses, little by little, centimeter by centimeter, and slowly they too will learn to give their very best without worry or fear.

If there is just one person in the family who is self-willed and always on guard, everyone else will automatically raise their defenses a little when they are around that person. It is almost like a reflex; as soon as we see people who are on guard we say, "He makes me feel uncomfortable." When we become comfortable with ourselves, we make everyone else comfortable too. The way to be permanently free from these tensions in personal relationships is to put the welfare of those around us first.

At Ramagiri some of our young men have become master carpenters. One of them is making an oddly shaped table which is full of angles and corners, but all the pieces fit so well that when they are together there are no angles or corners at all. When we try to manipulate someone else to fit into our angles and corners, we are actually making the corners sharper, and the sharper they get the more difficult it is to fit the pieces of our own life together into an harmonious whole. How much happier we would be if we could think less about everyone else's angles and corners and more about how we can dovetail into their lives: if we could concentrate less on others' reactions and more on how best to conduct ourselves. Even if others are irritable, we can be more generous. This is the attitude that comes from learning to see the Lord of Love in everyone.

Yesterday when I was taking our dog Muka for a walk I saw a jackrabbit in front of us seated on the road, full of confidence that none of us at Ramagiri would harm him. But seeing Muka, he became unsure and gave a couple of leaps, getting out of our way. Muka looked up at me as if to say, "Why does he have such abnormal legs? Why are the back two so much longer than the front ones?" Muka looks upon his four legs of equal length as normal, and he measures the world from this point of view; anything not conforming to his dimensions is abnormal. The jackrabbit is no different. Looking at the world from his vantage point, he would have said, "What strange legs your dog has—all equal length. How does he manage to hop?" Of course, from our point of view the rabbit's legs are just right for a rabbit and Muka's are just right for a dog.

Similarly, most of us live with people who have different opinions than ours. Everyone has different dimensions, and each walks or jumps forward in his own way; yet there is a common core in all of us. Twelve years ago, when I had just arrived in America, everyone asked me, "How do you like it here?" I always replied, "Just as I liked it there." There are no differences between people, no matter whether they are in India, Africa, America, or Europe. All our greatness comes from this common humanity, and when we constantly keep our eyes fixed on it, we discover the unity of life which is divine.

योगी युञ्जीत सततमात्मानं रहसि स्थितः ।
एकाकी यतचित्तात्मा निराशीरपरिग्रहः ॥१०॥

*10. The aspirant should constantly seek the Self within him through the practice of meditation. Controlling his body and his mind he should practice one-pointedness, free from expectations and attachments to material possessions.*

Meditation is a dynamic discipline by which we learn to focus our complete concentration at will. Every spiritual aspirant should try to practice *ekāgratā,* or one-pointedness of mind, at all times. In order to become one-pointed, it is necessary to do only one thing at a time, giving full attention to the job at hand. This is a discipline which can deepen our love and loyalty to everyone around us. There is a close connection between deep concentration and loyalty, and with the practice of meditation, we can greatly increase this precious capacity to remain loving and loyal no matter what the vicissitudes or circumstances.

One-pointed attention is something we have to train our minds to achieve, and a good place to begin is with our senses. Often the agitation of the mind is reflected in the restlessness of the eyes. We have only to look at people for a little while to see how tempestuous their minds are; their eyes are like the pendulum of a clock, swinging from one side to the other. As the eyes have never been trained, however, we cannot blame them for thinking their dharma is to be a pendulum. We should train them instead to stop when they get to one side, and keep all their attention there rather than swing immediately somewhere else. Finally, when the mind becomes still, the eyes will become still also. Sri Ramana Maharshi's eyes were extremely beautiful, for they were so still that to look into them was to fall fathoms deep into infinite love.

We can begin practicing one-pointed concentration today by giving our complete attention to whatever we are doing. While eating, for example, we can give our complete attention to our food and not to the newspaper or book we have brought with us. On one occasion in San Francisco we saw a businessman eating the *Wall Street Journal* for lunch. He wasn't paying any attention to his food, so only a few morsels went into his mouth; but he was gorging himself on the newspaper. The same principle of training applies to all the other senses too. Personal conversations give us a splendid opportunity to train our ears. If we are listening to a friend, even if a parrot flies down and perches on his head we should not get excited, point to the parrot, and break out, "Excuse me for interrupting, but there's a parrot on your head." We should be able to concentrate so hard on what our friend is saying that we can tell this urge, "Keep quiet and don't distract me. Afterwards I'll tell him about the bird."

Finally we come to the concept of nonattachment. This is where most of us are vulnerable, for just about everyone is caught and entangled in all sorts of selfish attachments to people and material objects. As long as we are susceptible to these attachments we are not aware that they are ropes tying us down. It is good to remember the picture of Gulliver lying on the ground, tied by innumerable little ropes to innumerable little pegs by innumerable little men that seem almost like hobgoblins. We, too, are prostrate when we are tied down by countless little selfish, self-willed, and separating attachments to people and to things. It is only when we have broken loose from these ties through the practice of meditation that we find freedom.

शुचौ देशे प्रतिष्ठाप्य स्थिरमासनमात्मनः ।
नात्युच्छ्रितं नातिनीचं चैलाजिनकुशोत्तरम् ॥ ११ ॥

*11. Establish yourself firmly in a clean spot, neither too high nor too low, seated on a cloth, a deerskin, and kusha grass.*

Here Sri Krishna advises us to choose a clean place for practicing meditation—clean in the sense of having pure air, quietness, and austerity. Next we should find a suitable way of sitting. It should not be too high, for if we are prone to bouts of sleep we may fall and hurt ourselves. It is wise to sit on the floor, or in a chair with arms. Then Sri Krishna mentions spreading *kusha* grass and a deerskin. This is how it is done in the traditional āshrams of India, but we can sit on an Acrilan blanket or on our bed and still attain spiritual awareness. What is important is to keep our mind one-pointed. To any question of whether we should sit in the full lotus, half lotus, or quarter lotus positions, we can apply Sri Ramana Maharshi's pungent comment that we should sit in the posture in which the mind is still.

Currently we are seeing all kinds of paraphernalia advertised for meditation: special incense, shirts, pillows, and even, I am told, kits for regulating brain waves. Please do not fall for this talk about chemical or mechanical grace; there is only one form of grace: that which comes from the Lord of Love within, which leads to self-purification, strengthening of the will, and selfless service.

तत्रैकाग्रं मनः कृत्वा यतचित्तेन्द्रियक्रियः ।
उपविश्यासने युञ्ज्याद्योगमात्मविशुद्धये ॥१२॥

*12. Having taken your seat, strive to still your
thoughts. Make your mind one-pointed in the practice
of meditation, and your heart will be purified.*

In order to sit for meditation one has to be firm, not only in body,
but in mind as well. Here firmness does not mean sitting rigid and
tense as if rigor mortis had set in; it means sitting with the firm resolve to train the mind to come gradually to rest in the Lord.

No matter whether you sit in a chair or on the carpet, the proper
posture for meditation is with the spinal column erect. Every time
your mind wanders away from the subject of meditation, or you get
drowsy or get into a deeper state of concentration, check to make
sure your spinal column is straight. Many people are not aware of
how their heads droop or turn in meditation, or of how their bodies
sway back and forth when a deeper level of consciousness is
reached; so without dwelling on it, please check your head and back
position occasionally during meditation to make sure they are correct.

Again, Sri Krishna emphasizes here the need to cultivate a one-
pointed mind. Our mind is like a grasshopper chirring and jumping
from one blade of grass to another, and to train the mind to be one-
pointed, we should do only one thing at a time. In our kitchen at
Ramagiri this is one of the main principles the women observe;
when they are cutting a vegetable, they keep their eyes completely
on the knife. On one or two occasions they didn't do this, and minor
first aid had to be rendered.

When our attention is wandering, we have to render first aid
mentally. People whose attention wanders easily are subject to one
of the greatest sources of suffering—boredom. There is nothing
more disastrous in life than to be bored, and one of the effective
ways to relieve boredom is to give more concentration to whatever
we are doing, because it is the quality of attention we give to a job
that makes it interesting. Unfortunately, most of us cannot give our

attention with complete freedom. We are likely to give it only to things we like. There are people who can give their attention freely to trigonometry, but when you give them poetry they will find it impossible to concentrate. My suggestion is that there is real challenge in doing something we do not like, especially when we are overcome by lethargy, backache, and all kinds of problems that seem to prevent us from getting down to work. At first the mind says, "*You may want to work on this project, but I'm not with you.*" But you tell it, "It isn't as bad as it looks, really. Let's just see what it is like. After all, there is no harm in putting our toes in the water and seeing what the temperature is like." Then, when the mind has touched the water, you go a little further and say, "Let's play about a little and see what happens." Little by little you can coax the mind to get so absorbed that it will say at last, "I'm not going to get out of the water. I like playing about."

The capacity to give our undivided attention is one of the essential ingredients of the learning process. All of us have unpleasant chores to do, and sometimes it is helpful to draw up a list of things which need to be done joyfully and without delay, including in this list the jobs we detest, the jobs we would rather delegate. By working at such jobs we gradually release ourselves from the tyranny of likes and dislikes, which means we can give our complete concentration to any task, whether it is pleasant or not.

समं कायशिरोग्रीवं धारयन्नचलं स्थिरः ।
संप्रेक्ष्य नासिकाग्रं स्वं दिशश्चानवलोकयन् ॥१३॥

*13. Hold your body, head, and neck firmly in a
straight line, and keep your eyes from wandering.*

To sit in meditation with the back, neck, and head in a straight line is not as easy as it sounds. As long as your eyes are open, everything is straight. But once you gently close your eyes and start going through the Prayer of St. Francis slowly in the mind, word by word, you begin to concentrate, which means you begin to sink below the surface level of consciousness. As your concentration increases and the mind begins to get one-pointed, forgetting all the distractions you have been occupied with throughout the day, your nervous system starts to relax. All your knots and taut nerves begin to loosen and there is a very natural sense of how good meditation feels. But simultaneously the trunk begins to shorten, the shoulders hump, the neck disappears, and before you know it, the chin has come to rest on the chest. This is just the time, when meditation feels so nice, so relaxing, to draw yourself up, move away from the back support, and sit again with the back, neck, and head in a straight line. The mind says, "I'm alert now. You can trust me." You start the memorized passage again, but it is the same old story. You have to keep straightening your posture over and over again until at last, when a wave of sleep comes near you, your will says, "Vanish. Go back where you came from."

The problem of sleep in meditation will haunt us for some years and as meditation deepens, the will must be strengthened in order to remain awake on a plane of consciousness on which we are not at home, on which we have not learned to travel. In the final stages of meditation, when we go down like a plummet into the depths of our unconscious, there is nothing we can do if we fall asleep. So from now on in meditation, when sleep is overcoming you, draw yourself up by sheer exercise of willpower, keep your spinal column erect, and if necessary open your eyes for a moment and repeat the mantram. At such times you may find it helpful also to look at a picture of Jesus, the Buddha, or some other inspiring spiritual figure. When you have overcome the obstacle of sleep, close your eyes and go back again to the passage.

Not only in meditation can the will be strengthened, but at breakfast, too, when we are eyeing the third piece of toast or the second cup of coffee. Even more effective, when we are greatly agitated and want to go our own way because our parents, partner, friends, or children differ from us, is to make a painful turnabout and go their way instead of ours. If we can do this, the following morning in meditation the wave of sleep will take one look at our will and subside without a murmur. For anyone who wants to overcome the problem of sleep in meditation, this is one of the surest ways to go about it: to make a sudden turnabout and violate one's own self-will in order to foster the happiness of others. Gradually this turnabout will bring a delicious satisfaction, although not unmixed with pain.

Another reason this erect posture must be maintained, according to the Hindu and Buddhist mystics, has to do with the vast mass of evolutionary energy called kundalinī that is located at the base of the spine. As meditation deepens, kundalinī rises up through the spinal column, activating the different centers of consciousness. According to this theory, keeping the spinal column erect in meditation, when accompanied by allied disciplines such as discriminating restraint of the senses and putting the welfare of others first, helps kundalinī to rise.

Sri Krishna also refers here to the position of the eyes, for this can indicate our state of mind. We can see from the eyes of a person whether he is angry, sorrowful, or restless, because in these states the pupils keep darting to and fro. Similarly, when the mind is at rest and the heart is full, the eyes become still and begin to shine. If we want the beauty of the eyes to shine forth, we have to learn to still the mind through the practice of meditation.

प्रशान्तात्मा विगतभीर्ब्रह्मचारिव्रते स्थितः ।
मनः संयम्य मच्चित्तो युक्त आसीत मत्परः ॥१४॥

*14. When his mind has ceased to wander, a man finds complete fulfillment in Me. In this state all fears dissolve in the peace of the Self, and all actions proceed toward Me.*

As our meditation deepens, the mind will become so calm that agitated people will find rest in our presence, and angry people will be forgiving. Even without preaching to others or advising them, our conduct and our unfailing sympathy and support will have a beneficial influence on all those around us. We are all concerned about external pollution, but internal pollution is equally dangerous. One angry person, for example, can upset a whole family. For some, anger is even a feast, a way of introducing excitement into a dull, torpid existence. When a person has been agitated for a long time, it is difficult for him to give up his agitation. We can help such people by never indulging in violence ourselves: by never retaliating, never using harsh words, and never failing to love even those who hate us.

It is difficult to understand that most angry people are frightened. As Gandhi told us, a man who carries a gun is really walking about in fear for his life. When we trust and respect others, all fear vanishes because those around us become our protector, our shield. Another fear that many have is of growing up. Many of us carry a big cradle on our backs, and wherever we go we put it down, get into it, and lie there saying, "You do what I want you to do, and if you don't I'm going to howl and howl and howl." Growing up means taking on life with all its responsibilities and facing whatever comes our way with courage, calmness, and security. We will lose all fears when we realize the Lord is in everyone, making them loving and merciful at heart.

Fear exists only when there is a division in the mind. In the mind there are deep crevices where little bugs of selfishness and separateness live, which thrive on all the minor irritations which occur day in and day out. To remove these little bugs we do not need to use pesticides; all we need to do is reduce our separateness by putting others first, by embracing in our consciousness not only those who support us, which is very easy, but also those who provoke and attack us. Meditation gradually transforms the negative capacity for resentment into a positive capacity for moving closer to our family, our friends, and finally our enemies. By overcoming the obstacles of separateness and self-will that come our way daily in all shapes and sizes, from little irritations to big storms, we eliminate all fear from our consciousness and move closer to the state of perfect peace which is union with the Lord.

युञ्जन्नेवं सदात्मानं योगी नियतमानसः ।
शान्तिं निर्वाणपरमां मत्संस्थामधिगच्छति ॥१५॥

*15. When he constantly controls his mind and*
*senses through the practice of meditation and seeks*
*the Self within, he attains nirvāna, the state of*
*abiding joy and peace in Me.*

The person who keeps his eyes on the Lord all the time, who practices meditation regularly with sustained enthusiasm, trains his
senses, and disciplines his mind to obey him, at last becomes established in nirvāna, the state of abiding joy, in which he sees that all
of us are one. Nirvāna is not to be found beyond the grave; it is
found right here in this life. As the Buddha teaches in the Dhammapada, the man of the world, who lives for himself, suffers in this life
and afterwards as well, while the man of nirvāna lives in joy both in
this life and in the life to come. It is possible to live in the world and
find nirvāna; it is possible to live within the family and yet be established completely in oneself and see the presence of the Lord everywhere.

नात्यश्नतस्तु योगोऽस्ति न चैकान्तमनश्नतः ।
न चाति स्वप्नशीलस्य जाग्रतो नैव चार्जुन ॥१६॥

*16. O Arjuna, they will not succeed in the practice*
*of meditation who eat too much or eat too little, who*
*sleep too much or sleep too little.*

We should always try to follow the middle path, which means we
should strive to be temperate in all we do. We should neither indulge our senses excessively nor mortify them excessively; we
should have neither too much wealth nor too much poverty, neither
too much learning nor too much ignorance, neither too much work
nor too much leisure. Striking this balance in all activities is an exhilarating discipline we all can learn to practice.

Most of us, for example, do not need as much food as we may
think we do. One of the finer points of the art of eating is to stop just

when you are about to ask for another helping: when your hand is outstretched, you should be able to get up and turn your back on the table. It can be a little distressing at the time, but afterwards you have much more appreciation of the meal. I would suggest that we eat just three times a day—a hearty breakfast after meditation, a moderate lunch, and a lighter dinner, based on the findings of modern nutrition rather than on fads or fancies.

There are all kinds of interesting ways in which we can keep the palate on the middle path. When it is craving candy or a hot fudge sundae, go for a walk repeating the mantram, and bargain for time with the mind by telling it, "In two hours when we are going home we can go to an ice cream parlor for a deluxe sundae." Interestingly enough, two hours later the mind has forgotten ice cream sundaes and is thinking about the movie it will enjoy tomorrow evening. All you need do is put just a little break of time between the palate and its desire, for you can count on the mind to change its desires. A more gentlemanly technique, whenever the mind asks for some unnutritious delicacy like a chocolate candy bar, is to try giving it raisins instead. Very soon it will stop asking for candy.

Playing these little tricks on the mind will bring no harm, but do not be violent with it. Treat it gently, patiently, and compassionately; since we have allowed it license for so many years, it is not fair to expect it to come to heel in a day or two. Occasionally, however, when there is a first-rate conflict—when you see a wave of resentment, anxiety, or frustration welling up—it is helpful to skip a meal. When this is done with discrimination, taking particular care that the body is not deprived of its energy, you will find that not only is the mind easier to control, the body benefits too.

Too much sleep, too, is bad for the body, mind, and meditation. When we sleep too much, we may be unable to face a challenge; then, instead of stretching out to meet the challenge, the will simply becomes paralyzed. Sleeping too much is like saying, "I don't like being human; I prefer to be inert like an old tree, or a rock." But too little sleep is equally an enemy of meditation. In order to live in harmony with the laws of life, we need to observe the rhythm of night and day by going to sleep as early as possible at night and getting up as early as possible in the morning. When you get into bed early, repeat the mantram until you fall asleep. Though at first you may not fall asleep easily, you will have no trouble after your body has had a little time to recondition itself. All our habits can be changed completely by using the immense learning tool we acquire through meditation. Going to sleep too early or too late, getting up too early or too late, eating too much or too little, bursting out in anger or crying in agitation—these are all just repeated patterns of thinking, speaking, and acting which can be altered through the practice of meditation.

युक्ताहारविहारस्य युक्तचेष्टस्य कर्मसु ।
युक्तस्वभाववबोधस्य योगो भवति दुःखहा ॥१७॥

*17. The person who has learned to be detached*
*in all his actions through the practice of meditation,*
*who is temperate in eating and sleeping, work and*
*recreation, will come to the end of sorrow.*

Sorrow is necessary for us only when we require it to grow to our full stature. We can think of the Lord as a physical education teacher; he looks us over carefully and selects those of us who are drooping with selfishness and self-will. To these he gives sorrow, saying, "Let me give you some special exercises to help you grow as tall and as straight as you can." When we have grown to our full height and can push ourselves out of the way to become sensitive to the needs of others, the Lord will say, "You don't require any more sorrow, any more ordeals. You have gone beyond all suffering by extinguishing your self-will and selfishness. Now you are ready to help reduce the suffering and sorrow of those around you."

If we start looking carefully at our own suffering, we shall find that it often comes to teach us to stop repeating our mistakes. In my young ignorance I committed many mistakes, and much sorrow came my way. But through my Grandmother's blessing came the desire never to be separate or selfish, and with it the horror of being angry or violent towards any living creature. I was able to learn the lessons of sorrow so that it became impossible for me to commit the same mistakes again. When we have learned not to commit selfish mistakes in life, not to impose our self-will upon our dear ones, our society, and even our enemies, there is no reason why personal suffering should come to us at all.

यदा विनियतं चित्तमात्मन्येवावतिष्ठते ।
निःस्पृहः सर्वकामेभ्यो युक्त इत्युच्यते तदा ॥ १८ ॥

*18. Through constant effort a person learns to withdraw the mind from selfish cravings to the Self within, and thus attains union with the Lord.*

In the early days of meditation we often seem to hear, as it were, two tape recorders playing in our consciousness at the same time. The first tape is the inspirational passage we are using in meditation; the second is a distraction expressing itself in words that contradict and distort the words of the passage. On such occasions all we have to do is give more and more attention to the words of the passage, which means that we are giving less and less attention to the second tape recorder. For a long, long time our meditation will be this dull, dreary discipline of bringing the mind back to the words of the passage and shunning associations and distractions. But if we persist the great day will come, through the grace of the Lord, when our mind will not wander once from the Upanishads or the Prayer of St. Francis. At that time we will not be aware of the jets roaring in the sky, or the trumpets blaring in our neighbor's apartment; we will not be aware of the body which we have always believed ourselves to be. Even if the rapture of this state lasts for only a few minutes, it is long enough for the Divine Physician to dissolve our tensions, resolve our conflicts, and give us the certitude that we can function with a new freedom no matter what problems come our way.

In this verse Sri Krishna tells Arjuna *viniyatam cittam:* "Have a completely disciplined mind; be the master of your senses and mind." The Buddha would say that most of us do not live intentionally. In fact, he would question whether most of us are actually alive; to him we are like puppets pulled by forces outside ourselves, running after what satisfies our senses and away from what violates our self-will. This is not living; this is being flotsam and jetsam on the sea of life. Only when we have brought our senses under control, when we have extinguished our self-will, can we say we live intentionally.

Just imagine what would happen if all the cars in a city were to roll out of their garages and roar out onto every road at top speed without a driver, without obeying signals or traffic rules. There would be hundreds of accidents. This is just what is happening today when people go about driven by their senses, controlled by their self-will instead of sitting in the driver's seat directing their body, senses, and mind. I admire the ease with which the good driver drives; it is almost as though he has eyes in the back of his head. In order to master the art of living we too need eyes in the back of our heads to be able to look at our behavior in the past and correct ourselves wherever we made mistakes. The person who has learned in this way to respect the freedom of all, who has learned never to manipulate others, never to attack others, has a driver's license which is valid always. This is the sign of the person established in himself: he does not collide with those who are angry but goes about with love and respect for others no matter what the circumstances.

यथा दीपो निवातस्थो नेङ्गते सोपमा स्मृता ।
योगिनो यतचित्तस्य युञ्जतो योगमात्मनः ॥ १९ ॥

*19. When meditation is mastered, the mind is unwavering like the flame of a lamp in a sheltered place.*

When I was at the University of Kansas I visited the President Truman Museum where I saw a little clay lamp from Israel, on whose pedestal were inscribed these words from Proverbs 20:27: "The spirit of man is the candle of the Lord." These clay lamps, common in ancient Jerusalem, are still used today in Kerala, where they are lit and placed in an alcove of the shrine. Since there is no wind in the protected niche, the tongue of the flame burns without a flicker.

In the depths of your meditation, when you are concentrating on an inspirational passage such as the Prayer of St. Francis, your mind should be like the tongue of a flame in a windless place, motionless and steady. At that time you will be concentrating completely on the words of the prayer, which means that you are slowly becoming like St. Francis in your daily conduct and consciousness. It requires enormous endeavor to do this, but through ceaseless effort I think every one of us can reach the state in which the mind, like the flame of the clay lamp, does not flicker or waver at all.

यत्रोपरमते चित्तं निरुद्धं योगसेवया ।
यत्र चैवात्मनात्मानं पश्यन्नात्मनि तुष्यति ॥२०॥
सुखमात्यन्तिकं यत्तद्बुद्धिग्राह्यमतीन्द्रियम् ।
वेत्ति यत्र न चैवायं स्थितश्चलति तत्त्वतः ॥२१॥
यं लब्ध्वा चापरं लाभं मन्यते नाधिकं ततः ।
यस्मिन्स्थितो न दुःखेन गुरुणापि विचाल्यते ॥२२॥
तं विद्याद्दुःखसंयोगवियोगं योगसंज्ञितम् ।
स निश्चयेन योक्तव्यो योगोऽनिर्विण्णचेतसा ॥२३॥

*20. In the still mind the Self reveals itself. From the depths of meditation a man draws the joy and peace of complete fulfillment.*
*21. Having attained that abiding joy beyond the senses, revealed in the stilled mind, he will never swerve from the eternal truth that all life is one.*
*22. In this state he desires nothing else, and cannot be shaken by the heaviest burdens of sorrow.*
*23. The practice of meditation frees him from all affliction. This is the path of yoga. Follow it with determination and sustained enthusiasm.*

In these verses Sri Krishna is trying to tell us, as far as words can convey, the state we reach when our mind becomes completely one-pointed. First of all, we see ourselves as we really are. Up until this point, the one person we have never seen is ourselves. When Nureyev appeared in San Francisco not long ago there were quite a few ballet fans who, I was told, flew all the way from New York to see him. The mystics would point out how fruitless it is to go to see important people when our first priority is to see ourselves. We think we know Tom, Dick, and Harry, but we really know everyone, including ourselves, only on the surface level. If we could see our real Self coming down Ashram Street, we would wonder who this beautiful, radiant, magnificent creature could be. We would not be able to take our eyes off him, we would be so full of love. Then he would come to us, slowly, step by step, and enter our consciousness. All of us are full of dazzling beauty just waiting to reveal itself, and in order to let this radiance emerge all we must do is throw off the mask of the self-willed, separate ego with which we identify ourselves today.

Once we have seen our real Self in all its glory, no treasure on earth, no achievement, no pleasure is even worth mentioning. When we look at money, it is only dull metal; when we look at pleasure, it is just dull tinsel; when we look at power and prestige, they are no more than dimestore jewelry. Today we can be excited about the pursuit of little satisfactions because we lack a frame of reference in which to evaluate them meaningfully. It is only when we have made a certain amount of progress on the spiritual path through meditation that we develop a standard of comparison. When we acquire this deeper, clearer point of view, we can compare the joy of St. Francis to the joy of going into a pizza parlor, or the joy of Meister Eckhart to that of going into a beer garden. Then we realize we have been penny-wise and pound-foolish in life, going after trivia when we could as well go after the supreme goal.

In the final stages of meditation the whole burden of regret, resentment, vague longing, and restlessness falls away. This is the end of all sorrow. We become established in the Lord and see him in the heart of every creature—human, beast, bird—and in all life. With this inspiring picture of the goal of meditation, Sri Krishna appeals to Arjuna: "Make your will resolute, and throw yourself into this spiritual endeavor so that you too will go beyond sorrow to become established in the indivisible unity that is divine."

संकल्पप्रभवान्कामांस्त्यक्त्वा सर्वानशेषतः ।
मनसैवेन्द्रियग्रामं विनियम्य समन्ततः ॥२४॥

*24. Renouncing wholeheartedly all selfish desires
and expectations, use your will to control the senses.*

In order to attain the supreme state of complete security and boundless joy, we have to renounce every trace of selfish desire and sweep away the last little selfish urge hiding in the cobwebs in the corner of the ego. For the vast majority of us, this takes a whole lifetime of sweeping with the broom of meditation.

Every morning my Grandmother used to sweep the veranda of our house, which was constantly threatened by the dust of tropical India. If she had neglected her sweeping, the dust would have grown thick after just one morning; and if left unswept for a few weeks, the entire veranda would have been hidden under the dust. Similarly, our minds get cluttered and covered with debris when we fail to have our daily meditation. We may be tempted to meditate only once or twice a week, so that on weekdays we can devote all our time to pursuing our pleasure and profit. But when we try to clean only on the weekend, it takes all day. Even then we sometimes add further difficulties by stimulating our senses. After a few weekends like this, we begin to clean only once a month, but at that point the pile of dirt and debris is too high for even a vacuum cleaner to clear away.

The way to keep the mind clean and pure is to spend half an hour every day, no matter what other responsibilities we have, in the practice of meditation. If we do this regularly every morning, we gradually shall find that it becomes easy to keep the place clean. By practicing meditation regularly and keeping our senses under control, we can clean away the debris of *sankalpa,* all our selfish desires, and make room for the Lord of Love. Without the practice of meditation, it is difficult to bring the senses under control, and without sense control, it is difficult to rise above the physical body; without rising above the physical body, it is not possible to discover the indivisible unity of life. From this we can see how important it is to devote a half hour every morning—such a small amount of time—regularly and enthusiastically to the practice of meditation.

शनैः शनैरुपरमेद्बुद्ध्या धृतिगृहीतया ।
आत्मसंस्थं मनः कृत्वा न किंचिदपि चिन्तयेत् ॥२५॥

*25. Keep your mind from wandering. Little by little, through patience and repeated effort, the mind will become stilled in the Self.*

Instead of being impatient and always wondering when the Lord will come, if we throw ourselves heart and soul into the practice of meditation and the allied disciplines of sense restraint and selfless service, gradually over the years we shall become complete master of every area of consciousness. On the spiritual path we must make every effort to move forward even if it is little by little, even if every day we keep making mistakes. Sometimes we are so insensitive and preoccupied with ourselves that when we try to put others first we simply are not aware of their needs. Our mistakes begin to haunt us; but rather than sitting in a corner and crying over the day's errors, or developing a comfortable guilt complex, we should repeat the mantram and make sure that we do not repeat the same mistakes the next day.

I remember how difficult it was for me to change my food habits, especially after years of highly spiced Indian food which was sadly lacking in nutrition. In the company of friends, seated around the table, you sometimes cannot resist temptation. When they are smacking their lips over french-fried potatoes or English muffins spread thick with butter, you find yourself joining in, and before you know it you have eaten food that will not help your body, mind, or intellect. In meditation, when I used to come to the verse in the Gita where the Lord says, "Anyone who allows his senses to sweep him away is like a little boat caught in a storm—he will never make harbor," it would stab me like a dagger. The memory of something I had eaten would try to prevent me from meditating, but I would concentrate more and more on the words of the passage as hard as I could. During the day, when I was tempted to indulge in some special sweet, all that I had to do was think of how I would have to go through all that conflict again. When the senses are trying to sweep us away from the path, when our self-will is disrupting relationships with those around us, it is good to remind ourselves that even though we may get some temporary satisfaction, we will have to go through the pain of ridding ourselves of these selfish desires all over again.

In learning to control the mind, the repetition of the Holy Name is an invaluable aid. When we get angry or afraid, we should not ask the mind why it is in such a state, because this gives it more attention and intensifies its anger or fear. The mind is something like a high-powered computer which sometimes goes out of order, and when it gets angry or afraid, this is just a mechanical breakdown which does not affect our real Self at all. If anger or fear is taking possession of the mind, the way to prevent a breakdown is to go for a long, brisk walk repeating the mantram, and anger will become compassion, fear will become courage, and hatred will become love.

By doing this for many years, we can correct our destructive responses and cultivate a positive, constructive state of mind. Even if our habits have been developing since we were two years old, they can be changed through the practice of meditation. In this sense meditation is the most powerful learning tool we have, and though it may take years of hard work to get hold of it, once we have acquired this immense skill nothing on earth can equal the satisfaction, the joy, and the sense of mastery it will bring. We are all subject to deep resentments going back to the early days of our childhood. Usually there is very little that we can do about these deep-seated problems, but with the learning tool of meditation we can travel into the depths of our consciousness and get rid of them once and for all.

When you are able to travel into deeper levels of consciousness, you may have an experience in your sleep in which something almost like a pistol shot goes off in your head. On the following morning, you can almost see your inhibitions lying at the foot of the bed. You get up and feel as if shackles have been taken off your feet, as if handcuffs have been removed from your hands. This will take place over and over again, because we have a list of fears to shed as big as a Sears Roebuck catalog, and it is only after we have shed all these fears and resentments that we will find ourselves in the supreme state, seeing the Lord everywhere, in everyone, all the time.

यतो यतो निश्चरति मनश्चञ्चलमस्थिरम् ।
ततस्ततो नियम्यैतदात्मन्येव वशं नयेत् ॥२६॥

*26. It is the nature of the mind to be restless and diffuse, always seeking satisfaction without. Lead it within; train it to rest in the Self.*

The nature of the mind is to desire, to desire, to desire, and most of us firmly believe that permanent joy can be found by satisfying our desires. The mind is such a cunning, clever customer that I have a sneaking admiration for it when it comes and says it will make us happy by giving us, say, Helen of Troy. We fall for the mind's tempting promise, but we find the Cyclopes instead. When we complain to the mind, "Mr. Desire, this is not what you promised—people with eyes in their foreheads trying to gobble us up," the mind says, "Well, that was just an experiment; here is a real offer for happiness, and if you will accept it, I'm sure you will be completely satisfied." Again we are convinced that we will not be led astray, but it is still the same story: we still haven't learned; we still go searching for joy outside ourselves. Some of the great mystics have thrown up their hands at the number of times we have to go around the world before we see that it is round, at the way we turn our back upon joy until we discover, through the grace of the Lord, that joy has been right here within us all the time.

One of the games I used to enjoy was ping-pong, and with concentration I mastered all sorts of styles of gripping the paddle and returning the ball. I haven't played ping-pong for many years now, but with the news of how table tennis tournaments between China and the United States have mended international relations, I had a little yearning to play the game again. Now when two people are arguing I can always bring them together and say, "Let's play ping-pong." When we were in Portland, Oregon, we visited Reed College, where we found a room with ping-pong tables and paddles but not a ball in sight. I felt a little frustrated having gone that far out of my way to play ping-pong and not being able to, but I repeated the mantram a few times and forgot all about the incident. Then yesterday at dinner one of our friends told us he had discovered a ping-pong table complete with balls and paddles in the barn at Ramagiri. Imagine going to Oregon and looking for ping-pong equipment when all the time it is lying right there in your barn! This is my illustration of Jesus' statement, "The kingdom of heaven lies within."

In order to realize this inner joy for ourselves, it is necessary to still the mind, to rid it of all selfish desires and expectations. This is what we are learning to do in meditation when we bring our mind back every time it wanders away from the words of the inspirational passage to the movie theater or the supermarket. As time goes on, the mind will wander less and less, so that after some years we may have to bring it back only two or three times. In deeper meditation the great day may come when it does not wander away at all but stays put on the words of the inspirational piece, which means the mind is so concentrated in all its power that it lights up the whole passage. In the mystical tradition this is described as the words opening their doors and taking us in. They are no longer just words we are repeating in our mind; they have become integrated into our consciousness, transforming our character and our daily lives. When we can concentrate completely on St. Francis's words, "It is in pardoning that we are pardoned," then instead of holding things against our parents, our children, or our friends, we will be able to open our arms wide to them. We will be able to stand steadfast with love and respect for those who oppose us, and our former enemy will come to us as a good friend. This steadfast love for all is abiding joy.

प्रशान्तमनसं ह्येनं योगिनं सुखमुत्तमम् ।
उपैति शान्तरजसं ब्रह्मभूतमकल्मषम् ॥२७॥

*27. Abiding joy comes to those who still the mind
and senses, who free themselves from the taint of
self-will and unify their consciousness in the Lord.*

The person who sees the Lord present in all life has unshakable
strength, for he is rooted in the Lord. Not all the dangers in the
world will shake such a person out of his security, because nothing
can agitate him: his mind is still, and his thoughts are completely
under control.

Every day we have opportunities for spiritual growth when
things happen to us which we do not like, which start the mind moving in all directions in agitation. There is no use getting mad at the
mind, because the angrier we get at the mind, the more we will be
agitated. The best thing to do is to keep the mind quiet by repeating
the mantram over and over again. If you cannot repeat the mantram in your mind, write it in a book kept for this purpose. We used
to have people dropping in at odd hours very agitated, and when
they would start telling me what so-and-so said and how they wish
they could have put him in his place, I would give them the mantram notebook and ask them to write the mantram in it two hundred times. When they had finished writing, they would leave with
their minds peaceful. It is not at all helpful to exchange agitating
stories, so when someone starts narrating his tale of resentments,
ask him to write the mantram a number of times instead.

Another secret for stilling an agitated mind is to throw yourself
into work with no thought of reward or remuneration. A necessary
part of spiritual discipline for most young people is hard physical
work, which when combined with the use of the mantram calms the
mind.

When all our selfish, agitating desires have been expelled from
our mind, what is left is pure joy, pure spirit, of which we have been
unaware all this time. Joy is imprisoned within us, just waiting to be
released from the jailer, our selfish desires. To release it, all we have

to do is eliminate every selfish craving and extinguish every selfish impulse, which takes tremendous effort and inexhaustible patience.

Spiritual joy is sometimes described as a bashful girl who is just waiting to tiptoe up and put her arms about us, while all we are trying to do is keep her away. Our selfish desires and cravings tell us not to let her come near us because then they will have to go; and since we are under an hypnotic spell of ignorance, we believe that these selfish urges, which make us miserable to the point of agony, are our real friends. It is astonishing that we can be so perverse as to do just the things that will make us unhappy. Resentment and retaliation tear us apart, yet we let ourselves be driven by them. Instead, we need to learn to accept joy, who is always ready to come to us. This is what we are learning to do through the practice of meditation, to throw open our arms and welcome the joy of living that has been waiting all this time to embrace us.

युञ्जन्नेवं सदात्मानं योगी विगतकल्मषः ।
सुखेन ब्रह्मसंस्पर्शमत्यन्तं सुखमश्नुते ॥२८॥

*28. This infinite joy of union with the Lord is easily attained by those who are free from the burden of self-will and established within themselves.*

It is wise to remind ourselves that our real Self is absolutely pure; in our natural state we are untainted by any selfish desires, completely free of self-will. Anger, fear, greed, lust, malice—these are all unnatural states that we have come to accept as natural. Today we are imprisoned by our passions and cravings, but through the practice of meditation we can break off these shackles and live freely like the eagle soaring in the air.

Several days ago at Ramagiri I watched six baby swallows learn how to fly. They were seated on the telephone wires observing the mother bird, who came flying slowly in front of them, doing the easier turns and showing them the basics of flying. There was no point in telling these baby swallows to read books or attend lectures on how to fly; they have an inborn instinct for flying. They learn the skills of flight by watching their mother, who was showing her babies that there was no need to sit there quaking as if they were going to fall. Learning to fly may not be easy, but this is what birds are born to do. This was the lesson she taught her little ones.

Likewise, Sri Krishna sees us sitting on a perch made of pleasure, profit, power, or prestige, quaking with every variation in our bank account and every critical comment that comes our way, and he asks us if we would not rather forget our failings, weaknesses, and insecurities and become united with him. This is what we are born to do: to turn our back on our selfish interests and give all our love to the Lord, so that all the faculties and resources which have been hidden in us can come into our lives to the great benefit of those around us. Then we will no longer be acting; the Lord will take hold of our arms and act through us.

Today at a park in San Francisco we saw a mime show in which a young man really illustrated, to my mind, how we can be transformed when we yield ourselves to the Lord's direction. At first the mime was seated on a bench, talking and eating like everyone else; then he started his performance, and all his movements changed as if some puppeteer were standing behind him pulling the strings. There were all sorts of people passing by, and he had an uncanny knack for imitating them. I enjoyed the performance so much because it showed what all of us are like when we are ego-driven. For example, a high-powered businessman was shooting along to the financial district repeating his Dow Jones mantram. He was annoyed at the mime's clever caricature of his self-important air, but the young fellow's gestures were so eloquent that he forgot his high-powered business freeze and became a human being again and walked on smiling. The only occasion on which the young fellow lost was when a buxom, middle-aged lady came along; when he tried to imitate her, she just hugged him.

When we are ego-driven, living for ourselves, revenging the wrongs others do to us and hating those who hate us, we are like the people the mime was imitating. But if we surrender ourselves to the Lord, when he picks us up and pulls the strings behind us we can make a tremendous contribution to the welfare of all those who come in contact with us.

सर्वभूतस्थमात्मानं सर्वभूतानि चात्मनि ।
ईक्षतेयोगयुक्तात्मा सर्वत्र समदर्शनः ॥२९॥

*29. They see that the Lord is enshrined in every creature, and that all creation comes from the Lord. With consciousness unified through the practice of meditation, they see the Lord everywhere.*

The mark of the man or woman who has become united with the Lord is that he or she sees the Lord in all fellow beings, in every form of life. In one of the delightful anecdotes in the *Mahābhā-rata,* Dharmaputra, the oldest of the Pāndavas, turns up at the gates of heaven with his dog. Dvārapāla, the gatekeeper, takes down all the vital information about Dharmaputra—name, address, siblings —and then he notices the dog. "Sorry," says Dvārapāla, "we don't admit dogs. See that little sign? It says Dogs Not Allowed." Then follows an awfully confusing situation: Dharmaputra is established in the Lord and should be admitted, but what should be done about the dog? Finally Dvārapāla gives Dharmaputra a choice: to enter heaven alone, without the dog, or to go back where he came from with his dog. Without the slightest hesitation, Dharmaputra chooses to be with his dog, who is then immediately revealed as Lord Krishna in disguise.

The illumined man sees the Lord in every creature and is inca-pable of exploiting any other being for his own profit or pleasure. When we were on the Blue Mountain, we once saw a little black calf, only a few months old, being led to slaughter. I looked at the calf, and it was as if tears were flowing from his eyes; he was trying to tell me in his dumb language, "See what your brother is going to do to me?" Right then I decided that at every opportunity I would put in a good word on behalf of all animals.

It is not easy to understand, when we are caught in cultural hab-its, that eating meat violates the indivisible unity of life. It used to be very difficult to find a restaurant that served vegetarian food. Now, however, there are good vegetarian restaurants springing up in many cities, and at every chance we get, we can recommend these restaurants to our friends. This is a simple way of showing our love and respect for the Lord, who lives in the lamb, the deer, the cow, and all other forms of life.

योे मां गह्गति सर्वत्र सर्वं च मयि पश्यति ।
तस्याहं न प्रणश्यामि स च मे न प्रणश्यति ॥३०॥

*30. I am ever present to those who have realized Me in every creature. Seeing all life as my manifestation, they are never separated from Me.*

Now the Lord tells us that when we see him in everyone, when we show everyone the same courtesy and consideration regardless of what they do to us, we will receive his guidance, and he will protect us against all the storms of life. We can cultivate this equal vision every day by trying to see the Lord in everyone around us.

If in spite of our best efforts we become angry, agitated, or afraid, we can bring our mind back to the state of calmness by going for a walk repeating the mantram. The rhythm of our footsteps and the rhythm of the mantram will blend and stabilize the rhythm of our breathing, which is closely connected with our state of mind. Angry people breathe irregularly; those who are calm, loving, and secure breathe like a little child, smoothly, slowly, and deeply.

Even if we turn to the Lord as a last resort, when all else fails, he is still content to receive us. When I was at the University of Minnesota I became friends with a young fellow from Kerala studying to be an engineer. He had always been a good student, but the night before his final examination he came to me afraid and anxious that he might fail. He had tried pep pills and lecture notes, but when they failed to dispel his fears he had come to see if there was anything in the Gita that could help him. I did not ask him why he had not come six years sooner; I just told him that the Lord is always glad when we come to him, always ready to help us when ruin is

staring us in the face and all other paths have failed. He was so relieved to hear this that he asked me what exactly Sri Krishna had to
say about engineering exams in the Gita. I told him that there was
no exact reference, but in times of danger— "Oh," he broke in,
"that's my final, all right. Real danger—I'll lose my scholarship and
my lifelong desire to be an engineer will never be fulfilled." So I
asked him to repeat the mantram while I took him for a walk from
Minneapolis to Saint Paul and then back again—a distance of about
twelve miles. He was so completely relaxed when we got home that
he was asleep before his head touched the pillow. The breathing exercise of walking with the mantram changed his anxiety and insecurity into calm assurance that he would do well in his exam, and he
did, too.

Whenever we have a difficult examination or a trying emotional
situation to face, the best thing we can do is repeat the mantram. In
going to sleep at night, it is simple to close our eyes and repeat the
Holy Name until we fall asleep. No matter how difficult the problems we have to face, this simple tonic will rest and refresh us so
that we will be at our best in meeting the day's challenges. I have
the responsibility of guiding the meditation of hundreds of people,
but when I go to bed now, after years of practice, I can just hand my
responsibilities over to the Lord. The mantram takes over so that I
hear it in my sleep, so that I see the Lord in my sleep; and when I
wake up I am refreshed in body, mind, and spirit, able to face whatever the day brings because I have placed my burden at the feet of
the Lord.

सर्वभूतस्थितं यो मां भजत्येकत्वमास्थितः ।
सर्वथा वर्तमानोऽपि स योगी मयि वर्तते ॥३१॥

*31. They worship Me in the hearts of all, and all
their actions proceed from Me. Wherever they may
live, they abide in Me.*

Outward signs of spiritual effort such as going to temple or church
are no substitute for the practice of meditation, for without meditation we will not have the capacity for transforming anger into com-

passion, ill will into goodwill, and hatred into love. A man may
have a brilliant intellect, may have won the Nobel Prize; but when
it comes to changing anger into sympathy or hostility into kindness,
he is helpless without the spiritual discipline of meditation.

You have probably seen that huge machine which demolishes old
buildings by hoisting a heavy metal ball high into the air and then
dropping it with a terrific crash. This is similar to what occurs in the
early stages of meditation, in which we destroy old habits of acting,
speaking, and thinking. This is a painful process; the joy comes
when we start rebuilding. At that point we do not have to drive
miles to pick up materials, cart them home, unload them, and store
them until we are ready to use them. The Lord has all the materials
ready, and he is waiting to hand them to us as we need them. We
have only to demolish our self-will and selfishness and he will give
us the materials of love, wisdom, patience, and endurance with
which to build a house that can never be destroyed.

If we continue to use our old house, built with selfishness, fear,
and anger, without a secure foundation, it is likely to crash and bury
us in its ruins. But if we tear down the old, creaking structure and
build a new one on firm foundations, with materials given by the
Lord, then we will live free from anxiety and fear. With such a
house, we will be able to offer shelter to more and more of those
around us. This is another way of phrasing the truth that Sri Krishna
never tires of repeating: "Do not depend on things outside yourself,
on money, possessions, power, or fame, for they will not bring lasting joy or security; they will bring only a temporary satisfaction
which will leave you weaker and weaker with the passage of time."

आत्मौपम्येन सर्वत्र समं पश्यति योऽर्जुन ।
सुखं वा यदि वा दुःखं स योगी परमो मतः ॥३२॥

*32. When a person responds to the joys and sorrows
of others as if they were his own, he has attained the
highest state of spiritual union.*

In this verse Sri Krishna sums up the entire art of living in one simple, practical suggestion: to understand how to behave towards others, all we have to do is understand that what gives us pain gives others pain also. Jesus uses similar language when he tells us, "All things whatsoever ye would that men should do to you, do ye even so to them."

We can apply this wise advice even to the smallest trifles of daily living. When we are waiting for a friend who is a few minutes late, for example, we look at our watch, shake it, and get more agitated as the seconds go by. But when we are half an hour late, we expect our friend to be patient and understanding. We expect others to overlook our few foibles because of our many virtues, yet at the same time we consider it our prerogative to point out everyone else's weaknesses and mistakes. To understand others, to be considerate towards others, we have only to recognize how much we appreciate consideration ourselves.

The person with real spiritual consideration will help others forget about their failings. Learning to make others comfortable, even when they have made a mistake, is another way of going beyond our petty little selves and becoming aware of everyone else's needs. The more we can forget ourselves by being sensitive and aware of everyone else, the more the Lord comes to life in us. The Compassionate Buddha was good at driving this point home to his disciples. He would tell them there was nothing to discourse or debate about in understanding other people: what offends you, offends others. It is that simple. When someone makes a sarcastic remark about us, we are not exactly delighted; therefore, we cannot afford to make sarcastic remarks to others.

Harsh thoughts, resentful thoughts, can wound others more deeply than knives. We are not used to thinking of thoughts as things; our idea of a thing is something we can put in a cup and rattle. We are unaware of the cacophony of the thoughts that rattle in our consciousness. If we could open our inner ear, we would be surprised to hear these hateful thoughts making such horrible noises in our consciousness: "I hate you, I hate you," or "Drop dead, drop dead." Such hateful thoughts injure others like a knife we throw at them over and over, and injure us too because each thought rankles and digs further into our consciousness as the days go by. Yet thoughts can be curative also. When a person bursts out in anger against us, if we can remain friendly, not hold his mistake against him, and move closer to him, we will bring him continual relief from his anger. This is true of even the roughest character; everyone responds to forbearance and forgiveness, which bless not only the one who gives them and the one who receives them, but everyone who associates with the man or woman who forgives.

अर्जुन उवाच
योऽयं योगस्त्वया प्रोक्तः साम्येन मधुसूदन ।
एतस्याहं न पश्यामि चञ्चलत्वात्स्थितिं स्थिराम् ॥३३॥

ARJUNA:
*33. O Madhusūdana, the complete stillness of
union which you describe is beyond my comprehen-
sion. How can the mind, which is so restless, attain
lasting peace?*

*Madhu* is the name of a demon, the ego demon; *sūdana* refers to one who destroys. This is a beautiful name for Sri Krishna: Madhusūdana, 'the slayer of the ego.' Arjuna addresses him in this way with great respect, confessing that he sees no way of conquering his restless, turbulent mind.

We know that in meditation there are days when we come confidently out of the meditation room thinking we have performed the funeral ceremony of the ego; but then, on the following morning in meditation, we hear a titter from the mind which says, "Fooled you, didn't I?" Sometimes we feel almost ridiculous for trying to conquer this demon called the mind; yet we must not let ourselves lapse into negative thinking, for it is completely within our power to reshape our mind, our conduct, and our destiny. We do this by making intentional choices about how we act, how we speak, and how we think, day in and day out. By using inspirational passages like the Prayer of St. Francis or the second chapter of the Gita, our choices in daily living will become wiser and more in harmony with the selfless ideal we are meditating upon. In this way we begin to transform our thinking from fear, anxiety, and despair into courage, love, and wisdom.

चञ्चलं हि मनः कृष्ण प्रमाथि बलवद्दृढम् ।
तस्याहं निग्रहं मन्ये वायोरिव सुदुष्करम् ॥३४॥

*34. O Krishna, the mind is restless, turbulent, and violent. Trying to control the mind is like trying to control the wind.*

Now Arjuna gets down to specifics by telling the Lord, "You might as well ask me to control the wind, to ride on a storm or to master a hurricane, as to control my mind." Even the expression "I think" is more a euphemism than a statement of fact: we do not think most of our thoughts; they think us. We sit in meditation with a deep desire to meditate on the Lord, but how is it our thoughts go to the local pizza parlor, or to the movie we saw? The answer is that the mind just thinks what thoughts it likes. When we at last become aware, through meditation, of the lack of liberty in our own realm, we get the incentive to drive the usurper, our ego, from the throne. The ego is seated there scepter in hand, and since we do not know that he really isn't king, we all say, "You command, we obey." Patanjali, the great teacher of ancient India, calls meditation *rāja yoga,* the 'royal path,' the way to depose the ego and reinstate the Lord as the true ruler of our body, mind, and spirit.

Having listened to Arjuna's lamentation that the battle of the ego is too fierce for him, and heard him say he can defeat others but not his own selfish passions, Sri Krishna now smiles lovingly, puts his arm around his friend, and encourages him to take on his greatest foe, his own selfishness and separateness.

श्री भगवानुवाच
असंशयं महाबाहो मनो दुर्निग्रहं चलम् ।
अभ्यासेन तु कौन्तेय वैराग्येण च गृह्यते ॥३५॥

SRI KRISHNA:

*35. It is true that the mind is restless and difficult
to control. But it can be conquered, O Mahābāho,
through regular practice and detachment.*

The Lord does not address Arjuna as "mister" here; he calls him
*Mahābāho,* 'you whose arms extend to the heavens.' Our arms, too,
can extend to the heavens if we try to reach beyond ourselves. Today we are leading selfish lives, going after what concerns us, ob-
livious of the needs of others, and this selfishness has crippled our
arms. But the Lord of Love tells us that if we stretch our arms wide
to embrace everyone, if we use them for comforting and strengthening others, we will find them growing longer and longer until finally
we will be able to reach out and catch the Lord.

Stretching our arms is not easy, for it takes untiring effort and
the grit to bear with others no matter how unlovingly they treat us.
We start strengthening our arms right with our family, with our
friends, and on our job, by doing little things for others. It is easiest
to begin by establishing good relationships with our family, because
they want to be loving and close as much as we do. Then, after we
have brought a cease-fire to the guerilla warfare in our own home,
we can gradually develop good relationships with our neighbors,
then with our city council, then on to the state capital; and finally,
when we have proven ourselves to be an unshakable negotiator for
peace, we can work on a national and international level.

Yesterday we took the children to start their swimming lessons,
and I was recalling how I learned swimming from my Grandmother
in just two easy lessons. First she showed me how; then she told me
to get into the water and swim like her, reassuring me that she
would rescue me if I needed help. I had such trust and faith in her
that I plunged right in and, after swallowing some water, started
swimming. In contrast, the gradual, incremental method of the

modern instructor is a safe and sure way of teaching a large number of people to swim. From what I saw yesterday, they start you out in the baby pool, blowing bubbles. Then they take you on to kicking, and when this is mastered, you learn to dog paddle. Likewise, on the spiritual path the incremental approach is the logical sequence for us. We gradually make our arms long and strong by setting our lives right, first in our own homes and then in our community and society.

The instructions we need to follow to develop selflessness are very simple. Practice meditation regularly every day. Repeat the mantram at every opportunity. Restrain the senses with temperate, moderate choices, and put the welfare of all those around you first. At the swimming pool I saw an object lesson in what is meant by carrying out instructions. An excellent instructor was teaching four children to dive by showing them all the movements they should follow to do a perfect dive. Although all four were listening to everything he said, and watching him closely, each gave a different performance. The little girl did such a perfect dive that I had to hold myself back from applauding loudly. She had the capacity to translate instruction into practice. Then came the little boys: one did a belly flop, another tried to curl into a ball, and the third, over-enthusiastic, landed on his back. For them, the capacity to translate instruction into practice was still in the making. Like the little girl, we should try to remember Sri Krishna's instructions exactly and follow them to the letter.

In the second line Sri Krishna tells us there are two essential aids for bringing the mind under control. One is *abhyāsa:* regular, systematic practice. Every day, no matter what problems try to interfere, we must get up as early as we can and meditate. When we do this regularly, our practice will become perfect. The other is *vairāgya:* detachment from our opinions, our actions, our ego. We are so entangled and embroiled in ourselves that we take everything personally. Once, after I had been talking about some of our human weaknesses, a lady in the audience indignantly asked me why I had been talking about her that way in public. Anger, jealousy, malice—

these are weaknesses we all have. Instead of giving in to them, however, we should turn our back on these petty demands for attention and go against our frustration and anger when these demands are not met. With sustained practice of meditation and sustained detachment from the ego, Sri Krishna reassures us that we will be able to reach him at last.

असंयतात्मना योगो दुष्प्राप इति मे मतिः ।
वश्यात्मना तु यतता शक्योऽवाप्तुमुपायतः ॥३६॥

*36. Those who lack self-control will find it difficult to progress in meditation. But those who are earnest in the practice of meditation and self-restraint will attain the goal.*

If we are prepared to base our lives on meditation and follow Sri Krishna's instructions exactly, union with the Lord is possible. But if we are lethargic or sporadic—if we start out on the spiritual path with a big bang and end up with a whimper—the unitive state is not possible. The Sanskrit word *ārambhashūra,* 'hero at the beginning,' describes this second type perfectly.

The person who succeeds on the spiritual path is the plugger, the one who will not give up. If he cannot run, he will walk; if he cannot walk, he will crawl. He will not take no for an answer. To reach a selfless goal, he is prepared to climb over any obstacle; whatever barriers are in his way, he will pile them up into a big heap to climb over an even greater barrier. If we keep trying to make the most of these opportunities, we will discover that there is joy in overcoming what seemed to be an immovable obstacle. At first these efforts to grow are extremely painful, because they usually require us to go against our self-will. But if we keep our eyes on the supreme goal, these agonizing stabs will turn into little pinpricks and finally into just the tickling of a feather. When we have such complete, unqualified dedication to the supreme goal, we shall find what joy there is in going forward on the spiritual path.

अर्जुन उवाच
अयतिः श्रद्धयोपेतो योगाच्चलितमानसः ।
अप्राप्य योगसंसिद्धिं कां गतिं कृष्ण गच्छति ॥३७॥

ARJUNA:

*37. Krishna, what happens to the man who has
faith, but who wanders from the path and loses
sight of the goal?*

Here Arjuna is very much our representative, giving voice to the
disquieting doubts that keep nibbling at little bits of our consciousness. Sounding like a skeptical modern man, Arjuna asks Sri
Krishna: "Supposing that after practicing meditation for some
years, a force beyond my control makes me give it up. Are all those
years of hard discipline wasted?" This is a question we are all likely
to ask in the early stages of meditation.

After we have been meditating for some years we will gradually
begin to see some of its great rewards. By bringing the senses under
control, we will come to have vibrant health; by bringing the mind
under control, we will find a state of quiet joy; and by bringing the
ego under control, we will develop more loving relationships with
our family and friends. If, after having a glimpse of these rewards,
we give up meditation for some reason, we will find there is nothing
in the world to take its place. We can throw ourselves into feverish
pleasure and excitement, into the driving pursuit of power, but
there will always be a little voice inside us saying, "You've lost the
path."

This verse is very apposite today, especially with respect to the
pressing problem of drug addiction. Thousands of young people
are being misled by the assertion that psychedelic drugs can bring
about spiritual awareness. Even well-known people have made
statements about Indian sages using drugs; but I have no hesitation
in saying that no sage worth his mantram has ever taken drugs for
spiritual purposes. Meher Baba, a great modern mystic, warned us
that not only do drugs not bring spiritual awareness, but when

taken for a long time they may damage our capacity for spiritual awareness. If we look for a chemical shortcut through drugs, there is a possibility we will reach a point where we will be unable to meditate. Meditation is such a demanding expedition into the world within that we must have a strong, resilient body, a fit nervous system, a calm mind, and a lucid intellect, all of which are likely to be impaired not just by drugs, but by any form of excessive indulgence in the senses and in self-will.

कच्चिन्नोभयविभ्रष्टश्छिन्नाभ्रमिव नश्यति ।
अप्रतिष्ठो महाबाहो विमूढो ब्रह्मणः पथि ॥३८॥
एतन्मे संशयं कृष्ण छेत्तुमर्हस्यशेषतः ।
त्वदन्यः संशयस्यास्य छेत्ता न ह्युपपद्यते ॥३९॥

*38. If a man becomes deluded on the spiritual path will he lose the support of both worlds, like a cloud scattered in the sky?*
*39. O Krishna, you who are the dispeller of all doubts, remove this doubt which binds me.*

Probably everyone has watched the wind break up a big billowy cloud into tiny pieces and scatter them all over the sky. Arjuna compares himself to such a cloud and asks Sri Krishna, "What will happen if some great calamity, some overwhelming desire, picks me up, cuts up my consciousness, and scatters my mind, my resolve, and my will in all directions, making my desire for the spiritual life disappear like a cloud? Will I have lost both the world of sense pleasure and the joy of the spiritual life?" This is a very practical question, which is likely to occur to all of us who have been used to indulging our senses and imposing our self-will on others. Having confessed his doubts, Arjuna here pleads with the Lord to give them a fatal blow. In samādhi, when the Lord of Love permeates our consciousness, all our doubts will cease, and there will come a tremendous inner certitude that will convey itself to everyone around us.

श्री भगवानुवाच
पार्थ नैवेह नामुत्र विनाशस्तस्य विद्यते ।
न हि कल्याणकृत्कश्चिद्दुर्गतिं तात गच्छति ॥४०॥

SRI KRISHNA:

*40. Pārtha, my son, spiritual work will never
be wasted, nor will one who does such work ever
come to a bad end, either here or in the world
to come.*

Now we can almost see Sri Krishna coming closer to Arjuna, putting his arm about him, and saying, "Never will meditation on Me be wasted, even if it has been done only for a short time. No step taken on the spiritual path is ever in vain." According to the Hindu and Buddhist scriptures, no person is ever lost, for we are all children of the Divine Father. We can find the most secluded place to hide and delay our reunion all we want; but whether we like it or not, one day we are going to go home to the Lord.

A beautiful aspect of the Hindu mystical tradition is that the word *damnation* never occurs. All of us, even though we are tardy and playing truant, are still children of the Lord. A good way to strengthen ourselves and ward off negative states of feeling is to remember that in spite of our outward acts and appearances we are pure, perfect, and ever divine in origin.

Many years ago I went to a church service where the minister delivered a very strong sermon. The congregation seemed to enjoy it tremendously, and I realized how, in today's world, we need someone who will occasionally shock us into the awareness that we are on the wrong path. Once in the pulpit this minister started hurling forked lightning in all directions; and when the climax of the sermon came, he started singling out members of the congregation whom he knew, telling them, "You're a sinner." I was cowering, hoping that he wouldn't call on me, because in the Hindu way I had always been told, "You're a saint." When everyone is in a conspiracy to convince us, even when it seems unjustified, that we are a saint, one day we give in and actually become one. On the other hand, when our negative behavior is emphasized, when we are told we are sinners, we develop guilt feelings. So please tell your children that they are little saints, even when they seem not to warrant it. We can help adults in this same way too by always emphasizing their bright side. Everyone has a favorable side, and when we are patient and forbearing, people will rise to our expectations.

प्राप्य पुण्यकृतां लोकानुषित्वा शाश्वतीः समाः ।
शुचीनां श्रीमतां गेहे योगभ्रष्टोऽभिजायते ॥४१॥

*41. When such people die, they go to other realms where the righteous live. They dwell there for countless years and then are reborn into a home which is pure and prosperous.*

In this verse Sri Krishna tells us that if we give up meditation after some years because of overpowering sense-desires or self-will, he will carefully store our sādhana for us so we can pick it up later. The Lord is a good storekeeper, and he will keep our sādhana in a packet carefully put away on the shelf until we come and reclaim it the next time we enter the human context. When we return to the store and ask him, "Will you look for something I forgot last time? It's a packet of six years' meditation," Sri Krishna will say, "I've kept it very carefully up on this shelf. It's a pretty good packet; weighs a good bit, you know."

As proof of this he tells us we will be born next time into a family with good parents, who will help us by their personal example to be patient and forgiving and to lead the spiritual life. This is perhaps why I had the great blessing to be born as the grandchild of my Grandmother. If you ask my mother how she accounts for her boy, who led such an ordinary life, becoming aware of his real Father, she will say that I have been looking for Him for many centuries, practicing meditation and calling, "Where are you, dad?" all the time, until one day He said, "Here I am, son."

अथवा योगिनामेव कुले भवति धीमताम् ।
एतद्धि दुर्लभतरं लोके जन्म यदीदृशम् ॥४२॥

*42. Or they may be born into a family where
meditation is practiced. To be born into such a
family is extremely rare.*

It is a sound law that whatever effort we put forward on the spiritual
path is never wasted. In accordance with the theory of rebirth or
reincarnation, Sri Krishna reassures us that if we find it too difficult
to meditate and lead the spiritual life, then in our next life we may
be born into a home where our parents meditate. There is no greater
privilege than this, for it gives us an early start in our search for
the Self.

According to the theory of reincarnation, we have chosen every
one of our relationships carefully, especially our relationship with
our parents. In Bardo, where according to the Tibetans we wait to
come into this life, all of us have scorecards, and we tally up our
samskāras to make sure we have a perfect match. Parents and children resemble each other in so many ways that it is unfair for us to
criticize our mother or father, for we are so much like them. In
Bardo nobody gets a lemon; there are good points about every parent and every child that we should always emphasize. Where the
parents support meditation, it is especially fortunate; and where the
family considers it a great boon for the son or daughter to be meditating, it is a blessing to the whole family. But even if our parents
are not meditating with us, they will come to have a certain gratitude that their child is striving to lead a life that will benefit everyone around him. Therefore it is good for all of us to begin or end
our meditation with a prayer for the welfare of our parents and all
the other members of our family.

तत्र तं बुद्धिसंयोगं लभते पौर्वदेहिकम् ।
यतते च ततो भूयः संसिद्धौ कुरुनन्दन ॥४३॥
पूर्वाभ्यासेन तेनैव ह्रियते ह्यवशोऽपि सः ।
जिज्ञासुरपि योगस्य शब्दब्रह्मातिवर्तते ॥४४॥

*43. The wisdom they have acquired in previous
lives will be reawakened, Arjuna, and they will strive
even harder for Self-realization.
44. Indeed, they will be driven on by the strength
of their past disciplines. Even one who inquires after
the practice of meditation rises above those who
simply perform rituals.*

For twenty or twenty-five years we may have been studying at
school, going surfing, and learning all kinds of skills, but never
thinking about meditation or the spiritual life because the need for
it seemed far away. Then one day we go to the Tilden Meditation
Room at the University of California, where someone is talking
about the Bhagavad Gita. Some words and phrases get into our consciousness, and we go home dazed. We think about what he said,
we ponder over it, and finally a little window in our consciousness
opens and we decide to give meditation a try.

There is a certain magnetism between us and the Lord which we
have been unaware of all this time. Until we come of age we are like
little magnets, trying by our own efforts to find fulfillment; but
when we bring ourselves close to the Lord, his immense magnetism
draws us on effortlessly.

According to the Gita, desire for the spiritual life is not a sudden
development. It lies within us, just waiting for us to remember it.
After meditating several years there is a sudden deepening in meditation, and we start regaining the memory of what we had already
learned; our values become more selfless, more noble, and more
spiritual. When this occurs, we are not adding anything new to our
knowledge or wisdom; we are remembering what has been within
us all the time. All of us who are meditating have had some previous
spiritual experience; and in certain cases this experience is rather

substantial, which explains some of the differences in progress in
meditation. These dissimilarities need never dishearten us, because
we all can pick up and go forward as rapidly as we want from wherever we stopped before.

When the power of our spiritual efforts in past lives begins to rise
up in our consciousness, it is often felt as restlessness, a condition
that is characteristic of many young people today. Restlessness is
really a call to meditation; and once we have regained our previous
knowledge, once we have recalled our previous sādhana, all our desires, all our motivation for the spiritual life will deepen tremendously. The first three or four years of meditation require a lot of
strenuous, often painful effort, but once we have regained our
knowledge, much of the pain and many of our doubts fall away.
Then we want to strive even harder and give all we can to the spiritual life, which is a sign that we have regained our spiritual heritage.
It is as if we were *vīnā* players who have not played for twenty-five
years. When we pick up the *vīnā,* it feels so strange; our fingers do
not know their way. But we go on practicing day after day, day
after day, and suddenly our fingers remember their skill and the
song comes out in all its sonorous glory: *Hare Rāma, Hare Rāma,*
*Rāma Rāma, Hare Hare; Hare Krishna, Hare Krishna, Krishna*
*Krishna, Hare Hare.*

प्रयत्नाद्यतमानस्तु योगी संशुद्धकिल्बिषः ।
अनेकजन्मसंसिद्धस्ततो याति परां गतिम् ॥४५॥

*45. Through constant effort over many lifetimes*
*a person becomes purified of all selfish desires and*
*attains the supreme goal of life, union with the Lord.*

One day Sri Ramana Maharshi was telling those around him that
they had been together for many, many centuries, and Major Chad-
wick, a good British disciple, said, "I don't believe it." Sri Ramana
Maharshi just smiled and told his disciple, "You have simply forgotten." We, too, have forgotten our previous sādhana; but even

if we try to lead a careless, sensate life, the power of our past efforts will turn all pleasure to ashes.

I have seen people plunging into the world of sense pleasure in the hopes that this would lead to joy, and I have seen these hopes turn into frustration and despair in a very short time. Sri Krishna says that these are people who are highly evolved but do not realize their true capacities, who are highly spiritual but like to think that they are very sensate. They go to every restaurant on Telegraph Avenue, but only find their palate clamoring to be controlled. Terribly bored, they ask if this is all there is to the pleasure of the senses. There are many such young people today who have forgotten their real spiritual stature, and it is a great pity that in spite of their boredom and frustration they should keep on trying to play the game of the senses, which I sometimes call the sad-go-round. Instead of criticizing such people, we should remind them of the joy which awaits them if they will only reclaim their spiritual heritage.

Sri Krishna tells us that when the power of our previous spiritual development forces us to turn to meditation as a last resort, even on these terms he will welcome us, saying: "This is one of my thousand names, the Last Resort. Far from holding it against you, I welcome you with open arms; for you have come in spite of yourself, driven by your true spiritual nature."

In order to claim our past sādhana, in order to recall our old disciplines, the family context is just right for us. Instead of trying to embrace the whole world at the outset, we should learn to love our family and then gradually extend this love more and more. We are living in a world racked with violence and agitation, and in the early days of our sādhana it is difficult to go against our self-will, say no to our senses, and put the welfare of others first. Yet we have to learn not only to swim in this sea of strife but to contribute to its calmness and peace. So Sri Krishna tells us to jump in and he will teach us to swim; and when we jump we find ourselves safe in his arms.

Yesterday at the swimming pool I played the role of instructor. Geetha, who had missed a number of swimming lessons because of a cold, made me promise to give her special instructions. First I had to get her to jump into the water, which naturally frightened her. She loves me very much, so I had only to tell her to jump into my arms and she jumped. Then, holding on to me tightly, she kicked her way across the pool. I told her that next time she should hold on to me with only one hand; then the third time, she should use both her arms and feet to swim. In this way she would soon discover she could swim, and I would be by her side all the time. Similarly, when we become completely self-reliant and depend on the Lord of Love within in order to live for those around us, we will find he is there all the time. Even if we try, we cannot be drowned.

Around the pool there were swimming instructors walking about with long poles to rescue anyone in trouble. To me, living today is like being in a swimming pool without knowing how to swim. When we hate those who hate us, when we burst out in anger against those who are angry against us, it is because we do not know how to swim. But when we try to swim—returning love for hatred and compassion for anger—even if we sink a little and gasp for air, Sri Ramana Maharshi, Sri Ramakrishna, St. Francis, and many others are there holding out a long pole to rescue us. There is no need to be afraid, for there is always some illumined person to rescue us from the sea of life called samsara.

तपस्विभ्योऽधिको योगी ज्ञानिभ्योऽपि मतोऽधिकः।
कर्मिभ्यश्चाधिको योगी तस्माद्योगी भवार्जुन ॥४६॥

*46. Meditation is superior to severe asceticism and the path of knowledge. It is also superior to selfless service. May you attain the goal of meditation, Arjuna!*

Here Sri Krishna tells Arjuna that the person who meditates is superior even to those who follow ascetic disciplines. The Buddha, who once underwent such disciplines, reminds us that by starving the body or breaking the senses we cannot attain illumination, but by treating the body with wisdom, by giving it what it needs and gently denying it what it does not need, we turn the body into a true servant.

Sri Krishna also says the person who meditates is superior to those who follow the path of knowledge. Knowledge is looked upon here as a steep slope up which ordinary people like us cannot climb, but meditation enables us to acquire wisdom gradually and become wise by developing a higher mode of knowing.

Finally, the Lord tells us that the person who meditates is superior to those who are devoted to selfless action, for without meditation, self-will can enter into the most loving relationships and distort the most selfless efforts. The verse ends with the Lord's blessing, given out of such love and compassion that it should be dear to everyone who seeks the Self: "May you attain the goal of meditation." So may we all attain the goal.

योगिनामपि सर्वेषां मद्गतेनान्तरात्मना ।
श्रद्धावान् भजते यो मां स मे युक्ततमो मतः ॥४७॥

*47. Even among those who meditate, that man or woman is dearest to Me who has become completely absorbed in Me, and worships Me with perfect faith.*

Even among meditators, Sri Krishna has a special favorite whom he loves to support, whom he wants united with him. This is the one who meditates on the Lord with a one-pointed mind, who does everything in life for the Lord's sake. Such a person will ask himself: "If I eat this, will it strengthen my body so that I can serve the Lord? If I act this way, will it strengthen my mind and my will so that I can serve the Lord?" Sri Krishna is deeply in love with such a man or woman, whose consciousness is permeated with the presence of the Lord.

Every one of us can become Sri Krishna's favorite through sustained, systematic, enthusiastic practice of meditation. In this sixth chapter, "The Practice of Meditation," the Lord has told us that without meditation it is not possible to acquire spiritual wisdom, to act selflessly, or to bring about the much-needed transformation of our character, conduct, and consciousness. When we take to meditation and persevere, no matter what the obstacles, we will find the

Lord's grace coming to us in many ways; we will be blessed with vibrant health, with increasing security, and with the ability to harness our creative resources to solve even the most difficult problems. By seeking the Self through meditation, we will come to live in awareness of the unity of life expressed in everyone, everywhere, every minute.

इति ध्यानयोगो नाम षष्ठोऽध्यायः ॥६॥

# Who Is the Illumined Man?

ARJUNA:

                   Tell me of those
Who live always in wisdom, ever aware
Of the Self, O Krishna; how do they talk,
How sit, how move about?

SRI KRISHNA:

                   They live in wisdom
Who see themselves in all and all in them,
Whose love for the Lord of Love has consumed
Every selfish desire and sense craving
Tormenting the heart. Not agitated
By grief or hankering after pleasure,
They live free from lust and fear and anger.
Fettered no more by selfish attachments,
They are not elated by good fortune
Or depressed by bad. Such are the seers.

Even as a tortoise draws in its limbs,
The wise can draw in their senses at will.
Though aspirants abstain from sense pleasures,
They will still crave for them. These cravings all
Disappear when they see the Lord of Love.
For even of those who tread the path,
The stormy senses can sweep off the mind.
But they live in wisdom who subdue them,
And keep their minds ever absorbed in Me.

When you keep thinking about sense objects,
Attachment comes. Attachment breeds desire,
The lust of possession which, when thwarted,
Burns to anger. Anger clouds the judgment;
You can no longer learn from past mistakes.
Lost is the power to choose between the wise
And unwise, and your life is utter waste.
But when you move amidst the world of sense
From both attachment and aversion freed,
There comes the peace in which all sorrows end
And you live in the wisdom of the Self.

The disunited mind is far from wise;
How can it meditate? How be at peace?
When you know no peace, how can you know joy?
When you let your mind heed the Siren call
Of the senses, they will carry away
Your better judgment as storms drive a boat
Off its safe-charted course to certain doom.

Use all your power to set the senses free
From attachment and aversion alike,
And live in the full wisdom of the Self.
Such a sage awakes to light in the night
Of all creatures. That which the world calls day
Is the night of ignorance to the wise.

As the rivers flow into the ocean
But cannot make the vast ocean overflow,
So flow the magic streams of the sense-world
Into the sea of peace that is the sage.

They are forever free who break away
From the ego-cage of *I, me,* and *mine*
To be united with the Lord of Love.
This is the supreme state. Attain to this
And pass from death to immortality.

# Glossary & Guide
# to Sanskrit Pronunciation

This is a glossary of the Sanskrit and other Indian terms used in The Bhagavad Gita for Daily Living. *For a more complete guide to Sanskrit terms and
their pronunciation, see* A Glossary of Sanskrit from the Spiritual Tradition
of India *(Berkeley: Blue Mountain Center of Meditation, 1970).*

## GUIDE TO THE PRONUNCIATION OF SANSKRIT WORDS

*Consonants.* Consonants are generally pronounced as in English, but there
are some differences. Sanskrit has many so-called aspirated consonants, that
is, consonants pronounced with a slight *h* sound. For example, the consonant
*ph* is pronounced as English *p* followed by an *h* as in ha*ph*azard. The *bh* is
as in a*bh*or. The aspirated consonants are *kh, gh, ch, jh, th, dh, ph, bh.*

| | |
|---|---|
| *c* as in *ch*urch | *g* as in *g*old |
| *h* " " *h*ome | *j* " " June |

The other consonants are approximately as in English.

*Vowels.* Every Sanskrit vowel has two forms, one short and one long. The
long form is pronounced twice as long as the short. In the English trans-
literation the long vowels are marked with a bar ( ¯ ). The diphthongs—*e, ai,
o, au*—are also pronounced twice as long as the short vowels. Thus, in the
words *nīla* 'blue' and *gopa* 'cowherd,' the first syllable is held twice as long
as the second.

| | |
|---|---|
| *a* as in *u*p | *ri* as in *wri*tten |
| *ā* " " f*a*ther | *e* " " th*ey* |
| *i* " " g*i*ve | *ai* " " *ai*sle |
| *ī* " " s*ee* | *o* " " g*o* |
| *u* " " p*u*t | *au* " " c*ow* |
| *ū* " " r*u*le | |

## SPELLING OF SANSKRIT WORDS

To simplify the spelling of Sanskrit words we have used a minimum of dia-
critical marks, retaining only the long mark ( ¯ ) for the long vowels and
omitting the other diacritics which are sometimes used in rendering Sanskrit
words into English. Some subtleties of Sanskrit pronunciation, such as the
difference between retroflex and dental consonants, are therefore lost. The
gain in simplicity, however, seems to far outweigh this loss.

*abhyāsa* Regular practice.

*advaita* ['not two'] Having no duality; the supreme Reality, which is the "One without a second." The word *advaita* is especially used in Vedānta philosophy, which stresses the unity of the Self (Ātman) and Brahman.

*ahamkāra* [*aham* 'I'; *kāra* 'maker'] Self-will, separateness, the fundamental barrier which prevents Self-realization and awareness of the unity of all life.

*Anasūyā* [*an* 'not'; *asūyā* 'jealous'] "She who is free from jealousy," a character in the ancient Indian drama *Shakuntala*. She is a symbol for devoted friendship, free from rivalry and envy.

*apara* [*a* 'not'; *para* 'beyond'] That which is not transcendent, i.e. lower knowledge, intellectual knowledge.

*Arjuna* One of the five Pāndava brothers. He is an important figure in Indian epic and legend, and is Sri Krishna's beloved disciple and friend in the Bhagavad Gita.

*āsana* A posture; a system of physical exercise taught in ancient India, designed to tone up the nervous system as a preparation for meditation.

*āshram* [Skt. *āshrama,* from *shram* 'to exert oneself'] A spiritual community where students live with a spiritual teacher as members of his family; a retreat where meditation and spiritual disciplines are practiced.

*Ātman* The Self, the innermost soul in every creature which is a spark of the divine essence.

*avatāra* [*ava* 'down'; *tri* 'to cross'] The descent of God to earth; the incarnation of the Lord on earth; the birth of the Lord, of divine consciousness, in the heart of man.

*Bardo* [Tibetan *bar* 'between'; *do* 'two'] In Tibetan mysticism, the state between two lives in which the soul awaits a proper body and context for rebirth.

*Bhagavad Gītā* [*Bhagavat* 'Lord'; *gītā* 'song'] The Song of the Lord, the name of the important Hindu scripture which contains the instructions of Sri Krishna.

*bhakti yoga* The Way of Love.

*Brahmā* The god of creation. *Brahmā,* the Creator, *Vishnu,* the Preserver, and *Shiva,* the Dissolver, make up the Hindu Trinity. (Note: *Brahmā,* which is a word with masculine gender, should not be confused with *Brahman,* the supreme Reality, which has the neuter gender.)

*Brahman* The supreme Reality underlying all life; the Divine Ground of existence; the impersonal Godhead.

*brahmin* [Skt. *Brāhmana*] One who seeks to know Brahman; also, a member of the priestly, learned caste in traditional Hindu society.

*Buddha* [from *budh* 'to wake up'] "The Awakened One." An enlightened being; the title given to the sage Siddhārtha Gautama Shākyamuni after he obtained complete illumination. The Buddha lived and taught in North India during the sixth century B.C.

*buddhi* Understanding, intelligence; correct view, idea, purpose.

*deva* A god.

*devī* A goddess.

*Dhammapada* [Pāli, from Skt. *Dharmapada*] Name of an important early Buddhist scripture.

*dhārana* The first stage in meditation.

*dharma* Law, duty; the universal Law which holds all life together in a unity.

*dhoti* A piece of cloth—wrapped around the body, drawn between the legs, and tied at the waist—which is worn as a lower garment.

*dhyāna* Meditation. Specifically, in Patanjali's yoga, the second stage in meditation.

*duhkha* Suffering.

*Duryodhana* The oldest son of Dhritarāshtra and the chief enemy of the Pāndavas and Sri Krishna.

*ekāgratā* One-pointedness; disciplining the mind to concentrate on only one thing at a time.

*Ganesha* The elephant-headed god of prosperity in the Hindu pantheon, symbol of divine power. He is the son of Shiva and Pārvatī.

*Gītā* "The Song," a shorter title for the Bhagavad Gita.

*guna* Quality; specifically, the three qualities which make up the phenomenal world: sattva, law; rajas, energy; and tamas, inertia.

*guru* A spiritual teacher.

*Hare* [vocative of *Hari*] The Lord Vishnu.

*Hastināpura* "City of the elephants," an important city in ancient India, located about sixty miles northeast of the modern Delhi. It was the capital city of the Pāndavas and their line.

*Himālaya* [*hima* 'snow'; *ālaya* 'abode'] The great mountain range which stretches across the northern border of India, important in mythology as the home of Shiva and other gods.

*Īshvara* The Lord; the Inner Ruler who guides from within.

*jnāna yoga* The Way of Wisdom.

*Kailāsa* Name of a peak in the Himālayas, in Indian myth the home of Shiva.

*kāma* Selfish desire, greed; sexual desire, sometimes personified as Kāmadeva, "god of desire."

*karma yoga* The Way of Action, the path of selfless service.

*karma yogī* One who does selfless work.

*Kauravas* "The sons of Kuru," usually referring to Duryodhana and his brothers, who are the enemies of the Pāndavas.

*Krishna* [from *krish* 'to draw to oneself'] The Lord of Love who dwells in the hearts of all.

*krodha* Anger.

*kundalinī* "The serpent power"; spiritual energy, evolutionary energy.

*Kurukshetra* "The field of the Kurus," where the Mahābhārata battle takes place.

*līlā* Game; the divine play of the Lord disguising himself as many.

*Madhyamārga* The Middle Path, the way of moderation taught by the Buddha.

*Mahābhārata* The great epic of ancient India which contains the Bhagavad Gita.

*manas* The mind; the faculty which registers and stores sensory impressions.

*mantram* A Holy Name or phrase; a spiritual formula.

*Māra* "The Striker"; in Buddhism, the Tempter, the Evil One who tries to prevent the Buddha's enlightenment.

*Māyā* Illusion; appearance, as contrasted with Reality. The creative power of the Lord.

*moksha* Liberation, salvation, illumination.

*neti, neti* [*na iti, na iti*] "Not this, not this," the refrain of the Upanishads, which teach that the supreme Reality is indescribable, undefinable, beyond the dualities of this world.

*nirvāna* [*nir* 'out'; *vāna* 'to blow'] Complete extinction of self-will and separateness; realization of the unity of all life.

*nirvikalpa samādhi* A state of spiritual awareness in which there is no perception of duality, of inside or outside, of subject and object; merger in the impersonal Godhead.

*Om* [or *Aum*] The cosmic sound, which can be heard in deep meditation; the Holy Word, taught in the Upanishads, which signifies Brahman, the Divine Ground of existence.

*Pāndavas* "The sons of Pāndu," a collective name for Arjuna and his four brothers: Yudhishthira, Bhima, Nakula, and Sahadeva.

*para* ['the beyond'] Higher knowledge; spiritual insight.

*prajnā* [from *jnā* 'to know'] A transcendental mode of knowing developed in deep meditation.

*prakriti* The basic stuff from which the mental and physical worlds take shape; nature.

*prāna* Breath; vital force.

*preya* That which is temporarily pleasing.

*purusha* ['person'] The inner soul, the spiritual core of man.

*Rādhā* Name of the milkmaid who is Sri Krishna's beloved while he sojourns in Vrindāvana. She represents the human soul longing for the divine Beloved.

*rāja yoga* The Royal Path, the path of meditation taught especially by Patanjali in the *Yoga Sūtras*.

*rajas* Passion, energy, the second of the three qualities (gunas).

*Rāma* [from *ram* 'to rejoice'] The Lord of Joy, the principle of joy within.

*Rāmagiri* "The Hills of Joy," name of the country retreat of the Blue Mountain Center of Meditation.

*sādhana* A body of disciplines, a way of life, which leads to the supreme goal of Self-realization.

*samādhi* [*sam* 'with'; *Ādhi* 'Lord'] Union with the Lord; a state of intense concentration in which consciousness is completely unified.

*samsāra* The world of flux; the round of birth, decay, death, and rebirth.

*samskāra* A personality trait conditioned over many lives or one life: a mental and behavioral pattern; a latency or tendency within the mind which will manifest itself if given the proper environment and stimulus.

*sat* [from *as* 'to be'] Truth, That which really is; the Good.

*sattva* Goodness, purity, law, the highest of the three qualities (gunas).

*shanti* Perfect inner peace, the "peace that passeth all understanding."

*Shiva* Third in the Hindu Trinity; he who destroys the ego and conquers death.

*shraddhā* Faith.

*shreya* The Good, that which is permanently beneficial.

*Sītā* The wife of Rāma and the ideal for womanly love and loyalty.

*Srī* [pronounced *Shrī*] A title of respect originally meaning 'Lord' or 'holy'; now, in modern India, simply a respectful form of address.

*sthūlasharīra* The gross body, the physical body.

*stūpa* A shrine containing a relic of the Buddha.

*sukha* Pleasure.

*sūkshmasharīra* The subtle body made up of samskāras, or mental impressions.

*svadharma* The duty appropriate to a particular person, one's own individual dharma.

*tamas* Inertia, ignorance, the lowest of the three qualities (gunas).

*tanhā* [Prākrit, from Skt. *trishnā* 'thirst'] The thirst for selfish satisfaction, the craving of the senses and the ego.

*tapas* Austerity, control of the senses; the spiritual power acquired through self-control.

*Upanishads* Ancient mystical documents to be found at the end of the Vedic canon.

*vīnā* An ancient South Indian stringed instrument used in classical music.

*Vishnu* Second in the Hindu Trinity; the Preserver who incarnates in age after age for the establishment of dharma and the welfare of all creatures.

*yajna* Sacrifice; selfless service; an offering.

*yoga* [from *yuj* 'to unite'] Union with the Lord, realization of the unity of all life; a path or discipline which leads to such a state of total integration or unity.

# Index

END

Library of Congress Cataloging in Publication Data:

Easwaran, Eknath.

    The Bhagavad Gita for daily living.

    Includes indexes.
    CONTENTS:   v. 1. The end of sorrow. —v. 2.
Like a thousand suns.
    1. Mahābhārata.   Bhagavadgītā.   I.   Mahābhārata.
Bhagavadgītā.   English & Sanskrit.   1979–
II.   Title.
BL1130.E2   1979       294.5 924       79–1448

ISBN 0–915132–03–6   v. 1.
ISBN 0–915132–17–6   v. 1. pbk.

ISBN 0–915132–04–4   v. 2.
ISBN 0–915132–18–4   v. 2. pbk.